UNFOLDING STAKEHOLDER THINKING

THEORY, RESPONSIBILITY AND ENGAGEMENT

Edited by Jörg Andriof, Sandra Waddock, Bryan Husted
and Sandra Sutherland Rahman

Unfolding Stakeholder Thinking

THEORY, RESPONSIBILITY AND ENGAGEMENT

with a Foreword by R. Edward Freeman

EDITED BY JÖRG ANDRIOF, SANDRA WADDOCK, BRYAN HUSTED
AND SANDRA SUTHERLAND RAHMAN

Routledge
Taylor & Francis Group

LONDON AND NEW YORK

First published 2002 by Greenleaf Publishing Limited

Published 2017 by Routledge
2 Park Square, Milton Park, Abingdon, Oxon OX14 4RN
711 Third Avenue, New York, NY 10017, USA

Routledge is an imprint of the Taylor & Francis Group, an informa business

Cover by LaliAbril.com.

British Library Cataloguing in Publication Data:
    Unfolding stakeholder thinking
        Vol. 1: Theory, responsibility and engagement
        1. Social responsibility of business 2. Business planning
        I. Rahman, Sandra Sutherland
        658.4 ' 08

    ISBN 978-1-874719-52-6 (hbk)

CONTENTS

FOREWORD

This book of essays symbolises the need for a new era of management thinking and theory: one based on the idea of stakeholders. In the 21st century, it should go without saying that organisations, especially business corporations, must be responsive and responsible to their stakeholders—groups and individuals who can affect or are affected by the organisation's purpose. Sadly, this is not the case.

Within the last year corporations have come under unprecedented criticism from many directions. Some critics decry the rise of 'globalism' and its effects on local culture. They believe that the drive for corporate profits can be said to undermine our human sense of community and solidarity. While it is difficult to see what the positive vision of these critics really is, make no mistake, they believe that the business corporation is the main culprit for many of the problems in the world. Yet another group of critics has suggested that companies have not gone far enough with respect to pursuing profits. They believe that companies are not run in the shareholders' interests, and that companies need to focus even more on 'maximising shareholder value'. In light of these groups of critics, we are treated to a daily barrage of news stories about Enron, Arthur Andersen, Xerox, WorldCom, Tyco, Firestone and others who have been accused of wrongdoings—often in the name of shareholders.

The main problem that we face is that our idea of 'good management' has been hijacked. 'Shareholder value' is the reigning orthodoxy, and many of the alleged ethical violations have been committed in the name of shareholders. The main problem with the shareholder value orthodoxy is that it appears to give us more precision in decision-making than there really is. Using the tools and techniques developed over the last 50 years, managers can calculate 'precise' effects on shareholder value on a project-by-project basis. 'If we settle these lawsuits and seal the court documents, then the effect on shareholder value is x.' 'If we move to a cheaper and less expensive raw material, and don't change our label, then the effect on shareholder value is x.' 'If we finance this deal as an "off-the-books" limited partnership, then the effect on shareholder value is x.' 'If we stretch the meaning of this accounting rule and smooth our earnings, then the effect on shareholder value is x.' Each of these statements simply ignores the effects on other stakeholders, and each assumes that executives have control over other variables, such as who finds out about these decisions. In today's world of ubiquitous communication and transparency which information technology makes possible, the precision of the shareholder value model is a false hope. What is to be done?

The answer lies in the essays in this book. First of all we need to take the idea of 'stakeholders', 'managing for stakeholders', 'stakeholder management', 'stakeholder dialogue', 'stakeholder capitalism', etc. very seriously. We need literally to rewrite management theory and practice so that these ideas are at the centre. We need to see the executive's job as how to get stakeholder interests to move in roughly the same direction. Of course, shareholders have to win, but customers, suppliers, employees and communities have to win as well. In order to build a sustainable enterprise, each of these stakeholder groups must be able to satisfy their interests in what we know as the business corporation. The corporation is just a clearinghouse, a vessel, a mere means, an instrument for satisfying the interests of stakeholders. The entrepreneur or the executive in a large firm must put together a deal so that customers, suppliers, employees, communities and financiers (shareholders, owners, banks and others) win over time. Of course, sometimes there are conflicts. The manager's job is to solve these conflicts in a way that preserves and enhances the basic structure of the deal. When managers fail at this job, then stakeholders withdraw their support for the enterprise and go elsewhere to satisfy their needs.

Second of all, we need to see business activity as a moral activity, an activity that affects the hopes and dreams and wellbeing of many human beings. The shareholder orthodoxy would have us believe that we can separate 'business' from 'ethics', but the real world tells us that we can't and shouldn't. Business is no different from other aspects of our lives, and we need to see executives and their stakeholders as fully fledged moral beings. 'Business ethics' should be a redundancy rather than an oxymoron.

The work that needs to be done in order to rescue business from the moral scrapheap is being done by the authors and editors of this volume as well as others. The burgeoning academic area of 'stakeholder theory' holds great promise. And the calls for reform ensure that now is a moment in history where it is possible to implement great change about the way we think about business. *Unfolding Stakeholder Thinking* is the right book at the right time.

R. Edward Freeman
Charlottesville, Virginia
July 2002

INTRODUCTION

Jörg Andriof
KPMG, Germany;
Warwick Business School, UK

Sandra Waddock
Boston College, Carroll School of
Management, USA

Bryan Husted
ITESM/Instituto De Empresa,
Mexico

Sandra Sutherland Rahman
Framingham State College,
USA

Just how has stakeholder thinking unfolded in the years since Ed Freeman popularised the concept of stakeholder thinking his seminal book, *Strategic Management: A Stakeholder Approach* (1984)? This two-volume series hopes to provide insight into the answers to that question by unfolding theorising and empirical research on the behaviour of businesses and stakeholders around the world through the fundamentals of stakeholder theory. From the original 'spoke-and-wheel' design of stakeholder interaction promulgated in Freeman's (1984) book, stakeholder thinking has evolved into the study of interactive, mutually engaged and responsive relationships that establish the very context of doing modern business, and create the groundwork for transparency and accountability.

The chapters in these volumes make clear that in today's societies successful companies are those that recognise that they have responsibilities to a range of stakeholders that go beyond mere compliance with the law or meeting the fiduciary responsibility inherent in the phrase 'maximising returns to shareholders'. If in the past the focus was on enhancing shareholder value, now it is on *engaging* stakeholders for long-term value creation. This does not mean that shareholders are not important, or that profitability is not vital to business success, but that in order to survive and be profitable a company must engage with a range of stakeholders whose views on the company's success may vary greatly. The *process* of engagement creates a dynamic context of interaction, mutual respect, dialogue and change, not one-sided management of stakeholders. Indeed, although some would argue with the phraseology, we believe the very term 'stakeholder *management*' to be outdated and corporate-centric in the recognition of engagement and consequent mutuality. Companies can manage their *relationships* with stakeholders, but frequently cannot actually manage the stakeholders themselves, because, as the activism and collaborative initiatives described in some of the papers in this volume suggest, company–stakeholder relationships go two ways and different institutions bring different agendas, goals and priorities to the engagement.

There are clear implications to the way in which stakeholder thinking is unfolding today. If in the past corporate 'social' responsibility was simply seen as profitability plus compliance plus philanthropy, now responsible corporate citizenship—or corporate responsibility—means companies being more aware of and understanding the societies in which they operate. Corporate responsibility means recognition that day-to-day operating practices affect stakeholders and that is in those impacts where responsibility lies, not merely in efforts to 'do good' (Marsden and Andriof 1998; McIntosh et al. 1998; Waddock 2002). Companies are faced with the challenge of reporting on the company's social and environmental impact alongside the financial performance. These challenges mean that senior executives and managers need to be able to deal with a wide range of issues including greater accountability, human rights abuses, sustainability strategies, corporate governance codes, workplace ethics, stakeholder consultation and management—and theorising, stakeholder thinking, needs to capture these new realities.

Below we will *very* briefly highlight some of the major developments in the unfolding of stakeholder theory as we see it today, hitting only key points (and very possibly overlooking others).

The emergence of stakeholder thinking

As it unfolds today, stakeholder thinking has deep roots in economic theory, beginning with Adam Smith, who was trained in the field of moral philosophy and applied his knowledge to explaining a unified system of economic life. Smith argued that societies function best when economic interests and ethical interests coalesce. His argument, eloquently made in *The Theory of Moral Sentiments* (1759) and in *The Wealth of Nations* (1776), established the notion that economic and ethical interests share a symbiotic relationship. Although the moral underpinnings of Smith's work are frequently overlooked today, stakeholder theory embraces both economic and ethical arguments and continues to develop ideas to assist business, governmental and non-governmental (NGO) organisations in recognising and maximising the full potential of their symbiotic relationship.

Since the beginning of recorded history, humans have attempted to explain the laws of nature and link them to human civilisation (cf. Frederick 1995). Philosophers ponder the natural forces that shape the dynamics of evolving species and civilisations. Charles Darwin's *Origin of Species* describes his global theory of the economy of nature that embodies the notion that all parts cohere in one system and are interdependent and that what affects one part will affect the rest (see also Capra 1995). This theory, which is grounded in the biological sciences, clearly describes the competitive nature of the dynamics of relationships in the natural environment. It served as a basis for understanding that everything in nature is important and that everything in nature serves a purpose. Darwin's theory of the survival of the fittest serves as a basis for understanding the cycle of life in nature. The process of natural selection is that the strongest and fittest will survive to carry on the species. Competition on the basis of strength and fit creates the evolutionary force that perpetuates a species that is continuously improving. In many respects, the business system, absent much stakeholder thinking, reflects this competitive dog-eat-dog world, yet recent biologists and physicists argue strongly for an alternative view: the reality of symbiosis or collaborative initiatives that ensure (along with competition) that the system as a whole survives (e.g. Maturana and Varela 1998; Capra 1995). Indeed, Smith himself integrated these perspectives, advocating 'that all the nations of the world should be considered as one great community' (Smith 1759). Smith's forward-looking view of the world seems to have laid the cornerstone for today's view of a borderless world of natural resources integrated by both competitive and symbiotic forces.

In the neoclassical economics view of the business environment, which derives from Smith (albeit largely overlooking the moral theory foundation of his work), the firm is viewed as a closed system with its only concern to satisfy stockholders. Somehow, the conception came to be that corporate walls and the boardroom defined the firm's environment, distinct from society. The very language of the field of scholarship that developed around business in its environment reflects that conception: business *and* society, as if business were and could be separated from the society surrounding it and on which it depends. From that relatively narrow perspective, increasing revenues is considered the primary (ethical and fiduciary) obligation of the firm and that obligation is aimed at satisfying the only salient stakeholder, the investor.

The popular phrase that characterised the responsibility of management prior to the 1960s was *caveat emptor* or 'Let the buyer beware'. If products were unsafe, it was up to the customer to take responsibility. If factors of production were 'exploited' in the process of manufacturing the good, then it was considered fair as long as companies were not violating any codified law. The events of the 1960s changed the dynamics of the business environment. The consumer and environmental movements empowered consumers' and other activists' 'voice'. Consumers formed protest marches and lobby groups to demand that firms take responsibility for offering the public safe products. Lawsuits against firms that sold products that harmed consumers began to clog the courts. Corporations that were considered 'individuals' in the eyes of the law were beginning to be forced by legislation to be responsible corporate citizens. Companies were, as a provocative book by S. Prakash Sethi (1977) was titled, 'up against the corporate wall' in terms of public perceptions of how they lived up to their responsibilities. Notably, in a new wave of stakeholder activism today there are also protests and anti-corporate demonstration, this time about issues that cross national boundaries, such as working conditions, labour rights and environment.

The consumer and environmental movements of the 1960s triggered recognition that other people and organisations can affect or are affected by business activities and, at some level, triggered a sense of empowerment for actors in those other institutions in society. The magnitude of this feeling of power is described by a global historian of this era when he says:

> the major actor or subject of global history is no longer the nation-state . . .
> [T]hey are movements, such as the women's environmental causes; non-governmental organisations (NGO's), such as Amnesty International or Human Watch (whose structures may rapidly be replacing those of religion in the setting up of an international conscience); and multinational corporations (Mazlish 1993).

While some civil-society observers could dispute this claim, what is clear is that the consumer and environmental movements triggered recognition that institutions other than business in society had different kinds of claims, goals and interests that were not always fully compatible with the objective of maximising shareholder wealth.

Business *and* society thinking unfolds

Prior to the first phase of stakeholder thinking, evidence of the need to link business and society had already begun to appear in the literature (Berle and Means 1932; Kapp 1950; Boulding 1953; Selekman and Selekman 1956; Tawney 1948; Galbraith 1958; Gordon and Howell 1959; Pierson 1959). Researchers focused on the relationship of business to society and corporate 'social' responsibility (Adams 1969; Austin 1965; Boulding 1968; Elbing 1970; Galbraith 1967; Lodge 1970a, 1970b). *The Social Responsibilities of the Businessman* by Howard R. Bowen (1953) and *Business and Society* by Joseph McGuire (1963) are early landmark books articulating the need for business to be, in some respects, responsible to society.

By the end of the 1970s and into the early 1980s, a new business and society paradigm had unfolded to shape scholarship, especially in the US. As Frederick argued (1987, 1994a) the field had moved from CSR1 or the corporate social *responsibility* concept triggered by the activism of the 1960s and early 1970s to CSR2, corporate social *responsiveness*. The business and society paradigm was articulated by, among others, Preston and Post (1975), Carroll (1979), Jones (1980), Wartick and Cochran (1985), Wood (1991a, 1991b) and Jones (1995). Still largely corporate-centric, the models presented by these authors generally argued for links between business and society, suggesting that businesses needed, through their structures and functions, to be *responsive* to issues and needs external to themselves, or what Frederick (1994a) termed CSR2, corporate social responsiveness.

The new corporate responsiveness was reflected in the conception of the public responsibilities of management articulated by Preston and Post (1975) and operationalised through boundary-spanning functions that were explicitly developed to allow companies to respond proactively to external issues and what were then called constituencies. Corporate units dealing explicitly with issues management (Wartick and Mahon 1994; Wartick and Cochran 1985) emerged during the 1980s, along with community relations functions (Burke 1999), and related functions proactively dealing with external stakeholders (e.g. media relations, customer relations, investor relations).

Stakeholder thinking emerges

Freeman (1984) initially popularised the stakeholder concept, which had originated in 1962 when the Stanford Research Institute first used the term 'stakeholder perspective'. The concept built on the theories of Darwin and Smith, and the realities of the changing environment in the 1960s, acknowledging that there are people and organisations other than stockholders who are affected by the operations of a firm. Freeman's 1984 book explicitly linked stakeholder theory to strategic planning, suggesting its centrality to the mission and purpose of the firm or what Freeman and Gilbert (1988) later called 'enterprise strategy', asking the question 'What do we stand for?' Freeman's class definition of a stakeholder is still widely used today, encompassing advances in stakeholder theorising and greater complexity of understanding of the roles and interactions of companies and stakeholders:

> A stakeholder in an organization is (by definition) any group or individual who can affect or is affected by the achievement of the organization's objective (Freeman 1984).

Stakeholder thinking, even in its early days, embodies a conceptual shift in management's perception of its environment, in part because Freeman (1984) framed stakeholders as part of the process of strategic management and such relationships as instrumentally useful (Freeman 1999). The literatures on corporate planning, systems theory, corporate social responsibility and organisation theory subtly began to merge (Freeman 1984) and give rise to a new way for strategic planners to view their business environment as the potential performance implications of better relationships with stakeholders became clear. Although stakeholder thinking unfolded along what many perceived to be a separate path from the more traditional business and society stream (and certainly from strategic management), over time efforts to link corporate performance and the way a company interacted with its environment empirically began to make the connection.

Much research in the business in society stream has focused on establishing the link between corporate 'social' and financial performance. Several comprehensive studies of this literature (e.g. Wood and Jones 1995; Pava and Krausz 1996; Griffin and Mahon 1997; Roman et al. 1999), and particularly the definitive study by Margolis and Walsh (2001a, 2001b), suggest that this relationship is likely, as Freeman hypothesised for stakeholder relationships, to be a positive one. Waddock and Graves (1997a) argued for the existence of a 'good management theory', suggesting that corporate 'social' performance (CSP) and financial performance were linked because the level of CSP and quality of management were correlated.

This link was extended to stakeholder theory by Waddock and Graves (1997b) (with corporate reputation as the dependent variable because shareholders were considered one of the stakeholders). Waddock and Graves (1997b) made the link between corporate 'social' performance and stakeholder thinking empirically by defining corporate responsibility as the way in which the company operationalises its treatment of stakeholders (see also Wood and Jones 1995 for a similar, albeit conceptual, linkage). Jones termed this linkage 'instrumental stakeholder theory', asserting 'the core theory—that a subset of ethical principles (trust, trustworthiness, and cooperation) can result in significant competitive advantage for the firm when operationalized' (Jones 1995).

Ethics gets 'added'

Although Freeman (1999) does not distinguish the normative (ethical), descriptive or instrumental 'versions' of stakeholder theory as Donaldson and Preston (1995), others do, including scholars working in the parallel corporate 'social' responsibility stream. By the end of the 1980s, recognition had dawned that, in a postmodern world where the very existence of value-neutrality is questionable, conceptualisation about ethics needed to be more closely linked into thinking about the business–society relationship, whether through the stakeholder or corporate 'social' performance (Wood 1991a, 1991b) lens.

Epstein (1987, 1998) integrates corporate responsibility, responsiveness and ethics through a process lens aimed at corporate social policy, in an effort to avoid what Freeman (1994) later calls the 'separation thesis': the idea that ethics *can* be separated from actions or stakeholder relationships. Jones and Wicks (1999b) attempt much the same for stakeholder theory in their convergent stakeholder theory, although Freeman (1999) argues that convergence would be unnecessary if separation had not occurred in the first place (see also Donaldson 1999; Gioia 1999; Trevino and Weaver 1999).

Berman *et al.* (1999, using the KLD corporate responsibility database) tested the Donaldson and Preston (1995) framework, and established evidence of a connection between the treatment of their stakeholders and the firm's financial performance (see also the comprehensive meta-studies cited above for similar evidence, especially Margolis and Walsh 2001a, 2001b). The Berman *et al.* study found support for the instrumental or strategic perspective, but not an intrinsic stakeholder commitment model.

The social issues in management field has recognised the need to more rigorously test and define the underpinnings of the relationship between social issues and management, hence the array of empirical studies that are now beginning to emerge. Considerable contributions continue to be made in the area of stakeholder theory development (such as books by Alkhafaji [1989], Anderson [1989] and Brummer [1991]; and articles by Brenner and Cochran [1991], Clarkson [1991], Goodpaster [1991], Hill and Jones [1992] and Wood [1991a, 1991b]).

Stakeholder thinking unfolds: engagement and responsibility

The chapters in this volume reflect several emerging conceptual and normative themes that are now unfolding. The second volume extends this discussion by focusing on the management of stakeholder relationships. Among the core topics that emerge in Part 1, 'Thinking about stakeholder theory', is the continuing tension between traditional economic theory and a stakeholder view of the firm.

Part 1 provides a range of conceptual frameworks that highlight current stakeholder thinking. In the opening chapter, Jörg Andriof and Sandra Waddock ('Unfolding stakeholder engagement') provide an overview of the ways in which concepts of stakeholder engagement have evolved—or unfolded—in recent years. K.E. Goodpaster, T.D. Maines and M. Rovang discuss, in 'Stakeholder thinking: beyond paradox to practicality', the stakeholder paradox in practical terms in the second chapter, providing a framework for Michael Jensen's critical chapter on the impracticality of companies' having multiple objective functions as is implied by stakeholder thinking, which is entitled 'Value maximisation, stakeholder theory and the corporate objective function'. Duane Windsor, in 'Jensen's approach to stakeholder theory', however, counters Jensen's arguments, arguing for the primacy of stakeholder-oriented as well as financial goals. In the final chapter in the first section, Suzanne Beaulieu and Jean Pasquero reintroduce the dynamic quality of stakeholder interaction as an ongoing, tension-filled and iterative process in their chapter, 'Reintroducing Stakeholder dynamics in stakeholder thinking: a negotiated-order perspective'. This chapter sets up a theoretical framework for the dynamic inter-action of stakeholder engagement processes that are the focus of Part 2 of the book

The second core element of unfolding stakeholder thinking today is thus a decided movement in practice and theorising toward stakeholder engagement strategies that evolve in dynamic interaction and create mutual (including *stakeholder*) responsibilities, reflected in Part 2: 'Stakeholder responsibility and engagement'. Fuelled by processes of dialogue and stakeholder engagement strategies, we can see the beginning of important shifts in understanding the role(s) of companies with respect to other actors in society in some of the chapters in this volume. This shift is toward a systems level of analysis that looks at the mutual interaction and engagement of multiple institutions in society, some businesses, and other representative of civil society or governmental organisations.

Stakeholder responsibilities create a situation of mutual engagement and responsibility. Stakeholders who place demands on firms or other organisations have some responsi-bility for assuring that their demands do not have significant unintended negative conse-quences. Consequences of stakeholder demands can apply to the firms themselves or other stakeholders whose interests and needs have not been fully understood or taken into account (cf. McGowan and Mahon 1995; Rahman 2000). While the issue of stake-holder responsibility is particularly notable in the global debate on environment, there are other issues, such as labour standards, working conditions and human rights, in which it also has significant importance. Stakeholder responsibilities suggests the need for an active process of mutual *engagement* reflected in many of the chapters, and in giving 'voice' and even a degree of influence (Frooman 1999) to activists and other outside stakeholders who may be critical of the firm.

Stakeholder demands create impacts, and sometimes unintended (and sometimes intended) consequences. For example, in international settings, where labour and human rights issues have gained considerable public attention in recent years, pressures have been brought to bear on some governments to reduce child labour. In Bangladesh, the government passed a law prohibiting child labour under significant international com-munity (activist and NGO) pressure, which resulted in children and sometimes their mothers being fired. The unfortunate outcome was that, with few schools to go to and families still in dire need of the children's income, they were frequently forced into the sex trades or the gruelling work of breaking bricks (Rahman 2000).

The mutuality of stakeholder engagement and responsibility creates the need to under-stand how these interactions occur. In 'Towards a Managerial practice of stakeholder engagement: developing multi-stakeholder learning dialogues', Stephen Payne and Jerry Calton focus on developing a better understanding of these interactions. In the next chapter, the lessons that can be learned by managers with respect to stakeholder respon-sibilities are discussed by Duane Windsor ('Stakeholder responsibilities: lessons for managers'). These chapters highlight the dynamic and interactive processes involved in stakeholder relationships in ways that go well beyond the usual static and one-sided wheel-and-spoke relationships typically considered.

These more conceptual chapters are followed by several case studies that highlight the interactive mutuality of stakeholder engagement processes either through company- or country-based case studies. For example, in an interesting study of one company's transition to employee ownership, Cecile Betit addresses 'The Carris Companies: making 100% employee governance the practice. Shifting stakeholder and citizen rights and responsibilities to the employees'. Anne Lawrence then explores why the transformation toward stakeholder engagement happened in the 1990s at Royal Dutch/Shell in 'The drivers of stakeholder engagement: reflections on the case of Royal Dutch/Shell'. Dennis Rondinelli and Ted London look at cross-sectoral stakeholder and company responsibilities through an environment lens in 'Stakeholder and corporate responsibilities in cross-sectoral environmental collaborations: building value, legitimacy and trust'. Gretchen Hund, Jill Engel-Cox, Kimberly Fowler and Howard Klee explore 'Two-way responsibility: the role of industry and its stakeholders in working toward sustainable development', in a study that focuses explicitly on the topical issue of sustainability. Debra King and Alison Mackinnon carry forward the issue of sustainability in their chapter, 'Who cares? Community perceptions in the marketing of corporate citizenship'.

In the final chapters in Part 2, the influence of activists from a range of perspectives becomes focal. Tamara Bliss explores how activists influence corporate decision-making in 'Citizen advocacy groups: corporate friend or foe?' In the final chapter in this section, James Mattingly and Daniel Greening also focus on activism's influence on companies in 'Public-interest groups as stakeholders: a "stakeholder salience" explanation of activism'.

Conclusion

Today's global strategic manager is encouraged to view the world as a resource and the stakeholders with whom he or she interacts as possible allies—or adversaries. To create the core competences (Prahalad and Hamel 1990) they will need to succeed, firms must assemble critically selected factors of production and they must develop their own sources of competitive advantage (Porter 1980). Increasingly, to cope with the global sprawl of multinational corporations in search of a profitable and competitive mix, we believe companies will need to develop the kinds of stakeholder engagement, relationship management, and assessment and reporting strategies dealt with by the authors in this book.

The global reach of multinational corporations has become the vehicle for bringing Darwin's and Smith's prediction of our 'economy of nature' to a reality for today's strategic business planner, and has only served to highlight the need for the (re)integration of business into society, relationships into stakeholder relations, and ethics into managerial practice. The rise in power of global activism involving NGOs, and global business involving multinational corporations (MNCs), according to Mazlish and Buultjers (1993), makes it even more critical today for companies to consider the power and interests of corporate stakeholders when developing strategic plans. The interactivity and mutuality of relationships described in the chapters in this book make it clear that firms and stakeholders *share* the power and responsibility to influence the profit potential of the firm and benefits of firms' success to a society.

Part 1
THINKING ABOUT STAKEHOLDER THEORY

UNFOLDING STAKEHOLDER ENGAGEMENT

Jörg Andriof
KPMG, Germany;
Warwick Business School, UK

Sandra Waddock
Boston College, Carroll School
of Management, USA

> If the unity of the corporate body is real, then there is reality and not simply legal fiction in the proposition that the managers of the unit are fiduciaries for it and not merely for its individual members, that they are . . . trustees for an institution with multiple constituents rather than attorneys for the stockholders (E.M. Dodd, Jr, 1932).

> Corporate Governance is concerned with holding the balance between economic and social goals and between individual and communal goals. The corporate governance framework is there to encourage the efficient use of resources and equally to require accountability for the stewardship of those resources. The aim is to align as nearly as possible the interests of individuals, corporations and society (Sir Adrian Cadbury at the Global Corporate Governance Forum, World Bank 2001).

Stakeholder theory as it has evolved—or unfolded—in recent years has begun to focus attention on the importance of the **relationships** that companies have with stakeholders, relationships that go well beyond those that companies naturally have with shareholders. Generally, perspectives on stakeholder theory have moved away from an entirely corporate-centric focus in which stakeholders are viewed as subjects to be **managed** towards more of a network-based, relational and process-oriented view of company–stakeholder engagement, where at least there is consideration of mutuality, interdependence and power. In this chapter we will argue that unfolding stakeholder relationships, and in particular emerging processes for stakeholder engagement, can best be understood by beginning to integrate corporate social performance/responsibility, stakeholder and strategic relationship theories.

The world that companies face today appears to many observers to be considerably more complex, chaotic and dynamic than the world of previous eras. Technological shifts have created instant global communications capacities that make corporate performance and behaviours in multiple arenas considerably more visible—more transparent—than they ever have been. Boundaries between companies have diminished as long supply chains, strategic alliances, joint ventures and partnerships of various types have evolved into virtual and network organisations. Similar erosion of boundaries can be found in the numerous collaborations and partnerships that companies now have with organisations in the civil society and governmental sectors (Waddell 2000; Waddock 2002). As boundaries have eroded and connectivity increased, demands for greater corporate transparency and accountability have multiplied. Companies have found themselves increasingly on the firing line of an intense anti-globalisation movement, fuelled by activism on issues such as labour and human rights, transparency and anti-corruption initiatives, and environmental protection and sustainability.

One response to these shifts by many companies has been to engage in partnerships and collaborations not only with other companies but also, increasingly, with stakeholders who represent interests that go well beyond traditional corporate interests. If companies are to cope effectively with the stakeholder issues and relationships that now confront them, they need better understanding of the dynamics and expectations fundamental to living, acting and working in a network of collaborative relationships. Drawing on the literatures of business in society, stakeholder theory and strategic relationships, we will attempt in this chapter to provide a framework that can enhance understanding of the dynamics of and rationale for the increased levels of stakeholder engagement witnessed today.

Three underlying theoretical areas help to establish the conceptual foundations unfolding stakeholder relationships and engagement: business in society, stakeholder theory and strategic relationships. This chapter builds a conceptual framework for linking these literatures by reviewing the history and influential ideas of these conceptual foundations to better understand how and why stakeholder engagement occurs.

Business in society refers to the field that describes, analyses and evaluates firms' complex societal and ecological links. Particularly relevant are the concepts of corporate (social) responsibility, corporate social performance and social capital. Stakeholder theory argues that managers of firms have obligations to a broader group of stakeholders than simply shareholders (or owners) and it is usually juxtaposed against stockholder theory. Strategic relationships are an integral part of most organisational activities in today's complex, uncertain environment, particularly as boundaries between organisations become more transparent and complexity of tasks demands interactive rather than unilateral action (Waddock 1989; Waddell 1998). The emergence of new stakeholder engagement strategies, including strategic alliances and partnerships, social partnerships and multi-sector collaborations, means that collaborative strategies (as opposed to purely competitive strategies) have become a critical basis for stakeholder engagement. Thus, partnerships can be described using networking processes that are conceptualised within a relational view of the firm. Within this context, partnerships and other forms of stakeholder engagement that have unfolded in recent years can be seen as trust-based collaborations that build social capital between individual companies and other social institutions working on objectives that can only be achieved jointly and interactively.

1.1 Unfolding business in society

1.1.1 Defining corporate (social) responsibility

The business in society literature, which is deeply intertwined with the emergence of stakeholder engagement strategies, has a long and rich history with two main streams, corporate (social) responsibility and corporate social performance. In this section we will argue that corporate 'social' responsibility has moved from a position where the responsibilities of the firm, originally rather broadly understood to be part of business's social contract (Derber 1998), moved to a narrow concept of maximising returns to shareholders. This narrow understanding has been re-broadened over the course of the 20th century to encompass what was called corporate 'social' responsibility and is currently moving to a new conception of corporate responsibility as embedded in the very practices involved in doing business (Waddock 2002).

Clark (1916) provides one of the earliest considerations of firms' economic and social responsibility, which was further elaborated by Dodd (1932): the concept that managers needed to accept their social responsibilities. Influential references of the 1930s and 1940s include Barnard's 1938 *The Functions of the Executive* and Kreps's 1940 'Measurement of the Social Performance of Business', both of which argued that managers' responsibilities went beyond simple returns to shareholders.

Bowen's 1953 landmark book *Social Responsibilities of the Businessman* is the beginning of a modern period of literature about corporate (social) responsibility (CSR). Bowen argues that 'businessmen' have an obligation 'to pursue those policies, to make those decisions, or to follow those lines of action which are desirable in terms of the objectives and values of our society' (1953: 6). As is suggested by Bowen's emphasis on the objectives and values of society, CSR rests on two fundamental premises. First, in a form of social contracting, business exists at the pleasure of society and, second, business acts as a moral agent within society. These two ideas (social contract and moral agency) provided the basic premises for the evolution of thinking about CSR.

Levitt, however, argues that 'welfare and society are not the corporation's business. Its business is making money, not sweet music. In a free enterprise system, welfare is supported to be automatic; and where it is not, it becomes government's job' (1958: 47). His objection centres on the fact that social responsibility would put business into fields not related to their 'proper aim', as Hayek (1960) stated. In perhaps the strongest, best-articulated and long-standing position against corporate responsibilities beyond maximisation of shareholder wealth, Friedman (1970) argues the social responsibility of business is to increase its profit.

Criticism of the concept of CSR has focused on its ambiguity. For example, Davis and Blomstrom's classic definition states that 'social responsibility is the managerial obligation to take action to protect and improve both the welfare of society as a whole and the interest of organisations' (1975: 6). The main concepts of 'obligation', 'welfare' and 'self-interest of obligations' in this definition are very broad and open to a range of interpretations.

Moving away from economic theory, McGuire (1963) and other authors such as Kohlberg (1969), Davis (1973), Stone (1975) and Frederick (1987) include not only economic and legal obligations but also certain responsibilities to society which extend beyond these obligations. Davis's definition of CSR demonstrates these concerns: 'The firm's consideration of and response to, issues beyond the narrow economic, technical and legal requirements of the firm . . . to accomplish social benefits along with the traditional economic gains which the firm seeks' (1973: 313).

Manne and Wallich (1972) take this definition further, by suggesting that the behaviour of the firm must be voluntary. Jones (1980) argues that corporations have an obligation to constituent groups in society other than shareholders and beyond that, as prescribed by law or union contract. Two facets of this definition are critical. First, the obligation must be voluntarily adopted and, second, the obligation is a broad one, extending beyond the traditional duty to shareholders and to other societal groups: that is, to groups we now call stakeholders (Freeman 1984).

Following this, Preston and Post (1975) and Buchholz (1977) introduced the notion of 'public responsibility of managers', proposing that the social impact of the firm should be guided and appraised within the context of external public policy. The public responsibilities of managers in corporations, in this view (Preston and Post 1975), extend to the ripple effects of business activities in society and on relevant stakeholders through what Preston and Post called interpenetrating systems. The advocates of public responsibility focus more on the social contract side of business and less on the question of morality.

Steiner (1975) conceptualised CSR as a continuum of responsibilities, ranging from 'traditional economic production', to 'government dictated', to a 'voluntary area' and incorporating 'expectations beyond reality'. Similarly, Carroll (1979) argued that companies have multiple responsibilities starting with economic and moving to legal, ethical and discretionary (which would generically be 'social') responsibilities.

In other conceptual developments during this era, Ackerman and Bauer (1976) and Sethi (1979) further extend the concept of CSR. Rather than providing a focus on 'social' responsibility, which assumes an obligation and emphasis on motivation rather than performance, their concept integrates the notion of 'social responsiveness'. Frederick (1987, 1998a) later termed this perspective CSR2, corporate social responsiveness, as opposed to the earlier CSR1, corporate social responsibility. The idea of corporate social responsiveness meant that companies were responsive to social pressures. Frequently, companies operationalised this responsiveness by establishing boundary-spanning functions, such as public affairs (Post et al. 1982), issues management (Wartick 1988) and community relations (Waddock and Boyle 1995; Burke 1999) functions, in the recognition that they play a long-term role in the social system. The responsiveness framework moved companies from a reactive to a more proactive posture with respect to their external (stakeholder) relationships (Preston and Post 1975). Notably, as the field of business in society developed it was and still is most of the time, called 'business and society', as if business were somehow separate and distinct from other elements of society.

Other writers such as Hay et al. (1976) and Zenisek (1979) place greater emphasis on the ethical perspective in modelling social responsibility, viewing it as the degree of 'fit' between society's expectations of the business community and the ethics of business. In 1987, Epstein (1987) provided a definition of CSR in his quest to equate social responsibility, responsiveness and business ethics. Epstein's article is one of the first attempts to integrate ethical responsibility into corporate behaviours, avoiding what Freeman (1999) has called the separation thesis and arguing, in effect, that ethics is integral to action.

Thompson et al. (1991), Warhurst (1998a) and Schwartz and Gibb (1999) have taken the standpoint that CSR should go beyond mere legal obligations. By the late 1980s, the concept of corporate (social) responsibility had evolved towards a more integrated perspective (see Carroll 1979; Epstein 1987; Frederick 1987) that encompassed all of the economic, legal and ethical obligations of business and even some of what Carroll (1979) had termed discretionary responsibilities.

Although CSR is a concept that was developed primarily in North America, it has been applied in Europe and in developing countries, albeit tentatively (Lash 1998).

During the 1990s, the concepts of corporate responsibility and citizenship began to take the place of corporate 'social' responsibility in both business and academic circles, in recognition of the reality that responsibilities are integral to corporate practices, behaviours and impacts, not separate from them (Waddock 2002). Corporate responsibility (CR) or corporate citizenship (CC) has emerged from the legalistic and reactive definitions of the early years through a time in which companies were thought to be obliged or, minimally, requested to 'do social good'. Corporate citizenship, particularly the stakeholder engagement process, is significantly more interactive, moving it beyond even proactive behaviour (see Preston and Post 1975; Waddock 2002). Early efforts to integrate ethics into the understanding of CSR have now evolved into integrated perspectives on CR and CC, such as those offered by Marsden and Andriof (1998):

> As Peter Drucker (1993: 155) says, however, citizenship is more than just a legal term, it is a political term. 'As a political term citizenship means active commitment. It means responsibility. It means making a difference in one's community, one's society, one's country'. Drucker might have added, in today's global economy, 'one's world'. Good corporate citizenship, therefore, is about understanding and managing an organisation's influences on and relationships with the rest of society in a way that minimises the negative and maximises the positive (Marsden and Andriof 1998: 329-30).

Or, as Logan *et al.* (1997) put it:

> Today the phrase leading companies are using to define their relationship with the wider society is 'corporate citizenship'. It implies a responsibility to provide useful goods and services while operating legally, acting ethically, and having concern for the public good. Corporate citizenship is a multi-faceted concept that brings together the self-interest of business and its stakeholders with the interests of society more generally.

These perspectives on CC and CR suggest a more integrated approach to companies' existence in society, a recognition that companies are part of, not separate from, society. Notably these emerging terms recognise the relationship of business to other stakeholders in a new way that is better expressed by the phrase 'business *in* society' than the earlier iteration 'business *and* society', which is still found in journals and textbooks. The evolution of the concept from CSR to CR and CC has a set of implicit features that need to be recognised. One important shift is the movement from reactive postures, to proactive but unilateral boundary-spanning functions, to interactive *engagement* with stakeholders (Preston and Post 1975; Waddock 2002). A second feature of this shift of definition is the recognition of power relationships and interdependences: that is, a movement towards a more systemic understanding of the relationships that exist among organisations and their stakeholders in societies, particularly important in any kind of relationship or engagement process.

In the next section, we will explore a second stream of literature—corporate social performance—which contributes to understanding the evolving roles of business engaged in society with stakeholders and how those roles are shifting.

1.1.2 *Modelling corporate social performance*

Business in society has also been viewed through the lens of corporate social performance more generically. Corporate social performance (CSP) theory is, in part, a response to neoclassical economics' somewhat narrow emphasis on maximising shareholder value. CSP scholars envision societies as complex webs of interconnected stakeholders, with multiple causes and effects in their interactions, and businesses as social institutions with both powers and responsibilities. Although CSP is often thought of as having a normative content, it is generally a theory of how corporations are held accountable to the societies in which they operate or, as Wood (1991a) argues, how they gain legitimacy. CSP's distinctive features are the enhanced development of ideas of corporate responsibility, coupled with the **integration** of responsibility and responsiveness through an approach involving principles, processes and policies in the corporation (Wood 1991b), or what can be collectively called practices (Waddock 2002). CSP models were developed in part to bring a more pragmatic orientation to the relationship between business and society.

Carroll's (1979) three-dimensional model integrates four aspects related to corporate responsibilities: economic, legal, ethical and discretionary responsibilities arranged in a hierarchical pyramid with broad economic responsibilities and relatively narrow discretionary responsibilities. Carroll offered a definition of social responsibility, an identification of social issues or topical areas to which these responsibilities are tied and a consideration of the philosophy, mode or strategy behind business response to social responsibility and social issues. A criticism of Carroll's model is that it fails to capture the processes of analysis, debate and modification that characterise actual corporate behaviour as well as scholarly enquiry (Wartick and Cochran 1985). Carroll, however, recognised the multifaceted complexity of corporations' responsibilities in society and identified topical areas of corporate involvement in society—and with stakeholders—for the first time.

Wartick and Cochran (1985) extended Carroll's model by proposing three underlying dimensions of CSP: **principles** of CSR, **processes** of corporate social responsiveness and **policies** regarding social issues management. These extensions are useful in that they help managers and scholars to appreciate the complementary aspects neglected in Carroll's model, although they still put corporations in the unilateral 'driver's seat' with respect to engagement with stakeholders.

Wood (1991a, 1991b) elaborated and reformulated Carroll's model (essentially by turning it upside down to suggest the importance of ethical and societal/discretionary responsibilities as a foundation for action) and Wartick and Cochran's extensions. According to Wood, social responsiveness is a set of processes, rather than a single process, and policies encompass the observable outcomes of corporate and managerial actions.

Swanson (1995) argues that businesses' economic and duty-aligned perspectives are not integrated as they need to be. Her model provides a research framework that can be applied to explore this integration. To that end, Swanson's model reorients that of Wood by recasting decision-making in terms of ethical and value-based processes that are able to link the individual, the organisation and society. Therefore, Swanson's model discards the assumption that the CSR principles are hierarchical, providing an interactive approach able to link principles, processes and outcomes integrally together (as earlier attempts by Epstein and Frederick, cited above, had also attempted to do).

Drawing on the international context of many modern businesses, Gnyawali (1996) suggests that in today's global environment CSP is shaped by a combination of firm-specific, country-specific and global factors. While some of these appear to be more common across countries, others are country-specific. Also, each firm's unique characteristics shape the response of that firm to given social issues. Thus, to understand the CSP of a firm, one needs to examine factors that shape CSP in the country in which the firm operates, global factors that shape CSP in every country and firm-specific factors that shape the CSP.

The aim of the intellectual field of business in society is to find and develop a constructive business relationship with society. This search is inherently normative, because it seeks to explain what corporations should or should not do on behalf of the social good as well as how they gain legitimacy (Wood 1991b; Buchholz *et al.* 1994; Frederick 1998a, 1998b). Such an endeavour necessarily involves factual accounts of corporate activity. To date, normative and descriptive approaches have not been satisfactorily blended into one theoretical perspective (Swanson 1999), though efforts to link corporate (social) performance with stakeholder theory (Wood and Jones 1995; Waddock and Graves 1997b) may prove fruitful in this regard. Many prominent scholars hold that until integration is forged between normative and descriptive approaches, a coherent theory of business in society will be kept at bay (see Frederick 1994b; Donaldson and Dunfee 1994; Quinn and Jones 1995; Dean 1998; Wicks and Freeman 1998; Jones and Wicks 1999a).

Jones (1996) criticises the fact that, although CSP models are rich in detail and thorough in coverage in their current versions, they offer no formal, empirically tested theory except for the extensive research that has been done to link financial and 'social' performance. Over the years, studies of the correlation between CSP and financial performance have produced varying results (see Ullman 1985; Wood and Jones 1995; Pava and Krausz 1995; Griffin and Mahon 1997). Whereas some studies conclude that a relationship does exist, others produce mixed results (see Cochran and Wood 1984; Aupperle *et al.* 1985; McGuire *et al.* 1988; Barton *et al.* 1989; Preston and Sapienza 1990; Griffin and Mahon 1997; Weaver *et al.* 1999). On the whole, however, recent studies of the studies suggest that, when measurement issues are properly taken into account, the relationship between financial and social performance appears to be neutral or positive (e.g. Wood and Jones 1995; Waddock and Graves 1997a). Indeed, a recent comprehensive meta-study of studies on the financial–social performance link concluded that the question is generally settled in favour of at minimum a neutral and quite possibly a positive relationship (Margolis and Walsh 2001a, 2001b).

Clarkson argued that the difficulties encountered in defining CSP could be attributed, in part, to the broad and inclusive meaning of the word 'social'. 'The connotation of social is society, a level of analysis that is both more inclusive, more ambiguous and further up the ladder of abstraction than a corporation itself' (1995: 102). Current research focuses on linking CSP to theories of stakeholders, ethics and organisations. This linkage systematises the assumptions and theoretical implications of the CSP model; empirically testing ideas on how people perceive, interpret and enact CSP; examining the validity of the CSP model in cross-cultural and multinational settings; and critiques of existing CSP theory. Indeed, studies that operationalise corporate responsibility as stakeholder relationships have begun the necessary integration process between these two streams of literature (e.g. Wood and Jones 1995; Waddock and Graves 1997b; Berman *et al.* 1999).

In the late 1990s, the term 'corporate citizenship' began to replace CSP (e.g. Carroll 1998; Andriof 1998; Goyder 1998; Miller 1998). Companies, as independent legal entities, are members of countries and can be thought of as corporate citizens with legal rights and duties—responsibilities. All companies, therefore, are corporate citizens but their citizenship performance varies just as it does for any individual citizen. As Drucker (1993) argues, citizenship is a political term. Positive corporate citizenship, therefore, can be defined as understanding and managing a company's wider influences on society for the benefit of the company and society as a whole (Marsden and Andriof 1998), and those influences invariable affect stakeholders, as we shall discuss in the next section. Corporate citizenship is closely associated with the idea of reputation management, sustainable development and managing risk (Fombrun 1996; McIntosh *et al.* 1998; Warhurst 1998b; Robertson 1999).

Andriof and Marsden (1999) argue that firms have a ripple effect on society, like a stone being thrown into a pond (see also Preston and Post 1975) (see Fig. 1.1). Firms have economic, environmental and social impacts, which Elkington (1997) referred to as the 'triple bottom line'.

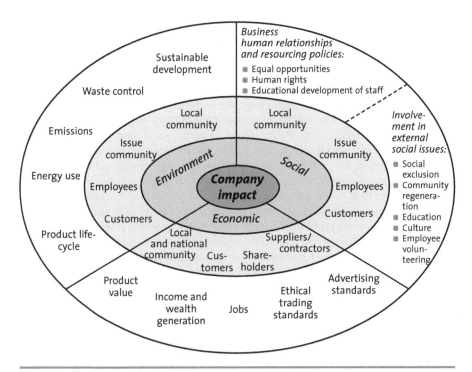

Figure 1.1 *A company's ripple effect*

Within the context of corporate citizenship, international business conduct is influenced by regulations, guidelines, standards and codes of conduct that have proliferated recently and lend a regulatory and principles-based framework to interrelationships of international business organisations, governments and communities at a global, regional and local level. Several observers have noted the need for uniform guidelines to inform transnational corporations' (TNCs') conduct (see Rugman et al. 1985; Struvidant and Vernon-Wortzel 1990; Post 1999) and to help companies deal with stakeholder demands.

Multiple new initiatives and forces are shaping current corporate citizenship initiatives by companies, including proliferating codes of conduct and standards, reporting schemes, demands for transparency and responsibility management systems (Waddock et al. 2001). Recent multiple NGO and stakeholder initiatives aim directly at monitoring TNC performance explicitly on corporate responsibility issues, including Social Accountability International's social accountability standard (SA 8000). Another is the Institute for Social and Ethical Accountability's (ISEA) systematic concept for a firm's social and ethical accountability (AA 1000) standards. One major initiative is the Global Reporting Initiative (GRI), which is attempting to develop social audit standards comparable to traditional accounting's generally accepted accounting principles. The initiative that may have received the most public attention is the UN's Global Compact, which asks companies to sign on to and live up to nine principles based on fundamental UN conventions in the areas of human rights, labour rights and environment.

These and related schemes, some of which are modelled on the quality movement's ISO standards (Waddock et al. 2001) and most of which are voluntary, link corporate 'social' performance or corporate responsibility and the way companies treat various stakeholder groups (in particular employees, customers, suppliers and communities). In addition, such initiatives (and there are many) are responsive to the growing demands from shareholder, labour rights, human rights and environmental activists for greater corporate transparency and accountability. In other words, such initiatives are aimed at helping companies to make real and measurable their responses to stakeholder demands for accountability and better governance (Zadek et al. 1997; Pruzan 1998; Johnson and Greening 1999).

Because multiple points of view are incorporated into the development and implementation of principles and these new reporting schemes, these initiatives can be viewed as responsive to increasing demands for companies to engage with stakeholders and assure corporate legitimacy. The result of these developments is greater recognition of interdependence among stakeholders from different sectors and significantly more collaborative or interactive approaches between companies and their stakeholders. To fully comprehend the implications of these interactive or stakeholder-engaged corporate activities we need to understand the role of social capital, as well as how strategic relationships are developed and sustained. We now turn to understanding the role of social capital in the processes of stakeholder engagement.

1.1.3 Building social capital

Social capital is the glue of connectivity that holds relationships together (e.g. Putnam 1995). Thus we argue that, in an era of networked stakeholder relationships, understanding social capital is essential to learning how to construct and maintain corporation–stakeholder connections. Initially, the term 'social capital' appeared in community studies, highlighting the central importance—for the survival and functioning of city neighbourhoods—of the networks of strong, cross-cutting personal relationships developed over time that provide the basis for trust, co-operation and collective action in communities (Jacobs 1965; Loury 1977). Recent research describes social capital as an asset embedded in relationships—of individuals, communities, networks or societies (Coleman 1990; Burt 1997; Nahapiet and Ghoshal 1998). Unlike other kinds of capital, social capital cannot be traded on the open market; rather, it can change as relationships and rewards change over time, disappearing when the relations cease to exist. Generally, social capital has also been treated as a moral resource, the supply of which increases rather than decreases with use. Nevertheless, some reservations about social capital remain. Locke (1999) criticises social capital theorists for believing that knowledge is primarily a social product, pointing out, for instance, a loss of objectivity and a weak established causality between social capital and other forms of capital.

Although researchers differ in the level of analysis used in describing social capital, it is frequently associated with societal, organisational or industry effectiveness and success. Social capital has been described as an attribute of successful nations or geographic regions (Porter 1990; Fukuyama 1995), communities and societies (Putnam 1993, 1995), individual workers (Burt 1992a), firms in their interactions with other firms (Baker 1990) and individual actors (Portes and Sensenbrenner 1993; Belliveau et al. 1996). Porter (1998), for example, found that companies best achieve competitive success when they are in 'clusters', which are defined by social capital. Extending social capital theory to stakeholder relationships, we argue that successful stakeholder engagement is premised on having high amounts of social capital in the network of company–stakeholder relationships. Trust and, as we shall see below, values are intimately associated with high levels of social capital and may well be paramount to successful stakeholder engagement as well (Svendsen 1998).

Researchers also vary with regard to the normative aspect of social capital implicit in their theories. Social network researchers, for example, assume Granovetter's (1973, 1985) position that individuals best develop social capital by pursuing numerous strategically positioned 'weak ties' with others. Burt (1992b, 1997) describes social capital in terms of 'brokerage opportunities' within a social system, whereby individuals who are able to bridge gaps between otherwise disconnected others (i.e. fill 'structural holes') enhance their stores of social capital. Conversely, writers such as Fukuyama (1995) argue implicitly for the value of trust-creating 'strong ties' among individuals within cohesive and bounded social networks or communities. Coleman (1990) also notes the importance of a closed system in maintaining social capital. Thus, different approaches to social capital alternatively stress density, redundancy or efficiency in social interactions and, in this regard, vary in terms of their implicit normative recommendations for building social capital.

The central premise in social capital theory is that networks of relationships constitute a valuable resource for the conduct of social affairs, providing their members with the 'collectivity-owned capital, a "credential" which entitles them to credit, in the various senses of the word' (Bourdieu 1986: 249). Resources are made available through contacts or connections that networks bring. For example, through 'weak ties' (Granovetter 1973) and 'friends of friends' (Boissevain 1974), network members can gain privileged access to information and to opportunities. Significant social capital, in the form of social status, can be derived from membership of specific networks (Bourdieu 1986; Burt 1992b; D'Aveni and Kesner 1993), including stakeholder networks.

Although these authors agree on the significance of relationships as a resource for social action, they lack consensus with regard to a precise definition of social capital. Nahapiet and Ghoshal (1998) define 'social capital as the sum of the actual and potential resources embedded within, available through and derived from the network of relationships possessed by an individual or social unit' (1998: 243). They present a theoretical model of how social capital facilitates value creation by firms. Building on Moran and Ghoshal's (1996) formulation of value creation as arising from the combination and exchange of resources, Nahapiet and Ghoshal identify three dimensions of social capital: structural, relational and cognitive, all of which can be expected to be present in engaged stakeholder relationships.

Although social capital takes many forms, each of these has two characteristics in common: social capital constitutes some aspects of the social structure, while facilitating the actions of individuals or social units within the structure (Coleman 1990). In addition, for firms' management of social risk, social responsiveness and stakeholder engagement, social capital might be an invaluable resource. Hence, it is important to build the right form of social capital—access information and opportunities or social status, particularly as companies attempt to meet external demands by engaging more directly with different stakeholder groups, the subject of the next section.

1.2 Developing a stakeholder theory of the firm

1.2.1 *Unfolding stakeholder thinking*

Stakeholder thinking is a way to see companies and their activities through constituency concepts and propositions. The idea is that 'holders' who have 'stakes' interact with the firm and thus make its operation possible (Blair 1998). The basic ideas behind this thinking are not new, even though the explicit formulation of the theory is in its relative infancy. It is possible to trace the main impulses back to Barnard (1938), March and Simon (1958), Cyert and March (1963), Thompson (1967) and Pfeffer and Salancik (1978). Freeman (1984) considers that the first definition of the stakeholder concept can be found in an internal memorandum of the Stanford Research Institute from 1963.

Since its introduction, stakeholder thinking has become a consistent dimension in organisational life and is therefore difficult to discount in any organisational model. It was not until Freeman (1984) integrated stakeholder concepts into a coherent construct, however, that stakeholder thinking moved to the forefront of academic attention. A number of scholars have since developed and enhanced Freeman's work. Carroll (1989) was one of the first to use the stakeholder approach explicitly as a framework for organising business in society topics. Brenner and Cochran (1991) and Hill and Jones (1992), meanwhile, offered stakeholder models as alternative approaches to Wood's (1991a) CSP framework. In Kay's 1996 formulation, strategy describes how companies respond to suppliers, customers, competitors and the wider society within which they operate. According to Kay, strategy involves values and expectations of those who can influence the company and its performance—the stakeholder.

Donaldson and Preston (1995: 70) argued that stakeholder thinking could potentially 'explain and guide the structure and operations of the established corporation'. Several authors (Brenner and Cochran 1991; Hill and Jones 1992; Donaldson and Preston 1995; Jones 1995) have treated stakeholder thinking as the foundation for a theory of the firm and as a framework for the business in society field. Thus, stakeholder thinking has matured from servant logic supporting the advancement of other theories to a theory of the firm in its own right. Whether a stakeholder 'theory' currently exists is a matter of debate (Harrison and Freeman 1999). Nevertheless, efforts to create testable stakeholder theory (Brenner and Cochran 1991; Jones 1995; Mitchell *et al.* 1997; Waddock and Graves 1997b; Berman *et al.* 1999; Sachs *et al.*1999; Post *et al.* 2002) are evidence of a movement towards theory that explains how organisations function with respect to various constituencies with whom they are inextricably embedded.

Stakeholder theory development has centred on two related streams: (1) defining the stakeholder concept and (2) classifying stakeholders into categories that provide an understanding of individual stakeholder relationships. One of the primary challenges in stakeholder analysis has been the construction of a universally accepted definition of the term 'stake' (Donaldson 1995). Starik (1994) notes that, although there has been an abundance of articles and books using stakeholder thinking, the meaning of the term 'stakeholder' has not been consistently applied. Freeman's definition of stakeholder— 'any group or individual who can affect or who is affected by the achievement of the firm's objectives' (1984: 25)—continues to provide the boundaries of what constitutes a stake.

Although debate continues over whether to broaden or narrow the definition, most researchers have utilised a variation of Freeman's concept. For example Hill and Jones define stakeholders as 'constituents who have a legitimate claim on the firm' (1992: 133). Carroll (1993) also argues that those groups or individuals can be stakeholders by virtue of their legitimacy, but he broadens the scope of the definition to include those who have power—the ability to impact the organisation. Clarkson (1995) suggests an alternative approach for identifying and evaluating stakeholder claims, which casts stakeholders more narrowly as risk-bearers. He argues that a stakeholder has some form of capital, either financial or human, at risk and, therefore, has something to lose or gain depending on a firm's behaviour. To these elements, Waddock (2002) adds a tie or tether that creates a bond of some sort.

Regardless of how Freeman's (1984) definition is modified, there is a core idea that underlies the unfolding of stakeholder thinking. Whatever the definition within the stakeholder perspective, organisations are required to address a set of stakeholder expectations and, increasingly, they find themselves engaged with stakeholder groups or their representatives in various ways as part of the process to meet these expectations. Thus, management choice is a function of stakeholder influences (Brenner and Cochran 1991; Mitchell *et al.* 1997). Consequently, the main objectives in stakeholder research have been to identify who a firm's stakeholders are and to determine what types of influence they exert (McGee 1998).

A stakeholder theory of the firm, however, requires not only an understanding of the types of stakeholder influence but also how firms respond to those influences or what we call engagement. Although focusing on individual stakeholder relationships is appropriate for classifying types of stakeholder, this analysis cannot be extended to describe a firm's behaviours, because each firm faces a different set of stakeholders, which aggregate into unique patterns of influence. Ambler and Wilson (1995) demonstrate that firms do not simply respond to each stakeholder individually; they respond, rather, to the interaction of multiple influences from the entire stakeholder set. Thus, explanations of how organisations respond to their stakeholders require an analysis of the complex array of multiple, interdependent relationships existing within the stakeholder environment.

Extant research has concentrated on producing classification schemes for categorising stakeholders according to the type of influence they exert on organisations. Several schemes exist, including Carroll's (1989) environmental sorting and Clarkson's (1995) primary and secondary classification; Freeman's (1984) internal and external change distinction; and the Scandinavian contribution, which focuses on types of transaction (Näsi 1995b). Yet, no matter how popular stakeholder analysis has become and how richly descriptive it is, there is no agreement on what Freeman (1994) calls 'The Principle of Who or What Really Counts'. In 1997, Mitchell *et al.* developed a theory of stakeholder identification and salience—incorporating normative and descriptive theory elements—focusing on three core variables: power, legitimacy and urgency. Berman *et al.* (1999) partly tested the stakeholder identification and salience theory. The results provide support for a strategic stakeholder management model, but no support for an intrinsic stakeholder commitment model, which suggests that companies may engage most directly with those stakeholders that exert significant pressures rather than simply for the sake of engagement or out of a values-based orientation.

Building stakeholder partnerships—stakeholder engagement—is an attempt to describe the behaviour of an organisation within its environment. The conceptual competition within stakeholder theory, between legitimacy and power, is reflected in virtually every major theory of the firm—particularly in agency, behavioural, institutional, population ecology, resource dependence and transaction cost theories (Argenti and Campbell 1997). Resource dependence theory suggests that power accrues to those who control resources needed by the organisation, thereby creating power differentials among parties (Pfeffer 1981, 1997b), and it confirms that the possession of resource power makes a stakeholder important to a firm. Legitimacy is achieved if patterns of organisational practice are in congruence with the wider social system (Scott 1987; Powell and DiMaggio 1991). Institutional theory describes this adaptation. Strategy processes deriving from resource dependence are primarily proactive; institutionalised processes are reactive (Mintzberg *et al.* 1998; Mintzberg and Lampel 1999); while stakeholder engagement is inherently interactive (Preston and Post 1975), based on mutual interdependence among actors. Figure 1.2 classifies research themes in terms of the two underlying rationales of stakeholder thinking.

Corporate responsibility and the maintenance of sound organisational ethics may not invariably depend wholly on the strategic behaviour induced by the anticipation of organisational gain. Organisations may act ethically or responsibly not only because of any direct link to a positive organisational outcome (e.g. greater prestige or more resources) but merely because it would be unthinkable to do otherwise. In this way, organisational behaviour may be driven not by processes of interest mobilisation (DiMaggio 1988) but by preconscious acceptance of institutionalised values or practices.

Within the resource dependence perspective, theory assumes that organisations may be interest-driven and that organisations exercise some degree of control or influence over the resource environment or the organisation's exchange partners for the purposes of achieving stability. Theorists argue that organisational stability is achieved through the exercise of power, control or the negotiation of interdependences for purposes of achieving a predictable or stable inflow of vital resources and reducing environmental uncertainty. From a resource dependency perspective, companies deal with the concerns of

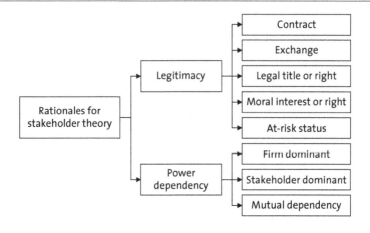

Figure 1.2 **Rationales for stakeholder theory**

stakeholders or engage with stakeholders because it is in their interest to do so. A power perspective suggests the importance of assessing the relative power balance between stakeholders and the focal company so that the company can gain legitimacy in the eyes of relevant stakeholders (or 'society') and so that the interaction can actually be mutual.

1.2.2 *Distinguishing stakeholder theory dimensions*

Freeman (1995) notes that the last 15 years can be characterised as a search for a full-blown theory of stakeholders able to replace the dominant theory in business schools, namely the stockholder theory. However, he believes 'that there is no one stakeholder theory of the firm' (1995: 35). Stakeholder theory has at least four types. These various theories are often intertwined in the literature and are rarely stated formally. Donaldson and Preston (1995) distinguish the theoretical dimensions implicit in stakeholder theory: descriptive/empirical, instrumental and normative—and make explicit what was merely implicit in early formulations of stakeholder theory. These early formulations simultaneously suggested that: (1) firms and/or managers actually behave in certain ways (descriptive/empirical); (2) certain outcomes are more likely if firms/managers behave in certain ways (instrumental); and (3) firms/managers should behave in certain ways (normative). Donaldson and Preston also point out that none of the theoretical formulations of stakeholder theory is formally stated or fully developed. Recognising and valuing Donaldson and Preston's perspectives on stakeholder theory, Freeman (1995) suggests a fourth use of stakeholder thinking—metaphorical or narrative. In this context stakeholder theory is a story rather than a theoretical construct. Freeman considers that the 'task is to take metaphors like stakeholder thinking and embed it in a story about how human beings create and exchange value' (1995: 45).

Donaldson and Preston (1995) conclude that the most promising area for the development of theory in stakeholder theory is in the normative realm. Indeed, they offer a normative justification for stakeholder theory based on property rights. Other normative justifications include social contract approaches, Kantian capitalism, agent morality and the normative arguments for CSR. Each of these normative positions is legitimate because each is falsifiable, presumably through logic, counter-argument and/or appeal to higher normative principle.

Instrumental stakeholder theory (Jones 1994) is developed in the extensive literature attempting to link corporate responsibility and financial performance indicators (Margolis and Walsh 2001a). Firms run by their top managers and embedded in markets which provide some discipline for inefficiency have relationships—called contracts—with many stakeholders (Jones 1994). Among the many mechanisms available for reducing contracting costs is the voluntary adoption of behavioural standards, which reduce or eliminate opportunism—that is, certain ethical norms. While systematic benefits are easy to identify, individual benefits are less so. Frank (1988) has argued that honest, trustworthy and co-operative people (or stakeholders with high levels of social capital with respect to companies) help to solve the problem of opportunism and, hence, are desirable partners in contracting relationships. A key to competitive advantage for firms is, therefore, mutually trusting and co-operative contracts with their stakeholders: that is, social capital. In the realm of descriptive/empirical stakeholder theory, several possibilities exist. One such statement could be phrased thus: 'Managers behave as if several stakeholder groups, not just shareholders, affect firm performance'. Again, this is an empirically falsifiable claim: that is, evidence could be accumulated to show that managers do not, in fact, behave as if stakeholders mattered in terms of the success of the firm. A semantically similar, but substantively distinct, descriptive statement could read: 'Managers behave as if stakeholders mattered because of the intrinsic justice of stakeholders' claims on the firm'.

Empirically, Clarkson (1995) has accumulated evidence that does not contradict either of these claims. Berman *et al.* (1999) provide support for a strategic stakeholder management model, but place little emphasis on an intrinsic stakeholder commitment model. Brenner and Cochran (1991: 57) make a theoretically more aggressive but empirically less traceable claim: 'The stakeholder theory of the firm posits that the nature of organisations' stakeholders, their values, their relative influence on decisions and the nature of the situation are all relevant information for predicting organisational behaviour.' Although Brenner and Cochran argue that 'values which are highly weighted should be favoured in actual choice situations' (1991: 44), they stop short of substantive prediction or description of the mechanism(s) through which the predicted behaviour might occur.

Despite these efforts, no descriptive theory of the firm has emerged that might imitate, or perhaps replace, the theories of neoclassical and managerial economics. A descriptive theory of the firm may not be forthcoming unless some member of the community of business in society scholars is willing to make some heroic assumption(s) about human behaviour (see Freeman and Liedtka 1997; Hutton 1997; Gioia 1999). The success of economic theory is premised on the behavioural assumptions of rational self-interest, which Etzioni (1988) and others have thoroughly demolished. Unfortunately, even though these same scholars have also documented a wide variety of human behaviour—some self-interested, some altruistic, some rational, some irrational—their models still leave enormous amounts of variation unexplained.

In 1999, Jones and Wicks developed a 'convergent stakeholder theory'. A convergent stakeholder theory incorporates elements of the social science approach and the normative ethics approach (Jones and Wicks 1999a). This theoretical view of organisations

		Rationale	Unit of analysis	Level of analysis	Underlying theory	Advocates
Narrative approach	Metaphorical	Stakeholder as part of a 'story' in broader narrative of corporate life	Participants of organisational processes	Macro-organisational market perspective as a system	Strategic management business policy	Mitroff 1983; Freeman 1995; Litz 1996
	Normative	Corporate social responsibility via fiduciary principle and principle of corporate legitimacy	Modern property rights	System-centred principles	• Utilitarianism • Libertarianism • Social contract theory	Donaldson and Preston 1995; Donaldson and Dunfee 1999
			Agent morality	Organisation-centred principles	Principal agency theory	Wood and Jones 1995; Yuthas and Dillard 1999
			Social contracts (welfare and justice)	System-centred principles	Social contract theory	Rawls 1971; Rousseau 1762; Child and Marcoux 1999
			Kantian capitalism	System-centred principles	Ethical theory (categorical imperative)	Freeman and Evan 1990; Wright and Ferris 1997
Analytical approach	Instrumental	Effect of stakeholder consideration on firm's bottom line	Efficient relationships/trans-actions/relational contracts	Competitive behaviour	• Social net-work theory • Positive agency theory • Transaction cost theory	Frank 1988; Preston et al. 1991; Hill and Jones 1992; Jones 1994, 1995
	Description	Organisational and managerial behaviour for stakeholder consideration	Extrinsic performance orientation and intrinsic justice/value orientation	Managerial behaviour	Managerial economics and organisational psychology/ sociology	Clarkson 1995; Etzioni 1988; Mitchell et al. 1997
			Nature of stakeholders and their values and their influence on decisions and nature of the situation	Organisational behaviour	Organisation theory/decision theory	Brenner and Cochran 1991; Logsdon and Yuthas 1997; Berman et al. 1999

Table 1.1 **Stakeholder theory dimensions**

helps to explain why managers can develop morally sound approaches to business and then ensure that they work (Donaldson 1999; Marens and Wicks 1999). Trevino and Weaver (1999), however, question Jones's and Wicks's (1999a) assertion that their convergent approach can be used to integrate divergences in stakeholder theory. They argue that Jones and Wicks have failed to prove the existence of any plausible empirical stakeholder theory that can be integrated with normative theory. Furthermore, Jones's and Wicks's attempt to create a convergent theory has done little to advance stakeholder research beyond its current limitations (Beaver 1999). Freeman (1999) views stakeholder theory as divergent, rather than convergent, claiming that there should be no separation between ethics and performance (i.e. some degree of responsibility is embedded in all action; see Waddock 2002). Freeman argues for multiple narratives or stories about companies and stakeholders. What is clear from all of this theorising about stakeholders is that they are important elements in the constitution of the firm and that attention must be paid to their interests to some degree or other. Companies that understand this reality recognise the network in which they are inextricably embedded and work to engage with relevant stakeholders to avoid surprises that might otherwise face them.

1.2.3 Engaging with stakeholders

Stakeholder groups can be assessed against strategic aims according to three sets of criteria—influence, impact and alignment (Harrison and St John 1996). Each of these is measurable, to a greater or lesser degree. Clearly, the higher the potential for business fortunes and the higher the business impact on stakeholder groups, the more important it is to maintain a constructive dialogue. The easier the dialogue becomes, the greater the alignment of values between the company and the stakeholder group (Scholes and Clutterbuck 1998). Managing stakeholder audiences as if they were discrete and unconnected is no longer a viable strategy. Many companies have found that to be effective in the complex and often chaotic world they now face they need to develop systems and approaches that enable them to prioritise stakeholders, align closely to them, integrate the messages to and from them, and build bridges between them rather than buffer impacts.

Stakeholder research has concentrated primarily on classifying individual stakeholder relationships and influential strategies rather than understanding stakeholder engagement. Vogel (1978) first addressed what Frooman (1999) calls stakeholder influence strategies, including proxy resolutions and boycotts. In recent years, stockholder resolutions (Davis and Thompson 1994), boycotts (Paul and Lydenberg 1992) and modified vendettas (Shipp 1987; Corlett 1989) have all been recognised as stakeholder influence strategies. In these empirical studies scholars have generally considered the effectiveness of the strategies, or the market's reaction to such strategies and have included examinations of boycotts (Garrett 1987; Pruitt et al. 1988), divestitures (Davidson et al. 1995) and letter-writing campaigns (Smith and Cooper-Martin 1997).

Frooman's 1999 stakeholder influence theory suggests the existence of four types of stakeholder influence and four types of resource relationship. It argues, further, that the balance of power implicit in the relationship determines which of the types of strategy a stakeholder will use. Still, this approach cannot explain how a firm engages with its stakeholders.

Each firm faces a different set of stakeholders, which aggregate into unique patterns of influence. Thus, firms do not engage with each stakeholder individually but, rather, must answer the simultaneous demands of multiple stakeholders. Rowley (1997) describes this simultaneous influence of multiple stakeholders in a two-by-two matrix: the density of the stakeholder network by the centrality of the focal organisation. The bedrock of this work is Oliver's (1991) effort to converge institutional and resource dependence theory and Rowley's attempts to predict how companies respond to stakeholders in a given configuration.

As noted above, recent developments external to the corporation have weakened conventional boundaries between internal and external stakeholders as they relate to management principles and systems. As a consequence, stakeholders require more, and different, management attention than they traditionally received: that is, there is increasing demand for engaged stakeholder relationships.

The instrumental perspective is that better stakeholder relationships result in higher profitability or increased firm value. Examples of instrumental outcomes include: improved predictability of changes in the external environment resulting from better communication with external stakeholders (which may also lead to greater control); higher percentages of successful innovations resulting from the involvement of stakeholders in product/service design teams; and fewer incidents of damaging moves by stakeholders (e.g. strikes, boycotts, bad press) owing to improved relationships and greater trust (Svendsen 1998; Moss Kanter 1999).

Stakeholders thus provide a lens for viewing and interpreting important trends in the operating environment. Therefore, 'proactive stakeholder engagement is simply the right thing to do' (Harrison and St John 1996: 49). One of the key factors that determines the priority of a particular stakeholder is its influence on the uncertainty facing the firm. For example, political power influences environmental uncertainty. In addition, it is important to understand the role of strategic choice in determining the nature of the interdependency that exists between a stakeholder and a firm. Strategic decisions at all levels influence the importance of various stakeholders.

When environments are more complex and uncertain, webs of interdependences are created among stakeholders. Additionally, the problems faced may look more like what Ackoff (1975) called 'messes': problems that require interaction among multiple stakeholders for resolution. In these environments, bridging (also called boundary-spanning) techniques are needed that build on interdependences rather than buffering them (Harrison and St John 1996), and collaborative strategies become important. As Pfeffer and Salancik argue, 'The typical solution to problems of interdependence and uncertainty involves increasing the mutual control over each other's activities' (1978: 43). Joint ventures with competitors, co-operative product development efforts involving suppliers and customers, and industry-level lobbying efforts are examples of partnering techniques that bring the firm into closer alliance with its critical stakeholders. Research suggests that strategic alliances are a device for reducing both the uncertainties that arise from unpredictable demand and the pressures that come from high levels of interdependences among organisations (Burgers et al. 1993) (see Fig. 1.3).

Harrison and St John (1996) postulate that firms should consider proactive partnering techniques (i.e. stakeholder engagement) not only to increase control in the face of environmental uncertainty but also to create organisational flexibility. Partnering and engagement activities allow firms to build bridges with their stakeholders in the pursuit of common goals, whereas traditional stakeholder management techniques (buffering) simply facilitate the satisfaction of stakeholder needs and/or demands. Further, as noted earlier, such interaction requires relatively high levels of social capital (trusting relationships) if it is to be effective.

The potential benefits of bridges between partners may be illustrated using relationships with customers as an example. Firms with a traditional buffering posture towards customers focus on arm's-length information-gathering about new product needs and expected demand, and compliance with current quality and service expectations, all in an effort to buffer the firm from uncertainty and customer complaints. With bridging techniques, a firm might choose to create stronger linkages with customers by involving them directly in the firm's product development programmes, continuous improvement

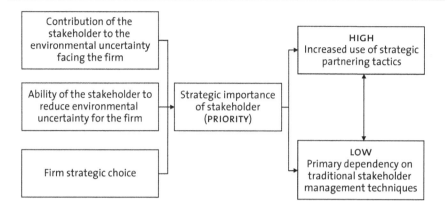

Figure 1.3 **Strategic importance of stakeholders**

Source: Harrison and St John 1996

programmes, and production planning and scheduling. Bridging builds on interdependency and engagement rather than buffering it. Thus, to fully understand stakeholder engagement, we also need to understand how strategic relationships are built and collaborative strategies work.

1.3 Reviewing strategic relationships

1.3.1 Appreciating collective strategies

For much of its history, business policy has characterised the organisational environment as an exogenous entity, or a set of external constraints delimiting what is possible in terms of strategic action. Managers must navigate within and around these constraints as lone pioneers negotiate an intractable terrain. Thus, strategic management is seen as an entrepreneurial adventure in which firms must circumvent 'threats' and exploit 'opportunities' (Andrews 1971). Organisations are basically viewed as solitary units confronted by faceless environments. This may be characterised by business policy's pioneering ethos.

More recently, organisational environments have been viewed as neither faceless nor intractable, but as constituted by specific interest groups or stakeholders with whom organisations may strike favourable bargains and thereby shape the basic nature of their operating domains (Ansoff 1965; Freeman 1984; Ocasio 1997). Astute manipulations of stakeholder resource dependency can afford organisations a degree of autonomy to exercise strategic choice in the forging of a 'negotiated environment' (Cyert and March 1963). Despite this mutual interdependence with others, however, organisations are still viewed as pitched against their environments in the sense that they act on their own behalf, pursuing localised interests rather than furthering the joint goal of the organisational collectives in which they are immersed. In business policy, analysis typically proceeds only from the point of view of the focal organisation rather than from the network of interrelated entities in which any organisation exists. Strategic choice is predicted on the independent actions and self-interested motivations of the focal units concerned. This may be characterised as business policy's 'egocentric organisation' (Astley and Fombrun 1983).

Some of this narrowness of focus on single units has been overcome with the importation of ideas from the field of industrial organisation and its emphasis on aggregates of organisations in whole industries. Again, this development has simply reinforced the notion that fundamentally alien environments confront organisations. The managerial task is viewed as one of devising a 'competitive strategy' for bettering rivals (Porter 1980). Business policy's debt to military science (Evered 1983) becomes evident here: policy-making approximates to a cut-throat game of 'warfare' (Porter 1980). In this warfare an astute choice of 'competitive weapons' (Uyterhoeven *et al.* 1973), 'strategic moves' (Hofer and Schendel 1978) and 'counterpunch plans' (MacMillan 1982) sorts out the 'winners' from the 'losers' (Allen and Hammond 1975). In other words, inter-organisational relationships are seen as ultimately competitive and antagonistic. This may be characterised as business policy's 'battlefield analogy' (Astley and Fombrun 1983).

Each of these characterisations is grounded in a particular conception of the nature of organisation–environment relationships. The pioneering ethos implies that the critical variable in organisation–environment relations is 'constraint', in that organisations are forced to adapt to sets of exogenous and rather intractable contingencies (Astley 1984). The egocentric orientation implies that the critical variable in organisation–environment relations is 'choice', in that strategic, self-serving action assumes a degree of autonomy on the part of organisations to select beneficial courses of action and to manoeuvre independently on their own behalf. The battlefield analogy implies that the critical variable in organisation–environment relations is 'competition'. Thus, organisations must constantly strive to do better than their rivals in order to survive. Constraint, choice and competition have been seen, respectively, as the central foci in the history of the field of strategic management.

Astley (1984) proposes, however, that the field has neglected one particular variable in organisation–environment relations. This is 'collaboration' or joint action by organisations on matters of strategic importance. Astley argues that collaboration should join constraint, choice and competition as being of central interest to strategic management theorists. It is to this end that scholars call for an appreciation of the role of collaboration as an integral part of what is termed 'collective strategy' (Bresser 1988).

Business policy should have, behind its pioneering ethos, a sentiment. This view is grounded in the conception of the environment as an exogenous constraint and recognises that organisational environments are primarily socially constructed environments that emerge from the milieu of interactions taking place among the collectivities of organisations pervading modern society. In this view, threats and opportunities are not so much found as created. Resources are not simply fortuitously discovered and exploited, but produced. The source of this creativity and production lies in collective organisational actions. Strategic networks increasingly influence contemporary environments. The stakeholder perspective, because it is premised on a network of relationships, inherently falls into the category of strategic networks.

1.3.2 *Towards strategic networking*

The broad, context-sensitive concept of strategic management emerging in modern strategy research is based on recognition that firms must be regarded as open systems, dependent on their environment for survival and goal achievement. In most businesses, the environment has changed from low competition and low complexity towards more turbulent, complex and demanding operating conditions (Drucker 1980; Ansoff 1984; Peters 1987). Increased interdependency makes it necessary to focus on a firm's strategic relations to a larger set of actors—stakeholders—in the task environment and to increase awareness of relevant contextual aspects behind the market scene. Accordingly, the stakeholder perspective on strategy highlights a major challenge to strategic management stemming from changed market conditions. This challenge incorporates ecological concerns, global aspects, CSR and long-term commitment and co-operations among various market participants, not to mention the demands on companies of critical external stakeholders.

Strategic network theory can contribute to new principles of management by:

- Including whole systems of organisations, the macro environment as well as the micro level of the individual network actors

- Regarding personal relations among managers as an important element in the contractual grounding of an exchange

- Discussing the role of long-term commitment, reciprocity and trust (social capital) to reduce uncertainty about the future consequences of relational investments

- Including not only economic and technical information related to price, product and market but also information flows about social behaviour, values, symbols and culture-specific authority criteria (Powell 1990)

Networks are complementary rather than counter to competitive relations and short-term contracts in the market (Dussauge and Garrette 1999). The benefits of networks include increased flexibility from the partners, a more open stream of confidential information between exchange partners and reduced conflict, as shown in Table 1.2 (Borch and Arthur 1995).

Stakeholder engagement recognises not only the complexity but also the potential benefits of strategic networks with key stakeholders because the firm in a strategic network benefits from cumulative processes including both increased dependency through exchange and the development of social capital. The partners in a network gradually build dependency on resources controlled by others in the network and position themselves to make future use of these resources (Johanson and Mattsson 1987).

The partners within a strategic network—or set of stakeholder relationships—must rely on each other to share unforeseen benefits and costs of the exchange. Such mutual trust can be achieved through the extension of exchange relations to incorporate deeper personal commitments among the participants. Shared values, norms, inter-personal affiliation and respect, which have been found important in helping the single firm to cope with increased complexity and uncertainty, need now to be extended to stakeholder contractual relations. Because of the complexity and turbulence of network relationships,

	Neoclassical principles of strategic management	*Strategic network management principles*
Flexibility	Low, limited to formal contract	High, based on openness to the consequences of trust
Conflict-reducing mechanisms	Power-oriented; based on formal agreement and law	Norm-oriented; based on communicative action and agreement
Range of relation	Limited in time and space through formal contracts	Long-range because of transaction-specific investments
Connection to personal and social life-worlds	None; instrumental and system-oriented	Several; co-ordination through involvement of personal affiliation and social norms

Table 1.2 *Neoclassical principles of strategic management versus strategic network management principles*

the formalised legal contract is not sufficient to co-ordinate and control such transactions (Granovetter 1985). A relation-based co-ordination can, however, reduce uncertainty and thereby transaction costs (Williamson 1991) in such networks.

In sum, a stakeholder perspective emphasising strategic network principles particularly for companies willing to engage with stakeholders transparently and interactively, suggests a broad analytical frame as well as new tools for solving strategic challenges. Included are knowledge of trust-building (social capital formation) and of creating an atmosphere to stimulate learning and adaptation processes (Johanson and Mattsson 1987) through engagement and collaborative interaction, mutuality and power sharing. Strategic networks may serve as a complementary solution to co-ordination through formal, legal contracts based on law, or through hierarchy and internal bureaucracy.

1.3.3 Stakeholder engagement as a source of competitive advantage

Scholars in the strategy field are concerned fundamentally with explaining differential firm performance (Rumelt *et al.* 1991). As strategy scholars have searched for sources of competitive advantage, two prominent views have emerged regarding the sources of supernormal returns. The first, market-based view (MBV), associated with Porter (1980), suggests that supernormal returns are primarily a function of a firm's membership in an industry with favourable structural characteristics. The second view, the resource-based view (RBV) of the firm, argues that differential firm performance is fundamentally due to heterogeneity, rather than industry structure (Rumelt 1984, 1991; Wernerfelt 1984; Barney 1991). Firms that are able to accumulate resources and capabilities that are rare, valuable, non-substitutable and difficult to imitate will achieve a competitive advantage over competing firms (Dierickx and Cool 1989; Barney 1991). Thus, extant RBV theory views the firm as the primary unit of analysis. As a further development of the RBV, the dynamic capabilities approach (Teece *et al.* 1997) also views the firm as the unit of analysis.

Although these two perspectives have contributed greatly to the understanding of how firms achieve above-normal returns, they overlook the important fact that the (dis)advantages of an individual firm are often linked to the (dis)advantages of the network of relationships in which the firm is embedded (Dyer and Singh 1998; Porter 1998). Proponents of the RBV have emphasised that a competitive advantage results from those resources and capabilities that are owned and controlled by a single firm. Competing firms purchased standardised (non-unique) inputs that cannot be sources of advantage, because these inputs (factors) are either readily available to all competing firms or the cost of acquiring them is approximately equal to the economic value they create (Barney 1986). However, a firm's critical resources may extend beyond firm boundaries.

Recent studies suggest that productivity gains in the value chain are possible when trading partners are willing to make relation-specific investments and combine resources in unique ways (Dyer 1996). Firms that combine resources in unique ways realise an advantage over competing firms who are unable or unwilling to do so. Thus, idiosyncratic inter-organisational linkages may be a source of relational rents and competitive advantage (Moss Kanter 1994).

Dyer and Singh's (1998) relational view of the firm suggests that a firm's critical resources may span firm boundaries and be embedded in inter-organisational routines and processes. The central thesis of the relational view is that a pair or network of organisations can develop relationships that result in sustainable competitive advantage. Inter-organisational relationships are the unit of analysis. The relational view extends the existing literature on alliances and networks in a number of ways. First, it attempts to integrate what is known regarding the benefits of collaboration by examining the inter-organisational rent-generating process. Dyer and Singh (1998) have argued that collaborating organisations can generate relational rents through relation-specific assets, knowledge-sharing routines, complementary resource endowments and effective governance. Second, the relational view has identified the isolating mechanism that preserves the relational rents generated through effective inter-organisational collaboration. The relational view introduces mechanisms not discussed previously in the literature on sustainability of rents: inter-organisational asset connectedness, partner scarcity, co-evolution of capabilities and institutional environment. As we consider stakeholder engagement strategies, clearly these mechanisms become relevant to determining whether stakeholder engagement can also potentially be a source of competitive advantage.

1.4 Unfolding stakeholder engagement

Business in society, stakeholder and strategic relationships theories comprise the conceptual foundations and key issues used to construct a framework with which stakeholder engagement can be analysed. From each theoretical area, a key message can be gained that reflects the theoretical development and its likely future direction. Unfolding stakeholder engagement is premised on the belief that progressive companies have moved from reactive compliance-oriented management of social issues through proactive boundary-spanning functions that cope more effectively with external matters and into interactive engagement strategies with a range of stakeholders important in a company's network. Such collaborative strategies depend on the establishment and maintenance of social capital, help a company to meet stakeholder demands and expectations (i.e. focus on corporate responsibility) and create a network of ongoing relationships. Stakeholder engagement can also potentially provide critical strategic information, resources and problem-solving capabilities not available to companies that still view themselves as lone rangers. The strategic relationship literature clearly indicates that a transition from a buffered dependency on stakeholders towards a bridging dynamic interdependency between a firm and its surroundings as well as influential stakeholders is taking place.

Stakeholder engagements and partnerships are defined as trust-based collaborations between individuals and/or social institutions with different objectives that can only be achieved together. The basis for successful partnerships is an agreement about rules for co-operation. A higher consensus or agreement, achieved through interaction, means less regulated partnering because of a minimised conflict potential and can best occur when social capital exists.

Stakeholder engagement can thus be viewed as a process for managing a company's social risk, connecting with stakeholders and building social capital. Stakeholder engagement today is an important aspect of many companies' business strategy. We have argued above that corporate responsibilities are integral or inherent in relationships with stakeholders, relationships enacted through operating policies and in the networks in which companies exist. Social capital encapsulates resources embedded in stakeholder relationships (Nahapiet and Ghoshal 1998) and is an important outcome of navigating social risk through connecting processes with stakeholders.

STAKEHOLDER THINKING
Beyond paradox to practicality

Kenneth E. Goodpaster, T. Dean Maines and Michelle D. Rovang
University of St Thomas, USA

This essay departs from two convictions: (1) that ethical values in any society must ultimately be oriented towards the common good (today, more than ever before, the common good of a global community); and (2) that, in the arena of business ethics, there is
a non-contingent connection between ethical values and 'stakeholder thinking', broadly
interpreted. The purpose of our reflections is to reveal the sometimes paradoxical nature
of that non-contingent connection, while describing a concrete tool (currently being
field-tested) for fostering stakeholder thinking (without paradox) in business enterprises.

2.1 Clarification of 'stakeholder thinking'

Many believe that 'stakeholder thinking' is important because it is through this kind of
thinking that specifically *ethical* values enter management decision-making. On this view,
business ethics is really about setting aside more conventional management frameworks
in favour of a stakeholder framework. It is our belief that this idea, while it contains an
important truth, can be very misleading.[1] To understand why, we will first define the term
'stakeholder' and then distinguish between two very different ideas with which it can be
associated: *analysis* and *synthesis*.

---

1   The inadequacy, as will become apparent, stems from several sources: (a) mistaking stake-
    holder analysis and stakeholder synthesis; (b) mistaking partial and impartial stakeholder
    synthesis; (c) mistaking fiduciary and non-fiduciary responsibility; and (d) mistaking constit-
    uency-based thinking and moral reflection based on the common good.

The term 'stakeholder' appears to have been invented in the early 1960s as a deliberate play on the English word 'stockholder' to signify that there are other parties who have a 'stake' in the decision-making of the modern, publicly held corporation besides those holding equity positions. Professor R. Edward Freeman (1984: 46) defines the term as follows: 'A stakeholder in an organisation is (by definition) any group or individual who can affect or is affected by the achievement of the organisation's objectives'. Examples of stakeholder groups (other than stockholders) are employees, customers, suppliers, communities and even competitors.

2.1.1 Decision-making: stakeholder analysis and stakeholder synthesis

Any rational decision-making process includes such steps as: (i) gathering information, (ii) sorting, (iii) weighing, (iv) integrating and, eventually, (v) acting on the processed information. 'Stakeholder analysis', as we shall use the phrase, includes the first two of these steps in relation to information about stakeholders, but does not go beyond them. In a stakeholder analysis of several options available to a decision-maker, the affected parties for each available option can be identified and the positive and negative implications for each stakeholder group can be clarified. But questions having to do with weighing and integrating this information in order to make a choice remain to be answered. These latter steps are not a part of decision *analysis* but of decision *synthesis*.

Analysis, then, is simply the first stage of a process that eventually calls upon the moral (or non-moral) values of the decision-maker. To be told that someone regularly makes stakeholder analysis part of his or her decision-making, is to learn very little about such a person's values. We learn that stakeholders are identified in relation to proposed courses of action and even that the implications for each stakeholder are identified, but we do not learn *why and by what criterion a decision will be made*. Stakeholder analysis, as a decision-making process, is incomplete and for the most part, morally neutral.[2]

The idea of 'stakeholder synthesis', on the other hand, includes the remainder of the decision-making steps, weighing the significance of the available options for the affected stakeholders and making a normative judgement that integrates this information into a decision. The key point is that stakeholder synthesis goes beyond simply *identifying* various affected stakeholder groups. It makes a normative response to this information, assigning relative weights to stakeholder interests and rights.

2.1.2 Stakeholder synthesis: prudential and impartial

A 'stakeholder synthesis', however, may not be *ethically* motivated. A politician or a management team, for example, might be careful to consider positive and (especially) negative stakeholder impacts for no other reason than that offended stakeholders might resist or retaliate. This kind of stakeholder thinking is not really done out of ethical concern. It simply manifests a concern about possible impediments to one's objectives. It is what we might call a *prudential* synthesis. On such a view, for example, negative effects on relatively *powerless* stakeholders (those who cannot retaliate) may be ignored or discounted in the

---

2   It is therefore a mistake to see it as a substitute for normative ethical thinking.

synthesis and eventual decision. Machiavelli is often interpreted as recommending such a discounting of the least powerful.[3]

So we can see: (i) that 'stakeholder analysis' is not a complete decision-making process to begin with; and (ii) that moving from stakeholder analysis to stakeholder synthesis is not necessarily moving towards *ethics*, especially if it amounts to treating merely prudentially the interests and rights of stakeholder groups other than stockholders.

Suppose we go beyond a prudential synthesis, however, treating all stakeholders *non-instrumentally*, just like stockholders? Would we then arrive at a more ethically satisfactory form of stakeholder synthesis? The answer, we believe, leads to some conceptual puzzles.

2.1.3 *What makes a synthesis ethical?*

In contrast to taking a prudential approach in stakeholder thinking, we can imagine a management team giving the same care to the interests of, say, employees, customers and local communities as to the economic interests of stockholders. This kind of synthesis might involve trading off the economic advantages of one group against those of another: for example, in a decision having to do with a plant closing or product safety. Using this type of synthesis, the interests and rights of all stakeholders would be treated equally, though 'equally' would be interpreted either along utilitarian lines (the greatest good for the greatest number of stakeholders) or along more 'contractarian' lines (maximising the wellbeing of the least-advantaged stakeholders).

Unlike the prudential or 'partial' view of stakeholder synthesis, such an 'impartial' view considers stakeholders apart from their instrumental, economic or legal clout. Here the word 'stakeholder' carries with it, by the deliberate modification of a single phoneme, a shift in managerial outlook. Some would say a shift from amoral to moral. Others, however, would disagree.

2.1.4 *Problems with impartiality*

Unfortunately, an *impartial* approach to stakeholder synthesis may be as incompatible in its way with our convictions about the nature of morality as the *partial* approach, leaving us in conceptual disarray. The underlying issues have to do with:

1. The special fiduciary obligations owed by management to stockholders

2. The nature of the 'common good' as more than a mere summation of numerous private goods

Behind (1) lies the belief that the obligations of agents (managers) to principals (stockholders) are either stronger or different in kind from those of agents to other (stakeholder) parties. Behind (2) lies the belief that simply adding up individual (or constituent) interests and rights is relevant but ultimately inadequate to discerning the 'common good' towards which organisations are expected to order their behaviour.

3   Were this kind of synthesis to be adopted in a business organisation, stakeholders (or at least those outside the stockholder group) would be viewed instrumentally, as factors that might advance the corporation's interests. *Moral* concern would avoid injury or unfairness to those affected by one's actions because it is wrong, regardless of the retaliatory potential of the aggrieved parties.

There are, then, *two* ways in which the idea of an 'ethical synthesis' can be problematic. One has to do with the way in which the interests and rights of stockholders are treated in relation to other stakeholders. The other has to do with the way in which the interests and rights of the full complement of stakeholders are combined into a unified whole.

It is hard to imagine that a practitioner who is looking to 'stakeholder thinking' for a decision procedure would find much encouragement in the face of these problems. Such a practitioner could, of course, simply ignore the two problems by (i) treating stockholders as having no more distinctive a claim on management than any other stakeholder; and (ii) treating the 'common good' as simply the aggregate or sum of constituency goods weighted by the number of individuals affected. But we believe this is a significant price to pay to achieve stakeholder synthesis.

2.1.5 Stakeholder paradox I

Practitioners who would simply pursue an *impartial* stakeholder synthesis first must come to terms with a strong moral intuition about the *legitimacy* of treating stockholders impartially, given the economic mission and legal constitution of the modern corporation. This anomalous situation has been referred to as the *stakeholder paradox* (but we will call it *stakeholder paradox* I, since there is a second, related paradox to be taken up below).

> **Stakeholder paradox I:** It seems essential, yet illegitimate, to guide corporate decisions by ethical values that go beyond prudential or instrumental stakeholder considerations to impartial ones.[4]

The issue arises from management's *fiduciary* duty to the stockholder, essentially the duty to keep not a profit-maximising promise but a promise of 'most-favoured' stakeholder consideration. An impartial stakeholder synthesis, in the eyes of some, cuts managers loose from certain well-defined obligations of accountability to stockholders and could lead to a betrayal of trust. If corporate responsibility is modelled on public-sector institutions with impartiality towards all constituencies, the provider of capital seems to lose status.

Stakeholder paradox I seems to call for an account of corporate responsibility that: (i) avoids surrendering moral relationships between management and multiple stakeholders as the prudential view does; while (ii) interpreting obligations to stockholders as fiduciary obligations (thus protecting the uniqueness of the principal–agent relationship between management and stockholders).

The responsibilities of management towards stakeholders can best be understood as extensions of the obligations that *stockholders themselves* would be expected to honour in their own right. No one can expect of an *agent* behaviour that is ethically less responsible than that expected of him or herself. I cannot (ethically) have done on my behalf what I should not (ethically) do myself.

This guiding principle does not, of course, resolve the synthesis for business decision-makers. But it does suggest that such conflicts are of a piece with those that face us all. It urges a form of stakeholder thinking different from both the prudential and the impar-

---

4 See 'Stakeholder Paradox' in the revised and expanded 2001 edition of Lawrence Becker and Charlotte Becker (eds.), *The Encyclopedia of Ethics* (Becker and Becker 2001).

tial approaches, one that both managers and institutional investors might apply to policies and decisions.[5]

2.1.6 Stakeholder paradox II

All this being said, practitioners face a second stakeholder paradox, in addition to the first puzzle about special fiduciary obligations to stockholders. This second paradox stems not from accommodating stockholders properly in the synthesis, but from approaching the synthesis as an aggregation problem. Behind the idea of stakeholder synthesis as an aggregation lies a view of the common good that many would question.[6] In the words of David Braybrooke and Arthur Monahan, the common good as an ideal in the history of ethics

> is clearly incompatible with the individualistic reckoning required by contractarianism. It takes as settled, moreover, a question that utilitarianism deliberately leaves open to determination by contingent facts . . . Theorists of the common good refuse, for purposes of working out an ethics, to contemplate the possibility that human beings might be fully happy apart from subordination [to the common happiness] (Braybrooke and Monahan 1992: 175).

The relevance of each stakeholder category to the common good is not in question—but the idea that individual destinies are first arrived at and then added to make an optimal common destiny is seen as backwards. The seeds of synthesis are planted in the analytical soil ahead of time, so to speak. A stakeholder group—for example, employees—may be called upon to make sacrifices for the common good (in wages or even lay-off arrangements) which would, from a more individualistic point of view, be difficult to defend. The situation is similar for customers in the context of acceptable risk in product safety debates. The concept of the common good invites a form of stakeholder thinking that looks at synthesis in a more organic or holistic way.

The conventional idea of stakeholder synthesis tends to view management as a trustee charged with balancing the diverse claims of a broad set of constituencies. Each constituency has its own special set of interests. Each seeks its own advantage, however enlightened its view of this advantage might be. What the stakeholder model describes is less a community than an assembly of fragmented interests. Stakeholder synthesis is supposed to *maximise* or *optimise the sum of these interests*. But, in the words of Naughton *et al.* (1996: 222): 'Because the stakeholder approach focuses on individual claims as its starting point, it has tremendous difficulty pursuing a collective notion of a common life in which goods are shared to enhance human development.'

---

5 The way out of the paradox seems to lie in understanding the conscience of the corporation as a logical and moral extension of the consciences of its principals. It is not an *expansion* of the list of principals, but a gloss on the principal–agent relationship itself. Whatever the structure of the principal–agent relationship, neither principal nor agent can claim 'moral immunity' from the basic obligations that apply to any human being (or human organisation) towards other members of the community.

6 'Putting together the clues that St Thomas [Aquinas] has left . . . shows that the common good specifically rules out a number of prospects licensed by utilitarianism and insists on things that contractarianism at best brings in as contingent superadditions to the basic plan of justice' (Braybrooke and Monahan 1992: 175).

The ideal of the *common good* is neither the particular good of one stakeholder group, nor the optimal aggregation of the goods of several stakeholder groups. Rather, it is 'the good of the community in which people develop' (Naughton *et al.* 1996: 221). This unitary good includes, yet transcends, the particular goods of each stakeholder group. It does not provide managers with a detailed blueprint for organisational life. But it does suggest a *normative orientation* for the firm's activities.[7] Companies are called to contribute to human development through the products and services they offer, the working environment they create and the collaborations and partnerships they form (Naughton *et al.* 1996: 208).

The upshot is that there appears to be a second barrier to the straightforward application of a synthesis-producing calculus for stakeholder thinking—a second 'paradox'.

> **Stakeholder paradox II:** It seems essential, yet problematic, to guide corporate decisions by a view of the common good arrived at by simply aggregating separate stakeholder costs and benefits.

While ethical responsibility clearly has something to do with impartial concern for affected parties, it is not at all clear that the pursuit of the common good is equivalent to the maximisation or optimisation of the separately calculated interests of various stakeholder groups. And, if this equivalence fails, then impartial stakeholder synthesis faces a second barrier, as puzzling as the barrier indicated by *stakeholder paradox I*.

2.1.7 Stakeholder thinking: beyond the paradoxes?

We now find ourselves in uncomfortable territory. Clearly multiple 'stakeholders' have a morally significant relationship to management, but that relationship (except in one case) is different from a fiduciary one. Management may never have promised customers, employees, suppliers, etc. a 'return on investment', but management is nevertheless obliged to take seriously its extra-legal obligations not to injure, lie to or cheat these stakeholders *quite apart from* whether it is in the stockholders' interests.

Clearly, too, the interests and rights of multiple 'stakeholders' are relevant to an organisation's understanding of the 'common good'. But corporate responsibility to customers, employees, suppliers and stockholders might involve asking certain of these stakeholder groups to make sacrifices for the sake of the common good that do not maximise the satisfaction of their interests, viewed *apart* from the common good.

What, then, is a practitioner to do? Motivated to think in stakeholder terms, but faced with paradoxes in any decision-making synthesis, the practitioner appears to be left with either a calculus of questionable legitimacy or business as usual. Is there any other way— a way beyond the conceptual paradoxes? We think the answer is yes.

Understanding that stakeholder analysis is different from stakeholder synthesis and that stakeholder synthesis can take many forms, some of which are more ethically plausible than others, but most of which face significant obstacles, may help us to clarify the challenge facing the responsible corporation. In Section 2.2 we shall examine in some detail an approach to stakeholder thinking that business leaders from around the globe have found persuasive, the Caux Round Table Principles for Business and their accom-

---

7   For a more thorough discussion of this point and a description of a model of the firm based on the concept of the common good, see Chapter 2 of Helen J. Alford and Michael J. Naughton, *Managing as if Faith Mattered* (Alford and Naughton 2001).

panying implementation guidelines, the Self-Assessment and Improvement Process (SAIP). Later, we shall reflect on how this approach may take us *beyond* the stakeholder paradoxes.

2.2 A stakeholder-based process for self-assessment

The acknowledgement that a business enterprise has responsibilities towards multiple stakeholders is an acknowledgement of the validity for corporations of the idea of conscience. Conscience generates what philosopher Josiah Royce once referred to as the 'moral insight': 'the realisation of one's neighbour, in the fullest sense of the word *realisation*; the resolution to treat him unselfishly'. He also noted that human frailty clouds this insight after only a short time:

> We see the reality of our neighbour, that is, we determine to treat him as we do ourselves. But then we go back to daily action and we feel the heat of hereditary passions and we straightaway forget what we have seen. Our neighbour becomes obscured. He is once more a foreign power. He is unreal. We are again deluded and selfish. This conflict goes on and will go on as long as we live after the manner of men. Moments of insight, with their accompanying resolutions; long stretches of delusion and selfishness: That is our life (Royce 1885: 155).

Surmounting the barriers to ethical awareness and action identified by Royce is no small task for individuals. For business organisations, it requires an *institutionalisation* of conscience. Institutionalisation facilitates the translation of ideals into action. It also sustains their presence within the firm as a source of moral suasion.

2.2.1 The Caux Principles: institutionalising conscience

Integral to the process of institutionalisation is the *progressive articulation* of ethical standards. By crystallising ethical values into principles, we capture and convey vital dimensions of human moral experience. Articulating principles helps overcome what Royce called the 'obscuring of neighbours' to which organisations are prone by making moral wisdom explicit, so that it can guide future decisions and actions. Furthermore, by explicating standards with specific measures, companies are better able to judge whether their behaviour truly embodies their ideals. Progressive articulation helps an organisation to assess the 'fit' between the demands of conscience and its deeds. Any discrepancy between aspiration and action then serves as a point for organisational reflection and learning, as well as a spur to improvement.

2.2.2 The Caux Round Table Principles for Business

This process can be illustrated through one of the best-known sets of transcultural ethical principles available today. The Caux Round Table Principles for Business were officially launched in July 1994 (see Appendix, page 60). These principles emerged from discussions among Japanese, European and American executives and were fashioned in part from a document called the Minnesota Principles.[8] The Caux Principles (as they are called) articulate a comprehensive set of ethical norms that could be embraced by a business operating internationally and in multiple cultural environments. To meet this challenge, the Caux Principles had to formulate core values in such a way that both Eastern and Western mind-sets could find them intelligible and acceptable.

The Caux Principles rest on two broad ethical ideals: human dignity and the Japanese concept of *kyosei*. The former witnesses to the significance of each person as an end. It implies that a person's worth can never be reduced to his or her instrumental utility or value as a means to the fulfilment of another's purpose. The ideal of *kyosei* was defined by Ryuzaburo Kaku, the late chairman of Canon, Inc., as 'living and working together for the good of all' (Kaku 1997: 55). *Kyosei* is a subtle and complex concept that tempers individual, organisational and even national self-interest with concern for more embracing 'common goods' (Goodpaster 1998: 530).

These two ideals emphasise distinct yet complementary aspects of Royce's moral insight. Human dignity underscores the moral reality of our neighbour, the innate worth he or she has by virtue of being human. It establishes our neighbour as deserving of our concern. In contrast, *kyosei* heralds behaviour that recognises and honours our resolve to treat our neighbour as ourselves. The realisation of our neighbour is achieved by pursuing in solidarity the good we have in common—through co-operative action that promotes justice, prosperity and community.

The Caux Principles express these ideals in a format that progresses towards greater specificity. The document's Preamble establishes the vital need for corporate conscience in a world that is interdependent and an economy that is increasingly transnational. The next section outlines seven General Principles; these begin to clarify how the values of human dignity and *kyosei* inform business practice within a global context. The third and final section of the Caux Principles utilises a stakeholder framework to supplement these general norms with more detailed guidelines. The 'Stakeholder Principles' specify how the ideals of human dignity and *kyosei* may be activated practically in a company's relationships with customers, employees, investors, suppliers, competitors and communities. The Stakeholder Principles thus function as a battery of more detailed aspirations that point executives and managers towards specific practices. The implementation of these practices helps bring the ideals of the Caux Principles for Business to life within an enterprise. A further development in this progressive articulation, the SAIP, will be discussed below.

The Caux Principles give meaning to the phrase 'principled business leadership'. The progressive articulation of standards for responsible business conduct, however, must continue. What is needed is a more direct assessment of the fit between the principles and a company's operations. Managers would then be able to identify behaviour inconsistent with the principles and to craft new initiatives in keeping with the principles' letter and spirit (see Fig. 2.1).

---

8   In language and form, the Minnesota Principles provided the substantial basis for the Caux Round Table Principles for Business. To obtain a copy of the Minnesota Principles, contact the Center for Ethical Business Cultures (CEBC), Minneapolis, Minnesota, www.cebcglobal.org.

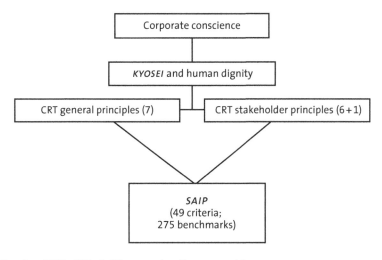

CRT = Caux Round Table; SAIP = Self-Assessment and Improvement Process

Figure 2.1 **Progressive articulation**

2.2.3 Corporate self-awareness

An individual conducts a journey towards self-awareness by discovering meaning and values. A corporation proceeds on a similar quest—finding self-awareness in its cultural identity and shared values. In his classic book on leadership, Philip Selznick wrote that:

> There is a close relation between 'infusion with value' and 'self-maintenance'. As an organisation acquires a self, a distinctive identity, it becomes an institution. This involves the taking on of values, ways of acting and believing that are deemed important for their own sake. From then on self-maintenance becomes more than bare organisational survival; it becomes a struggle to preserve the uniqueness of the group in the face of new problems and altered circumstances (Selznick 1957: 21-22).

Selznick describes a search for self-awareness that transforms an organisation into an institution. Clearly, a necessary first step towards this self-awareness is articulation of responsible business standards. Rather than merely espousing values and standards, an institution must find ways to transform its initial principled commitment into a progressively more specific self-assessment process.

The Caux Principles may serve as an expression of a company's goals for conduct, or as a template for assessing a company's current norms. More importantly, the progressive articulation of these principles suggests an organisational cycle of communication, which includes educating, listening, reflecting and learning (Goodpaster 1998: 534).

The idea of self-awareness is reminiscent, on an organisational level, of Plato's famous cave allegory (Jowett 1920: 514-17), which depicts an underground cave that eventually opens towards the light of the sun. People are chained within the cave, forcing them to see only its back wall, illuminated by a fire projecting shadows of objects before them.

Truth and reality for the prisoners consist only of shadowy images and darkness because they know nothing else. If one of the inhabitants left the cave, however, he would realise the more profound reality outside. If this enlightened cave dweller were then to return to the cave, he would not be able to view the situation as before. Plato suggests further that if the enlightened escapee attempted to share his new knowledge with the rest of the prisoners, they might feel a heightened sense of intimidation and danger about his new convictions. Thus, the cave represents the world of appearances and shadows, while the journey outside stands for the ascent to knowledge and transparency.

2.2.4 A newly developed tool for organisational self-awareness

Corporations need objective criteria, or self-awareness benchmarks, to assist them in escaping the cave. The Caux Round Table recently initiated the development of the Self-Assessment and Improvement Process© (SAIP), a tool designed to progressively articulate the Caux Principles. The SAIP is ultimately dialogical, focused on internal conversation and positive change. It offers a pathway towards enhanced corporate self-awareness, translating the aspirations articulated by the Caux Principles into detailed questions about company practices.

The SAIP allows senior leaders to 'score' the firm's conduct in relation to an acknowledged global standard for responsible behaviour. It helps the company to identify past patterns of behaviour and areas of strength and weakness. It also facilitates awareness of emerging concerns and issues, thus functioning as an early warning system for senior leaders. By promoting internal disclosure and effective oversight, the SAIP assists with such critical management tasks as communications, corporate control and strategic planning.

The net effect of the process is to strengthen confidence in management on the part of groups affected by the company's decisions and activities. The specific benefits that can accrue include enhanced loyalty on the part of customers and employees, and improved relationships with shareholders, union representatives, government officials and community leaders. Another benefit can be a positive assessment of the firm's stock price by analysts.

Perhaps even more vital, however, is the transformative journey that such self-appraisal represents. By pursuing self-awareness in this way, executives become more informed and enlightened. They are then in a position to undertake improvements in the spirit of the Caux Principles that will benefit corporate stakeholders.

The SAIP is structured around the Caux Principles. A company's performance against each of the seven general Caux Principles is evaluated from seven distinct perspectives: how well the firm has fulfilled the fundamental duties that flow from a principle, and how well it has realised the aspirations articulated by that principle in its relations with six stakeholders—customers, employees, owners, suppliers, competitors and communities. The result is a 7-by-7 matrix of assessment criteria (see Table 2.1).

To illustrate the use of the SAIP, let us consider a company's self-assessment regarding the general principle 'The Economic and Social Impact of Business' and a critical stakeholder group: customers. To perform this appraisal, the company must reflect on the assessment criterion contained in cell 2.2 in Table 2.1 and the five specific questions ('benchmarks') that amplify and elaborate this criterion (see Box 2.1).

Category	1 Fundamental duties	2 Customers	3 Employees	4 Owners/ investors	5 Suppliers/ partners	6 Competitors	7 Communities
1. Responsi- bilities of business	Criterion 1.1	Criterion 1.2	Criterion 1.3	Criterion 1.4	Criterion 1.5	Criterion 1.6	Criterion 1.7
2. Economic and social impact of business	Criterion 2.1	Criterion 2.2	Criterion 2.3	Criterion 2.4	Criterion 2.5	Criterion 2.6	Criterion 2.7
3. Business behaviour	Criterion 3.1	Criterion 3.2	Criterion 3.3	Criterion 3.4	Criterion 3.5	Criterion 3.6	Criterion 3.7
4. Respect for rules	Criterion 4.1	Criterion 4.2	Criterion 4.3	Criterion 4.4	Criterion 4.5	Criterion 4.6	Criterion 4.7
5. Support for multilateral trade	Criterion 5.1	Criterion 5.2	Criterion 5.3	Criterion 5.4	Criterion 5.5	Criterion 5.6	Criterion 5.7
6. Respect for the environment	Criterion 6.1	Criterion 6.2	Criterion 6.3	Criterion 6.4	Criterion 6.5	Criterion 6.6	Criterion 6.7
7. Avoidance of illicit operations	Criterion 7.1	Criterion 7.2	Criterion 7.3	Criterion 7.4	Criterion 7.5	Criterion 7.6	Criterion 7.7

Table 2.1 **SAIP assessment criteria**

2.2 Customers

How does the company contribute to the social wellbeing of its customers through its marketing and communications?

 2.2.1 How does the company respect the integrity of the culture of its customers?

 2.2.2 How does the company address situations where prevailing evidence deems a product harmful in any country? What role does disclosure play in this strategy?

 2.2.3 How does the company provide remedies for customer dissatisfaction? Describe applicable mechanisms for redress through recalls, warranties, and claims procedures.

 2.2.4 How does the company follow relevant consumer codes to protect vulnerable consumer groups?

 2.2.5 What are the company's current levels and trends in key measures of product/service performance and applicability?

Box 2.1 *Some sample SAIP questions*

The SAIP identifies the maximum possible score a company can receive for its performance against these interrogatories. By comparing relevant data against a set of quantification guidelines, the firm can generate a score characterising its current level of performance for this general principle and stakeholder group. By totalling the scores for all 49 cells, the company can generate an overall indication of its performance against the requirements of the Caux Principles.[9]

The SAIP is modelled after the Malcolm Baldrige National Quality Award, a comprehensive and flexible process for measuring total quality. The Baldrige process represents some of the best thinking available today on self-assessment, incorporating feedback from business leaders, academics and corporate observers. The SAIP attempts to capture and capitalise on this thinking.

2.2.5 Self-knowledge through sharing

As corporations complete self-assessment journeys, journeys mapped by stakeholder co-ordinates, something much more than a 'score' will be the result. For during such a process, if it is done honestly and carefully, a new kind of corporate mind-set is likely to emerge. Just as Plato's cave dweller found a less shadowy, more three-dimensional world at the conclusion of his upward trek, the company will come to see its policies and their implementation, as well as its measurements of progress, in a 'new light'.[10] Also, like the

9 The maximum possible score of the SAIP is 1,000 points. The SAIP scorecard indicates how this total is allocated across the general principles and, within a given principle, to each stakeholder. In other words, it highlights the maximum possible score that a company can receive for its performance against each principle and how these points are distributed across the seven distinct perspectives represented within the self-assessment. These allocations involve differential weightings of the criteria.

10 To quote Plato again: '[M]y opinion is that in the world of knowledge the idea of good appears last of all and is seen only with an effort; and, when seen, is also inferred to be the universal

escapee from the cave, such a company may eventually want to share its experience with others.

We have seen how stakeholder thinking can be translated into a set of aspirational principles for guiding corporate conduct worldwide. And we have seen further (in the previous section) how a corporate self-assessment process (SAIP) using benchmarks can help to make aspirational principles more specific and more 'actionable'. Indeed, self-assessment based on credible benchmarks and measures can be a culturally transformative process—strengthening ethical integrity in organisations that undertake such an effort.

The significance of the self-awareness to which the SAIP gives rise can hardly be overstated. It gives senior leaders and employees throughout the organisation a dispassionate, empirical and consciousness-raising profile of the company's ethical culture, rooted in policies, their implementation and their measurable results. Beyond consciousness-raising, such a self-assessment provides a platform for whatever future interventions may be necessary to improve the culture.

Now, one of the key attributes of the SAIP is its *privacy* or company *confidentiality*. This attribute has many benefits, but it also has some costs that may lead organisations to pursue something less private—thereby changing *self-awareness* into something more, what we will call *self-knowledge*.

2.2.6 *Benefits of a private SAIP*

The fact that the SAIP is conducted *privately* and *confidentially* by the companies that choose to use it is beneficial in many ways:

- It lowers the threshold of risk for companies to undertake the SAIP in the first place, because it does not involve revealing any negative findings that might publicly embarrass the company.[11]

- It encourages the use of otherwise confidential data in the assessment, increasing its candour and reliability.

- It allows for comparisons and contrasts between business units within a company, as well as between the same business units at different times, so long as the application of criteria and scoring are handled consistently.

- It systematically identifies areas in need of improvement and intervention by senior company leadership and/or the board.

Such benefits lower the risk and enhance the utility of the SAIP, leading to significant self-awareness. What (if anything), therefore, might encourage a corporation to consider an approach to this process that was less than fully private or confidential?

---

author of all things beautiful and right, parent of light and of the lord of light in this visible world and the immediate source of reason and truth in the intellectual; and that this is the power upon which he who would act rationally either in public or private life must have his eye fixed' (Plato, *The Republic*, Book VII: 517).

11 It may also lower the risk of involuntary exposure due to legal discovery interventions, since the process is carried on with some degree of attorney–client privilege.

2.2.7 Costs of a private SAIP

Such a question has an analogue in the lives of individuals: What, if anything, would encourage a person to consider less than fully private or confidential treatment of candid ethics-related information about himself or herself? The traditional answers to this question include:

- That sharing such information with others (or a least one other, such as an impartial counsellor or confessor) improves one's *perspective* on both the data and on underlying causes (think again of the cave allegory)

- That exchanging such information with others through dialogue allows one to benefit from the *experiences* of those others

- That self-assessment measures, if they are to have genuine *validity* and provide a basis for improvement, call for comparability across persons

These traditional observations about the 'downside' of privacy in the context of individual persons (loss of perspective, experience and validity) apply to organisations in natural ways. Corporations, like individuals, can lose perspective and exaggerate both positive and negative self-assessments. Without a counsellor or consultant familiar with other company self-assessments, it is difficult to get beyond the subjectivity of the self-scoring process. How a company stands ethically is difficult to discern unless there is some impartial quality control on the methods of measurement used. Privacy, while it may allow for comparability between old and new assessment scores for a given company, does not allow for comparability in scoring *across* companies.

Corporations, again like individuals, can benefit enormously from sharing in the experiences of other corporations. Such 'best practices' dialogues benefit all parties, not only by providing a marketplace of ideas for improvement but also by providing motivation to 'stay the course'. How a company stands ethically in relation to other companies may influence its decisions about what and how to change over time.

Finally, corporations, like individuals, often benefit from third-party scrutiny in the conventional arenas of market competition and government regulation. Why should it be different in the arena of principled business conduct? But such third-party scrutiny, if it is to have any validity, depends on comparable, minimally subjective measures of corporate responsibility.

The fact that one company achieves a certain score and another company achieves a lower or higher score cannot, because of the subjectivity involved in the scoring process, reliably be used to draw any ethical comparisons between the two companies. And being able to demonstrate how it stands ethically in relation to other companies can be helpful to a company trying to defend itself against unreasonable charges of wrongful behaviour.

So we can see that if the SAIP is conducted privately and confidentially by the companies that choose to use it, there are certain benefits—and certain costs. The benefits have a lot to do with achieving self-awareness while lowering publicity risks and enhancing the completeness of the information base. The costs, as with personal privacy, are primarily opportunity costs—*perspective*, shared *experience* and third-party *validity*.[12]

---

12 To return to Plato's *Allegory*, the way out of the cave involved dialogue and discovery, eventually a more substantial kind of knowledge than the shadows on the wall permitted.

It is our belief that, in the near term, most companies will value the benefits of privacy over its opportunity costs, but, in the long run, especially as the number of companies doing such self-assessment increases, they (and their investors) will become less interested in these benefits and more interested in what *shared* assessments make possible. The trend will be from corporate self-awareness to a more 'transparent' corporate self-knowledge.[13]

While we have not attempted here to explore the logic in the 'trend' just hypothesised (from privacy and corporate self-awareness to transparency and corporate self-knowledge), we believe it is consistent with and a natural outgrowth of developmental patterns in human behaviour. Moral maturity seems to carry with it a willingness for greater self-disclosure, once it becomes clear that such disclosure is a significant asset to the individual (or organisation) involved.[14] Taking one's own 'moral inventory' leads naturally to a desire for feedback from (at least some) others, if only to gain perspective and insight into strategies and tactics for *responding* to the inventory (self-improvement). Research in social psychology would be required to support this hypothesis, of course.

2.3 From decision procedure to cultural discipline

It should be clear from the foregoing that the SAIP is not intended to be a decision-procedure for business leaders. Rather, it is a transformative activity. It fosters greater ethical self-awareness and self-knowledge through internal and (ultimately) external dialogue and catalyses actions that strengthen and invigorate the conscience of the corporation. Using the SAIP, senior leaders and employees embark on a reflective journey that offers the possibility of changing not just how they view their own company, but how they understand the nature of business. A manager's conception of the human value added by the enterprise may shift as a result of insights garnered from the SAIP.

This returns us to a question implicit at the end of Section 2.1: How is it possible, *if* it is possible, to avoid the paradoxes associated with stakeholder synthesis while still acknowledging the central importance of 'stakeholder thinking' in business ethics? Our excursion in Section 2.2 into the realm of organisational self-assessment promised certain benefits which in Plato's time would have been called *enlightenment*.

But does the enlightenment fostered by the SAIP *remove* the paradoxes of stakeholder synthesis? In our view, the answer to this last question is *no*. The silver lining of this cloud may be that at the end of the day, the paradoxes do not *need* to be removed.

---

13 The litigation environment, of course, could negatively influence this trend.

14 Within Cummins Engine Company, one time-honoured guideline for addressing ethical problems states that 'facts are friendly'. It suggests that an accurate and fair description of the situation in question, however painful or embarrassing, will help the company resolve such matters consistent with its ethical obligations. The maxim indicates a level of moral maturity where self-disclosure is embraced as a virtue, one the organisation should exercise and cultivate.

2.3.1 A path around paradox

When we originally introduced the ideas of stakeholder analysis and synthesis, we said that any rational decision-making process included such steps as: (i) gathering information, (ii) sorting, (iii) weighing, (iv) integrating and, eventually, (v) acting on the processed information. The assumption behind the scenes was that, if stakeholder thinking was to enter into the decision-making of business executives, the most obvious point of entry was a *decision-making process*, a guideline invoked or applied whenever significant options presented themselves.

We saw fairly quickly, however, that the demands of a decision-making process included not only analysis, but synthesis—and that the challenge of synthesis carried with it some barriers (paradoxes). We were not optimistic about finding an algorithm that gave proper weight to the interests and rights of *stockholders* and which then combined the weights of all stakeholders into some approximation to the *common good* in an increasingly global community.

We are now in a position to appreciate that the paradoxes emerge only if we insist that 'stakeholder thinking' be parsed as a decision-making process. But what if 'stakeholder thinking' entered into the ethical outlook and behaviour of an organisation in a different way? What if, instead of providing a decision-making process, 'stakeholder thinking' was undertaken as a cultural discipline in a company, much as a periodic moral inventory is often part of the discipline of individuals? (See Fig. 2.2.)

2.3.2 Stakeholder thinking as a cultural discipline

This is in fact the interpretation of 'stakeholder thinking' that permeated our discussion of the Caux Principles and the SAIP in Section 2.2. The SAIP is not offered as a decision-making process. Instead, it functions as a cultural audit, a systematic review of a com-

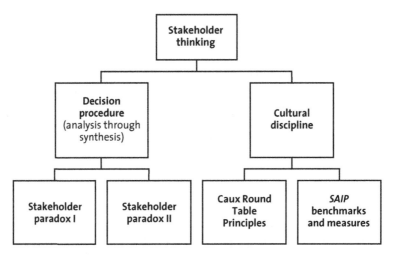

SAIP = Self-Assessment and Improvement Process

Figure 2.2 **Perspectives on stakeholder thinking**

pany's stakeholder awareness. Based on such a review, the company's leadership can encourage informed dialogue aimed at improvement.

It has often been remarked that ethics in the modern (not to mention postmodern) period is preoccupied with decision-making, in contrast to the Greek and Mediaeval emphasis on character and virtue. The organisational analogue to this observation hints at why 'stakeholder thinking' might instinctively be interpreted as a decision procedure today. But the more classical approach to ethics, epitomised in a remark attributed to St Augustine—'Love and do what you will!'—offers an alternative interpretation. Perhaps a cultural discipline aimed at stakeholder awareness provides a company's source of character or virtue, *without* a decision-making formula. Perhaps stockholders are properly served by companies with a fiduciary discipline, and perhaps the common good in an increasingly global community is also properly served.

2.4 Summary and conclusion

We began this chapter in search of an interpretation of 'stakeholder thinking' that might both clarify the idea and make it practical. Instead, we discovered that there were some significant barriers (paradoxes) to both clarification and practicality.

We then offered an account of a transcultural set of ethical principles (the Caux Principles) for business organisations, along with a Self-Assessment and Improvement Process that enables a company to understand very concretely how it measures up to these principles.

The SAIP actually served two purposes at once. It helped us to institutionalise the idea of conscience or 'moral insight' through a progressive articulation of general ethical principles. And it offered us an alternative interpretation of 'stakeholder thinking' as a cultural discipline, less vulnerable to paradox, through a Socratic process reminiscent of Plato's cave allegory.

The direction of business enterprise in the 21st century is clearly towards globalisation, which means that the concept of corporate citizenship is undergoing fundamental change. We know that citizenship, to be meaningful, presupposes a *community* with a *common good*. Business ethics in this new century, therefore, calls for a culture of corporate citizenship with a *global* perspective on the common good. We hope our pursuit of 'stakeholder thinking' beyond paradox to practicality helps respond to this call.

Appendix
The Caux Round Table Principles:
business behaviour for a better world

Section 1: preamble

The mobility of employment, capital, products and technology is making business increasingly global in its transactions and its effects. Laws and market forces are necessary but insufficient guides for conduct. Responsibility for the policies and actions of business and respect for the dignity and interests of its stakeholders are fundamental. Shared values, including a commitment to shared prosperity, are as important for a global community as for communities of smaller scale. For these reasons, and because business can be a powerful agent of positive social change, we offer the following principles as a foundation for dialogue and action by business leaders in search of business responsibility. In so doing, we affirm the necessity for moral values in economic decision-making. Without them, stable business relationships and a sustainable world community are impossible.

Section 2: general principles

Principle 1. The responsibilities of corporations: beyond shareholders towards stakeholders

The value of a business to society is the wealth and employment it creates and the marketable products and services it provides to consumers at a reasonable price commensurate with quality. To create such value, a business must maintain its own economic health and vitality, but survival is not a sufficient goal. Businesses have a role to play in improving the lives of all of their customers, employees and shareholders by sharing with them the wealth it has created. Suppliers and competitors as well should expect businesses to honour their obligations in a spirit of honesty and fairness. As responsible citizens of the local, national, regional and global communities in which they operate, businesses share a part in shaping the future of those communities.

Principle 2. The economic and social impact of corporations: towards innovation, justice and world community

Businesses established in foreign countries to develop, produce or sell should also contribute to the social advancement of those countries by creating productive employment and helping to raise the purchasing power of their citizens. Businesses should also contribute to human rights, education, welfare and vitalisation of the countries in which they operate. Businesses should contribute to economic and social development not only in the countries in which they operate, but also in the world community at large, through effective and prudent use of resources, free and fair competition, and emphasis on innovation in technology, production methods, marketing and communications.

Principle 3. Corporate behaviour: beyond the letter of law towards a spirit of trust

While accepting the legitimacy of trade secrets, businesses should recognise that sincerity, candour, truthfulness, the keeping of promises and transparency contribute not only to their own credibility and stability but also to the smoothness and efficiency of business transactions, particularly on the international level.

Principle 4. Respect for rules: beyond trade friction towards co-operation
To avoid trade frictions and promote freer trade, equal conditions for competition, and fair and equitable treatment for all participants, businesses should respect international and domestic rules. In addition, they should recognise that some behaviour, although legal, may still have adverse consequences.

Principle 5. Support for multilateral trade: beyond isolation towards world community
Businesses should support the multilateral trade system of the World Trade Organisation and similar international agreements. They should co-operate in efforts to promote the progressive and judicious liberalisation of trade and to relax those domestic measures that unreasonably hinder global commerce, while giving due respect to national policy objectives.

Principle 6. Respect for the environment: beyond protection towards enhancement
A business should protect, and, where possible, improve the environment, promote sustainable development, and prevent the wasteful use of natural resources.

Principle 7. Avoidance of illicit operations: beyond profit towards peace
A corporation should not participate in or condone bribery, money-laundering and other corrupt practices; indeed, it should seek co-operation with others to eliminate them. It should not trade in arms or materials used for terrorist activities, drug traffic or other organised crime.

Section 3: stakeholder principles

Customers. We believe in treating all customers with dignity, irrespective of whether they purchase our products and services directly or otherwise acquire them in the market. We therefore have a responsibility to:

- Provide our customers with the highest-quality products and services consistent with their requirements

- Treat our customers fairly in all aspects of our business transactions, including a high level of service and remedies for customer dissatisfaction

- Make every effort to ensure that the health and safety of our customers, as well as the quality of their environment, will be sustained or enhanced by our products or services

- Assure respect for human dignity in products offered, marketing and advertising

- Respect the integrity of the culture of our customers

Employees. We believe in the dignity of every employee and in taking employee interests seriously. We therefore have a responsibility to:

- Provide jobs and compensation that improve workers' living conditions

- Provide working conditions that respect employees' health and dignity

- Be honest in communications with employees and open in sharing information, limited only by legal and competitive constraints

- Listen to and, where possible, act on employee suggestions, ideas, requests and complaints

- Engage in good-faith negotiations when conflict arises

- Avoid discriminatory practices and guarantee equal treatment and opportunity in areas such as gender, age, race and religion

- Promote in the business itself the employment of differently abled people in places of work where they can be genuinely useful

- Protect employees from avoidable injury and illness in the workplace

- Be sensitive to the serious unemployment problems frequently associated with business decisions, and work with governments, employee groups, other agencies and each other in addressing these dislocations

Owners/investors. We believe in honouring the trust our investors place in us. We therefore have a responsibility to:

- Apply professional and diligent management in order to secure a fair and competitive return on our owners' investment

- Disclose relevant information to owners/investors subject only to legal and competitive constraints

- Conserve, protect and increase the owners'/investors' assets

- Respect owners'/investors' requests, suggestions, complaints and formal resolutions

Suppliers. Our relationship with suppliers and subcontractors must be based on mutual respect. We therefore have a responsibility to:

- Seek fairness and truthfulness in all our activities including pricing, licensing and rights to sell

- Ensure that our business activities are free from coercion and unnecessary litigation

- Foster long-term stability in the supplier relationship in return for value, quality, competitiveness and reliability

- Share information with suppliers and integrate them into our planning processes

- Pay suppliers on time and in accordance with agreed terms of trade

- Seek, encourage and prefer suppliers and subcontractors whose employment practices respect human dignity

Competitors. We believe that fair economic competition is one of the basic requirements for increasing the wealth of nations and ultimately for making possible the just distribution of goods and services. We therefore have a responsibility to:

- Foster open markets for trade and investment

- Promote competitive behaviour that is socially and environmentally beneficial and demonstrates mutual respect among competitors

- Refrain from either seeking or participating in questionable payments or favours to secure competitive advantages

- Respect both tangible and intellectual property rights

- Refuse to acquire commercial information by dishonest or unethical means, such as industrial espionage

Communities. We believe that as global corporate citizens we can contribute to such forces of reform and human rights as are at work in the communities in which we operate. We therefore have a responsibility in those communities to:

- Respect human rights and democratic institutions, and promote them wherever practical

- Recognise government's legitimate obligation to the society at large and support public policies and practices that promote human development through harmonious relations between business and other segments of society

- Collaborate with those forces in the community dedicated to raising standards of health, education, economic well-being and workplace safety

- Promote and stimulate sustainable development and play a lead role in preserving the physical environment and conserving the Earth's resources

- Support peace, security, diversity and social integration

- Respect the integrity of local cultures

- Be a good citizen through charitable donations, educational and cultural contributions, and employee participation in community and civic affairs

3

VALUE MAXIMISATION, STAKEHOLDER THEORY AND THE CORPORATE OBJECTIVE FUNCTION[*]

Michael C. Jensen
The Monitor Group and Harvard Business School, USA

In most industrialised nations today, economists, management scholars, policy-makers, corporate executives and special-interest groups are engaged in a high-stakes debate over corporate governance. In some scholarly and business circles, the discussion focuses mainly on questions of policies and procedures designed to improve oversight of corporate managers by boards of directors. But at the heart of the current global corporate governance debate is a remarkable division of opinion about the fundamental purpose of the corporation. Much of the discord can be traced to the complexity of the issues and to the strength of the conflicting interests that are likely to be affected by the outcome. But also fuelling the controversy are political, social, evolutionary and emotional forces that we don't usually think of as operating in the domain of business and economics. These forces serve to reinforce a model of corporate behaviour that draws on concepts of 'family' and 'tribe'. And, as I argue in this chapter, this model is an anachronism—a holdover from an earlier period of human development that nevertheless continues to cause much confusion among corporate managers about what it is that they and their organisations are supposed to do.

At the level of the individual organisation, the most basic issue of governance is the following. Every organisation has to ask and answer the question: What are we trying to accomplish? Or, to put the same question in more concrete terms: How do we keep score? When all is said and done, how do we measure better versus worse?

[*] Earlier versions of this chapter appear in Michael Beer and Nithan Norhia (eds.), *Breaking the Code of Change* (Boston, MA: Harvard Business School Press, 2000) and Michael C. Jensen, *Journal of Applied Corporate Finance* 14.3 (2001): 8-21. This research has been supported by The Monitor Group and Harvard Business School Division of Research. I am indebted to Nancy Nichols, Pat Meredith, Don Chew and Janice Willett for many valuable suggestions.

At the economy-wide or social level, the issue is this: If we could dictate the criterion or objective function to be maximised by firms (and thus the performance criterion by which corporate executives choose between alternative policy options), what would it be? Or, to put the issue even more simply: How do we want the firms in our economy to measure their own performance? How do we want them to determine what is better versus worse?

Most economists would answer simply that managers must have a criterion for evaluating performance and deciding between alternative courses of action, and that the criterion should be maximisation of the long-term market value of the firm. (And 'firm value', by the way, means not just the value of the equity but the sum of the values of all financial claims on the firm—debt, warrants and preferred stock, as well as equity.) This value maximisation proposition has its roots in 200 years of research in economics and finance.

The main contender to value maximisation as the corporate objective is called 'stakeholder theory'. Stakeholder theory says that managers should make decisions that take account of the interests of all the stakeholders in a firm. Stakeholders include all individuals or groups who can substantially affect, or be affected by, the welfare of the firm—a category that includes not only the financial claimholders but also employees, customers, communities and government officials.[1] In contrast to the grounding of value maximisation in economics, stakeholder theory has its roots in sociology, organisational behaviour, the politics of special interests and, as I will discuss below, managerial self-interest. The theory is now popular and has received the formal endorsement of many professional organisations, special-interest groups and governmental bodies, including the current British government.[2]

But, as I argue in this chapter, stakeholder theory should not be viewed as a legitimate contender to value maximisation because it fails to provide a *complete* specification of the corporate purpose or objective function. To put the matter more concretely, whereas value maximisation provides corporate managers with a single objective, stakeholder theory directs corporate managers to serve 'many masters'. And, to paraphrase the old adage, when there are many masters, all end up being short-changed. Without the clarity of mission provided by a single-valued objective function, companies embracing stakeholder theory will experience managerial confusion, conflict, inefficiency and perhaps even competitive failure. And the same fate is likely to be visited on those companies that use the so-called 'Balanced Scorecard' approach—the managerial equivalent of stakeholder theory—as a performance measurement system.

---

1   Under some interpretations, stakeholders also include the environment, terrorists, blackmailers and thieves. Edward Freeman (1984), for example, writes: 'The . . . definition of "stakeholder" [is] any group or individual who can affect or is affected by the achievement of an organisation's purpose . . . For instance, some corporations must count "terrorist groups" as stakeholders.'

2   See, for example, The Clarkson Centre for Business Ethics (1999). For a critical analysis of stakeholder theory, I especially recommend the articles by Elaine Sternberg (1996, 1999). See also Sternberg's (2000) recent book, *Just Business: Business Ethics in Action*, which surveys the acceptance of stakeholder theory by the Business Roundtable (1990) and *The Financial Times*, and its recognition by law in 38 American states. On the latter issue, see also James L. Hanks (1994).

But, if stakeholder theory and the Balanced Scorecard can destroy value by obscuring the overriding corporate goal, does that mean they have no legitimate corporate uses? And can corporate managers succeed by simply holding up value maximisation as the goal and ignoring their stakeholders? The answer to both is an emphatic no. In order to maximise value, corporate managers must not only satisfy, but enlist the support of, all corporate stakeholders—customers, employees, managers, suppliers, local communities. Top management plays a critical role in this function through its leadership and effectiveness in creating, projecting and sustaining the company's strategic vision. And even if the Balanced Scorecard is likely to be counterproductive as a performance evaluation and reward system, the *process* of creating the scorecard can add significant value by helping managers to understand both the company's strategy and the drivers of value in their businesses.

With this in mind, I clarify what I believe is the proper relation between value maximisation and stakeholder theory by proposing a (somewhat) new corporate objective function. I call it **enlightened** value maximisation, and it is identical to what I call **enlightened** stakeholder theory. Enlightened value maximisation uses much of the structure of stakeholder theory but accepts maximisation of the long-run value of the firm as the criterion for making the requisite trade-offs among its stakeholders. Enlightened stakeholder theory, while focusing attention on meeting the demands of all important corporate constituencies, specifies long-term value maximisation as the firm's objective. In so doing, it solves the problems arising from the multiple objectives that accompany traditional stakeholder theory by giving managers a clear way to think about and make the trade-offs among corporate stakeholders.

The answers to the questions of how managers should define better versus worse, and how managers in fact do define it, have important implications for social welfare. Indeed, the answers provide the business equivalent of the medical profession's Hippocratic Oath. It is an indication of the infancy of the science of management that so many in the world's business schools, as well as in professional business organisations, seem to understand so little of the fundamental issues in contention.

With this introduction of the issues, let me now move to a detailed examination of value maximisation and stakeholder theory.

3.1 The logical structure of the problem

In discussing whether firms should maximise value or not, we must separate two distinct issues:

1. Should the firm have a single-valued objective?

2. And, if so, should that objective be value maximisation or something else (for example, maintaining employment or improving the environment)?

The debate over whether corporations should maximise value or act in the interests of their stakeholders is generally couched in terms of the second issue, and is often mistakenly framed as stockholders *versus* stakeholders. The real conflict here, though this is rarely stated or even recognised, is over the first issue—that is, whether the firm should have a single-valued objective function or scorecard. The failure to frame the problem in this way has contributed greatly to widespread misunderstanding and contentiousness.

What is commonly known as stakeholder theory, while not totally without content, is fundamentally flawed because it violates the proposition that a single-valued objective is a prerequisite for purposeful or rational behaviour by any organisation. In particular, a firm that adopts stakeholder theory will be handicapped in the competition for survival because, as a basis for action, stakeholder theory politicises the corporation and leaves its managers empowered to exercise their own preferences in spending the firm's resources.

3.1.1 Issue 1: purposeful behaviour requires the existence of a single-valued objective function

Consider a firm that wishes to increase both its current-year profits and its market share. Assume, as shown in Figure 3.1, that, over some range of values of market share, profits increase. But, at some point, increases in market share come only at the expense of reduced current-year profits—say, because increased expenditures on R&D and advertising, or price reductions to increase market share, reduce this year's profit. Therefore, it is not logically possible to speak of maximising both market share and profits.

In this situation, it is impossible for a manager to decide on the level of R&D, advertising or price reductions because he or she is faced with the need to make trade-offs between the two 'goods'—profits and market share—but has no way to do so. While the manager knows that the firm should be at the point of maximum profits or maximum market share (or somewhere between them), there is no purposeful way to decide where to be in the area in which the firm can obtain more of one good only by giving up some of the other.

3.1.1.1 Multiple objectives is no objective

It is logically impossible to maximise in more than one dimension at the same time unless the dimensions are what are known as 'monotonic transformations' of one another. Thus, telling a manager to maximise current profits, market share, future growth in profits and anything else one pleases will leave that manager with no way to make a reasoned decision. In effect, it leaves the manager with no objective. The result will be confusion and a lack of purpose that will handicap the firm in its competition for survival.[3]

---

3   For a case study of a small non-profit firm that almost destroyed itself while trying to maximise over a dozen dimensions at the same time, see Michael Jensen, Karen H. Wruck and Brian Barry, 'Fighton, Inc. (A) and (B)', Harvard Business School Case #9-391-056, 20 March 1991; and Karen Wruck, Michael Jensen and Brian Barry, 'Fighton, Inc. (A) and (B) Teaching Note', Harvard Business School Case #5-491-111, 1991. For an interesting empirical paper that formally tests the proposition that multiple objectives handicap firms, see Kees Cools and Mirjam van Praag 2000. In their test using 80 Dutch firms in the 1993–97 period, the authors conclude: 'Our findings show the importance of setting one single target for value creation' [emphasis original].

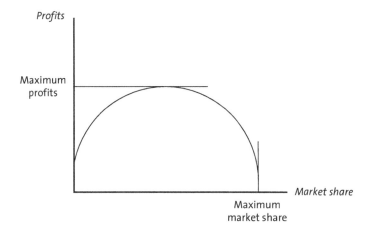

Figure 3.1 **Trade-off between profits and market share. A manager directed to maximise both profit and market share has no way to decide where to be in the range between maximum profits and maximum market share.**

A company can resolve this ambiguity by specifying the trade-offs among the various dimensions, and doing so amounts to specifying an overall objective such as $V = f(x, y, \ldots)$ that explicitly incorporates the effects of decisions on all the performance criteria—all the goods or bads (denoted by $(x, y, \ldots)$) that can affect the firm (such as cash flow, risk and so on). At this point, the logic above does not specify what V is. It could be anything the board of directors chooses, such as employment, sales or growth in output. But, as I argue below, social welfare and survival will severely constrain the board's choices.

Nothing in the analysis so far has said that the objective function f must be well behaved and easy to maximise. If the function is non-monotonic, or even chaotic, it makes it more difficult for managers to find the overall maximum. (For example, as I discuss later, the relationship between the value of the firm and a company's current earnings and investors' expectations about its future earnings and investment expenditures will often be difficult to formulate with much precision.) But, even in these situations, the meaning of 'better' or 'worse' is defined, and managers and their monitors have a 'principled'—that is, an objective and theoretically consistent—basis for choosing and auditing decisions. Their choices are not just a matter of their own personal preferences among various goods and bads.

Given managers' uncertainty about the exact specification of the objective function f, it is perhaps better to call the objective function 'value seeking' rather than value maximisation. This way one avoids the confusion that arises when some argue that maximising is difficult or impossible if the world is structured in sufficiently complicated ways.[4]

4 I'd like to thank David Rose for suggesting this simple and more descriptive term for value maximising. See Rose 1999.

It is not necessary that we be able to maximise, only that we can tell when we are getting better—that is, moving in the right direction.

3.1.2 Issue 2: total firm value maximisation makes society better off

Given that a firm must have a single objective that tells us what is better and what is worse, we then must face the issue of what that definition of 'better' is. Even though the single objective will always be a complicated function of many different goods or bads, the short answer to the question is that 200 years' worth of work in economics and finance indicate that social welfare is maximised when all firms in an economy attempt to maximise their own total firm value. The intuition behind this criterion is simple: that value is created—and when I say 'value' I mean 'social' value—whenever a firm produces an output, or set of outputs, that is valued by its customers at more than the value of the inputs it consumes (as valued by their suppliers) in the production of the outputs. Firm value is simply the long-term market value of this expected stream of benefits.

To be sure, there are circumstances when the value-maximising criterion does not maximise social welfare—notably, when there are monopolies or 'externalities'. Monopolies tend to charge prices that are too high, resulting in less than the socially optimal levels of production. By 'externalities', economists mean situations in which decision-makers do not bear the full cost or benefit consequences of their choices or actions. Examples are cases of air or water pollution in which a firm adds pollution to the environment without having to purchase the right to do so from the parties giving up the clean air or water. There can be no externalities as long as alienable property rights in all physical assets are defined and assigned to some private individual or firm. Thus, the solution to these problems lies not in telling firms to maximise something other than profits, but in defining and then assigning to some private entity the alienable decision rights necessary to eliminate the externalities (see Coase 1960; Jensen and Meckling 1992). In any case, resolving externality and monopoly problems, as I will discuss later, is the legitimate domain of the government in its rule-setting function.[5]

Maximising the total market value of the firm—that is, the sum of the market values of the equity, debt and any other contingent claims outstanding on the firm—is the objective function that will guide managers in making the optimal trade-offs among multiple constituencies (or stakeholders). It tells the firm to spend an additional dollar of resources to satisfy the desires of each constituency as long as that constituency values the result at more than a dollar. In this case, the payoff to the firm from that investment

---

5   In the case of a monopoly, profit maximisation leads to a loss of social product because the firm expands production only to the point where an additional dollar's worth of inputs generates incremental revenues equal to a dollar, not where consumers value the incremental product at a dollar. In this case the firm produces less of a commodity than that which would result in maximum social welfare.

In addition, we should recognise that, when a complete set of claims for all goods for each possible time and state of the world does not exist, the social maximum will be constrained; but this is just another recognition of the fact that we must take into account the costs of creating additional claims and markets in time/state-delineated claims. See Kenneth J. Arrow 1964 and Gerard Debreu 1959.

of resources is at least a dollar (in terms of market value). Although there are many single-valued objective functions that could guide a firm's managers in their decisions, value maximisation is an important one because it leads under most conditions to the maximisation of social welfare. But let's look more closely at this.

3.2 Value maximising and social welfare

Much of the discussion in policy circles about the proper corporate objective casts the issue in terms of the conflict between various constituencies, or 'stakeholders', in the corporation. The question then becomes whether shareholders should be held in higher regard than other constituencies, such as employees, customers, creditors and so on. But it is both unproductive and incorrect to frame the issue in this manner. The real issue is what corporate behaviour will get the most out of society's limited resources—or, equivalently, what behaviour will result in the least social waste—not whether one group is or should be more privileged than another.

3.2.1 Profit maximisation: a simplified case

To see how value maximisation leads to a socially efficient solution, let's first consider an objective function, profit maximisation, in a world in which all production runs are infinite and cash flow streams are level and perpetual. This scenario with level and perpetual streams allows us to ignore the complexity introduced by the trade-offs between current and future-year profits (or, more accurately, cash flows). Consider now the social welfare effects of a firm's decision to take resources out of the economy in the form of labour hours, capital or materials purchased voluntarily from their owners in single-price markets. The firm uses these inputs to produce outputs of goods or services that are then sold to consumers through voluntary transactions in single-price markets.

In this simple situation, a company that takes inputs out of the economy and puts its output of goods and services back into the economy increases aggregate welfare if the prices at which it sells the goods more than cover the costs it incurs in purchasing the inputs (including, of course, the cost of the capital the firm is using). Clearly, the firm should expand its output as long as an additional dollar of resources taken out of the economy is valued by the consumers of the incremental product at more than a dollar. Note that it is precisely because profit is the amount by which revenues exceed costs—by which the value of output exceeds the value of inputs— that profit maximisation [6] leads to an efficient social outcome.[7]

Because the transactions are voluntary, we know that the owners of the inputs value them at a level less than or equal to the price the firm pays—otherwise they wouldn't sell them. Therefore, as long as there are no negative externalities in the input factor mar-

---

6   Again, provided there are no externalities.
7   I am indebted to my colleague George Baker for this simple way of expressing the social optimality of profit maximisation.

kets,[8] the opportunity cost to society of those inputs is no higher than the total cost to the firm of acquiring them. I say 'no higher' because some suppliers of inputs to the firm are able to earn 'rents' by obtaining prices higher than the value of the goods to them. But such rents do not represent social costs, only transfers of wealth to those suppliers. Likewise, as long as there are no externalities in the output markets, the value to society of the goods and services produced by the firm is at least as great as the price the firm receives for the sale of those goods and services. If this were not true, the individuals purchasing them would not do so. Again, as in the case of producer surplus on inputs, the benefit to society is higher to the extent that consumer surplus exists (that is, to the extent that some consumers are able to purchase the output at prices lower than the value to them).

In sum, when a company acquires an additional unit of any input(s) to produce an additional unit of any output, it increases social welfare by at least the amount of its profit—the difference between the value of the output and the cost of the input(s) required in producing it.[9] And thus the signals to the management are clear: Continue to expand purchases of inputs and sell the resulting outputs as long as an additional dollar of inputs generates sales of at least a dollar.

3.2.2 Value and trade-offs through time

In a world in which cash flows, profits and costs are not uniform over time, managers must deal with the trade-offs of these items through time. A common case is when a company's capital investment comes in lumps that have to be funded upfront, while production and revenue occurs in the future. Knowing whether society will be benefited or harmed requires knowing whether the future output will be valuable enough to offset the cost of people giving up their labour, capital and material inputs in the present. Interest rates help us to make this decision by telling us the cost of giving up a unit of a good today for receipt at some time in the future. So long as people take advantage of the opportunity to borrow or lend at a given interest rate, that rate determines the value of moving a marginal dollar of resources (inputs or consumption goods) forwards or backwards in time.[10] In this world, individuals are as well off as possible if they maximise their wealth as measured by the discounted present value of all future claims.

In addition to interest rates, managers also need to take into account the risk of their investments and the premium the market charges for bearing such risk. But, when we add uncertainty and risk into the equation, nothing of major importance is changed in this proposition as long as there are capital markets in which the individual can buy and sell risk at a given price. In this case, it is the risk-adjusted interest rate that is used in calculating the market value of risky claims. The corporate objective function that maxi-

---

8   An example would be a case where the supplier of an input was imposing negative externalities on others by polluting water or air.
9   Equality holds only in the special case where consumer and producer surpluses are zero, and there are no externalities or monopoly.
10 For those unfamiliar with finance and present values, the value one year from now of a dollar today saved for use one year from now is thus $1 \times (1 + r)$, where r is the interest rate. Alternatively, the value today of a dollar of resources to be received one year from now is its present value of $1 / (1 + r)$.

mises social welfare thus becomes 'maximise current total firm market value'. It tells firms to expand output and investment to the point where the present market value of the firm is at a maximum.[11]

3.3 Stakeholder theory

To the extent that stakeholder theory says that firms should pay attention to all their constituencies, the theory is unassailable. Taken this far stakeholder theory is completely consistent with value maximisation or value-seeking behaviour, which implies that managers must pay attention to all constituencies that can affect the value of the firm.

But there is more to the stakeholder story than this. Any theory of corporate decision-making must tell the decision-makers—in this case, managers and boards of directors—how to choose among multiple constituencies with competing and, in some cases, conflicting interests. Customers want low prices, high quality and full service. Employees want high wages, high-quality working conditions and fringe benefits, including vacations, medical benefits and pensions. Suppliers of capital want low risk and high returns. Communities want high charitable contributions, social expenditures by companies to benefit the community at large, increased local investment and stable employment. And so it goes with every conceivable constituency. Obviously any decision criterion—and the objective function is at the core of any decision criterion—must specify how to make the trade-offs between these demands.

3.3.1 The specification of trade-offs and the incompleteness of stakeholder theory

Value maximisation (or value seeking) provides the following answer to the trade-off question: Spend an additional dollar on any constituency provided the long-term value added to the firm from such expenditure is a dollar or more. Stakeholder theory, by contrast,[12] contains no conceptual specification of how to make the trade-offs among stakeholders. And, as I argue below, it is this failure to provide a criterion for making such trade-offs, or even to acknowledge the need for them, that makes stakeholder theory a prescription for destroying firm value and reducing social welfare. This failure also helps to explain the theory's remarkable popularity.

11 Without going into the details here, the same criterion applies to all organisations whether they are public corporations or not. Obviously, even if the financial claims are not explicitly valued by the market, social welfare will be increased as long as managers of partnerships or non-profits increase output so long as the imputed market value of claims on the firm continue to increase.

12 At least as advocated by Freeman 1984, The Clarkson Centre for Business Ethics 1999 and others.

3.3.2 Implications for managers and directors

Because stakeholder theory leaves boards of directors and executives in firms with no principled criterion for decision-making, companies that try to follow the dictates of stakeholder theory will eventually fail if they are competing with firms that are aiming to maximise value. If this is true, why do so many managers and directors of corporations embrace stakeholder theory?

One answer lies in their personal short-run interests. By failing to provide a definition of 'better', stakeholder theory effectively leaves managers and directors unaccountable for their stewardship of the firm's resources. Without criteria for performance, managers cannot be evaluated in any principled way. Therefore, stakeholder theory plays into the hands of managers by allowing them to pursue their own interests at the expense of the firm's financial claimants and society at large. It allows managers and directors to devote the firm's resources to their own favourite causes— the environment, art, cities, medical research—without being held accountable for the effect of such expenditures on firm value. (And this can be true even though managers may not consciously recognise that adopting stakeholder theory leaves them unaccountable—especially, for example, when such managers have a strong personal interest in social issues.) By expanding the power of managers in this unproductive way, stakeholder theory increases agency costs in the economic system. And since it expands the power of managers, it is not surprising that stakeholder theory receives substantial support from them.

In this sense, then, stakeholder theory can be seen as gutting the foundations of the firm's internal control systems. By 'internal control systems', I mean mainly the corporate performance measurement and evaluation systems that, when properly designed, provide strong incentives for value-increasing behaviour. There is simply no principled way within the stakeholder construct (which fails to specify what 'better' is) that anyone could say that a manager has done a good or bad job. Stakeholder theory supplants or weakens the power of such control systems by giving managers more power to do whatever they want, subject only to constraints that are imposed by forces *outside* the firm—by the financial markets, the market for corporate control (e.g. the market for hostile takeovers) and, when all else fails, the product markets.

Thus, having observed the efforts of stakeholder theory advocates to weaken internal control systems, it is not surprising to see the theory being used to argue for government restrictions, such as state anti-takeover provisions, on financial markets and the market for corporate control. These markets are driven by value maximisation and will limit the damage that can be done by managers who adopt stakeholder theory. And, as illustrated by the 1990s campaigns against globalisation and free trade, the stakeholder argument is also being used to restrict product-market competition as well.

But there is something deeper than self-interest—something rooted in the evolution of the human psyche—that is driving our attraction to stakeholder theory.

3.4 Families versus markets: the roots of stakeholder theory

Stakeholder theory taps into the deep emotional commitment of most individuals to the family and tribe. For tens of thousands of years, those of our ancestors who had little respect for or loyalty to the family, band or tribe were much less likely to survive than those who did. In the last few hundred years, we have experienced the emergence of a market exchange system of prices and the private property rights on which they are based. This system of voluntary and decentralised co-ordination of human action has brought huge increases in human welfare and freedom of action.

As Friedrich von Hayek points out, we are generally unaware of the functioning of these market systems because no single mind invented or designed them—and because they work in very complicated and subtle ways. In Hayek's words:

> We are led—for example, by the pricing system in market exchange—to do things by circumstances of which we are largely unaware and which produce results that we do not intend. In our economic activities we do not know the needs which we satisfy nor the sources of the things which we get. Almost all of us serve people whom we do not know, and even of whose existence we are ignorant; and we in turn constantly live on the services of other people of whom we know nothing. All this is possible because we stand in a great frame-work of institutions and traditions—economic, legal, moral—into which we fit ourselves by obeying certain rules of conduct that we never made, and which we have never understood in the sense in which we understand how the things that we manufacture function (Hayek 1988).

Moreover, these systems operate in ways that limit the options of the small group or family, and these constraints are neither well understood nor instinctively welcomed by individuals. Many people are drawn to stakeholder theory through their evolutionary attachment to the small group and the family. As Hayek puts it:

> Constraints on the practices of the small group, it must be emphasised and repeated, are *hated*. For, as we shall see, the individual following them, even though he depends on them for life, does not and usually cannot understand how they function or how they benefit him. He knows so many objects that seem desirable but for which he is not permitted to grasp, and he cannot see how other beneficial features of his environment depend on the discipline to which he is forced to submit—a discipline forbidding him to reach out for these same appealing objects. Disliking these constraints so much, we hardly can be said to have selected them; rather, these constraints selected us: they enabled us to survive (Hayek 1988: 13, 14; emphasis original).

Thus we have a system in which human beings must simultaneously exist in two orders, what Hayek calls the 'micro-cosmos' and the 'macro-cosmos':

> Moreover, the structures of the extended order are made up not only of individuals but also of many, often overlapping, suborders within which old instinctual responses, such as solidarity and altruism, continue to retain some importance by assisting voluntary collaboration, even though they are incapable, by themselves, of creating a basis for the more extended order. Part of our present difficulty is that we must constantly adjust our lives, our thoughts and

our emotions, in order to live simultaneously within different kinds of orders according to different rules. If we were to apply the unmodified, uncurbed rules of the micro-cosmos (i.e. of the small band or troop, or of, say, our families) to the macro-cosmos (our wider civilisation), as our instincts and sentimental yearnings often make us wish to do, we would destroy it. Yet if we were always to apply the rules of the extended order to our more intimate groupings, *we would crush them*. So we must learn to live in two sorts of worlds at once. To apply the name 'society' to both, or even to either, is hardly of any use, and can be most misleading (Hayek 1988: 18; emphasis original).

Stakeholder theory taps into this confusion and antagonism towards markets and relaxes constraints on the small group in ways that are damaging to society as a whole and (in the long run) to the small group itself. Such deeply rooted and generally unrecognised conflict between allegiances to family and tribe and what is good for society as a whole has had a major impact on our evolution. And, in this case, the conflict does not end up serving our long-run collective interests.[13]

3.5 Enlightened value maximisation and enlightened stakeholder theory

For those intent on improving management, organisational governance and performance, there is a way out of the conflict between value maximising and stakeholder theory. It lies in the melding together of what I call 'enlightened value maximisation' and 'enlightened stakeholder theory'.

3.5.1 Enlightened value maximisation

Enlightened value maximisation recognises that communication with and motivation of an organisation's managers, employees and partners is extremely difficult. What this means in practice is that, if we simply tell all participants in an organisation that its sole

---

13 It is useful here to briefly summarise the positive arguments (those refutable by empirical data) and normative arguments (those propositions that say what should be rather than what is in the world) I have made thus far. I have argued positively that firms that follow stakeholder theory as it is generally advocated will do less well in the competition for survival than those that follow a well-defined, single-valued objective such as value creation. I have also argued positively that if firms follow value creation, social welfare will be greater and, normatively, that this is desirable. I have argued positively that the self-interests of managers and directors will lead them to prefer stakeholder theory because it increases their power and means they cannot be held accountable for their actions. I have also argued positively that the self-interest of special-interest groups that wish to acquire legitimacy in corporate governance circles to enhance their influence over the allocation of corporate resources will advocate the use of stakeholder theory by managers and directors. This leads to the positive prediction that society will be poorer if they are successful, and to the normative conclusion that this is undesirable. For a discussion of the role of normative, positive (or instrumental) and descriptive theory in the literature on stakeholder theory, see Thomas Donaldson and Lee E. Preston 1995.

purpose is to maximise value, we will not get maximum value for the organisation. Value maximisation is not a vision or a strategy or even a purpose; it is the scorecard for the organisation. We must give people enough structure to understand what maximising value means so that they can be guided by it and therefore have a chance to actually achieve it. They must be turned on by the vision or the strategy in the sense that it taps into some human desire or passion of their own—for example, a desire to build the world's best automobile or to create a film or play that will move people for centuries. All this can be not only consistent with value seeking but a major contributor to it.

And this brings us up against the limits of value maximisation per se. Value seeking tells an organisation and its participants how their success in achieving a vision or in implementing a strategy will be assessed. But value maximising or value seeking says nothing about how to create a superior vision or strategy. Nor does it tell employees or managers how to find or establish initiatives or ventures that create value. It only tells them how we will measure success in their activity.

Defining what it means to score a goal in football or soccer, for example, tells the players nothing about how to win the game; it just tells them how the score will be kept. That is the role of value maximisation in organisational life. It doesn't tell us how to have a great defence or offence, or what kind of tactics to use, or how much to train and practise, or whom to hire and so on. All of these critical functions are part of the competitive and organisational strategy of any team or organisation. Adopting value creation as the scorekeeping measure does nothing to relieve us of the responsibility to do all these things and more in order to survive and dominate our sector of the competitive landscape.

This means, for example, that we must give employees and managers a structure that will help them to resist the temptation to maximise short-term financial performance (as typically measured by accounting profits or, even worse, earnings per share). Short-term profit maximisation at the expense of long-term value creation is a sure way to destroy value. This is where enlightened stakeholder theory can play an important role. We can learn from stakeholder theorists how to lead managers and participants in an organisation to think more generally and creatively about how the organisation's policies treat all important constituencies of the firm. This includes not just the stockholders and financial markets but employees, customers, suppliers and the community in which the organisation exists.

Indeed, it is a basic principle of enlightened value maximisation that **we cannot maximise the long-term market value of an organisation if we ignore or mistreat any important constituency**. We cannot create value without good relations with customers, employees, financial backers, suppliers, regulators and communities. But, having said that, we can now use the value criterion for choosing between those competing interests. I say 'competing' interests because no constituency can be given full satisfaction if the firm is to flourish and survive. Moreover, we can be sure—again, apart from the possibility of externalities and monopoly power—that using this value criterion will result in making society as well off as it can be.

As stated earlier, resolving externality and monopoly problems is the legitimate domain of the government in its rule-setting function. Those who care about resolving monopoly and externality issues will not succeed if they look to corporations to resolve these issues voluntarily. Companies that try to do so either will be eliminated by competitors who choose not to be so civic-minded, or will survive only by consuming their economic rents in this manner.

3.5.2 Enlightened stakeholder theory

Enlightened stakeholder theory is easy to explain. It can make use of most of what stakeholder theorists offer in the way of processes and audits to measure and evaluate the firm's management of its relations with all important constituencies. Enlightened stakeholder theory adds the simple specification that the objective function—the overriding goal—of the firm is to maximise total long-term firm market value. In short, the change in the total long-term market value of the firm is the scorecard by which success is measured.

I say 'long-term' market value to recognise the possibility that financial markets, although forward-looking, may not understand the full implications of a company's policies until they begin to show up in cash flows over time. In such cases, management must communicate to investors the policies' anticipated effect on value, and then wait for the market to catch up and recognise the real value of its decisions as reflected in increases in market share, customer and employee loyalty, and, finally, cash flows. Value creation does not mean responding to the day-to-day fluctuations in a firm's value. The market is inevitably ignorant of many managerial actions and opportunities, at least in the short run. In those situations where the financial markets clearly do not have this private competitive information, directors and managers must resist the pressures of those markets while making every effort to communicate their expectations to investors.

In this way, enlightened stakeholder theorists can see that, although stockholders are not some special constituency that ranks above all others, long-term stock value is an important determinant (along with the value of debt and other instruments) of total long-term firm value. They would recognise that value creation gives management a way to assess the trade-offs that must be made among competing constituencies, and that it allows for principled decision-making independent of the personal preferences of managers and directors. Also important, managers and directors become accountable for the assets under their control because the value scorecard provides an objective yardstick against which their performance can be evaluated.

3.5.3 Measurability and imperfect knowledge

It is important to recognise that none of the above arguments depends on value being easily observable. Nor do they depend on perfect knowledge of the effects on value of decisions regarding any of a firm's constituencies. The world may be complex and difficult to understand. It may leave us in deep uncertainty about the effects of any decisions we may make. It may be governed by complex dynamic systems that are difficult to optimise in the usual sense. But that does not remove the necessity of making choices on a day-to-day basis. And to do this in a purposeful way we must have a scorecard.

The absence of a scorecard makes it easier for people to engage in value-claiming activities that satisfy one or more groups of stakeholders at the expense of value creation. We can take random actions, and we can devise decision rules that depend on superstitions. But none of these is likely to serve us well in the competition for survival.

We must not confuse optimisation with value creation or value seeking. To create value we need not know exactly what maximum value is and precisely how it can be achieved. What we must do, however, is to set up our organisations so that managers and employees are clearly motivated to seek value—to institute those changes and strategies that are most likely to cause value to rise. To navigate in such a world in anything close to a purposeful way, we must have a notion of 'better', and value seeking is such a notion. I know of no other scorecard that will score the game as well as this one. Under most circumstances and conditions, it tells us when we are getting better and when we are getting worse. It is not perfect, but that is the nature of the world.

3.6 The Balanced Scorecard

The Balanced Scorecard is the managerial equivalent of stakeholder theory. Like stakeholder theory, the notion of a 'balanced' scorecard appeals to many, but it suffers from many of the same flaws. When we use multiple measures on the Balanced Scorecard to evaluate the performance of people or business units, we put managers in the same impossible position as managers trying to manage under stakeholder theory. We are asking them to maximise in more than one dimension at a time with no idea of the trade-offs between the measures. As a result, purposeful decisions cannot be made.

The balanced scorecard arose from the belief of its originators, Robert Kaplan and David Norton, that purely financial measures of performance are not sufficient to yield effective management decisions (Kaplan and Norton 1992, 1996). I agree with this conclusion though, as I suggest below, they have inadvertently confused this with the unstated, but implicit conclusion that there should never be a *single* measure of performance. Moreover, especially *at lower levels of an organisation*, a single pure financial measure of performance is unlikely to properly measure a person's or even a business unit's contribution to a company. In the words of Kaplan and Norton:

> The Balanced Scorecard complements financial measures of past performance with measures of the drivers of future performance. The objectives and measures of the scorecard are derived from an organisation's vision and strategy. The objectives and measures view organisational performance from four perspectives: financial, customer, internal business process, and learning and growth . . .
>
> The Balanced Scorecard expands the set of business unit objectives beyond summary financial measures. Corporate executives can now measure how their business units create value for current and future customers and how they must enhance internal capabilities and the investment in people, systems, and procedures necessary to improve future performance. The Balanced Scorecard captures the critical value-creation activities created by skilled, motivated organisational participants. While retaining, via the financial perspective, an interest in short-term performance, the Balanced Scorecard clearly reveals the value drivers for superior long-term financial and competitive performance (Kaplan and Norton 1996: 8).

As Kaplan and Norton go on to say:

> The measures are *balanced* between the outcome measures—the results of past efforts—and the measures that drive future performance. And the scorecard is *balanced* between objective, easily quantified outcome measures and subjective, somewhat judgmental performance drivers of the outcome measures . . .
>
> A good balanced scorecard should have an appropriate mix of outcomes (lagging indicators) and performance drivers (leading indicators) that have been customised to the business unit's strategy (Kaplan and Norton 1996: 10, 150; emphasis original).

The aim of Kaplan and Norton, then, is to capture both past performance and expected future performance in scorecards with multiple measures—in fact, as many as two dozen of them—that are intimately related to the organisation's strategy (Kaplan and Norton 1996: 162). And this is where my misgivings about the Balanced Scorecard lie. For an organisation's strategy to be implemented effectively, each person in the organisation must clearly understand what he or she has to do, how their performance measures will be constructed, and how their rewards and punishments are related to those measures.

But, as we saw earlier in the case of multiple constituencies (or the multiple goals represented in Fig. 3.1), decision-makers cannot make rational choices without some overall single dimensional objective to be maximised. Given a dozen or two dozen measures and no sense of the trade-offs between them, the typical manager will be unable to behave purposefully, and the result will be confusion.

Kaplan and Norton generally do not deal with the critical issue of how to weight the multiple dimensions represented by the two dozen measures on their scorecards. And this is where problems with the Balanced Scorecard are sure to arise: without specifying what the trade-offs are among these two dozen or so different measures, there is no 'balance' in their scorecard. Adding to the potential for confusion, Kaplan and Norton also offer almost no guidance on the critical issue of how to tie the performance measurement system to managerial incentives and rewards. Here is their concluding statement on this important matter:

> Several approaches may be attractive to pursue. In the short term, tying incentive compensation of all senior managers to a balanced set of business unit scorecard measures will foster commitment to overall organisational goals, rather than suboptimisation within functional departments . . . Whether such linkages should be explicit . . . or applied judgementally . . . will likely vary from company to company. More knowledge about the benefits and costs of explicit linkages will undoubtedly continue to be accumulated in the years ahead (Kaplan and Norton 1996: 222).

What the Balanced Scorecard fails to provide, then, is a clear linkage (and a rationale for that linkage) between the performance measures and the corporate system of rewards and punishments. Indeed, the Balanced Scorecard does not provide a scorecard in the traditional sense of the word. And, to make my point, let me push the sports analogy a little further. A scorecard in any sport yields a single number that determines the winner among all contestants. In most sports the person or team with the highest score wins. Very simply, a scorecard yields a score, not multiple measures of different dimensions like yards rushing and passing. These latter drivers of performance affect who wins and who loses, but they do not themselves distinguish the winner.

To reiterate, the Balanced Scorecard does not yield a score that would allow us to distinguish winners from losers. For this reason, the system is best described not as a scorecard but as a dashboard or instrument panel. It can tell managers many interesting things about their business, but it does not give a score for the organisation's performance, or even for the performance of its business units. As a senior manager of a large financial institution that spent considerable time implementing a Balanced Scorecard system explained to me:

> We never figured out how to use the scorecard to measure performance. We used it to transfer information, a lot of information, from the divisions to the senior management team. At the end of the day, however, your performance depended on your ability to meet your targets for contribution to bottom-line profits.

Thus, because of the lack of a way for managers to think through the difficult task of determining an unambiguous performance measure in the Balanced Scorecard system, the result in this case was a fallback to a single and inadequate financial measure of performance (in this case, accounting profits)—the very approach that Kaplan and Norton properly wish to change. The lack of a single, one-dimensional measure by which an organisation or department or person will score their performance means that these units or people cannot make purposeful decisions. They cannot do so because, if they do not understand the trade-offs between the multiple measures, they cannot know whether they are becoming better off (except in those rare cases when all measures are increasing in some decision).

In sum, the appropriate measure for the organisation is value creation, the change in the market value of all claims on the firm. And, for those organisations that wish a 'flow' measure of value creation on a quarterly or yearly basis, I recommend economic value added (EVA). But I hasten to add that, as the performance measures are cascaded down through the organisation, neither value creation nor the year-to-year measure, EVA, is likely to be the proper performance measure at all levels. To illustrate this point, let's now look briefly at performance measurement for business units.

3.6.1 Measuring divisional performance

The proper measure for any person or business unit in a multi-divisional company will be determined mainly by two factors: the company's strategy and the actions that the person or division being evaluated can take to contribute to the success of the strategy. There are two general ways in principle that this score or objective can be determined: a centralised way and a decentralised way.

To see this let us begin by distinguishing clearly between the measure of performance (single-dimensional) for a unit or person, and the drivers that the unit or person can use to affect the performance measure. In the decentralised solution, the organisation determines the appropriate performance measure for the unit, and it is the person's or unit's responsibility to figure out what the performance drivers are, how they influence performance and how to manage them. The distinction here is the difference between an outcome (the performance measure) and the inputs or decision variables (the management of the performance drivers). And managers at higher levels in the hierarchy may be able to help the person or unit to understand what the drivers are and how to manage them. But this help can only go so far because the specific knowledge regarding the drivers will generally lie not in headquarters but in the operating units. Therefore, in the end it is the accountable party, not headquarters, who will generally have the relevant specific knowledge and therefore must determine the drivers, their changing relation to results and how to manage them.

At the opposite extreme is the completely centralised solution, in which headquarters will determine the performance measure by giving the functional form to the unit that lists the drivers and describes the weight that each driver receives in the determination of the performance measure. The performance for a period is then determined by calculating the weighted average of the measures of the drivers for the period.[14] This solution effectively transfers the job of learning how to create value at all levels in the organisation to the top managers, and leaves the operating managers only the job of managing the performance drivers that have been dictated to them by top management. The problem with this approach, however, is that it is likely to work only in a fairly narrow range of circumstances—those cases where the specific knowledge necessary to understand the details of the relation between changes in each driver and changes in the performance measure lies higher in the hierarchy. Although this category may include a number of very small firms, it will rule out most larger, multi-divisional companies, especially in today's rapidly changing business environment.

3.7 Closing thoughts on the Balanced Scorecard and value maximisation

In summary, the Kaplan–Norton Balanced Scorecard is a tool to help managers understand what creates value in their business. As such, it is a useful analytical tool, and I join with Kaplan and Norton in urging managers to do the hard work necessary to understand what creates value in their organisation and how to manage those value drivers. As they put it:

> [A] properly constructed Balanced Scorecard should tell the story of the business unit's strategy. It should identify and make explicit the sequence of hypotheses about the cause-and-effect relationships between outcome measures and the performance drivers of those outcomes. Every measure selected for a Balanced Scorecard should be an element in a chain of cause-and-effect relationships that communicates the meaning of the business unit's strategy to the organisation (Kaplan and Norton 1996: 31).

But managers are almost inevitably led to try to use the multiple measures of the Balanced Scorecard as a performance measurement system. And, as a performance measurement system, the Balanced Scorecard will lead to confusion, conflict, inefficiency and lack of focus. This is bound to happen as operating managers guess at what the trade-offs might be between each of the dimensions of performance. And this uncertainty will generally lead to conflicts with managers at headquarters, who are likely to have different assessments of the trade-offs. Such conflicts, besides causing disappointments and confusion

---

14 And of course I do not mean to imply that the functional relationship between the value drivers and the performance measure will always be a simple weighted average. Indeed, in general it will be more complicated than this.

about operating decisions, could also lead to attempts by operating managers to game the system—by, say, performing well on financial measures while sacrificing non-financial ones. Moreover, there is no logical or principled resolution of the resulting conflicts unless all the parties come to agreement about what they are trying to accomplish; and this means specifying how the score is calculated—in effect, figuring out how the balance in the Balanced Scorecard is actually attained.

As we saw earlier, even if it were possible to come up with a truly 'optimising' system where all the weights and the trade-offs among the multiple measures and drivers were specified—a highly doubtful proposition—reaching agreement between headquarters and line management over the proper weighting of the measures and their linkage to the corporate reward system would be an enormously difficult, if not impossible, undertaking. In addition, it would surely be impossible to keep the system continuously updated so as to reflect all the changes in a dynamic local and worldwide competitive landscape.

A 1996 survey of Balanced Scorecard implementations by Towers Perrin gives a fairly clear indication of the problems that are likely to arise with it (Perrin 1996). Perhaps most troubling, 70% of the companies using a scorecard also reported using it for compensation, and an additional 17% were considering doing so. And, not surprisingly, 40% of the respondents said they believed that the large number of measures weakened the effectiveness of the measurement system. What's more, in their empirical test of the effects of the Balanced Scorecard implementation in a global financial services firm, a 1997 study by Christopher Ittner, David Larcker and Marshall Meyer concluded that the first issue their study raises for future research is 'defining precisely what "balance" is and the mechanisms through which "balance" promotes performance' (Ittner *et al.* 1997). As I have argued in this chapter, this question cannot be answered because 'balance' is a term used by Balanced Scorecard advocates as a substitute for thorough analysis of one of the more difficult parts of the performance measurement system—the necessity to evaluate and make trade-offs. They and others have been seduced by this hurrah word (who can argue for 'unbalanced'?) into avoiding careful thought on the issues.

In fact, the sooner we get rid of the word 'balance' in these discussions, the better we will be able to sort out the solutions. Balance cannot ever substitute for having to deal with the difficult issues associated with specifying the trade-offs among multiple goods and bads that determine the overall score for an organisation's success. We must do this to stand a chance of creating an organisational scoreboard that actually gives a score—which is something every good scoreboard must do.

3.7.1 *Closing thoughts on stakeholder theory*

Stakeholder theory plays into the hands of special interests that wish to use the resources of corporations for their own ends. With the widespread failure of centrally planned socialist and communist economies, those who wish to use non-market forces to reallocate wealth now see great opportunity in the playing field that stakeholder theory opens to them. Stakeholder theory gives them the appearance of legitimate political access to the sources of decision-making power in organisations, and it deprives those organisations of a principled basis for rejecting those claims. The result is to undermine the foundations of value-seeking behaviour that have enabled markets and capitalism to generate wealth and high standards of living worldwide.

If widely adopted, stakeholder theory will reduce social welfare even as its advocates claim to increase it—much as happened in the failed communist and socialist experiments of the last century. And, as I pointed out earlier, stakeholder theorists will often have the active support of managers who wish to throw off the constraints on their power provided by the value-seeking criterion and its enforcement by capital markets, the market for corporate control and product markets. For example, stakeholder arguments played an important role in persuading the US courts and legislatures to limit hostile takeovers through legalisation of poison pills and state control shareholder acts. And we will continue to see more political action limiting the power of these markets to constrain managers. In sum, special-interest groups will continue to use the arguments of stakeholder theory to legitimise their positions, and it is in our collective interest to expose the logical fallacy of these arguments.

© 2002 Michael C. Jensen
Harvard Business School Working Paper #00-058, revised 2/2002

JENSEN'S APPROACH TO STAKEHOLDER THEORY

Duane Windsor
Rice University, USA

The proper meaning of the term 'theory' can be a matter of controversy. The author treats theorising as essentially synonymous with objective and systematic thinking or reasoning drawing on validated standards for logic and evidence. Where there is controversy, not readily resolved by evidence, there must be reference to the rigour of logic used and how well that logic stands up to scrutiny, searching out fanciful speculation. In this sense, at least, management theory is not strictly divorced from management practice. In stakeholder thinking, theorising can address, as Donaldson and Preston (1995) explain, descriptive, instrumental or normative dimensions. Descriptive theory is characterisation of reality, behaviour and possibility. Instrumental theory is development of if–then causal relationships for prescribing goal-directed action, especially by management as stewards of assets owned by others. Normative theory is evaluation, typically moral, of ends and means. Donaldson and Preston (1995) view stakeholder theorising as akin to an 'onion' with a normative core linked to a descriptive surface by an intervening instrumental dimension. (They propose a normative core that is a broadened theory of stakeholders' property rights in which stakeholders are viewed as investors-at-risk akin, and morally equal, to financial claimants.)

The stakeholder theory of the firm, in recognisable modern form, originated (Freeman 1984: 31, 49 n. 1) at the Stanford Research Institute (in a 1963 SRI internal memo), but it received active academic interest and managerial acceptance following Freeman's seminal book (see Emshoff and Freeman 1981). In origin, stakeholder theorising was explicitly and intentionally a softening of (if not implicitly a fundamental challenge to) strict (or strong) stockholder doctrine (Freeman 1984: 32) then prevailing in US (i.e. state-level) corporate-governance law since at least *Dodge v. Ford* (Michigan Supreme Court, 204 Mich 459, 170 N.W. 668, 1919; the legal history is summarised in ALI 1994: 70-71 nn. 1, 2). Stockholder doctrine posits that shareholder return is the *primary* purpose of a business corporation (other purposes, if any, are then strictly secondary); such return is certainly the primary purpose of financial claimants. 'The SRI researchers argued that unless executives understood the needs and concerns of . . . stakeholder groups, they could not formulate corporate objectives which would receive the necessary support for the continued survival of a firm' (Freeman 1984: 32; cf. Clarkson 1995).

Freeman conceded that, despite strictly product-market theories of efficiency and effectiveness (1984: 4), 'Business has always dealt with non-marketplace stakeholders' (1984: 28 n. 3). Drucker (1999: 59) states that managerial balancing of stakeholder interests dates to the 1920s. In retrospect, one can identify some earlier stakeholder-like reasoning approaches (e.g. Dodd 1932; Barnard 1938; Papandreou 1952), post-1945 management–labour arrangements in Germany and Japan that could be characterised as stakeholder-like (Donaldson and Preston 1995: 76; see Drucker 1999: 59, for a criticism that the arrangements were simply to avoid industrial strife), and parallel Scandinavian theory efforts (Rhenman 1964, 1968; Rhenman and Stymne 1965; Danielsson 1979; see Näsi 1995b). Freeman (1984: 50 n. 15) provides evidence that Rhenman visited Stanford in the 1960s, and assigns priority of innovation to SRI; Freeman (1984: 41) also criticises Rhenman's conception as too narrow.[1]

A large and diverse stakeholder literature has blossomed since 1984, with a marked surge of stakeholder publications in and after 1995, partly in connection with the Sloan Foundation-supported Redefining the Corporation research project operated through the University of Toronto's (Max E.) Clarkson Centre for Business Ethics. Important stakeholder articles have appeared in the *Academy of Management Review* (Clarkson 1995; Donaldson and Preston 1995; Jones 1995; Jones and Wicks 1999a) and the *Academy of Management Journal* (Harrison and Freeman 1999), in addition to forming a key stream of publication in the annual *Proceedings of the International Association for Business and Society* (IABS) and *Business and Society* (published by IABS). The stakeholder viewpoint has been partly captured in so-called constituency statutes adopted in some 29 US states (Orts 1992: 72-73 n. 381; Jensen 2000: 55 n. 1, citing Sternberg 1994). Orts argues, however, that such statutes merely increase the discretion of managers while weakening the power of owners without increasing the power of other stakeholders. Corporate-governance reform reports issued during the 1990s (ALI 1994; Dey 1994—Toronto Exchange; Peters 1997—Amsterdam Exchange; Hampel 1998—London Exchange) all included language highlighting in some form stakeholder considerations as well as improved accountability of management to shareholders. Jensen (2000: 55, n. 1) cites Sternberg (1996) on the acceptance of stakeholder theory by the Business Roundtable and *The Financial Times* (of London). The Blair government (Labour Party) in the UK endorsed a stakeholder theory of the economy (Jensen 2000: 55 n. 1; see *Economist* 1996).

This chapter addresses the question of whether the evidently successful spread of stakeholder reasoning—among academic, managerial and political circles—masks an impending intellectual crisis in stakeholder theorising. And the chapter addresses the follow-on question of what, if there is indeed such a crisis, can be done about the situation from a stakeholder viewpoint, and what are the implications for managerial practice. The question is sparked by two developments—one external, the other internal to the stakeholder literature. The external development is a strong (intendedly fatal) counter-attack by respectable and intelligent advocates of the financial-economics alternative to

---

1 Rhenman defined 'stakeholders' in terms of dependence; Freeman defined stakeholders broadly in terms of dual effect or influence. Jensen (2000: 38) returns to a narrower definition focused, in effect, on power to affect the firm; the firm's effects on stakeholders are absorbed into social welfare improvements due to wealth creation.

stakeholder theory. (From the viewpoint of stakeholder reasoning, financial-economics theory may be less an alternative and more one dimension of a 'triple'-bottom-line performance evaluation framework.) The chapter uses Jensen (2000) as a starting point for stakeholder thinking; Jensen mounts a strong financial-economics counterattack on stakeholder reasoning and its practice by managers. The internal development, less readily characterised and interpreted, is a set of controversies within and around the stakeholder literature that may represent intellectual fermentation for reformulation and progress, or may represent unresolved difficulties not hampering the financial-econom-ics alternative. This chapter builds stakeholder theory from a financial-economics start-ing point rather than as an alternative. But the fundamental role of stakeholder reasoning remains to blunt the force of a purely financial-economics argument concerning managerial conduct.

4.1 The state of the field

The external development is readily characterised. Advocates of the financial-economics alternative to stakeholder theory have counterattacked against stakeholder theory in recent years on two bases, described below. The term 'financial-economics alternative' is somewhat artfully used here. The financial-economic theory of the firm has substantially evolved beyond the legalistic stockholder doctrine and short-run profit maximisation model at which stakeholder theorising in its origin was directed.

One basis for criticism is a corporate governance argument harking back in effect to the strict stockholder doctrine. This argument (see Sternberg 1994, 1996, 1999) holds that owners organised (or alternatively purchased) the firm (a presumption posited in financial-economics theory) and are ('constitutionally') entitled to the (residual) fruits of their financial investment; otherwise the organisation is definitionally not-for-profit. (This principle effectively prevails in the 31 US states that have not adopted so-called constituency statutes.) The argument essentially portrays stakeholder theorising as theft of extant (and morally justifiable) property rights of owners (cf. Friedman 1970, who criticises discretionary corporate social responsibility by managers as theft from con-sumers, employees and owners). This corporate-governance argument may be contrasted with Donaldson and Preston's (1995) formulation of a broader theory of property rights, taking into account the investment 'equities' of stakeholders other than financial claimants; and Blair's (1995) formulation of an argument for extending (on both motivational and equity grounds) ownership shares (not necessarily with voting rights) to knowledge workers. For Sternberg, stakeholder rights (if any) are strictly secondary (i.e. subordinated) to the property rights of owners.[2]

The other basis for criticism is a social-welfare argument (see McTaggart *et al.* 1994; Jensen 2000) holding that total long-run market value (i.e. financial-claim) creation by management is the best path to social wealth creation ultimately benefiting all stake-

---

2   Sternberg's argument is doctrinaire in the sense that what property law concerns is not who has ownership, i.e. actual possession, but rather who possesses the best right, i.e. claim to such ownership. Otherwise progressive taxation of income and wealth, in the sense of net negative transfers, is not possible.

holders. (Financial claimants include equity, debt, preferred stock and warrants; Jensen 2000: 38.) Jensen argues that the 'value maximisation proposition . . . has its roots in 200 years of research in economics and finance' in contrast to stakeholder theory's 'roots in sociology, organisational behaviour, the politics of special interests, and managerial self interest'.[3] Supporting the social welfare argument, moreover, is the apparent success of shareholder value, economic value or profit, and market value maximisation strategies in recent decades (cf. Mayer 1996).

In keeping with the tradition established by Friedman's (1970) criticism of discretionary corporate social responsibility practice by managers, holding that the responsibility argument is ambiguous and illogical, Sternberg (1996) and Jensen (2000: 39) both criticise the illogic or incomplete logic of stakeholder theorising. A response to this line of criticism is that made by Keynes (1936: 378), that it was not the logic of classical economics that was at fault but rather the failure of its tacit assumptions to correspond to the real world. Jensen adds a wrinkle to the financial-economics approach by arguing first that managers and employees require (logically and behaviourally) a single-valued objective function (i.e. bottom-line value creation), and then that attention to stakeholder interests is necessary for motivation of managers and employees to pursue long-term value creation. The wrinkle admits to an important psychological dimension to managerial and employee conduct (cf. Donaldson 1999). Even so, Jensen argues, essentially, that stakeholder practices and processes, properly understood (i.e. some 'enlightened stakeholder theory'), are a handmaiden of an 'enlightened value maximisation' theory. At best, the former are subordinated to and embedded within the latter, rather than vice versa. Jensen both accepts long-term value creation through stakeholder engagement practices (viewed instrumentally) and rejects multiple-bottom-line theory (viewed as a set of goals) for managerial conduct. That one disagrees with Jensen and Sternberg is not sufficient grounds for dismissal of their intelligent and well-considered arguments out of hand.

The internal development is not so readily characterised or interpreted. Freeman's view of stakeholder theorising dominated the literature for a decade. The surge of stakeholder publications in 1995, cited above, marked not simply a triumph of the approach, but deliberate efforts at explicit reformulation or extension. At least three main and unresolved tensions may be delineated. (Donaldson and Preston [1995: 70] argue that much of stakeholder literature has engaged in implicit theorising through lack of separation of descriptive, instrumental and normative arguments.)

One tension has concerned the proper definition or scope of stakeholdership. Whereas Freeman emphasised capacity to affect or be affected by a focal firm (i.e. a concept of dual or two-way influence), the Sloan Foundation-funded project has emphasised a broadened theory of property rights (relative to stockholder doctrine) treating various stakeholders as (or 'as if' morally) holding investments-at-risk in the focal firm, equal morally and practically in importance to the investments of financial claimants. (The argument is that all 'investments' are equally necessary to success of the firm; see Clarkson *et al.* 1994; Preston *et al.* 1999; Clarkson Centre for Business Ethics 2000.) Mitchell *et al.* (1997) introduced a useful three-dimensional definition built around the

---

3   Jensen's distinction is in reality perhaps not so strictly sharp in the literature. The economics literature on the theory of the firm is considerably more diffuse than the arguably mainstream financial-economics perspective and includes behavioural, managerial and evolutionary approaches—see Papandreou 1952; Thorelli 1965—that have indirectly influenced stakeholder theorising.

combinatorial possibilities of legitimacy, power and urgency as stakeholder attributes. The definitional controversy is not a minor matter. Jensen (2000: 38) appears to focus the definition of stakeholdership only on interests that can substantially 'affect the welfare of the firm'—a definition implicitly abandoning the 'affected' component of Freeman's definition.[4]

A second tension has concerned the status of nature: can, and, if so, should nature be defined as or treated as if enjoying stakeholder rights or status? Starik (1995) has been a prime proponent that nature 'is' the most important stakeholder of all. (Jensen [2000: 38] is dubious.) The alternative view, grounded ultimately in Kant (Rachels 1999: 132), is that only humans can be stakeholders, so that the role of nature must be apprehended in terms of human stakeholders' interests.

A third tension has concerned the relationship among descriptive, instrumental and normative approaches to stakeholder theorising. While Freeman (1984: 47) explicitly emphasised a descriptive grounding, he viewed 'management theory' as 'inherently pre-scriptive'. While Jones and Wicks (1999a) forecast an instrumental–normative integration, they doubt the prospects of a descriptive stakeholder theory akin to the economic theory of the firm. Donaldson (1999) responded that the true target of stakeholder theorising was the psychology of the manager.

While internal disagreements are not sufficient to indict a theory (on the contrary, disagreements may signal intellectual ferment), the disagreements may reinforce Jensen's point that 'stakeholder theory is incomplete as a specification for the corporate purpose or objective function' (2000: 38).

The business and society field, the home base for stakeholder theory, itself can be described as a hotchpotch or jumble of partly overlapping approaches rather than being well integrated; the situation in stakeholder literature is symptomatic. Frederick (1999) explicitly casts aside the developmental history of business and society studies. In his view, corporate social performance (CSP) and stakeholder theories (cf. Freeman 1999) have been thoroughly mined and must now be abandoned. (In his view, the appropriate path to take concerns the roles of nature and spirituality.) In contrast to the marked success of managerial strategies grounded in financial-economics theorising, the empirical evidence available on stakeholder theorising tends to suggest that managers are wholly instrumental (Agle *et al.* 1999; Ogden and Watson 1999) and that stakeholder-like practices in Europe involve significant efficiency costs (Mayer 1996).

4.2 Some considerations in stakeholder theorising

Figure 4.1 depicts an intersection of two continua. (The constructs are 'pure' only at the extrema or poles. In between, there is a varying mix.) The vertical continuum depicts a tension or trade-off between market exchange and political action—the essential theme

---

4   That Jensen (2000: 55 n. 2) quotes Freeman's definition suggests that the redirection is not simply inadvertent. He reintroduces the influence of stakeholders on the firm, but does so indirectly through the interests of managers and employees in the welfare or concerns of those stakeholders. Owners have interest in motivating managers and employees, whose motivation is a function of their psychology regarding others.

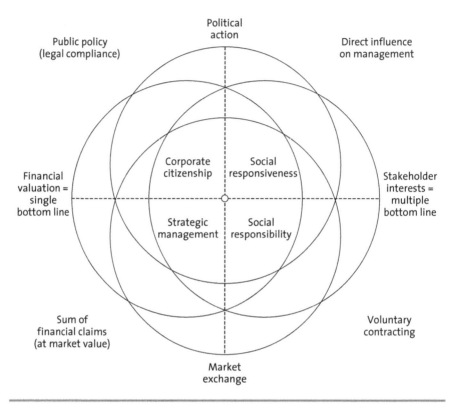

Figure 4.1 *Relationships among key considerations*

of Adam Smith (1776). Political action is explicitly defined to be broader than governmental action (i.e. public policy). Thorelli 1965 was an earlier effort at addressing this relationship in a political-economic theory of the firm. The horizontal continuum analogously depicts a tension or trade-off between financial or market valuation (i.e. Jensen's single-value bottom line or objective function) and stakeholder interests (i.e. a multiple-value bottom line or multiple objectives function). This trade-off problem is the basis of Jensen's criticism of stakeholder theory. Overlapping circles (cf. Mitchell *et al.* 1997: 872) along the two axes reflect an admittedly crude classification schema. One may characterise financial-economics and stakeholder theories as alternatives, or work towards their integration on some basis (and Jensen does both, by the device of 'enlightened' reformulations); one may similarly characterise market exchange and political action as alternatives (Jensen 2000: 47-48, quotes Hayek 1988: 13, 14, 18, extensively), or work towards their integration on some basis.

The design of Figure 4.1 delineates four quadrants. The north-west quadrant isolates public policy (i.e. legal compliance), that Jensen focuses narrowly on externalities and monopolies, although he notes the existence of so-called constituency statutes. (Preston and Post [1975] argued for a public policy solution to responsibility issues.) The north-east quadrant isolates stakeholder efforts at direct influence on managers and directors. Political action has the broad meaning of public policy and/or direct influence. Jensen, in effect, absorbs the latter into managerial decision-making. The south-west quadrant isolates the financial-economics theory of single-value decision-making. This theory presumably functions within legal and moral parameters or constraints (cf. Friedman 1970), such as public policy on externalities and monopolies, and in the direction of social welfare improvements without respect to the motives of economic actors (Smith 1776: Book 4 Ch. 2). Smith properly viewed voluntary market exchange, albeit grounded in self-interest motives, as superior to bad legal institutions such as feudalism, serfdom and slavery and to bad public policy such as mercantilism; but he also stipulated conditions of justice, security and relative social harmony (cf. Heilbroner 1953: 71). It should be noted here that the present dispute occurs within a constitutional democracy anchored on a (regulated) market economy. The south-east quadrant isolates voluntary contracting (cf. Nunan 1988), although such contracts can, in principle, embed views concerning multiple bottom lines.

The overlap of the four circles, at the intersection of the two continua, is by nature ill defined. As a matter of expositional convenience, the central circle (defined by overlap) is subdivided into four quadrants roughly corresponding to the outer quadrants. This author suggests that here, precisely, is where lies the matter of addressing business ethics and corporate social responsibility, corporate social responsiveness (conjoined responsibility in corporate social performance theory), global corporate citizenship, and their relationship to long-term strategic management of the firm. There is both a duty to obey the law (ALI 1994: 60) and extra-legal (i.e. moral) responsibilities (Friedman 1970). The latter are, however, voluntarily accepted as constraints on freedom of conduct (see Banfield 1985: 337). A problem evident in Jensen is an assignment of non-market issues to public policy processes without explicitly addressing ethical matters (cf. Heilbroner 1953: 314, arguing that such politicisation means making the electorate the judges of good and evil). A difficulty in such an approach is that it places no explicit moral constraint on the efforts of business to then influence public policy to self-interested advantage. Wealth, generated in markets, may work to affect public policy more than any moral consideration.

Figure 4.2 is a three-dimensional extension of Jensen (2000: 40, his Figure 1.1, which is strictly two-dimensional). His original two-dimensional depiction is shown (here relabelling the horizontal axis and adding some critical value labels) embedded as the two-dimensional plane in Figure 4.2 generated by the vertical and horizontal axes only (ignoring the third axis used below for a three-dimensional analysis). Jensen's depiction is shown using the financial value axis (labelled V1) and environmental improvement axis (labelled V2), the latter simply substituted for the market share dimension used in Jensen's own example. The reader here need focus initially only on the two-dimensional V1–V2 plane created by the vertical and horizontal axes. Jensen depicts a two-dimensional trade-off between two competing objectives: profits on the vertical axis (more properly for Jensen financial or market value creation, here V1) and market share on the horizontal axis (here, V2, relabelled environmental improvement). The design of Jensen's two-dimensional trade-off problem is such that maximum (attainable) profit occurs at less than maximum (attainable) market share (an argument for which reasonable empirical evidence exists). It is plain that the firm should select maximum profit over maximum market share—unless, of course, higher market share leads over time to

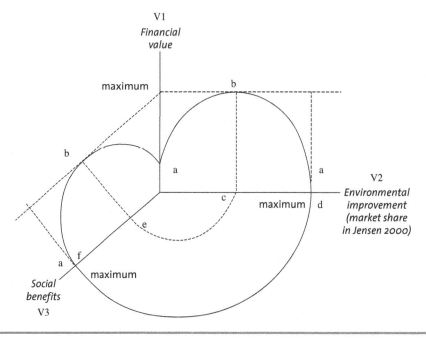

Figure 4.2 **Depiction of the triple bottom line**

higher value creation, but in such an instance market share is not a goal but purely an instrument for value creation. The selection of market share as a goal is strategically incompetent in comparison to value creation. (The transformation function or schedule, in effect, holds all other factors constant.)

Jensen's chief point is that it is not logically possible for managers to solve two conflicting goals. Maximising one dimension leads to a reduction on the other dimension. He then makes an argument as to why financial or market valuation is more important socially. There is a vital difference, however, between market share (strictly an instrument) and moral responsibility (which each individual must choose to treat as a goal or a constraint on some superior goal). Where there are multiple goals, the issue is one of prioritising among those goals. A difficulty with Jensen's approach is that the argument is instrumental: financial value creation is justified on the basis that it best achieves social welfare increases.

Jensen's depiction identifies, for simplicity of exposition, only two critical values (which he does not label): attaching labels in Figure 4.2 (indicated within inverted commas throughout the text), market value 'a' < 'b' occurs where the horizontal and third dimensions (whatever they are) are zero; market value 'b' is the maximum; and, where the horizontal and third dimensions reach a maximum, market value is again 'a'. (The recurrence of 'a' is by design yielding the simplest possible case. Where financial valuation differs from critical value 'a' here, the three-dimensional geometry becomes unnecessarily complex.) Jensen's point becomes, for purposes here, that managers cannot decide what to do between the range 'c' to 'd' (considered along the horizontal axis) with respect to market share (or environmental impact). The Jensen illustration is shown on the two-dimensional V1–V2 plane of Figure 4.2; only the labelling of the vertical and horizontal axes is changed here in preparation for a three-dimensional extension. (Otherwise the depiction is the same on this plane as Jensen's original illustration.) A three-dimensional problem, taken up below, is obviously that much more difficult for managers—illustrating Jensen's contention.

Figure 4.2 further depicts a three-dimensional trade-off reflecting the so-called triple bottom line of financial performance and reporting on social and environmental impacts (see Fombrun 1997; Elkington 1997; Bowden *et al.* 2001). Assignment of axis has no particular importance here. The vertical axis is labelled V1. (Jensen places valuation on the first or vertical dimension to indicate its priority, as that axis is conventionally the outcome dimension in economic analysis.) The second or horizontal axis, labelled V2, becomes environmental impact (in place of market share), where the firm ought to report social value creation in the form of environmental improvements (including reductions of adverse environmental impacts). The third axis, labelled V3, is social impact, where the firm ought to report social value creation in the form of community improvements (including reductions of adverse social and stakeholder impacts). While, in principle, there could be a multiple bottom line exceeding three dimensions, the depiction (and mathematics) would become difficult but conceptually unnecessary; Figure 4.2 simply aggregates all likely goals into three categories for easier representation.

To generate a physical depiction of a three-dimensional version of Jensen's trade-off problem, the reader can simply visualise the financial-value maximum rotated through an arc of 90 degrees towards the reader from the flat page. (Technically, Jensen's two-dimensional transformation curve or function is one of an infinite number of slices through a three-dimensional volume.) By construction (for simplicity of exposition), the two-dimensional transformation curve lying between the vertical (market value) and third (social benefit) axes is a mirror image of the two-dimensional transformation curve lying between the vertical and horizontal (environmental improvement) axes, because critical values 'a' < 'b' > 'a' are the same points rotated through space.[5] Allowing the financial values 'a' and 'b' to vary according to the other two dimensions simply generates a more complex surface (not needed for any expositional purpose here).

As Jensen (2000: 41) points out, the problem (so addressed) becomes one of defining trade-offs within an overall objective function definable (here adapted from Jensen) as $V = v (V1, V2, V3)$. He argues that V must be single-valued (i.e. financial performance), so that V2 and V3 are subordinated to V1, rather than being something unavoidably aggregative such as $V = V1 + V2 + V3$. But Jensen argues further that social welfare S is a function of V, such that $S = s (V)$. In effect (the present author seeks to systematise Jensen's evident views in relationship to business and society literature), Jensen's argument becomes that corporate social performance (CSP) must be a function of S and hence of V, as in $CSP = c (S) = s (V)$, such that $CSP = d(V) = c (s (V))$, absent of course externalities and monopolies. And Jensen reduces V to V1. The business and society literature (cf. Wood 1991a) proposes instead that $CSP = V1 + V2 + V3$ in some (ill-

---

5 Technically, the horizontal and third dimensions do not need to be on the same measurement scales; they differ of course from the dollar scale used for financial valuation on the vertical dimension. All that is necessary is that the relative proportions, i.e. the relationships, are the same by construction.

specified) manner. Jensen does not, strictly speaking, posit either value maximisation or a reasonably competitive market economy. Rather, he addresses managerial decision-making under uncertainty and a market game played from existing conditions. Managers need only pursue value creation, definable as moving up the transformation curve from 'a' towards 'b' (corresponding to a movement from the origin outward towards 'c' along the horizontal axis). Public policy, a political game also played from existing conditions, operates simultaneously to grapple with externalities and monopolies. A growing economy (generating higher market values for firms) in association with reductions in externalities and monopolies is (more or less) moving in the direction of greater social welfare.[6]

Jensen is entirely right to point out the resulting complexity for decision-makers (i.e. managers) inherent in multiple goals. Papandreou 1952 was an early effort at tackling the problem of multiple dimensions of V (treated, however, independently of social welfare S). The problem was addressed in somewhat different form by Brenner (1995: 80), who formulated a stakeholder value matrix allowing for variation in stakeholder values (an array V_j, such that values are defined by participants in the firm), stakeholders' weights on those values (an array W_{ij}) and the relative influence of stakeholders (an array R_i). Brenner (1995: 81) argued:

> The use of a choice process which explicitly deals with the needs of all stake-holders and which makes use of, at least, three decision criteria (economic, legal and moral) should more likely result in decisions which lead to the long term health of both the organisation and its society.

Jensen argues that a single-value function together with 'enlightened' motivation of managers and employees is superior. But, as noted earlier, moral issues cannot be equated with market share.

Jensen makes two important assertions that are highly relevant here. One assertion is that stakeholder practices amount to nothing more than what managers must do in any case for long-run strategic performance of the firm: deal with important stakeholders to their satisfaction (Jensen 2000: 42, 44, 50), as must occur in voluntary contracting (see Fig. 4.1, south-east quadrant). Another assertion, in connection with the argument concerning the logical and practical necessity of a single-valued objective function, is that a theory of the firm must address trade-offs between differing values through 'principled decision making independent of the personal preferences of managers and directors' in order to yield accountability for assets measured against 'an objective yardstick' (Jensen 2000: 51). Such 'principled decision making' presumably makes managers and directors stewards of long-term value creation. Jensen does not so much reject what would be Brenner's viewpoint in this context as argue that managers do such evaluations naturally as part of decision-making, and in effect will be thwarted by formalisation of responsibilities for any two, much less multiple, goals. Jensen's point is that managers' choices should be guided by and accountable for the long-term market value of the firm. These arguments are made (in the present author's interpretation) within state-conditions determined by public policy concerning externalities and monopolies (as addressed below).

---

6 Public policy is not here perfect. Rather, with respect to externalities and monopolies, market activities and changes in public policy are moving in parallel over time from whatever starting point historically.

4.3 Formulation of a stakeholder theory of the firm

In favour of stakeholder thinking (see Campbell 1997) is Carroll's argument that 'Stakeholder thinking is a powerful way of visualising organisations and their social responsibilities' (1995: 71). Critical of stakeholder thinking (see Argenti 1997) is Campbell and Alexander's observation that the approach does not determine any specific business strategy (1997: 3-4). The distinction between goals and constraints may prove to be a vital matter of contention. Jensen rejects multiple goals for managers, but implicitly admits other goals in the form of socially determined constraints on managerial conduct and also the views of managers and employees concerning stakeholder interests; thus, he models what becomes in effect constrained value creation as the essence of management.

Figure 4.3, still in three-dimensional form, interprets the decision-making problem in different form. The vertical axis V1 remains financial valuation. The horizontal axis V2 is relabelled as stakeholders' interests. The third axis V3 is relabelled stakeholders' power and/or public policy: this axis conveys that stakeholders may constrain the firm directly (through market action or political action) or indirectly through the present content of and changes in the content of public policy. The transformation curve retains the critical values 'a' < 'b' > 'a' as in Figure 4.2. From 'a' (at the origin) to 'b', value creation and increase in stakeholders' satisfaction work together (but, for Jensen, the latter is strictly an instrument for achieving the former). However, a conflict between firm welfare and stakeholders' interests is posited over the range beyond 'b' towards the recurrence of 'a'. Jensen admits to such conflicts (2000: 45) as the problem that managers must resolve. Where managers choose between financial valuation and stakeholders' interests, Jensen instructs them (on logical and social-welfare grounds) to select the former over the latter. (Naturally, managers' financial self-interest operates to the same effect.) Yet this trade-off does not occur independently of any other considerations.

The third dimension V3 indicates state-conditions for stakeholders' power and the content (and power) of public policy. Financial value maximisation 'b' occurs (by way of illustration) at state-condition 'Y'. (Jensen uses this kind of assumption, analogously, in making externalities and monopolies the subject of public policy.) By construction, an increase in stakeholders' power or a change in public policy adverse to the firm's welfare (i.e. a change in state-condition from 'Y' to 'Z') reduces the firm's market value (moving from 'b' down towards the recurrence of 'a'). A reduction in stakeholders' power or a change in public policy advantageous to the firm's welfare does not work analogously here. Due to the construction of the transformation curve, state-condition 'X' would also yield a reduction in market value moving from 'b' back towards 'a' on the vertical axis. By construction, then, purely to correct this defect in the physical depiction, Figure 4.3 shows an upward change in the transformation curve (shown as a dashed line) so that a new maximum market value 'g' higher than 'b' is feasible.[7] From Jensen's perspective, an increase in stakeholders' power and/or public policy restraint on managerial conduct can come only at a 'cost' to the firm's welfare measured as a decrease in financial valuation.

---

7 The effect of state-condition 'Z' could be handled in the same manner, by showing a downward change in the transformation curve. The author has here used the simplest exposition in each instance. The entire analysis is illustrative and obviously not a specific method of calculation or theorising.

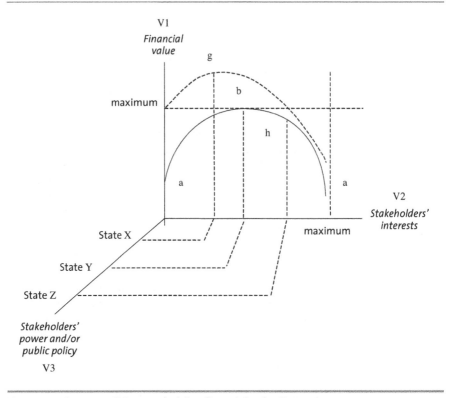

Figure 4.3 *State-conditions underlying financial valuation outcomes*

The Mitchell–Agle–Wood (1997) framework considers legitimacy, power and urgency from the perspective of managers. Jensen (2000: 38) narrows the conception of stakeholdership from that of Freeman: 'stakeholders include all individuals or groups who can substantially affect the welfare of the firm, including not only the financial claimants, but also employees, customers, communities, governmental officials, and under some interpretations the environment, terrorists, blackmailers, and thieves' (citing, at 55 n. 2, Freeman 1984: 53, on definition and inclusion of 'terrorist groups'). Since terrorism cannot be regarded as legitimate, it must be attributes of power and urgency that are at work to compel inclusion of terrorists in the list of stakeholders. What has happened in the USA since the Social Darwinism-oriented Gilded Age (between the Civil War and the Progressive Era) is that managers have come to accept, as they did not do then, the legitimacy of stakeholders other than owners. But, within that acceptance (whatever it signals being subject to interpretation), as the empirical studies of Agle *et al.* (1999) and Ogden and Watson (1999) noted earlier seem to indicate, stakeholders are regarded instrumentally rather than from within a moral frame of reference. (Smith [1776] expected rising wealth and moral education to work over time on people's natural sympathy for others.)

As Jensen is highly critical of the non-economic foundations of stakeholder thinking, the exposition of stakeholder theory here begins with a laissez-faire market economy. It is well recognised that such an economy, considered statically, does not maximise social wealth where significant unpriced externalities (particularly negative), information asymmetries and persistent monopolies are present. The conventional exposition, then, is to introduce such distortions. (For present purposes, it is simpler to ignore information issues to focus on externalities and monopolies.) Externalities are confined here, for simplicity of exposition, to negative impacts on the environment. Monopolies directly affect consumer welfare. (The term 'monopoly', as used in Jensen, is perhaps ambiguous, in that it is not strictly clear whether he means a true monopoly—such as Microsoft in practice holds over PC operating software—or more broadly some significant degree of monopoly power. The latter sense will be used here.)

The exposition involves at this point reference to Figure 4.4. The figure is simply a variation on a simple two-by-two game-theoretic matrix. The vertical stub (or axis) concerns the welfare of the firm (i.e. managers and financial claimants); the horizontal stub (or axis) concerns the welfare of the other stakeholders. There are four possible outcomes: win–win; win–lose (in favour of financial claimants); win–lose (in favour of other stakeholders); and lose–lose (prisoner's dilemma). A win–win solution, a solution without direct trade-offs, in which the three bottom lines are both additive and move together positively, would be highly desirable (if not always feasible). In Figure 4.2, there is a range in which such a solution is feasible: the range from 'a' at the vertical origin to 'b' at the maximum market value. The win–win solution is not automatically the effect of co-operation among the participants, but rather simply a set of conditions in which satisfaction of stakeholders results in value creation.

Husted (2001) and Husted and Allen (2001) have been working on integration of strategic management and social responsibility in a win–win setting; but the object is to persuade managers of possibilities rather than to restrict their conduct to particular standards. Jensen is concerned, strictly speaking, only with value creation—which can occur over the range from 'a' to 'b' (from the origin outward). The lose–lose outcome may reflect miscalculation, greed or class warfare. Jones (1995), invoking a prisoner's dilemma context, argues that trust is a desirable attribute leading on to co-operation and social welfare improvement. Olson (2000) comments, however, that prisoner's dilemma analogies have been overworked. The win–lose outcomes reflect conditions in which

Stakeholder welfare

		WIN	LOSE
Firm welfare	WIN	Mutual advantage	Producer exploitation
	LOSE	Producer stewardship	Prisoner's dilemma

Figure 4.4 **Four outcomes of interaction**

either the firm or its stakeholders gain some relative advantage. Unpriced externalities and monopolistic practices by the firm characterise producer exploitation. It is not, however, possible to characterise the opposite outcome as stakeholder exploitation of the firm. On the contrary, Smith (1776) was clear that the consumer was properly the beneficiary of the market economy and production-distribution only an instrument to consumption:

> Consumption is the sole end and purpose of all production; and the interest of the producer ought to be attended to only so far as it may be necessary for promoting that of the consumer. The maxim is so perfectly self-evident that it would be absurd to attempt to prove it. But in the mercantile system the interest of the consumer is almost constantly sacrificed to that of the producer; and it seems to consider production, and not consumption, as the ultimate end and object of all industry and commerce (Book 4 Ch. 8).

Therefore the term 'producer stewardship' (cf. Preston 1998) is invoked in Figure 4.4. The term conveys that the producer exercises stewardship with respect to stakeholder interests, such that some balancing occurs short of full producer exploitation. The co-opetition approach of Brandenburger and Nalebuff (1996) tries to combine partly competitive and partly co-operative conditions. However, Campbell and Alexander 1997, cited earlier, should be a caution that such an approach is apt to be no guide to specific choices. The approach rather identifies a state-condition that alone cannot be determinative of outcomes; strategic choice is the mediating dimension.

The long-term dynamics of a capitalist market economy are somewhat more difficult to characterise, as profit motive for entrepreneurial innovation may be the active driver of economic development (Schumpeter 1934; cf. Hirschman 1982 for a review of the issue). There is, nevertheless, in addition to the difficulties of externalities, information asymmetries and monopolies, a persistent trade-off problem:

> It is the dynamic nature of capitalism—very tough on specific individuals in the short run, highly beneficial for almost everyone in the long run. In place of the jobs lost will be new jobs from upstart companies and from large companies that are doing well (Tobias 2001: 5).

As Wilson (1989: 63) points out, capitalism is not moral but it has a morally desirable outcome: reduction of poverty for many (not creation of wealth for some) in the long run. A difficulty in this line of reasoning is defining the long run, which may be so far off as not to matter (cf. Keynes 1936).

The difficulty in capitalist development is that the dynamics can violate the win–win assumption posited in one quadrant of Figure 4.4. This violation can be camouflaged under the notion of hypothetical compensation, which amounts to a relaxation of the well-known Pareto efficiency principle. This principle states that overall welfare is increased where one party benefits and another party is not harmed: the second party can have no rational objection to the gain of the first party. The hypothetical compensation relaxation states that so long as the benefits to one party outweigh the costs to another party, such that the beneficiary could hypothetically compensate the loser (but does not actually do so), then there is an overall efficiency gain. But this efficiency gain ignores distributive effects (someone loses so that another gains) and can be morally suspect depending on the circumstances. The US Constitution (Amendment V) requires just (i.e. fair market) compensation for public taking of private property through the power of eminent domain (a clause that avoids the loser's veto inherent in the Pareto principle); the hypothetical compensation principle in effect would permit public taking of private property without compensation (as one or more states have tried to do in recent years on environmental rationales). Win–lose outcomes of this type are embedded, short-term, in capitalist development dynamics. One might assert a line of reasoning in which the social contract, agreed to by all parties, includes the possibility of such losses (just like investing in the stock market). Stakeholder theory addresses these short-term matters: stakeholdership includes those on whom losses are imposed by the gains of others.

The various stages in evolution of corporate social performance (CSP) theorising (see Wood 1991a) may be interpreted as attempting to address separation of financial valuation and social welfare. In principle, the CSP framework attempts to combine multiple dimensions: profit seeking, legal compliance, moral responsibility, stakeholder responsiveness and satisfaction, corporate philanthropy, environmental stewardship, and human rights stewardship. The key difficulty has been not so much the number of dimensions to be addressed but more whether those dimensions are constraints or goals. If they are constraints, then financial valuation is a matter of constrained maximisation (i.e. value creation). Carroll (1991) structured multiple dimensions of responsibility as a pyramid grounded in economic responsibility (i.e. profit seeking, goods and services production, employment) and moving through steps of legal responsibility and moral responsibility to discretionary philanthropy. While economic and legal responsibility are required, moral responsibility is expected and philanthropy is desired (and desirable). Jensen (2000) explicitly restricts attention to fiduciary and legal responsibility. Carroll (1995: 45) was explicit that the non-ethical dimensions of responsibility were nevertheless 'infused or embedded with ethical issues or overtones'. Wood (1991a) was explicit that individual managers must exercise any discretion morally. The posture taken by Jensen results, even if inadvertently, in elimination of moral responsibility: once managers obey the law, they are free to act and instructed only to create market value for the firm. This posture is to treat law as a set of constraints only and not as a set of principles (see Dworkin 1978). By this statement, the present author means that individuals treat the law as limits judged by some form of cost–benefit calculus concerning odds of having to face enforcement (criminal or civil) and the likely costs of such enforcement. Law as a set of principles should guide decision-making with respect to the broader intentions of the law.

4.4 Conclusion

The general approach in Jensen is to emphasise financial economics and strategic management, with problems of context (i.e. state-conditions in the sense defined here) shunted aside to public policy. The approach (although generally consistent with Preston and Post 1975) effectively side-steps business ethics (the author does not contend that such an effect was Jensen's intention). The general stance in economics has been to assume self-interested actors, but that stance does not address, however inadvertently, whether such actors are moral or amoral (cf. Carroll 1995). Self-interest can be duty-abiding and benevolent. Dodd (1932; see Weiner 1964) was critical of increasing the discretionary responsibility of managers for stakeholders' interests. If all economic actors are self-interested, managers could not be reliable stewards. Jensen affords scope for the possibility that managers and employees can themselves take stakeholder interests into account.

To this extent, at least, Jensen has a significant point concerning stakeholder reasoning: it has been directed at the psychology of managers in an effort to influence their behaviour through either or both of moral education (win–lose choices should favour the losers by voluntary self-restraint) or opportunism (there are win–win possibilities). Both Dodd and Jensen favour making managers more accountable to something external and arguably more objective. Dodd advocated increasing the legal rights of consumers and employees, in particular. Where they differ is that Jensen absorbs much of stakeholder reasoning directly into managerial choice, guided by value creation, whereas Dodd preferred something more reliable at law.

The key difficulty in strong economic cases for market action is that they tend to shunt the problems over to public policy, while leaving firms (their managers and owners) free to influence that context through the use of wealth. The approach reduces everything to markets and laws, on a tacit assumption that the combination will work well enough in the long run. The argument may turn out to be strongly valid. As Jensen rightly argues, the evidence favouring that combination is strong over the past 200 years and more since 1776. Treating nature 'as if' a stakeholder, in effect, raises vital questions about the long-run effects of the working of the combination. (The present author does not concur that nature 'is' a stakeholder.) Markets are not the same thing as the market system (Heilbroner 1953: 18). J.S. Mill demonstrated that distribution of wealth is a moral and not an economic question, the latter properly restricted to production (Heilbroner 1953: 121, 307). The vital purpose of stakeholder reasoning is to remind everyone that it is inescapable that they must address the moral issues arising in the short-term losses admittedly imposed by market dynamics; and that the purposes of wealth may be a matter of value judgements by the stakeholders. There is considerable danger that self-interested managers, imbued with the mental model that capitalism is the salvation of the world (cf. Werhane 2000), akin to an 'economic theology' (Heilbroner 1953: 314, citing J.K. Galbraith), will simply treat all stakeholders as abstractions (see Selekman 1958).

However ramshackle the present edifice of business and society studies, including stakeholder theorising (and critics have good points to make), its location is always extraordinarily valuable real estate (paraphrasing an oral statement by Professor Kenneth D. Mackenzie, at the 8th International Conference on Advances in Management, Athens, Greece, July 2001). Stakeholder management may be viewed as a constraint or as a goal. Professor Jensen takes the former approach in large measure, so that stakeholder practices are essentially instrumental (a view according with the empirical evidence about managers' conduct). The present author inclines to the view that stakeholder management should be more goal-oriented. However, it should be emphasised that Jensen permits some movement in this direction to the extent that he argues that managers and employees are concerned with the interests of other stakeholders. The managers and employees might themselves view stakeholder management as goal-oriented activity. If so, stakeholder theory aims at educating that tendency, as Adam Smith (1776) intended moral education to work.

REINTRODUCING STAKEHOLDER DYNAMICS IN STAKEHOLDER THINKING
A negotiated-order perspective

Suzanne Beaulieu
Université de Sherbrooke, Canada

Jean Pasquero
Université du Québec à Montréal, Canada

Stakeholder thinking (Näsi 1995b; Clarkson 1998) has contributed significantly to the interorganisational literature by demonstrating the importance of the environment in managing organisations. With a few exceptions, however (Vaara 1995; Pasquero 1996), it is in many ways still largely static. Combining it with other perspectives, especially actor-based perspectives, can help us understand more fully the organisational dynamics at play in the management of stakeholder relationships. Using several examples taken from a larger case study, we will illustrate how all participants in an issue (and not just managers) share responsibility in its resolution and how the interactive dynamics between participants can be viewed as the construction of a negotiated order. In the fluidity of relations between an organisation and its stakeholders, some negotiated orders break down and others emerge. We suggest that extending stakeholder theory through a perspective based on interaction, such as negotiated-order theory, allows a richer understanding of the dynamics.

This chapter is divided into four parts. In the first section, we present our conceptual framework. In the second, we introduce the context and methods of the case study on which the chapter is built. The third section develops the analysis of the case. In the fourth part, we discuss our conclusions.

5.1 Conceptual framework

The chapter focuses on how a professional corporation manages its organisational legitimacy. Our conceptual framework consists of three parts. We first discuss the related concepts of professional legitimacy and legitimation, which directed data collection throughout the case. We then present the two theories that we will use concurrently to analyse the processes at work: stakeholder theory and negotiated-order theory.

5.1.1 *Legitimacy and legitimation*

From its early institutionalist accounts, down to more power-based perspectives, organisational legitimacy has long been considered as an essential part of an organisation's continued existence (Pfeffer and Salancik 1978; Scott and Meyer 1994). Legitimacy is not an easy concept to grasp, for theoreticians as well as for managers. It is both intangible and fluid. Definitions abound. In his landmark paper on the subject, Suchman (1995: 574) proposed the following definition: 'Legitimacy is a generalised perception or assumption that the actions of an entity are desirable, proper, or appropriate within some socially constructed system of norms, values, beliefs and definitions.' Despite their differences, most authors agree that legitimacy is an essential resource to organisations, and that as such it needs to be managed. The critical point is to note that, to an organisation, legitimacy is not given, it is a resource conferred by its stakeholders.

For the purpose of our study, we have defined professional legitimacy as follows:

> Professional legitimacy is a multidimensional construct whose existence is linked to a profession's socio-economic relevance. Relevance is related to the expectations regarding the corpus of knowledge required of members, individual competencies, and market and social considerations. Six dimensions were identified as constituents of the concept of legitimacy: legal, identity, moral, technical, institutional and perceptual (Beaulieu 2001: 470).

Legitimacy, however, is not a static resource. It is the outcome of a construction process, which we call the legitimation process. Since the environment of a professional organisation is constantly changing, the management of its legitimacy requires continual attention. 'The legitimation process involves both the shaping of behaviour according to beliefs about what is proper and the moulding of knowledge according to prevailing beliefs about what constitutes social reality' (Hybels 1995: 243).

For the present study, five legitimation modes were used to describe how the organisation managed its legitimacy over time: initial construction, preservation, reinforcement, restoration and renewal (Beaulieu 2001: 471). These modes constitute a portfolio from which the organisation can choose the most appropriate.

5.1.2 *Stakeholder theory*

Stakeholder theory is particularly helpful when addressing the ongoing quest for legitimacy. In fact, legitimacy cannot be managed without identifying the relevant stakeholders since it depends greatly on their perceptions. 'Legitimacy is conferred upon or attributed to the organisation by its constituents—like beauty it resides in the eye of the beholder' (Ashforth and Gibbs 1990: 177, citing Perrow 1970).

The literature diverges on the definition of stakeholders, and it is not the aim of this chapter to clarify this issue (Donaldson and Preston 1995; Harrison and Freeman 1999). Consequently, like many authors before us, we have adopted Freeman's (1984) instrumental definition: 'any group or individual who can affect or is affected by the achievement of the organisation's objectives'.

What is more important in our view is that mainstream stakeholder theory suffers three limitations. One is its static character. A few authors have insisted on the importance of considering the multilateral construction of the relationships between the organisation and its stakeholders (Pasquero 1996; Berman *et al.* 1999; Frooman 1999). Stakeholder theory, however, is still not well equipped to account for the dynamics of multi-stakeholder interaction. A dynamic vision of how interactions emerge, how they evolve, and how issues are framed in the process is therefore needed.

The second weakness concerns the role assigned to stakeholders in the theory. Mainstream theory, especially in its instrumental versions, generally suggests that, to achieve success, an organisation must identify, classify and rank its stakeholders by priority, so that their demands can be fulfilled (Mitchell *et al.* 1997). In our view, this prescription is still anchored in the old pressure–response reactive paradigm, wherein the organisation is dominated by the elements of its environment. We believe it can be misleading, since to us 'stakeholder management'[1] is a process of mutual contribution rather than one of unilateral accommodation. We hold that the aim of an organisation is not only to 'manage' the relationships with its stakeholders; it is also, and maybe foremost, to reach specific goals, taking into consideration their presence and the influence they can exert on the decision-making process. We therefore argue that the theory should not focus exclusively on managers. Stakeholders must be reintroduced at the core of the theory.

The third limitation regards the bias of stakeholder theory towards the implicit assumption that stakeholders constitute homogeneous groups. In contrast, we hold that stakeholder heterogeneity is a more realistic assumption than homogeneity for both theory and practice. The theory does suggest that we can identify many different stakeholder groupings around the same organisation. We agree with this premise but we believe it must be developed further, taking into consideration the heterogeneity within stakeholder groups.

5.1.3 Negotiated-order theory

Negotiated-order theory was developed by Anselm Strauss and his colleagues in the context of small-group collaboration (Strauss 1978; Gray 1989; Maines 1991). It adds the process dimension that is missing in much stakeholder thinking. Namely, it rejects the perspective of organisations as rigid, static systems largely constrained by regulations, structures and hierarchical chains of command. Rather, negotiated-order theory emphasises the fluid characteristics of the organisation and the changing configuration of interactions woven between actors. Organisations are social constructions: fragile constructs subject to temporal and contextual events. Negotiated order exists when involved stakeholders share a common definition of a problem or situation, and recognise that common perceptions and interests link them together. 'A negotiated order exists when organisations have jointly determined the terms of their future interactions with one

---

1   In this chapter, 'stakeholder management' is used for convenience as a short cut for 'the management of the relationships between the organisation and its stakeholders'. Strictly speaking, the organisation does not 'control' or 'manage' its stakeholders. Rather, it negotiates with them to develop a common view of their respective duties, responsibilities and needs.

another' (Nathan and Mitroff 1991: 164). Negotiated order supposes a continuous renewal. In their synthesis paper, for example, Day and Day (1977: 129) emphasise this point (citing Strauss *et al.* 1963): 'The basis of concerted action (social order) must be reconstituted continually.'

Negotiated-order theory does not specifically discuss legitimacy. However, we hold here that at any given time a profession's legitimacy is the product of a negotiated order implying several stakeholders.

To conclude, we argue that stakeholder theory and negotiated-order theory complement each other and together offer a more dynamic and realistic vision of the interplay between parties both inside and outside the organisation. To manage legitimacy implies a constant effort at nourishing favourable perceptions from a wide variety of stakeholders. This requires negotiating consensual agreements in which each party will stay in the negotiated order because it has something to gain from it.

5.2 The case study: context and method

The empirical data used in this chapter is drawn from a larger case study carried out on a professional corporation (Beaulieu 2001). We first present the site of the study and then highlight two of its specificities. We conclude with an overview of the methodology.

5.2.1 *The 'CA Corporation'*

The corporation studied is the Chartered Accountants' Corporation of Québec (*Ordre des comptables agréés du Québec*, henceforth designated as 'the CA Corporation'). This corporation benefits from a 'reserved title' (no non-member can use the title of chartered accountant) and an 'exclusive field of practice' (that is, a monopoly) in auditing public corporations and some non-profits. Professions in the province of Québec (Canada) are controlled by a provincial government body (*Office des professions du Québec*, henceforth designated as 'the Board of Professions') which is responsible for supervision, regulation and granting of privileges. At the time of the study, out of 44 professions only 24 benefited from a reserved title and an exclusive field of practice, while the others benefited solely from a reserved title (which means that their fields of practice could be entered by non-members). Professional status brings with it obligations and duties (Dubar and Tripier 1998), whose extension depends on the vantage points of the stakeholders involved. For the regulatory body, the recognition and existence of a profession serves one single purpose: the protection of the public. From the CA Corporation's point of view, however, while the protection of public interest is obviously central, it does not exclude protecting members' interests. This duality of function often results in contradictions and conflicts.

The CA Corporation represents one of the most influential professions in Québec. Like many organisations in this era of change, it is facing new and difficult challenges. These include: growing competition within and outside the profession (in the fields of practice outside its monopoly), proliferation of specialised services, emergence of new territories of expertise, recruitment difficulties, challenges to the monopoly status, changing markets and new client expectations. These factors also affect the structure and character-istics of the membership of the Corporation itself (i.e. individual chartered accountants), which follow the evolution of the market.

Our case study therefore offers a particularly rich field to analyse the dynamics of stakeholder management, and to explore the joint responsibility of all the parties involved in furthering their interests.

5.2.2 *Two specificities*

The accounting field is marked by two specificities. One is the prominence of intangi-bles. Professionals sell competences and trust. In their vocabulary, they use terms such as 'reputation', 'identity', 'performance', 'ethics', 'morality' and 'credibility'. To this list we can add 'legitimacy', recognising, however, that this is a term that they will not nor-mally use. For an organisation such as the CA Corporation, stakeholder management, and therefore the management of its legitimacy, is not only important, it is crucial.

The second specificity is related to the major component of the structure of a professional organisation: its membership. The members of a professional corporation are not its employees. They are independent from the corporation; they pay an annual membership fee and earn their own living. The Corporation is run by a few permanent employees, whose job is to attend to the profession's objectives. The CA Corporation membership in Québec is now at 16,300, while permanent employees amount to around 60 people.

One original trait of a profession such as the chartered accountants is that its mem-bers are simultaneously internal and external stakeholders. As external stakeholders, they support their Corporation, at times criticise its stands, and eventually adopt the positions it takes. As internal stakeholders, they must comply with the rules defined by the Corporation itself; they also act as 'representatives' of their profession with outside entities, either as auditors, consultants, teachers or employees, or as guests to sit on tech-nical committees. Members are therefore important players in sustaining the legitimacy of the Corporation.

5.2.3 *Method*

Studies of organisational legitimacy are scarce in the literature. The case study on which this chapter rests was conducted over two years. It was inductive and exploratory. A his-torical study permitted an understanding of how the Corporation constructed its legitimacy over time. A current-events study helped to corroborate the historically derived findings. This dual approach provided a comprehensive outlook on the Corporation's legitimation process and how this process was incorporated into strategic management. Open interviews and secondary source data were used for the collection of data. Interviews were carried out in two sequences: the first round served to understand the finality of the organisation, and the actors' perceptions of their circumstances. In the second round, the main objective was to deepen the understanding of specific issues. Secondary source documents were used to select pertinent issues, to document these and to reinforce and triangulate evidence collected in interviews. Data analysis was carried out with the aid of a computer program, and in conformity with the constant comparison method. Studying legitimation was accomplished through an analysis of stakeholder strategies and actions across various issues.

5.3 Empirical evidence

We now proceed to apply our conceptual framework to our case study. We will analyse four issues faced over time by the CA Corporation and its stakeholders. They will allow us to demonstrate the interplay between the various actors involved as well as the richness gained in integrating the two streams of organisational theory discussed above. Three of these issues are historical and the last one is contemporary. For each issue, we use the same analytical framework. We first provide a short historical account. We then elaborate on the challenges at stake. We follow with a discussion of the main stakeholders involved. We finally analyse how the relevant negotiated orders were constructed as the Corporation and its stakeholders tried to meet the challenges they were facing. In each instance, the analysis emphasises the relationships between the parties involved.

5.3.1 Issue 1: (1946)
A new law reinforces the position of the CA Corporation

5.3.1.1 A brief historical account

During the 1940s, after several decades of existence, the CA profession was facing a vast array of new challenges. The government considered the profession too 'closed' and unrepresentative of Québec society of the time, in particular not including enough French-speaking members (the demographic majority in the province). Its political contacts were scant. Competition in the accounting field was increasingly severe, with many new professional associations being formed. Six accounting associations shared the market, with varying standards of quality and no government control. For chartered accountants, who wished to differentiate themselves and protect their territory, the solution was not to 'open' but to 'close' (restrict access to) the profession even further.

5.3.1.2 What were the main challenges facing the CA Corporation?

- To distinguish itself as a profession (to become a recognised profession on the same level as that of lawyers or physicians)

- To protect its territory and privileges (preserving public confidence, enhancing its growing prestige)

5.3.1.3 Who was involved and what were their respective stakes? (see Table 5.1)

The Corporation recognised that its influence with government was insufficient. It was facing competing organisations that wished to obtain the same legal protection as it

Stakeholders	Stakes
The CA Corporation	Too little political power
	Too few francophone members
	Too many competitors (risk of lessening the title's prestige, division of territory . . .)
Universities	Wish to increase their clientele
	Wish to obtain recognition of new programmes (allows widening of their market)
Competing associations	Wish to obtain recognition from the state equivalent to the CA Corporation
Government	Wants to promote social order, equity and protection of the public

Table 5.1 *Who was involved and what were their respective stakes? (Issue 1)*

already had. It realised that, alone, it would not make progress in obtaining the recognition it sought.

5.3.1.4 How were negotiated orders constructed?

In this example, we can identify three types of negotiated order with as many stakeholders.

- **With competing associations.** In the early 1940s the six accounting associations that existed in Québec were creating a complex and disconcerting situation for the profession. The chartered accountants had until then always refused to associate with other groups, judging their status 'inferior'. After a realistic evaluation of the situation, however, the CA Corporation came to the conclusion that collective action was the only feasible solution. In a dramatic policy reversal, it decided to form alliances with two competing associations. The price to pay was to open up: that is, to compromise on its closed-shop policy and accept members from these groups. Six years of laborious negotiations ensued, and in 1945 a joint proposal was submitted to the government, which accepted it. The sacrifice had paid off: the CA profession was now duly confirmed as the dominant profession in accounting.

- **With the universities.** Aspiring chartered accountants had to pass a qualifying exam. Universities wanted to keep their right to present candidates and assume a major role in this examination process, while CAs held out for their right to control the examination and accreditation processes throughout. This point brought on years of debate regarding who was responsible for the training of accountants. Universities, however, enjoyed growing clout at the time. They had close links with government, and university training was increasingly becoming the norm for accountants in the province. The Corporation eventually recognised the value of a partnership with the universities. It had to compromise again. By associating itself with the two main universities established at the time, the Corporation was then able to reach its dual goal: first, to have accounting recognised as a distinct scientific discipline; and, second, to be recognised as a true profession. As for the two universities, they gained the authorisation to award bachelor degrees in accounting.

▪ **With the government.** As seen above, by opting for an alliance with two competing associations, the CA profession was eventually able to convince the government to grant it the protection it had been seeking for so long. In 1946 a law was adopted, giving birth to the new organisation of the CA Corporation. Above all, the law recognised that expertise in accounting held a professional status equivalent to that of law or medicine. This law has been governing the practice of public accounting ever since.

In the previous case, the triggering threat arose from outside the organisation: a massive growth in competition that jeopardised the future and the status of the Corporation. The Corporation had to act. To realise its goals, it had to make compromises (notably in access to the profession), it had to prepare a policy statement in order to convince the government of its case, and finally it had to find a solution with the universities in the area of training. It was through these negotiations that a common ground was eventually found. Obviously, to succeed, the Corporation had had to take into account the respective interests of its various stakeholders. It did not do so, however, by simply yielding to these interests. Rather, it asserted a new position through a lengthy process of negotiation with a number of equally strong stakeholders. A negotiated order takes form when common goals can be recognised by various parties. In 1946, a new and lasting negotiated order was born in the accounting profession in Québec.

5.3.2 Issue 2: (1973)
A new governing structure upsets the established order

5.3.2.1 A brief historical account

In 1973 the Québec government saw two reasons to put some order into the world of professions in the province. One concerned the protection of the public. If some professions were known to fulfil their public duties well (especially the responsibilities concerning ethics and discipline), others had been found negligent in these matters. The second reason was the proliferation of demands for professional status in the province. An increasing number of associations demanded recognition from the state, while areas of expertise remained poorly defined. The debate, which had taken shape around the health system and its professions, had spread to other professions. The government chose to establish a new regulatory board, which we call here the Québec Board of Professions (*Office des professions du Québec*). It also promulgated a professional code and a specific act for each recognised profession, including of course a chartered accountants act. At the time, three accounting corporations were legally recognised and were in competition with each other. The never-ending debate over the fusion of the professional accounting corporations resurfaced. Once again, the CA Corporation stood in strong opposition to this option. In arguing that its standards were superior to those of its two competitors, it was successful in blocking it.

5.3.2.2 What were the challenges faced by the Corporation?

Until then, the CA Corporation had enjoyed complete autonomy. The new law changed this situation. It imposed on all professional corporations the same rigid structure, regardless of their field of activity. For the Corporation, this was a major point of contention. It tried to secure an exemption. Despite numerous solicitations to government bodies, it was not successful. It eventually had to yield to the government's requirements, accept losing part of its autonomy, make the necessary adjustments to its governing structure and modify some of its procedures to conform to the new order. All was not lost, however, since with the new law the CA Corporation emerged as the only one of the three accounting corporations to obtain an exclusive field of practice.

5.3.2.3 Who was involved and what were their respective stakes? (see Table 5.2)

Stakeholders	Stakes
The CA Corporation	Preservation of privileges (prestige, authority in the accounting field, autonomy)
The provincial government (Québec)	Finding a new structure of governance for all professions, after having experienced difficulties with the medical sector
	More control over the professions (a question of public interest)
Other accounting corporations	Maintaining a professional status and associated privileges
	Obtaining same recognition as the CA Corporation

Table 5.2 **Who was involved and what were their respective stakes? (Issue 2)**

5.3.2.4 How were negotiated orders constructed?

Two situations emerged in this case. One did not end on a negotiated order: that of merging all the accounting corporations into a single body. The other situation did come to a negotiated order, albeit a somewhat imposed one: the establishment of a new government regulatory body. It illustrates how one of the stakeholders (in this case, government) was able to exercise its power to eventually gain acceptance for its policy. The latter was indeed the central issue of the time for the Corporation.

What we observe in this case is a situation in which the powers of negotiation were sharply unequal, with government on one side and the Corporation on the other. This explains why the Corporation did not oppose the new structure for long. It quickly understood that, to demonstrate its goodwill, it needed to protect its reserved title and other advantages laboriously gained over time. Indeed, it emerged as the only one of the three accounting professions to be granted an exclusive field of practice. In the final analysis, while the Corporation had lost ground with respect to its autonomy, it had successfully manoeuvred to preserve a considerable advantage.

5.3.3 Issue 3: (1989) A major crisis shakes the CA Corporation

5.3.3.1 A brief historical account

Each year across Canada, a highly competitive national exam is held for all accounting students desiring to qualify for the title of chartered accountant. It is conducted by the Canadian Institute of Chartered Accountants (CICA), in collaboration with the provincial (state) bodies. The 1989 sitting opened an unprecedented crisis for the Québec Corporation. Inexplicably, the results for students from Québec were disastrous, especially those of students from French-speaking universities. Totally puzzled, the Corporation tried to gain time, and announced its desire to review the correction process thoroughly to ensure that students from French universities were not disadvantaged (training requirements may vary across universities). To pre-empt the impending uproar, it awkwardly decided not to publish the results on the announced date. This preventative move only prompted protests from students, universities and the other provincial corporations. The media picked up on the story and a climate of crisis quickly evolved. Emergency teams were assembled and a myriad of studies carried out. Among much controversy, the exam results were finally publicly released without change in February 1990. This move did not put the situation to rest.

With the support of their universities, discontented students resolved to bring proceedings against the Corporation in the spring of 1990. The universities also claimed that the Corporation had abdicated its right to inspect the exam. Simultaneously, the Corporation had to defend itself, demonstrate the rigour of its exam procedure and its training requirements, and publicly justify its role in this whole situation. This came as a hard blow for the organisation, since the universities had long been its partners in training. The judge eventually ruled in its favour. The Corporation then set out to renew contact with the universities in a hostile, tense atmosphere. It proposed to find a mutually satisfactory solution, but much friction remained between the parties. Subsequent student recruitment also suffered from the crisis, which had weakened the prestige and attractiveness of the profession. The CA Corporation was going through some of its more sombre days. Most parties had lost something in this unprecedented crisis.

Following months of analysis and numerous discussions between members of the Corporation, the universities and the CA exam authorities, a solution finally emerged: a fourth year of student training seemed desirable. In the Québec educational system, however, the first university degree is earned in three years. Graduate studies start on the fourth year. The universities were ready to consider the proposal only if this fourth year took place at the graduate level. The regulatory Board of Professions, whose authorisation was needed, objected and sharply rejected this proposal. The Corporation then decided to bypass it and apply to a higher authority. The overseeing minister eventually agreed to support the proposal, and the Corporation devised a pilot project, which in turn had to gain the students' approval. Support from the employers agreeing to train accounting students was also necessary. After three years the trial was deemed conclusive and a fourth year of studies became compulsory. Once again, the Corporation had come out a successful player. The crisis had put its credibility at risk, but its efforts had finally paid off. With the solution of a 'fourth year', it had simultaneously restored and strengthened its legitimacy.

5.3.3.2 What were the principal challenges faced by the Corporation?

- Restore the Corporation's credibility (the perceived legitimacy was strongly shaken)

- Review the exam correction process and verify whether it was fair for all

- Rebuild its partnership with the universities

- Rebuild the attractiveness of the profession

- Improve training (since competence was at the core of the profession's identity)

5.3.3.3 Who was involved and what were their respective stakes?

This issue went through three phases. The first two were crisis situations. The last one was a positive phase of legitimacy reconstruction.

Phase 1: the crisis erupts (see Table 5.3)
In this first phase of crisis, the organisation was not seeking a negotiated order; rather, it was merely defending its legitimacy.

Stakeholders	*Stakes*
The CA Corporation	Defends its credibility
Students	Defend their interests
Professors	Defend their credibility
Media	Alert the public
The public	Questions the CA profession's credibility

Table 5.3 **Who was involved and what were their respective stakes? (Issue 3): the crisis erupts**

Phase 2: students bring charges against the Corporation (see Table 5.4)
Again, in this second phase of crisis, the Corporation did not seek to reach a negotiated order; it was once more defending its legitimacy. In the face of daunting opposition, it simply wanted to demonstrate that the legal proceedings brought against it were not credible.

Stakeholders	Stakes
The CA Corporation	Wants to defend its credibility
Students	Want the exam to be recognised as void
Professors	Want to avoid blame
Judicial system	Has to clarify the situation (with authority and fairness)

Table 5.4 **Who was involved and what were their respective stakes? (Issue 3): students bring charges against the corporation**

Phase 3: the Corporation proposes a fourth year of study (see Table 5.5)

Stakeholders	Stakes
The CA Corporation	Has to rebuild confidence between all parties and find a solution to avoid a similar situation in the future
Students	Will be attracted to the profession if they have a better chance of succeeding
Board of Professions	Involved in changes in education; the law could not easily be changed
Ministry of Education	Involved in education; decision power
CA members and CA firms	Involved in this proposal in two ways: want their candidates to be successful and must consider a shortage of trainees because of changes in the educational system

Table 5.5 **Who was involved and what were their respective stakes? (Issue 3): the corporation proposes a fourth year of study**

5.3.3.4 How were negotiated orders constructed?

This last phase is fertile for examining how the CA Corporation jointly constructed new negotiated orders with its stakeholders.

- **With the universities**. A new negotiated order had to be established between the Corporation and the universities. First, the relationship between the two parties had to be rebuilt, since it had been completely destroyed in the first two phases. The Corporation took the initiative. In autumn 1990, it re-established contact with the universities, hoping to convince them of the necessity of formulating a new method for training students. Discussions were tense initially, but eventually normality was restored and the two resumed working together. The Corporation defended its interests and the universities theirs (it is noteworthy that the universities showed unusual solidarity among themselves during this process). The Corporation, however, proved intransigent in the need for change. It had too much to lose in abdicating. Gradually a common vision emerged, and all stakeholders agreed on a proposal to be defended before the Board of Professions and the Ministry of Education.

- **With the Board of Professions**. The Board of Professions refused to consider the proposal of a fourth year of study. Saddled with the responsibility to supervise 44 very different professional corporations, it did not want to create a precedent by granting an ad hoc exemption to the provincial university curriculum just for one of them. Training requirements and equivalences for professional membership are traditionally the object of sharp negotiations with each corporation, and one can understand why the board was unwilling to upset this equilibrium. The CA Corporation, for its part, had a crisis to resolve and would not give in, to the point of infuriating the regulators on which it depended.

- **With the Ministry of Education**. Strong from the backing of universities, the Corporation presented its proposal directly to the Ministry of Education, going above the normal authority of regulators of the Board of Professions. The Ministry accepted a pilot project to be carried out over three years. This decision definitively settled the issue. The Corporation used provisions in the Chartered Accountants Act, which gave it the necessary latitude to impose the new training programme. After nearly a decade of political manoeuvring, the programme finally became compulsory in 1998.

This issue demonstrates well how stakeholder thinking and negotiated-order theory complement each other. Interactions between stakeholders and an organisation take place around a stake. Each party has its interests to defend. The universities gained a new graduate programme, which required much effort to set up, but which also brought in new revenue and added credibility. The Corporation confirmed its authority in training and demonstrated its determination to see candidates succeed without sacrificing quality, so invaluable for the profession.

5.3.4 Issue 4: (1999) A new project for the future: the CA specialist

5.3.4.1 A brief historical account

In the early 1990s the Canadian CA authorities carried out a broad study on the accounting profession, market trends, and services the profession could provide. A report was presented in 1996. It revealed the challenges the profession was facing at the turn of the 20th century. The study confirmed that sweeping changes must be implemented if the CA profession was to preserve its privileges and prominence.

The report has since been instrumental in shaping the future of the profession. Among other findings, the main conclusion was that specialisation seemed inevitable. New knowledge was necessary to ensure the services of the future. In addition, the boundaries defining professional expertise were becoming inextricable. For example, chartered accountants (CAs) and certified management accountants (CMAs) were now directly entering management services. At the same time, new professional associations (for example, financial planners or information systems specialists) were competing with accountants in a host of services. These encroachments created confusion among the public, as it was becoming increasingly difficult to determine who was a specialist in a particular domain and who was not. Confronted with these chaotic trends, the CA Corporation clearly had to act. One upshot is that it is currently examining ways to establish an accreditation process for its members to develop specialities in addition to their CA title.

5.3.4.2 What were the principal challenges?

- Redefine the CA identity
- Redefine the CA's mission
- Review training thoroughly
- Establish specialisation criteria conforming to the CA philosophy
- Convince the parties involved of the proposal's validity

5.3.4.3 Who were the stakeholders and what were their respective stakes? (see Table 5.6)

Stakeholders	Stakes
The CA Corporation	Seeks to protect its territory and predominance
	Wants to loosen regulations that impede the profession from responding to changing markets
	Informs and convinces members of the proposal's relevance. Part of the Québec Corporation's and its Canadian counterpart (CICA)'s mandate is to protect and promote the profession and to provide opportunities for members, even if gains are not immediate.
Other professions and associations	All seek to widen their territory. New domains open up to many organisations.
Board of Professions	Must supervise the performance of professions. A project such as specialisation is encumbering. The regulatory structure is complex, and delays long. This project is currently before the Board of Professions.
Members	Some believe this will lead to divisions within the profession; others do not see the need for further specialised titles because other professions can grant specialisation within their original professional title.

Table 5.6 *Who was involved and what were their respective stakes? (Issue 4)*

5.3.4.4 How were negotiated orders being built?

The proposal to create specialties within the CA profession is a long-term project, still under development. It must gather the support of a host of stakeholders. With each of them, the Québec CA Corporation entertains specific strategies.

- **With the CICA and its provincial counterparts across Canada.** Significant regional differences exist across Canada, including differing provincial regulations and methods of professional practice. A minimum of nationwide co-ordination is therefore necessary. The CA Corporation of Québec must thus come to an agreement with CICA (Canadian Institute of Chartered Accountants) and its national counterparts on what the specialisations will be in Québec, and on issues such as their characteristics, training requirements, the accreditation process and how to grant specialisation titles.

- **With the Québec Board of Professions.** The Board must be convinced of the proposal's validity and change regulations to permit the recognition of specialities.

- **With CA members and CA firms.** The Corporation must provide them with ample information, obtain their input and, of course, their commitment to the proposal. The members are, in effect, critical representatives of the profession in the field. No general support for the report can be garnered if they are not first and foremost convinced of its value.

- **With universities.** Obviously, specialisation will also involve the universities. One year off schedule, a pilot project has recently been launched at a major business school in Montréal in investigative and forensic accounting.

Four main stakeholders, each important in its respective role, are involved in this proposal. Since the project has national ramifications, the major stakeholders are the other provincial CA organisations of Canada, and the nationwide CICA, which is responsible for directing the proposal. Much discussion is therefore necessary before a consensus is reached across the land, and the Québec CA Corporation is part of the process.

Another important stakeholder, at least for the CA Corporation of Québec, is the provincial regulatory Board of Professions, whose final approval is always necessary. The Board, however, is regarded by the Corporation as an inflexible and slow-moving body, whose regulations constitute a hindrance to its development. For example, as it has not yet been able to obtain the necessary legal and regulatory changes from the Board, the Corporation has had to find alternative paths to go ahead with its specialisation dossier. The unusual solution has been to use the federal Trademarks Law to protect its new specialisation titles, a situation unheard of in the rest of the country.

This case concerning the introduction of new accounting specialities is different from the three other issues we have examined in that it needed first to be resolved at an internal level, inside the profession, and then across the country. It exemplifies the evolution of a complex project that is still under way. Building from so many perspectives, a common vision has had to be developed, not only in methodology but also in working definitions, pace of implementation and accreditation requirements. For the project to go ahead, multilateral consensus has had to be established, involving numerous meetings and discussions among the participants. Interactions among stakeholders were a determining factor for the project to take shape. In this case, surprisingly, none of the stakeholders has tried to impose its views on the others and a common vision has gradually emerged through years of collaboration.

Once again, we can observe the development of several negotiated orders simultaneously between the organisation and its expanding list of stakeholders, each time through specific, issue-driven strategies.

5.4 Conclusions

The purpose of this chapter has been to study the dynamic relationships between an organisation and its stakeholders in a real-world context. The case demonstrates the volatility of stakeholder management. Relationships often shift when a new issue is put on the agenda of an organisation. The outcome is not easy to foresee because of the indeterminacy of the interplay between the participants, which is driven by the idiosyncrasies of the stakeholders involved, by the criticality of the issues at play and by circumstantial events. Overall, we draw four main conclusions from this study.

First, the case analysis confirms that, for a better comprehension of the real life of stakeholder management, stakeholders must be placed at the heart of the management process and not be considered as static players or as interfering external claims makers. They are an integral part of the management process. Strategic management implies stakeholder management. Stakeholder management is not limited simply to classifying stakeholders by priority, neither is it to answer their demands blindly; rather, it concerns how an organisation should act to attain its goals, what specific issues it must resolve for its own sake, and with whom the management game is to be played.

Second, issues must be understood in the context of stakeholder interactions, and not as given entities with independent properties of their own. The outcome of any issue is influenced by the interrelations between the organisation of interest and the stakeholders with whom it must enter into contact around this particular issue. Consequently, both the managers and the stakeholders involved share responsibility for the development and outcome of this issue. Each issue is different. Each issue involves a specific set of stakeholders. Each issue is related to a new challenge and so to different strategies and actions. Thus, to each issue will correspond a new negotiated order that emerges from these interactions. Issues are not, therefore, packages of claims thrown onto the organisation. They are co-constructed by the organisation and its stakeholders.

Third, the case shows that recognising the heterogeneity of stakeholders is of critical importance to the management process. Different groups come into salience, depending on the context. As the context shifts, so do the relevant stakeholders. We can identify three types of heterogeneity: synchronic, diachronic and spatial. Synchronic heterogeneity expresses the variability among the stakeholders making up the stakeholder set that the organisation has to face simultaneously at any given time. This set is made not only of several classes of stakeholders separated by conflicting interests but also within each class of stakeholders with very varied sets of interests, motivations or understandings. Diachronic heterogeneity reflects that the composition of the stakeholder set to be attended changes over time. As it moves from one issue to the next, the organisation may find itself in contact with new stakeholders; at the same time, former stakeholders whose interests have shifted may switch sides from previous issues, while other former stakeholders will stay clear of the new issue. Finally, spatial heterogeneity refers to the density of the stakeholder set under consideration; rarely are all stakeholders involved in any single issue—usually only a few stakeholders, and sometimes only one sub-group or even a lone individual, are involved. Therefore, focusing on a single stakeholder set made of the same stakeholder groupings over time would be misleading for the corporation, as it would miss the dynamics of stakeholder relationships.

For example, the case illustrates how different the stakeholders that constitute the CA membership group can be. It also shows that many stakeholders from the same generic group may not have the same understanding of the issues, to a point where their own organisation must at times help them define what their true interests are, as we saw in the case of specialisation, and even take unsolicited measures to protect their long-term interests. It is important that theory consider these various forms of stakeholder heterogeneity because they can have a major impact on the outcome of an issue and on the strategies to be adopted. In some sense, 'stakeholder management' is akin to governmental policy-making and implementation, in that rallying convictions around a new initiative is a major component of the activity. This description is a far cry from the conventional textbook, somewhat botanical, presentation of classifying and attending statically defined stakeholder claims.

Fourth, the case reveals two decisive factors that need further study in the analysis of stakeholder relationships. The first factor is issue criticality. The case shows it has a direct impact on the way negotiations evolve. Obviously, the more critical an issue is for a particular group, the more this group will invest resources to defend its interests. In so doing, however, it raises the interest of other parties for this same issue, which generates various levels of criticality feeding off each other. For any given group, the criticality of an issue is often not readily apparent. It is constructed through the confrontation with other stakeholders, and is therefore evolutive. Usually, it is revealed as the issue is played out among the stakeholders affected. As we have seen, no one can control an issue in its entirety and no one can predict the final outcome. Only an action-based perspective, such as negotiated-order theory, permits a clear understanding of the importance of this factor.

The second factor concerns the substantial impact an initiator can have on the evolution of an issue. Understanding the initiator's motivations, resources, capabilities and constraints allows a sharper grasp of the interactions among participants. As we have observed in at least two instances, this does not mean that the initiator always comes out the winner. It does mean, however, that initiators play a leading role, and that their motivations and the potential resources they may invest to preserve their interests can significantly influence both the issue and the circumstances of the other participants. Knowing this, participants can at any time change their strategies to be able to counteract. Through a retrospective analysis of these actions, interactions and retroactions, the underlying dynamics become clearer. Here again the two perspectives of stakeholder theory and negotiated-order theory reveal their complementarity and usefulness.

In 1946, for example, the CA Corporation was the initiator. To gain sufficient political power it decided to forge an alliance with other associations and came out a leader. In 1973 the state, perhaps the ultimate powerful stakeholder, was the initiator. The CA Corporation tried its best to stand up to it but eventually had to yield. In 1989, the initiator was again the Corporation. With a crisis demanding immediate action, it decided to forge ahead even though it could not calculate where its actions would lead. The risks were immense and the Corporation lost control of the issue several times. However, the motivations were strong, and its administrators persisted until the crisis was satisfactorily resolved.

Stakeholder thinking, when associated with a perspective such as negotiated-order theory, becomes in our view much more powerful, for together they can bring managerial dynamics to light. There is no such divide as the organisation on one side and its stakeholders on the other, especially when some stakeholders are both internal and external to the organisation; rather, there are issues that arise in the common part of the environment they have to deal with. To some extent, issues pick their stakeholders as much as the other way round. To understand their interplay, to see clearly that both the organisation and its various stakeholders are co-constructors of their reality and that they share responsibility in shaping this reality, combining the two perspectives used in this chapter is not superfluous. It permits us to reintroduce stakeholder dynamics at the core of stakeholder thinking, and therefore to escape some of the more restrictive limitations of stakeholder theory.

Part 2
STAKEHOLDER RESPONSIBILITY AND ENGAGEMENT

TOWARDS A MANAGERIAL PRACTICE OF STAKEHOLDER ENGAGEMENT
Developing multi-stakeholder learning dialogues

Stephen L. Payne
Georgia College and State University, USA

Jerry M. Calton
University of Hawaii–Hilo, USA

Stakeholder theory development by academicians has been a more-or-less genteel struggle to influence the sense-making perspectives and actions of business managers. Many social scientists in the field of business and society have aspired to measure the instrumental benefits to the corporation of good stakeholder relations (Waddock and Graves 1997a; Berman *et al.* 1999). Their intent has been to convince managers that the 'facts' will prove that they can 'do good' for society while also 'doing well' by the firm's shareholders. Those with a traditional philosophical turn of mind have tried to define the 'normative core' of stakeholder theory in terms of foundational or universal ethical duties that managers owe to the firm's other stakeholders (Goodpaster 1991; Evan and Freeman 1993). Both of the above approaches are limited by a shared assumption that managers need to control stakeholder relationships in a manner calculated to assure positive social, as well as financial, performance by the firm.

Recent trends in theory and practice appear to reflect a significant shift in assumptions concerning manager–stakeholder relations. This shift has been from the need for unilateral managerial cognition and control to a perceived need by some for reciprocal engagement and new dialogic forms of collective cognition or 'learning together' (Isaacs 1999) to achieve 'relational responsibility' (McNamee and Gergen 1999). This reorientation explains the growing interest in corporate 'citizenship' practice (e.g. Waddock 2002). Stakeholder engagement requires the extension of citizenship rights and responsibilities to a more inclusive set of stakeholders. One of the most important rights of political citizenship in a democratic society is the right to exercise one's voice in the shaping of public policy. An intriguing, and as yet unanswered, question is the extent to which the metaphor of citizenship can or should be applied to the corporate realm (Wood and Logsdon forthcoming). A related question is the extent to which stakeholders should have a voice in the shaping of corporate policy.

The historical record does not provide much confidence that stakeholder voices have been raised often, or to much effect, within the corporate governance process. However, an emerging conception of organisational relationships as an unfolding network of conversations lends a new urgency to the empowering of stakeholder voices. Ford (1999: 5) argues that 'we can define the state of an organisation at any point by its network of conversations and the actions, behaviours, and practices associated with those . . . conversations'. Recent reports of 'multi-stakeholder dialogues' suggest a potential model for stakeholder engagement to improve corporate governance. These multi-stakeholder dialogues (MSDs) have emerged within the domain of 'messy' problems that have not been amenable to unilateral attempts at managerial 'solutions'. Ackoff (1999: 13) defines messes as 'complex systems of strongly interacting problems'. These messes extend beyond the boundaries of the firm and create conditions necessary for the formation of stakeholder networks. We define this network as an interactive field of organisational discourse occupied by all stakeholders who share a complex, interdependent, ongoing problem domain and who want/need to talk about it. Within this domain, the corporation is not so much a system within itself as a participant in a larger system that includes other stakeholder citizens.

Stakeholder perceptions of excessive corporate influence and impact on their shared domain have led in some cases to calls for improved corporate citizenship practice. Efforts to grapple collectively with a shared mess require an expansion of sense-making capabilities. Among these capabilities is engaging dialogic learning from multiple stakeholders. Complex, interdependent problem domains are often framed by stakeholders from their initial interests and assumptions as a set of simplistic 'either–or' dichotomies. A paradox according to Lewis (2000) is a cognitive construct that juxtaposes apparent opposites while suggesting that contrasting notions such as 'self' and 'other' are somehow related in meaningful ways. The paradox of interdependent relations is inherent in stakeholder theory and practice (Aram 1989). MSDs may be a step towards improved collective learning by uncovering shared meanings and relational responsibilities (McNamee and Gergen 1999) beyond paradox.

MSDs are already occurring in two important problem domains. The first and more frequently reported domain involves global concerns about how economic development can be reconciled with environmental or system sustainability. Another domain concerns how scientific and technological advances can be assimilated within the imperative of human and social wellbeing. The potential for stakeholder engagement and improved corporate citizenship practice, though, is by no means limited to these particular messes.

Our chapter reviews some early examples of multi-stakeholder dialogues and the criticisms that have been raised concerning these processes. We believe such interactions must be further explored and developed to realise a corporate citizenship practice based on reciprocal engagement between managers and stakeholders. We particularly introduce a form of MSD called a multi-stakeholder learning dialogue (MSLD) that could contribute to the emergence of corporate citizenship practice and improved corporate governance.

6.1 Multi-stakeholder dialogues

A wide variety of stakeholder communication processes exist to fulfil many different purposes. Some of these purposes are more narrow, focused or instrumental in nature, while others are much more encompassing and directed towards relationship exploration, maintenance or improvement. Yosie and Herbst (1998) summarise stakeholder processes ranging from those in which stakeholders participate directly in making and implementing organisational decisions to those stakeholder processes merely intended for managers to obtain their perspectives or attitudes on selected topics. One type of stakeholder process that is generating increasing interest and actual applications has been called a multi-stakeholder dialogue (MSD). The following examples illustrate the diversity of groups and organisations involved in forms of MSDs.

6.1.1 *Consulting assistance and training*

William Isaacs and his associates have recently been using forms of multi-stakeholder dialogue, based on assumptions from Argyris, Bohm and others, for consulting assignments and training/development sessions. One continuing multi-stakeholder dialogue facilitated by Isaacs and his consulting firm 'DIA-logos' addressed stakeholder disputes for a local healthcare system in Grand Junction, Colorado. The system was threatened by competitive suspicions, declining resources, over-dependence on expensive medical technologies, growing public health needs, and by the potential takeover of a local hospital by an outside, expansion-minded managed care company. The dialogue facilitated by Isaacs and his associates involved multiple stakeholders, including an elected government official. From this dialogue participants came to realise that survival required a collective strategy.

> With DIA-logos' consulting and dialogue intervention work, the group was able to launch a new initiative that blended the strengths of the providers as allies, enhancing efficiency and staving off entrance of national providers. As a result of the success of this project, Dialogue has been introduced into medical school curricula in Colorado.[1]

The DIA-logos website describes multi-stakeholder dialogues initiated by DIA-logos to meet the needs of corporations such as ARMCO (GS Technologies). The firm also offers basic and advanced training programmes for individuals interested in studying dialogic practices, action learning and professional development.

Other consulting firms are also offering services to help companies establish and conduct multi-stakeholder dialogues. The four partners in New Context Consulting[2] seek to bring people together to deepen understanding about important and sometimes emotional issues through its multi-stakeholder dialogues and community-building activities. AIDEnvironment, a Dutch independent research and management consultancy on natural resource issues, advertises its considerable global 'experience with the management of complex multiple stakeholder dialogues involving many experts with different intellectual backgrounds' (AIDEnvironment 2001). They feature an interactive, online,

---

1   www.thinkingtogether.com
2   www.newcontextconsulting.com/service_text_1tier.htm

multiple-stakeholder dialogue for strategic environmental analysis using 50 participants located in 20 different countries. In this area of environmental concerns, RAND Environment (Environmental Science and Policy Center) 'conducts multi-stakeholder dialogue projects to enhance consensus building, win–win decision making, public understanding, and planning policy-relevant research' (RAND Environment 2001). RAND Environment designs and conducts stakeholder dialogues that are tailored for each client and work to bring stakeholders who 'have much to gain from interaction but do not historically communicate'.

The Centre for Innovation in Management[3] within Simon Fraser University's Faculty of Business is an example of a university-based programme created to foster stakeholder responsiveness and responsible engagement. It seeks world leadership in stakeholder identification, engagement and measurement, from both a research and an applied perspective. The Centre focuses on the enhancement of stakeholder relationships. Among its services, the Centre facilitates collaborative learning and organises and hosts multi-stakeholder dialogues.

6.1.2 Business coalitions applying stakeholder dialogues

The World Business Council for Sustainable Development (WBCSD 2001) was formed in January 1995 through a merger between the Business Council for Sustainable Development (BCSD) in Geneva and the World Industry Council for the Environment (WICE), an International Chamber of Commerce (ICC) initiative, in Paris. Those two parent bodies had been spearheading business's response to the challenges arising from the Earth Summit in Rio de Janeiro in 1992. The WBCSD, as a coalition of some 150 international companies from 30 countries and more than 20 major industrial sectors, has become a leading business voice on sustainable development.

Björn Stigson (2000), President of the WBCSD, claims that corporate social responsibility has become an institutionalised element in the debate about what civil society expects from business. He goes on to suggest that business, government and civil society must engage in partnerships to find solutions together with other stakeholders. As part of these efforts, the WBCSD has multi-stakeholder dialogues to try to develop and agree on new solutions to issues of sustainable development. An important aspect of the WBCSD's work and ongoing learning was refined through dialogues with stakeholders such as shareholders, employees, investors, government development organisations, labour unions, human rights groups, religious groups and education and aid foundations. An initial stakeholder dialogue was held in September 1998. Several stakeholder dialogues with various interested parties in Africa, Asia and Latin America throughout 1999 gained greater input from non-OECD countries. The appropriate dialogic process was considered very important. Study within a working group helped to determine what specific topics were to be addressed, who the stakeholders were, and what was thought realistically achievable. A report, *Corporate Social Responsibility: Making Good Business Sense*, was published in January 2000, based on the findings of the stakeholder dialogues held in developing countries (WBCSD 2001).

---

3   www.cim.sfu.ca/workshop/page5.html

6.1.3 NGOs and interest group involvement

Other environmental and sustainability coalitions are organising membership networks and helping members develop skills to engage in MSDs. European Partners for the Environment (EPE 2001), based in Brussels, advises organisations that they should initiate multi-stakeholder dialogues to 'test ideas that will form the basis of your organisation's long-term strategy. Practising the dialogue will prepare you in the event of a pressured event, where the dialogue skills will come in handy.' EPE suggests to those organisations already engaging in stakeholder dialogues and/or belonging to the WBCSD that 'EPE involves the greatest breadth of stakeholders under one umbrella. You can reach all of them in one go through EPE . . . You have a wider group giving input, with whom to test ideas.' EPE welcomes NGOs, trade unions, institutes, academic organisations, networks, global and local companies, and public authorities to discover truly sustainable solutions including economic competitiveness, environmental excellence, equity and multi-stakeholder co-operation.

Other organisations such as the State of the World Forum (2001) are trying to 'establish a more compassionate, just, non-violent, and ecologically sustainable world order', by conducting multi-stakeholder dialogues. They have reportedly been 'including new, more diverse voices in dialogues on globalisation, extending the breadth and depth of the inquiry process'. The International Forum on Capacity Building (IFCB) is encouraging and trying to conduct multi-stakeholder dialogues at the national, regional and global levels. The IFCB website[4] reports that such dialogues are happening at the national level in many countries, but these dialogues are not working as expected at the regional level and only to a minimal degree at the global level. Plans for the next global conference include extracting lessons from earlier MSDs on capacity-building and examining different dialogic models as well as designing the global conference itself as a multi-stakeholder process. Identifying the critical mechanisms in an enabling environment that allows multi-stakeholder processes to work is another IFCB concern. From the MSDs conducted at national levels, the IFCB is studying issues such as:

- How preparation helped to ensure the involvement of different stakeholders

- The sociopolitical and regulatory context in which these dialogues took place

- Interpersonal relationships among different stakeholders

- How different perspectives of different stakeholders were accommodated

- How differential power relationships among different stakeholder groups could be minimised

According to McLaughlin and Davidson (1994),

> Multi-stakeholder dialogues, which involve all parties in a collaborative dialogue, are proving to be the most effective way to develop viable policies and reduce conflict on divisive issues such as race, abortion, and the environment. For example, The Institute for Multi-Track Diplomacy in Washington, DC, helps resolve ethnic conflicts worldwide through involving all stakeholders in dialogues—government, business and non-profit groups—and listening deeply to all perspectives.

4 www.alop.or.cr/ifcb/ifcb4sc.htm

6.1.4 Government and UN sponsorship

Government-related applications of MSDs are also being reported. Richardson (1999) describes the US Patent and Trademark Office (PTO)'s first-ever dialogue on outcome performance goals and indicators with major customers and stakeholders in October 1998 and January 1999. Together with information collected from another project, the National Academy of Public Administration used this stakeholder dialogue to formulate a report for PTO use in continuing its efforts to develop outcome-oriented performance goals and measures. Salomon *et al.* (1994) explore technology assessment through MSDs involving suppliers, donors and users of technology, including multinational companies, as well as many different groups potentially affected by possible unforeseen side-effects of technology policies. They review debates about the extent and form of public participation in decisions about technology development, deployment and regulation. The most participative approaches found include MSDs as well as open judicial hearings or public referendums that are occasionally encountered in countries such as Austria, Denmark, Italy, Norway and Switzerland. Based on their analysis of US experiences with successful stakeholder dialogues, the authors make a number of recommendations for government-sponsored stakeholder dialogues for technology assessment.

Within the United Nations and its many constituent groups, MSDs have become common. For example, the UN Centre for Science and Technology for Development (CSTD) worked to define and act on the concept of endogenous capacity. It came to the resolution in 1986

> that endogenous capacity is the capacity to make decisions on science and technology for development, which are sensible and well informed and taken at the level of the society, engaging all relevant stakeholders. A basic tenet in this resolution was the paraphrase that 'science and technology for development are too important to be left to scientists and technologists alone'. The whole of society must participate in decision making and implementation (Climate Friendly Technology 2001).

This served to promote stakeholder dialogues concerning the relationship of science and technology to mainstream practice in developmental forums on a national and global level.

The powerful Organisation for Economic Co-operation and Development (OECD) and its Development Assistance Committee picked up this theme in a meeting in May 1990. It published a booklet proposing a new paradigm for development assistance, based on technology missions resulting from MSDs at the national level. Pilot stakeholder dialogue projects in Cape Verde, the Daqing region of China, Jamaica, Jordan, Nepal, Pakistan, Tanzania, Thailand, Togo, Uganda and Vietnam have been held. By 1991 the concept of participatory decision-making based on stakeholder dialogues had taken root in development discourses as well as in practical actions (Climate Friendly Technology 2001). Other UN and international agencies have also applied MSDs. One example is the World Bank's engagement in recent years of stakeholders to participate in issues related to resource development and dam construction (Yosie and Herbst 1998).

6.2 Criticisms and concerns for multi-stakeholder dialogues

Despite the increasingly widespread use of multi-stakeholder dialogues, there have been criticisms of these processes. Yosie and Herbst (1998) describe strengths, limitations and challenges of these dialogues for considering environmental and developmental issues. Their analysis of research and participant experiences in these stakeholder processes led them to conclude that these processes are frequently not well managed due to the lack of experience and knowledge of effective dialogic practices among many convenors, facilitators and participants. Without such experience and knowledge, 'unrealistic expectations' about the potential outcomes of MSD processes can occur as well as ineffective use of resources, including stakeholders' time. Concerns raised by these researchers include:

- Difficulties encountered by the scientific community in participating more effectively so as to better communicate and inform in stakeholder deliberations, resulting in insufficient knowledge and insight from scientists and less scientifically rigorous risk-based decisions

- Potential for abuses by those facilitating or controlling stakeholder processes who are directed by their clients to engage in unethical practices, such as unrepresentative selection of stakeholders, exclusions of some questions or issues from dialogues, and bias in report writing that favours clients

- Use of techniques that work in developed nations, but do not build on traditional community and cultural assets such as community organisations and women's groups

- Stakeholder burn-out and possible backlash from their continuous involvement in specific stakeholder dialogues that may not meet their lofty expectations or not result in practical results

- The need for better matches between the choice of a particular form of stakeholder process and the problem it is attempting to solve

These and other potential concerns for the application of MSDs certainly exist, though they have been relatively under-emphasised alongside enthusiastic reports on the potentials of these processes. In policy and decision-making applications of MSDs, procedural and distributive injustice may be perceived by some stakeholders. Inappropriate or questionable choices by facilitators can lead to undesired outcomes for some stakeholders, particularly for those who do not have the power or voice to clearly articulate their positions. Despite opportunities for creativity in generating alternatives, unfair resource trade-offs are possible even within well-facilitated stakeholder processes. For such stakeholder processes involving and invoking relationship responsibilities, significant levels of trust and risk-taking must be present. Confidence in such dialogues is vulnerable to abuses or perceived threats. Lack of faith in the fairness of processes within MSDs can be observed in certain cases. One example comes from reports by a group called the Low-Level Radiation Coalition (LLRC) in its participation in a multi-stakeholder dialogue.

The web page for LLRC (2001) describes its experiences with a stakeholder dialogue sponsored by CIRIA (the Construction Industry Research and Information Association).

CIRIA is a UK-based, independent research association committed to improved performance for those involved in construction with concerns about environmental issues. CIRIA oversaw an MSD to develop guidelines for managing land contaminated with radioactivity and chemicals. It sought to obtain consensus on how such land sites should be handled in terms of de-licensing and/or other actions. It sponsored dialogues among present licensees, government agencies with environmental responsibilities, potential contractors, and community interests such as county councils, NGOs, environmentalists and other stakeholders. LLRC reported that about 60 people attended a CIRIA forum in June 2000. Of those attending, only two representatives were from NGOs, two were from local authorities and one was from the Nuclear Free Local Authorities. Most attendees were from the industry and from regulatory agencies. Although CIRIA claimed the forum was a great success, LLRC questioned the absence of NGOs such as Greenpeace and site-specific interest groups. LLRC's major concern was that it was denied access to post some written material on the topic under discussion to the website that CIRIA organisers had arranged to facilitate information-sharing among stakeholders. LLRC concluded that problems with such MSDs commissioned by the government and run by groups such as CIRIA were:

- Domination of the process by industry and other groups with lesser environmental commitment

- Exclusion from steering committee membership of stakeholders with alternative views

- Inadequate human and financial resources to enable environmental stakeholders to participate fully

Perhaps the most significant concern in the foregoing descriptions of recent MSDs is the nature of the dialogic process by which stakeholders interact. Some of these and other so-called MSDs may hardly be dialogues at all, according to definitions of dialogue found in communication and other disciplinary literatures. Within the field of management and the social sciences, renewed interest in collective or organisational learning through dialogue is often connected to the work of Peter Senge (1990). He makes a distinction between forms of discourse and describes the special properties and limitations of dialogue in contrast to 'discussion'.

> In a discussion, decisions are made. In a dialogue, complex issues are explored. When a team must reach agreement and decisions must be taken, some discussion is needed . . . When they are productive, discussions converge on a conclusion or course of action. On the other hand, dialogues are diverging; they do not seek agreement, but a richer grasp of complex issues . . . The ground rules are different. The goals are different. Failing to distinguish them, teams usually have neither dialogue nor productive discussions. A unique relationship develops among team members who enter dialogue regularly. They develop a deep trust that cannot help but carry over to discussions (Senge 1990: 247).

An assessment of MSDs in their early stages of use seems complicated by a frequent lack of information concerning their particular assumptions, goals and processes. Do these stakeholder communication processes foster higher-order learning and enhanced relationship-building, or are these MSDs actually forms of communication or discourse that Senge would refer to as discussion among stakeholders rather than dialogue?

6.3 Multi-stakeholder learning dialogues and other stakeholder processes

There are many dialogic traditions and concepts of dialogue as a process of learning, beyond more commonly recognised Socratic roots. Some theorists, such as Bohm (1996), view forms of dialogue as raising and changing the tacit infrastructure of thought enabling potential forms of learning. Anderson *et al.* (1994) examine many distinct, if not unrelated, dialogic traditions. Among these are Bakhtin's (1981) view of dialogue as a cultural form of human knowing, as well as Buber's (1970) regard for dialogue as being essential to the formation of human relationships by engendering in the self an appreciation of other. McNamee and Gergen (1999), building on some philosophical contributions of Levinas (1989), focus on ethical obligations and responsibilities as being co-constructed through dialogue. They explore relational responsibilities that are awakened through the process of more genuine and participative forms of dialogue.

Although the notion of individual duties and responsibilities is well established in American social and work life, processes for building a shared sense of relational responsibilities are under-developed. In the absence of compelling national crises, such as that triggered by the terrorist attack on the World Trade Center in New York City, many Americans may experience a vague sense of complacency or guilt when confronted by 'messy' interdependent problems, such as environmental degradation or a crisis in public education. A positive duty of care and a broader and deeper sense of moral agency among stakeholders might be enhanced through certain forms of MSD (Calton 1997). The creation of multi-stakeholder learning dialogues (MSLDs) might facilitate increased exploration and recognition of relational responsibilities. This interactive learning process could bring into play a broader appreciation of ways in which pluralist social values and norms found in the diverse social roles assumed by various stakeholders can contribute to a shared appreciation and understanding of the interdependent dimensions of messy problems. Such role examination or play through stakeholder dialogue should stimulate the stronger emergence of moral values, moral imagination (Werhane 1999) and moral learning needed to mobilise relational responsibilities in addressing shared messes.

6.3.1 Strategic management and organisational development

Relevant to any discussion of the theory of stakeholder engagement is the study of processes through which stakeholders actually, and conceivably might, interact. In what organisational and business contexts do stakeholders actually interact? Obviously much of this occurs in bilateral or dyadic stakeholder exchanges, such as between customers and organisational marketing/sales representatives, employees and organisational managers. Such exchanges usually occur as company managers or employees interact, in their established roles or functions, with individual stakeholders or a group of stake-holders with similar interests. Even top managers who interact with diverse sets of stakeholders usually meet at one time and place with specific subsets of stakeholders. Multi-stakeholder interactions or dialogues are much less common. These are often more complicated and intimidating experiences for organisational managers. Common tendencies for self-presentation and impression management are more difficult for managers to apply and control. Stating particular managerial positions can lead to 'whipsaw' effects, by which what is intended to satisfy or meet the demands of one set of stakeholders can have contrasting implications for other stakeholders who are present. Seldom do most managers have an opportunity to learn from open dialogues at which very diverse groups of stakeholders are present and capable of responding. Often busi-ness executives have sought buffers from stakeholder 'intrusions', time for 'considered' responses, and guidance from public relations or public affairs staff.

Two common and important processes within public- and private-sector organisations are strategic management (planning, implementation and control) and organisational development/change. How might such common forms of managerial interaction and involvement with stakeholders be related to the potential for the creation of MSLDs? Increasingly, managers are being urged to seek broader stakeholder inputs for strategy formulation and control. More active stakeholder involvement or participation in both social performance planning and social auditing has long been advocated to guard against managerial myopia and 'groupthink' (Robin and Reidenbach 1988). The dialogic processes and shared learning outcomes from MSLDs could certainly inform aspects of the strategic management process, particularly issues management and stakeholder analysis, used in many companies (Swanson 1999).

Another organisational process that has a history of theory and practice for organisa-tional management is organisational development/change (OD/C). Even undergraduate college students with a business major often have basic courses and textbook coverage in both strategic management and OD/C. The roots of OD/C go back at least to the National Training Lab in the 1940s and theorists such as Kurt Lewin. Many OD/C approaches involve the participation of multiple stakeholders in communication processes designed to diagnose potential challenges/problems for the organisation and to suggest change initiatives. Forms of multi-stakeholder learning dialogues would seem to enhance learning potential for certain OD/C methods.

The 1980s and '90s saw OD/C move beyond its traditional focus on small-group change, and techniques such as sensitivity training and survey feedback, towards exploration of a number of methods for managing 'whole-systems' change involving large, diverse groups of stakeholders who are actually present and interacting. As a sub-field within OD/C, the study of large-group interaction methods (LGIMs) has generated a recent literature of its own. Bryson and Anderson (2000) as well as Manning and Binzagr (1996) offer reviews of many major LGIMs and describe both overall LGIM assumptions and characteristics of individual LGIM methods.

6.3.2 Large-group interaction assumptions and methods

Among the common values and assumptions underlying LGIMs, according to Manning and Binzagr (1996), are:

- A 'whole-systems' orientation

- Creation of dialogue among all organisational stakeholders

- Focus on the processes/procedures of organising rather than on the reified organisation

- Perception of a collective organisational reality as the organisation that becomes created

- Capacity of individuals within organisations to self-organise and redefine their reality

- A set of universal values that are inherently 'good', shared by humanity, and ultimately influence voluntary collective action

Other common elements of LGIMs that Bryson and Anderson (2000) add are:

- Single applications of a particular method usually last from a few hours to three days and can involve a series of workshops or conferences over time.

- The need in almost all cases for a skilled individual or team facilitating the workshops

- Extensive planning as well as 'buy-in' from key decision-makers and opinion leaders

- An external 'process-design' consultant to sketch overall process design on which participants can build detail and meaning

- Considerable logistics (invitations, food, equipment, etc.) to support the method

- Potential for follow-up efforts to implement decisions or make action plans developed by participants

Bryson and Anderson (2000) claim that LGIMs are empowering and provide a kind of 'technology of democratisation' with pragmatic philosophical roots from theorists and activists working both in the streams of community and in organisational development. They add that most LGIMs were developed by practitioners who were less concerned with articulating or clarifying the theory supporting their methods than with addressing pragmatically the problem at hand. For such reasons, certain LGIMs seem to work in particular circumstances and do not work in others, but it is far from clear why this is so. Their particular advantage, as change methods, is fostering broader participation by key stakeholders in dealing with important issues. The increasing application of these methods has almost everything to do with the intense challenge, sense of involvement, spirit of fun and vivid memories experienced by participants (Bryson and Anderson 2000). Holman and Devane (1999) expect that, due to their success and popularity, LGIMs will become much more common and a standard practice in the public and non-profit sectors.

Although there are common assumptions underlying LGIMs, there are differences in these techniques. Some of the more apparent differences, according to Manning and Binzagr (1996), relate to: (1) their focus on enactment versus adaptation; (2) broad and actual involvement versus limited stakeholder participation and merely psychological representation for others; and (3) very structured interventions versus more open, self-designed methods. LGIMs are a developing phenomenon and 'hybrid' combinations of existing methods or new ones emerging can certainly be expected. Among more common LGIMs are Real-Time Strategic Change, Search Conferences with Participative Design, Future Searches, Strategic Options Development and Analysis, Strategic Choice, Technology of Participation, Open-Space Technology, Simu-real, Fast-Cycle Full Participation and the Conference Model. These methods are summarised and extensive citations for these techniques are provided in Bryson and Anderson 2000 and Manning and Binzagr 1996. Certain LGIMs, and particularly Real-Time Strategic Change, Strategic Options Development and Analysis and Strategic Choice, offer a whole-systems and broader stakeholder perspective for aspects of strategic management. Such methods tend to be fairly structured as strategic processes. Fast-Cycle Full Participation and the Conference Model approaches concentrate more on issues of organisation and work design. Search Conferences and Future Searches tend to engage stakeholders on a particular issue for which they try to plan and respond. Of these LGIMs, the least structured and most flexible is Open-Space Technology.

Recent applications of LGIMs seem to be change initiatives stressing improved stakeholder learning and relationship-building practices. The multi-stakeholder dialogues (MSDs) discussed above, as well as new initiatives, might gain greater change and learning potentials by incorporating processes being explored in certain LGIMs. Open-Space Technology seems a particularly appealing LGIM for generating alternative stakeholder assumptions concerning knowledge construction and for involving those who are less powerful, previously silent and more marginalised.

6.3.3 Open-space approaches

Rouda (1995) summarises basic characteristics associated with open-space approaches developed by Harrison Owen. These approaches try to enhance learning, networking and community-building through open dialogue and an 'idea marketplace'. Reeler (2001) states that the essence of open space and its lessons for other participative processes include the following:

> All stakeholders must be invited, but none must be forced to attend. The more the agendas are designed by participants, the more participation is likely to ensue. Expert inputs must be very carefully and clearly separated from participative processes . . . Expert input can be a resource to participative processes but should not serve to define them. Both a flexible structure and a complimentary [sic] culture of participation must be created in the process through the physical design (e.g. seating in circles, use of chaotic association around walls, etc.) and through participative principles based on personal choice, free association . . . and personal responsibility for both process and product.

Manning and Binzagr (1996) stress that stakeholders 'come to these interventions because they choose to and they advocate their ideas in a manner that all participants can hear openly, develop advocacy and support, and exert influence on the whole system'. Of all LGIMs, it has the fewest restrictions on who or how many participants attend and how they interact. Harrison Owen has summarised this method as: 'whoever comes', 'whatever happens', 'whenever it starts' and 'when it is over it's over' (Rouda 1995).

Bryson and Anderson (2000) suggest that the unstructured nature of the method can place greater burden and stress on participants for creating agendas and self-organising. The approach requires a facilitator who 'holds the space' so that participants can do their work. Facilitator interventions are minimal, potential for tapping stakeholder energy/creativity may be greater, and logistical demands are lower than with other LGIMs. They warn, however, that the less-structured process can occasionally be very frustrating to participants and may increase the chances of failure. Although there are published, reasonably well-documented descriptions of the method in practice (Owen 1991, 1997a, 1997b) and many enthusiastic accounts of its success (Owen 2001), Bryson and Anderson (2000) admit that a strong theoretical base from which open-space approaches derive is not well articulated. Their further concerns for this method include:

- Not necessarily involving content experts when they might be needed

- The quality of the 'quiet' facilitation required 'to hold the space'

- The expense of participant time required

They conclude that the method is probably best for generating ideas and not necessarily taking action on the ideas so generated.

6.4 MSLD as a stakeholder communication process

The emergence of MSDs, and increasing participation in such dialogues by diverse organisations and groups, may be a case of practice leading the development of significant theory about this phenomenon. The more appropriate forms of MSD for particular conditions and challenges confronting stakeholders remain in some question. One suggested form for MSDs is the multi-stakeholder learning dialogue (MSLD). The clear focus of the MSLD is improved stakeholder learning opportunities through dialogic processes that explore and move beyond initial stakeholder assumptions about facts and values surrounding 'messy' problems. MSLDs can be particularly helpful in coping with a variety of pluralist paradoxes, such as those of learning and belonging, as identified by Lewis (2000: 766, 769). In effect, stakeholders learn from each other the different ways that a shared messy problem can be defined. In the struggle to gain a cognitive grip on the mess, preconceived relationships between self and others change as new learning occurs.

MSLDs are hardly suggested as a panacea for all organisations and groups confronting any complex or divisive set of issues. Depending on factors such as the life-cycle of a particular issue facing a set of stakeholders and the characteristics of these specific stakeholders, other stakeholder processes might be considered. For example, Lampe (2001), drawing on feminist ethical theory, suggests mediation as an appropriate process for resolving certain stakeholder disputes. Yet mediation as an alternative for stakeholder interaction on messy problems may be unable to overcome entrenched and adversarial mind-sets/positions. Mediation by outside parties may still poorly connect stakeholders to 'the identities, emotions, needs and perceptions of particular individuals' (Wicks *et al.* 1994: 481). It may neglect the voices of certain marginalised stakeholders. It may be largely reactive, leading to emphasis on outcomes at the expense of concerns for relationship-building and learning from the other. Related managerial cognition and language, such as stakeholder negotiation and bargaining, can also focus our attention on outcomes (even win–win ones) and put the 'cart before the horse' of relationship-building and learning. According to McCoy (1992: 22), negotiation may lead to gaming attitudes and approaches that inhibit collaborative and accommodative impulses of stakeholders.

One impetus for considering mediation as well as a MSLD is the perceived need to circumvent power gridlocks and the attending 'win–lose' tactics of powerful stakeholders. However, MSLDs focus more on extended learning opportunities by exploring potentials for reframing and reformulating stakeholder issues, problems and questions. Another element that might jump-start the consideration of a MSLD is the presence of leadership and/or organisational cultures among stakeholders having values and underlying assumptions encouraging openness and relationship-building. Under these circumstances, MSLD could generate the reciprocal trust needed to build a sense of relational responsibility.

Still, there remains a paradoxical tension between MSLDs and traditional corporate processes such as strategic management and organisational development/change. MSLDs could inform and transform, rather than merely be co-opted by or inserted into existing organisational cultures and practices. For MSLDs to fulfil a more emancipative and empowering notion of 'strategic control' over the deficiencies and excesses of organisational politics, such as Quinn seems to suggest (1996: 390), these dialogues might be both separated and connected to existing practices. Strategic management processes might surely be informed by MSLDs and assisted by their relationship-building and learning capabilities. However, the often strongly instrumental or rationalistic nature of strategic management can tend to subvert the time and relationship demands as well as the somewhat contrasting knowledge construction characteristics of MSLDs. Stakeholder networks might engage in forms of MSLDs and open-space interaction methods without an emphasis on one particular focal organisation for development and change.

MSLDs offer several advantages for improving stakeholder processes and dialogue. These perspectives and approaches:

- Extend the scope of existing stakeholder theory/practice to suggest dialogic processes to more fully legitimate, surface and integrate the assumptions and claims of actual organisational stakeholders

- Are influenced by social science learning assumptions/methods, such as action research, participative action research, action science, action learning and collaborative enquiry, which seek to more closely integrate continuing enquiry and activities taken as a result of enquiry

- Expand typically more micro-level theory development to macro-level organisational and inter-organisational contexts through the involvement of relevant stakeholder networks implicated in particular problems/issues

- Offer potential means for engaging existing OD/C approaches towards large-scale or whole-systems change

- Allow opportunities for diverse forms of cognitive, aesthetic and affective learning to suit the learning styles and expressive needs of participating stakeholders

- Enhance discovery and creativity through provision for generative metaphors, narratives and diverse forms of cognitive construction (from traditional to radical notions of knowledge creation)

Such advantages associated with MSLDs seem to justify the investment of time and resources to develop a communicative interface for stakeholder networks to grapple with complex or messy issues.

MSDs will evolve through a trial-and-error process of pragmatic experimentation (Wicks and Freeman 1998) and assessment by participating stakeholders. Such an evolution, however, might benefit from experimentation with forms of MSLD that emphasise long-term relationship enhancement and extended enquiry and learning processes that are both separated from and connected to existing organisational processes. Large-group interaction methods, such as open-space methods, along with action research and action science perspectives, appear to offer guidelines for those considering or initiating multi-stakeholder learning dialogues.

STAKEHOLDER RESPONSIBILITIES
Lessons for managers

Duane Windsor
Rice University, USA

Much of business ethics boils down to exhortation concerning proper managerial conduct, in various circumstances, or defences of managerial practices generally based on the economic development benefits of markets (see Wilson 1989). Thinking about ethics from a manager's perspective is perhaps more difficult. The essential task is learning to reason morally about varying circumstances concerning duties, rights, consequences and virtues. This volume addresses a perceived, or proposed, imbalance in the prevailing conceptualisation of business responsibilities. The idea is to establish the responsibilities of stakeholders other than managers and owners, including duties to the firm. There is substantial merit in the proposed thesis. Constructs such as corporate social responsibility, corporate social responsiveness, corporate social performance and global corporate citizenship all emphasise—as they were intended to do—the duties of and constraints on the motives (or goals) and conduct (or actions) of firms: i.e. the managers and owners of joint-stock public corporations or privately held companies.[1] In an effort

1 There is a vital distinction between managers and owners. Owners are, conceptually at least, the organising element of the firm: it cannot come into existence absent owners' action. At law (not necessarily morally), owners are jointly the residual claimants on the firm's assets. In a privately held firm, ownership is concentrated; in a public corporation, ownership is more diffuse. In the latter, directors (typically holding shares) are elected as stockholders' representatives for 'management' of the firm; they in turn hire managers. (In German practice, a supervisory board representing more than one constituency selects a management board.) One or more top executives (typically holding shares) commonly are inside directors. (Other managers may or may not hold shares.) Management (whether board, management committee or chief executive officer) has effective control of operations until dismissed. The board's roles are appointment and dismissal of executives, audit and evaluation of conduct and performance, policy and compensation; the board is typically advisory with respect to strategy. A long-standing dispute concerns whether managers are fiduciary agents of the owners (i.e. representatives) or stewards for the long-term viability of the firm (i.e. trustees). In the US, the wider spread of corporate ownership arguably makes the classic distinctions among types of stakeholder (e.g. customer, employee, owner) hazier.

to rebalance conceptualisation of responsibilities, this volume considers the duties of and constraints on the motives and conduct of stakeholders (other than managers and owners, themselves stakeholders) defined in relationship to both the focal firm and other stakeholders of that firm. Stakeholders also have a collective impact on nature, and either collectively or in national groups joint responsibility for one or more commonwealths.

For managers, that other stakeholders should have some duties—towards the firm, in particular—should presumably be a pleasant relief from widespread assault, on various grounds, by business critics and calls for greater corporate responsibilities and global citizenship activities. This author suggests, however, that there are some key lessons for managers in the proposed reconsideration of stakeholders' responsibilities. Responsibilities towards the firm will require that managers first conduct themselves morally, and existing notions of corporate responsibility and citizenship do not necessarily obtain that pattern of conduct. Other stakeholder responsibilities often involve moral and citizenship duties requiring collective action, such that managers will often need to lead the way—as in child labour and environmental protection issues.

The stakeholder role cannot be readily separated from general considerations of moral reflection and citizenship. A difficulty is that the stakeholder role must be considered by case and circumstance. While responsibilities towards other stakeholders are arguably stronger than responsibilities to the firm (such that managers must demonstrate by moral conduct worthiness to be the object of such responsibilities by others), those responsibilities, while interdependent, often do not occur at first hand but rather often through a chain of distant repercussions. It is therefore an additional step, conceptually and practically, to add accountability for specific outcomes beyond simple notions of motivations and actions.[2] The distinctions among motives, actions and outcomes form the essential thread around which Wood (1991a, 1991c) reformulated the corporate social performance perspective. The simplest approach, which is taken here, is to posit and hold constant the duties of and constraints on managers and owners in order to study those of the other stakeholders of a focal firm. The theme of the special issue is, in effect, that stakeholder interdependence, i.e. a web of positive and negative impacts (or *consequences*) among individuals generated by interactions beginning with a focal firm, creates 'mutual engagement and responsibility'.

Stakeholders who make 'demands' on firms—or on other non-business organisations (i.e. governmental and non-profit)—presumptively bear '*some* responsibility' (emphasis added here) of assurance that their 'demands' do not generate '*unintended* negative consequences' for the firm or other (emphasis added here). This chapter both expands on this theme and suggests some important caveats to ponder. These caveats become most diffi-

2   The distinction between actions and outcomes is the essential problem over which US antitrust law has been and remains deeply divided. 'To widen the market and to narrow the competition, is always the interest of the dealers. To widen the market may frequently be agreeable enough to the interest of the public; but to narrow the competition must always be against it, and can serve only to enable the dealers, by raising their profits above what they naturally would be, to levy, for their own benefit, an absurd tax upon the rest of their fellow-citizens' (Smith 1776: Book I Ch. XI). The profit motive is plain enough, and natural. US antitrust law is confused concerning whether what matters is specific conduct (i.e. deliberate monopolisation through, for example, predatory pricing, on account of expected future consequences) or outcome (i.e. effective monopoly however obtained). Both forms of litigation have been pursued. The case against Microsoft involves, effectively, both complaints. There have been business attempts to use antitrust arguments to stifle competition and innovation.

cult in the instance of consumers, the firm's final customers. Other stakeholders form part of the sociopolitical environment within which market exchange occurs, or part of the consumer's supply chain (i.e. the firm, its distributors and suppliers). Low-cost responsibilities do not create major difficulties for consumers. Responsibilities with significant costs attached do create major problems, not the least of which is redistribution: transfer of consumer wealth and/or welfare to other economic actors. The redistribution is less significant where it is a part of the consumers' preferences, but preferences are a matter of moral education and bear more strongly on the wealthier. The proposed expansion involves taking account of the circumstance that stakeholders are, in addition to being interdependent (i.e. subject to 'mutual engagement'), already subject to general moral duties and citizenship duties. That is, taking a stakeholder role with respect to a focal firm—voluntarily or involuntarily—means either additional responsibilities, or giving specific direction (and perhaps reinforcement) to existing responsibilities. Some moral duties and many citizenship duties are joint (i.e. collective) as distinct from mutual, and involve collective action problems (see Olson 1965). Stakeholdership may less impose new duties and more define specific opportunities for benevolence grounded in natural sympathy for others (Smith 1776).

Some serious caveats arise in the nature of consequentialism. 'Consequence' must be read here as outcome or result. Consequence must be explicitly defined in order to identify duties and opportunities for benevolence. By the definition generally accepted in the stakeholder literature, any direct or indirect consequence relating to the focal firm defines stakeholdership. Anyone positively or negatively affected by a focal firm, directly or indirectly, is a stakeholder of that firm; anyone who can positively or negatively affect a focal firm, directly or indirectly, is a stakeholder of that firm. Only someone who neither affects nor is affected by a focal firm is *not* its stakeholder. This classical definition may be too broad including as it does competitors and media (Donaldson and Preston 1995: 86). For the purposes of this chapter, nature can be regarded 'as if' holding stakeholder status; it has in any case great destructive power (see Fig. 7.4 on page 151). Direct consequence means acting immediately on another. Indirect consequence implies, however, the possibility of a long chain of repercussions on nature and throughout the steadily globalising economy. The consequentialism framework, for that is what the volume's theme defines, obliges any stakeholder of a focal firm to consider the various impacts or effects of his or her actions, if not, strictly speaking, his or her motives, in addition to considering what rules should govern action or conduct. If a stakeholder's impacts are *negative* and *unintended*, the stakeholder faces a definable moral problem. This language implies prevailing conditions of ignorance concerning impacts of stakeholder conduct, such that a stakeholder has a duty not to act deliberately within a veil of ignorance (to adapt language from Rawls 1971). The issue then becomes one of cost of correction. But, presumptively at least, some *intended* negative consequences are also suspect, and then cost is no longer the issue.

The most obvious instances of stakeholder responsibility involve the global natural environment, global labour standards and basic human rights; these naturally are the subject of the UN Global Compact (which is discussed further below). But these instances may oblige collective action, such as the Kyoto international accord on climate change, which the Bush administration has conspicuously declined to approve. There is a strong case for universal moral standards, stated in terms of a minimum set of natural (i.e. inalienable) human rights (see Donaldson and Dunfee 1999); such rights may arguably not include labour standards. Even so, global labour standards may be seen as minimum wage, collective bargaining and public education traditions—well established in the advanced economies—extended to the world economy. The case for environmental protection is the destructive power of nature. The global natural environment is an instance of joint moral responsibility as distinct from stakeholder responsibility (the latter adds little on this score except perhaps to direct attention to specific issues). Definition and enforcement of global labour standards may levy what amount to private taxes on both higher-wage labour and consumers (see footnotes 2 and 4). The volume's theme is stated in terms of (1) the dangers of ignorance, and (2) the reasonable standard that a stakeholder should bear at least 'some' responsibility for consequences of conduct. 'Some' is what requires definition; a general criterion is not likely to suffice. There is sharp division over the advisability of child labour in developing countries, notwithstanding the UN Global Compact statement. The thesis of stakeholders' responsibilities has a very democratic and ethical ring to it, drawing as it does implicitly on the Declaration of the Rights of Man and the Citizenship (1789, a manifesto adopted by the revolutionary National Assembly of France as preamble for a draft constitution). A principle of the Declaration, criticised and revised later by Mill (1859), was that individual liberty is limited only by harm to others (the idea is older; see Barker 1960: 305 n. 29).[3]

This chapter does *not* take a distinctly contrarian position on the theme, which has substantial merit. Rather, the chapter is cautionary, and addresses the inherent difficulties and limits of the argument. (A sound argument will stand up to criticism.) The key matter is to what forms of actions, by whom, the thesis leads. The argument itself is stated in the weakest and, therefore, most defensible form; it is barely rejectable. Stakeholders *voluntarily* making demands (in effect, a market demand for purely luxury consumption is voluntary) thereby bear *some* responsibility (i.e. a responsibility greater than zero), which is otherwise ill defined in general and definable only by reference to specific circumstances, and only for *unintended* negative consequences. The thesis of the special theme can be restated readily in stronger form: 'The right to exercise free choice is necessarily accompanied by the responsibility to accept the consequences of choosing' (Wood 1991c: 71). Thus, the form of the argument might be strengthened to address *unavoidable* requirements (i.e. of necessity), *substantial* responsibilities and *intended* negative consequences. A stronger argument is correspondingly more difficult to justify, and more contingent on circumstances. It would seem appropriate here to consider both the weak and the strong form of the theme. The acid test of the thesis is with respect to consumers and consumption. The impact of economic action on nature and other stakeholders begins with final demand or consumption, from which other economic activities are derived (Smith 1776).

---

3   Mill (1859) proceeded (Rapaport 1978: xv-xvii) by seeking to distinguish between harm to others that should be prevented by social coercion and harm to others that should be tolerated (as in effect social coercion would be worse). He first delineated the principle of the French Revolution: that there must be no harm to others. Mill regarded the principle as inadequate. He then defined a second principle that social coercion must be to prevent violation of some 'distinct and assignable obligation to any other person or persons'. In the context of the present chapter, Mill can be read as being concerned with violation of rights held by others, a scope narrower than the notion of harms to others.

7.1 Framework for analysis

Enough difficulties are intuitively identifiable to warrant more careful analysis of the volume's thesis. Table 7.1 presents a simple two-by-two matrix. The horizontal stub distinguishes between the weak form and the strong form of the theme. The vertical stub distinguishes between voluntary demands and necessary requirements. (In effect, the former can be regarded as akin to luxuries, which one could do without; the latter can be regarded as akin to necessities, which one cannot do without. But the difference between luxuries and necessities may prove a matter of dispute and subjective definition. Water is a necessity; the only issue is abundance of supply and hence price of consumption.) As the table illustrates, voluntary demands involve avoidable negative consequences: forgoing the demand can obviate these consequences. The two cells within the row for voluntary demands concern unintended consequences versus intended consequences. The former involves *some* responsibility; the latter must involve, relatively, more *substantial* responsibility. The volume's thesis is restricted to the north-west quadrant of the table. Necessary requirements may likewise concern unintended and intended consequences. But neither can now be said to impose evident responsibility; rather, necessary requirements impose choice (i.e. a genuine moral dilemma). To choose between luxury and duty is one matter; to choose between necessity and consequence is another matter. Unintended consequences may or may not be avoidable at relatively little cost; the matter turns on the nature of the consequences in each instance. Intended consequences do not involve a condition of ignorance.

	WEAK FORM	**STRONG FORM**
VOLUNTARY DEMANDS	*Unintended* Avoidable negative consequences imply some responsibility.	*Intended* Avoidable negative consequences imply substantial responsibility.
NECESSARY REQUIREMENTS	*Unintended* Avoidable negative consequences are ambiguous with respect to responsibility.	*Intended* Avoidable negative consequences are ambiguous with respect to responsibility.

Table 7.1 *Forms of the thesis*

Figure 7.1 provides an abstract depiction of the general situation of stakeholders in a focal firm, from a manager's perspective. The purpose here is to capture the key dimensions or elements of the mutual and joint responsibility notions. The horizontal line depicts a one-way chain (or sequence) of purely economic activities involving the transformation of resources (i.e. inputs) through production and distribution (i.e. throughput) into final consumption goods and services (i.e. outputs). Demand for resources (ultimately resolving into labour and nature) is 'derived' from demand for consumption goods and services. There is, coinciding with this economic value-added chain (all economic

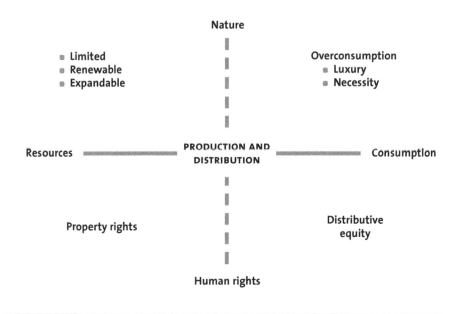

Figure 7.1 *Relationships among key dimensions*

values are determined by market demand-and-supply exchanges), a question of property rights (who owns what, and also how and why). The vertical line, intersecting the value-added chain at production and distribution, adds issues raised by humanity's relationship to nature and by human or natural rights (i.e. rights naturally inherent in all human beings). This vertical link (shown as a dashed line for distinction) depicts linkage or connectedness: the relationship of nature and humanity must be described in greater detail. That relationship may be hostile or fruitful, and contingent (see Fig. 7.4 on page 151).

The design of Figure 7.1 yields four quadrants. The north-west quadrant (relating nature as a whole and specific resources) involves considerations of whether resources are strictly limited, partly renewable and expandable by technology (i.e. invention). Resources originate either in nature or in labour, but technology can both extend and create resources (such as a third form of carbon invented by chemists at Rice University). The south-west quadrant involves considerations of property rights (in resources) and also whether human rights supersede (i.e. yield superior claims on) such property rights. The firm functions in a sense as an unavoidable logical linkage (as well as a profit-seeking action entity) between inputs and outputs; it is a market 'intermediary' between supply and demand. The north-east and south-east quadrants will be addressed later in connection with consumers' roles. The north-east quadrant isolates the problem of over-consumption: the impact of consumption, taken in aggregate, on nature. There is embedded here a free-rider problem, the tragedy of the commons (Hardin 1968; Hardin and Baden 1977): each consumer's impact is, considered individually, negligible until aggregation of effects strikes an irreversible ecological tipping point (see Fig. 7.4). The south-east quadrant isolates the problem of the consumer's responsibilities with respect to human rights of others.

It has long been recognised that there are certain difficulties with the doctrine of liberty, some addressed by Mill (1859; see footnote 3 on page 140). First, what is the definition of **harm**? Death, injury and deprivation of liberty or property ('inalienable rights [of] . . . life, liberty and the pursuit of happiness' in the US Declaration of Independence preamble) are plain enough; but in this context does harm include restriction of freedom of action or economic loss or lack of economic opportunity? Second, is harm objective or subjective? Suppose two individuals disagree over some valuation; if A proceeds anyway, is B then (psychologically at least) 'harmed'? Harm to nature is reasonably objective; human rights can presumably be an agreed set (see Donaldson and Dunfee 1999); labour standards may turn out to be highly subjective, if not part of human rights. Third, is one obliged to prevent **self-harm** by another, and, if so, at what cost to one's self? Mill's approach (detailed in footnote 3) places limits on personal liberty, but requires that specific rights of others define those limits. In other words, the problem is to identify the rights of others rather than one's own duties. In retrospect, one may see that Mill could not readily develop a general theory of duty to prevent and/or avoid harm to others. The reasons are discussed below.

There is inherent in a consequentialism approach a danger that, in any sufficiently strong form to matter, it indicates a unanimous-consent principle along the lines of the Pareto no-harm principle for economic efficiency. The danger is reduced, of course, by the weak form of the volume's thesis, which serves as a marked limitation. The Pareto principle specifies that a reallocation of resources that increases the welfare of A without reducing the welfare of B is morally acceptable: indeed, B can have no objection, other than envy, to A's gain. In case of harm, B is morally entitled to veto the reallocation of resources. The hypothetical compensation principle was a relaxation of the Pareto standard along the following lines: a reallocation of resources is acceptable if the increase in A's welfare is greater than the decrease in B's welfare such that A could compensate B and still be better off. This compensation is, however, hypothetical: A could act but is not obligated to do so. The US Constitution (Amendment V) requires just (i.e. fair market) compensation for public taking of private property through the power of eminent domain (a clause that avoids the loser's veto inherent in the Pareto principle); the hypothetical compensation principle in effect would permit public taking of private property without compensation (as one or more states have tried to do in recent years on environmental rationales).

Pushed in this way, the doctrine of universal personal liberty becomes a doctrine of universal personal veto, if the notion of harm is expanded. In effect, before acting, one must ask publicly whether there is *any* reason to suppose that someone else would object to the action on account of an unintended negative consequence. (To re-emphasise, non-intentionality denotes ignorance here. The strong form of the volume's thesis pushes well beyond such a limit.) In principle, one must broadcast one's intention and discern whether there are negative consequences, direct or indirect, objective or subjective. The doctrine of personal liberty is thus turned, in the extreme, on its head to become a doctrine of global unanimous consent. In strong form, the doctrine of global unanimous consent is akin to Calhoun's (1853) theory of concurrent majorities in a federal republic, where majorities were defined by the states of the American union. Of course, Calhoun was concerned, under the guise of states' rights, to preserve the evil of slavery.[4] Here, however, the presumption is of universal human rights and the ultimately destructive power of nature. In the Kyoto dispute, the US is, in effect, invoking the notion of concurrent majorities. President Bush stated that his primary responsibility was to the economic welfare of US citizens. Business firms favouring the Kyoto provisions do so, according to reports, in part because they hold (relative to the accord) tradable pollution rights whose value might be lost under the US position. The logical extreme of the doctrine of consent is the so-called Polish veto (*liberum veto*), a problem studied by Rousseau (*Considérations sur le Gouvernement de Pologne*). In this case any member of the Polish-Lithuanian parliament could veto action; the result, given a corrupt nobility, was disastrous, as no action producing harm could be adopted and, because of corruption, often no action producing even a general benefit (see Lukowski 1991). The weak form of the volume's theme does not reach this far, of course; but the direction of the argument becomes clear in pushing the argument in an extreme direction.

Issues of distributive equity and perception of extortion fundamentally explain the opposition of the Bush administration to the Kyoto agreement on climate change. The US, like other advanced industrial economies, is asked to reduce specified emissions, while developing economies are not. A difficulty is that twin goals are bundled into the agreement—climate change and economic development—in such a way that pollution is shifted from advanced to developing economies, and possibly as a result national wealth. In relationship to the Kyoto agreement, a straightforward example of stakeholder responsibility reasoning concerns the potential of wind power for electricity generation (see Furlong 2001, citing Jacobson and Masters 2001). Wind provides less than 1% of US energy; coal 52%. Wind energy cost per kilowatt-hour is about the same as using coal (3–4 cents), and there are government incentives for coal, gas and oil industries. However, the total social costs of coal are about 5.5–8.3 cents per kilowatt-hour taking into account the deaths of some 2,000 US mineworkers annually and the accumulated taxpayer costs since 1973 of about US$35 billion (in monetary and medical benefits to former miners). Jacobson and Masters (of Stanford University) propose building something between 214,000 and 236,000 wind turbines at a cost of US$338 billion. That level of installation would cut coal-based generation by two-thirds and reduce greenhouse gas emissions below 1990 levels in accordance with the US goal identified in the 1997 UN Kyoto Protocol, which the Bush administration has rejected. (The present author, for purposes of exposition, simply accepts the viability of the wind generation technology proposal.) For consumers and employees of electricity, the problem is both diffused and concealed within a veil of ignorance. No one consumer can directly influence the situation. Rather the government policy-making process (doubtless dominated by producer interests) must grapple with the problem. (US$338 billion is a lot of money, in the face of a recession, undeclared war and large national debt. Presumably there may be significant

---

4   'Calhoun denied the whole concept of social contract and natural rights, both of which had had long and respectable careers. Society, Calhoun argued, was not created by contract; society has always existed, and man [*sic*, humanity] has never existed outside of society. A state of nature, as described by the contract writers, never existed; nor were men [*sic*, people] ever endowed with natural rights. The only rights men [*sic*, people] have ever known, were those granted by society. It was thus that Calhoun could repudiate equality and uphold slavery' (Post 1953: xxi).

land acquisition issues.) The collective action problem is in part a diffusion of moral responsibility.[5]

7.2 Stakeholder responsibilities

The weak form of the volume's theme may be interpreted, in this context, as arguing that a stakeholder must take account of possibilities of harm, but is not obligated to act: that is, the stakeholder is not obligated to be subject, in advance, to veto or to be obligated to pay just compensation. The weak form of the thesis begins to look a lot like a case for informed benevolence, which can be regarded as a moral duty, particularly for the wealthy, but one much weaker than certain other moral duties, and defined in particular circumstances by stakeholder relationships. If this duty exists, it does so without there being generated a corresponding right on the part of someone else: benevolence is a virtue and not someone else's entitlement.

It is necessary to address stakeholder responsibilities concretely, by type of stakeholder and within specific circumstances. Otherwise, one cannot answer the vital question: Do customers, employees and suppliers, for instance, have responsibilities to the focal firm, beyond any established at law or by contract; or to other stakeholders, beyond any established by general moral and citizenship responsibilities? Mutual and joint responsibilities for stakeholders separate into four general categories or types of situation:

- Between the firm and its stakeholders
- Among stakeholders themselves
- Concerning common pool resources (including nature as a whole)
- Concerning the commonwealth

These responsibilities are those of interdependent actors, moral individuals and citizens. With respect to other stakeholders, a stakeholder must consider proper conduct and distributive equity. There are identifiable rules for personal conduct, applicable to managers, owners and other stakeholders alike. For example, there is no purpose in personal abuse of a waiter by a customer. Abuse is not the proper conduct of anyone. This rule, however, is a general one rather than one specific to a definable stakeholder status.

How much one should tip a waiter may be a different matter. Tipping is an illustration of Donaldson's (1989) principle that economic conduct, at least, can vary by stage of

---

5   One may think of Rousseau in *The Social Contract* (1762) as stepping around these problems in his notion of 'the general will' (*volonté générale*): a kind of ill-defined supermajority on socially important policy matters (Barker 1960: 260). The notion gets around both representative institutions and unanimity. The citizenry, in the role of a legislature or national referendum, recognises what is, effectively, crystal clear to everyone. (The notion is dangerous, of course.) The advantage of wind technology may be crystal clear (if in fact it is so); that clarity does not result in collective action. Assuming away problems of collective action, Rousseau merely presumes that recognition leads on (that is, it should lead on) to action. Olson (1965) is an important corrective to such a simplistic view.

economic development of a society.[6] There are generally established local standards for tipping: depending on location and type of service, ordinary service may warrant 10% or 15% or 18% tipping, whereas in some locations taxi drivers are commonly tipped and in other locations they are not; poor service should be undertipped and outstanding service should be overtipped. (In Stockholm, the gratuity is built into the price by established practice and the issue is the effect on service quality.) Is there then a duty to tip, or a duty to tip at the commonly prevailing standard? Is not failure to tip, or undertipping, tantamount to theft of someone's property right—to a living wage?

The commonwealth, for present purposes, is joint (i.e. collective) action by the citizenry to provide public goods (including justice and security) that markets would not supply (or would undersupply). Does this notion of public goods extend to distributive equity? Is such equity a matter of minimum standards (for wages, social security, medical care, housing, education, etc.) or of greater equality exceeding such minimum standards? Is distributive equity founded in human rights, or in the need of the majority of citizens for all to be equipped at certain minimum levels of public goods for the safety of society?

The UN Global Compact calls on firms to accept a set of principles on human rights, labour and the environment. Several hundred companies, and other organisations, have pledged support to date in a Global Compact network. There is useful moral authority in the standards of the Global Compact, as targets at which to aim. The nine principles ask business to:

- Support international human rights (see Donaldson and Dunfee 1999)

- Avoid complicity in human rights abuses

- Support freedom of association and collective bargaining

- Support elimination of forced and compulsory labour

- Support abolition of child labour

- Eliminate discrimination in employment and occupation

- Support 'a precautionary approach to environmental challenges'

- Promote greater environmental responsibility

- Encourage environmentally friendly technologies

The moral authority of these precepts should be self-evident. But commitment by a firm is voluntary. Obviously, where the cost of compliance is low, firms (and hopefully their stakeholders) will tend to adhere to the Global Compact: adherence is good for business reputation and does not materially affect the bottom line. Where cost of compliance is significant, some element of compulsion (e.g. embarrassment, if nothing else) must be added. Added cost must become an added burden to someone somewhere.

---

6 Donaldson states the principle in the form of what would have been acceptable in a society when it was at a similar stage of development. The principle does not address sufficiently, the present author suggests, the difficulty that more advanced societies may morally prefer to apply their present, and not their historical, standards, unless there are significant economic costs in doing so.

Mitchell *et al.* (1997) identified legitimacy, power and urgency as attributes of stakeholder identification and salience, from the perspective of management. Legitimacy and power can, however, be treated further as objective conditions. Legitimacy is a function of the definition of stakeholdership used above. Power is the capacity of stakeholders to affect the welfare of the firm and each other. Stakeholders, in an interdependent situation, must consider both the reactions of others (what Friedrich [1963: Ch. XI] characterised as the rule of anticipated reactions) holding power and also moral duties towards those same others. The relationship between self-interest and concern for others is one of partial overlap. Any individual's preference function may include concern for others as a dimension of self-interest. The perception of urgency is always the fundamental matter in directing action.

7.3 Consumers' responsibilities

The author argues that it is difficult, at best, to establish clear-cut responsibilities for customers, except by moral education or collective action. Indeed, consumers are likely to be the test case for the limits of the thesis of stakeholder responsibility. The reason is the peculiar relationship of consumers to the firm and its other stakeholders, forming jointly the consumers' supply chain.[7] Consumers retain a general freedom of choice. A difficulty is that customer responsibilities may readily become monopoly elements favouring producers, who may not be morally reliable; here, the moral conduct of managers is essential to establishing corresponding customer responsibilities. The argument is addressed below by two cases demonstrating difficulties in developing a general theory of consumers' responsibilities.

A classic situation is airlines' treatment, in recent years, of customers with respect to pricing and conditions of service. The prevailing circumstances in the airline industry are by now notorious. Elliott (2001) cites an instance in which a customer could save as much as 60% on the fare between two cities (travelling on business for his employer) by tacking on an extra leg, not used (i.e. a 'hidden city' itinerary). The airline, on discovery of this conduct, threatened to remove the customer's frequent-flier miles and bill his employer for the highest full-fare price. 'But a backlash against the airlines has begun' through pressure by consumer groups, Congress and competitors (Elliott 2001: 34). The competition and a revolt by business travellers concerning the common Saturday stay-over rule, together with the slumping economy, may be forcing changes in airline practices. Where in any of this mess is a consumer obligated by self-interested industry rules?

7 Considered statically, for Adam Smith, *The Wealth of Nations* (1776), there was no justification for monopoly (i.e. economic) rent: 'Consumption is the sole end and purpose of all production; and the interest of the producer ought to be attended to only so far as it may be necessary for promoting that of the consumer. The maxim is so perfectly self-evident that it would be absurd to attempt to prove it. But in the mercantile system the interest of the consumer is almost constantly sacrificed to that of the producer; and it seems to consider production, and not consumption, as the ultimate end and object of all industry and commerce' (Book IV Ch. VIII). Considered dynamically, the issue is more complex, in that profit-seeking may be the necessary motive for entrepreneurial innovation as the driver of economic development (Schumpeter 1934).

Software piracy is more difficult to defend. The Business Software Alliance (see Barlow 2001) is a non-profit organisation funded by software companies for the purpose of preventing software piracy (i.e. illegal copying). The principal target of the Alliance is other businesses (which avoid purchasing general licences or copies for each computer by illegal copying). The Alliance evidently receives many hundreds of tips monthly (without compensation), most likely provided by disgruntled employees. (It is not operating systems, but popular applications that tend to be pirated. Microsoft already controls most of the PC operating system market by selling directly to PC manufacturers, a matter of recent federal antitrust litigation.) The estimated piracy rates (according to Alliance data) in 2000 were 37% worldwide (down from 46% in 1995), 25% in the US, 34% in Europe and 98% in Vietnam (2% presumably purchased largely for copying). Naturally, the Alliance members would like global enforcement of anti-piracy rules. The Alliance members also work to reduce the lag time for global software introduction and to increase global user support. (In other words, there are defects in supply, in addition to cost to purchasers. Copying is also easy enough, for those with expertise.) US law is, of course, very clear. (It is common practice for US universities to post warnings to students against software piracy.) At law, piracy is an offence; it is doubtless, for a customer with money, dishonourable and potentially hazardous. To label software piracy immoral—an instance of theft of someone else's property—is rather more awkward (in the author's view). There is a distributive equity issue: smaller businesses are more likely to practise piracy than larger businesses. The issue becomes rather more problematic in the instance of developing countries, facing difficulties of poverty and defects in supply. In effect, one aspect of reduction of piracy is greater competition—both better supply and lower prices—in the software industry. Theft is presumably less appealing where less profitable. (For issues concerning free, or freer, availability of software code from a social welfare perspective, see Windsor 2002; Jussawalla 1992.)

The matter now becomes one of establishing the essence of these examples as a more general argument, which must include managerially defined 'cheating' as acceptable consumer conduct under certain circumstances as a form of resistance to arguably improper and self-interested business practices, often operating in parallel among firms dominating an industry (cf. Laulan 1981). Figure 7.2 provides a standard demand-and-supply or market exchange model with conventional downward-sloping demand (i.e. declining marginal benefit or utility of consumption) and upward-sloping supply (i.e. rising marginal cost of production and distribution). Market price P is determined simultaneously with market volume Q. For the present exercise, the producer enjoys some persistent degree of monopoly power relative to the consumer (depicted in the downward-sloping demand function), arising in barriers to competition and/or information asymmetries favouring the producer, such that the producer extracts a surplus or rent in excess of competitive cost.[8]

The consumer is 'entitled'[9] to lowest-cost consumption, cost being a function of the profit necessary to obtain supply, whether considered statically or dynamically. The

---

8   For expositional simplicity, here competition includes 'ordinary profit' or competitive profit. It is not the case under atomistic or workable competition that profit, in an accounting sense, is driven to zero, but rather that pure economic profit, or rent, is driven towards zero. Ordinary or competitive profit is just sufficient to prevent the producer from exiting the industry. The manager's goal is sustainable rent, and the laws can be bent to achieve and sustain that goal.

9   On Adam Smith's 1776 representation, see footnotes 2 (page 138) and 4 (page 144).

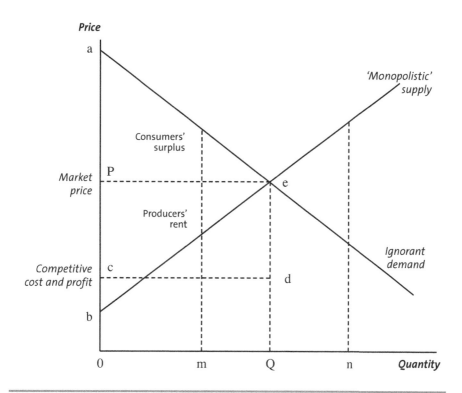

Figure 7.2 **Demand and supply illustration**

consumer is, of course, not entitled to impose negative externalities (unpriced effects) on others, including nature, any more than the producer would be entitled to do so. Here, however, duties are equally binding on consumer and producer. Negative externalities affecting nature do not involve moral responsibility, as towards other stakeholders, but rather the danger that the commonwealth will be destroyed through the power of nature.

In Figure 7.2, the demand function is labelled as **ignorant** (i.e. imperfectly informed): consumers' willingness to pay is partly a function of information asymmetries, including ignorance regarding unintended negative consequences. Given conditions of 'monopolistic' supply and 'ignorant' demand, in market equilibrium at point 'e', the producer extracts rent (or surplus) (the area marked 'Pcde' that is in excess of competitive cost) including ordinary profit (the area marked 'cdQ0'). Due to absence of perfect price discrimination by the producer, consumers retain some welfare surplus ('consumers' surplus'), the area marked 'aPe': consumers pay less than they are willing to pay.[10] The

10 Increased competition would shift the supply function to the right across the quantity axis, towards 'n', such that price and rent would fall towards the competitive level. The incentive of the producer is to find a means to shift the supply function to the left across the quantity axis, towards 'm', such that price and rent rise, and consumers' surplus is reduced.

consumer has an economic incentive to remain ignorant of certain information, despite the questionable morality of such conduct. If the consumer understood that demand resulted in unintended negative externalities, then the demand function would shift to the left across the quantity axis, towards 'm', such that price and rent fell towards the competitive level, or even below, resulting ultimately in the latter instance in the exit of the producer from the industry.

A classic instance was the migrant workers' effort (under the leadership of Cesar Chavez) to organise a US grape boycott in order to force better wages and working conditions. The intended strategy was a temporary drop in demand compelling producer concessions, followed by a restoration in demand; the change in cost of production and distribution must be absorbed out of the profit margin of producers or passed on to the consumers through higher prices.

Price and quantity are relative, so that a decline in demand in one industry or to one firm presumably is linked to an increase in demand in another industry or to another firm. The consumer presumably has to work out the chain of repercussions in terms of consequences for other stakeholders. For example, Friedman (2001) argues that, in order to address the US trade deficit (US\$400 billion), for the preservation of a US manufacturing base, 'A good place to start would be to insist that the labour, health, regulatory and environmental rules that Americans impose on their domestic producers be observed by our trading partners, too.' One example would be standards eliminating child labour in developing countries (whether such standards are globally appropriate or not, which is a matter of current controversy). With respect to Figure 7.2, informed demand shifts to the right along the quantity axis, towards 'n', such that price, but desirably not rent, rises relative to the competitive level; in this instance, the intention is that the change in price should go to labour.[11] (Shifts in either demand or supply schedules function to produce 'm' and 'n'; demand and supply simply work in opposite directions.)

Figures 7.3 and 7.4 illustrate two vital aspects of economic development. One aspect is the historical record of presently advanced economies in which, arguably, the welfare of the least-advantaged individuals or groups (cf. Rawls 1971) initially declined with industrialisation. There were a number of reasons for this circumstance, associated with the 'release' of excess agricultural labour to the growing cities, where supply of labour exceeded demand for labour, and population growth. As Figure 7.3 suggests, the welfare of the disadvantaged arguably declined to some nadir of fortunes and then recovered, and exceeded, pre-capitalist welfare. (The recovery may reflect both market forces and governmental actions.) The same process, roughly speaking, may be under way in many developing countries. In contrast, the welfare of the more advantaged has risen steadily

---

11 There are limits on consumers' capacity to handle additional economic burdens. In 1993 (Preston and Windsor 1997: 35, based on World Bank data), the world population was about 5.5 billion and still growing, of which 85% was outside the industrial market economies (accounting for 15%), which with the rest of Europe including Russia (stretching to the Pacific) accounted for 23%. The world gross national product, at market prices, was then about US\$23.7 billion (of which 78% was generated in the industrial market economies, and another 3% in the rest of Europe including Russia), or about US\$4,293 per capita. The average GNP per capita was about US\$22,800 in the industrial market economies, to be contrasted with US\$275 in India and US\$362 in the Asian socialist economies (including China). As Wilson (1989: 65) observes, capitalism is not moral: it is a process working, however, to a profoundly moral outcome—the alleviation of poverty through wealth creation, over time.

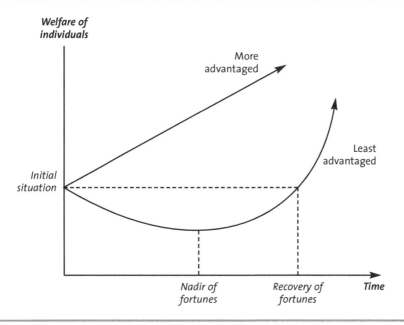

Figure 7.3 **A theory of capitalist economic development**

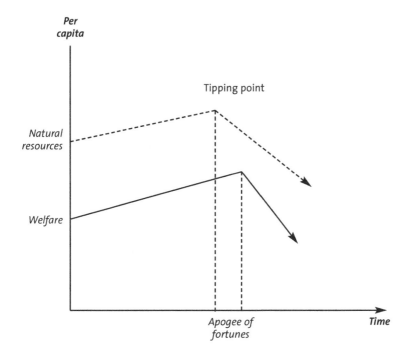

Figure 7.4 **A theory of ecological tipping point**

with economic development. The key issue now is whether the gap between more advantaged and least advantaged is closing or increasing. Moral responsibility is partly a function of the movement of the gap and, even if the gap is closing, the speed of that closing.

As articulated here, a consequentialism conception of stakeholder responsibilities leads on to an anti-consumption posture, one that must be considered carefully before accepting unreservedly. Figure 7.4 suggests that the welfare of the average individual in relation to usable natural resources per capita could decline in the future, perhaps past an ecological tipping point from which nature is not recoverable. Relative to pre-capitalist welfare, average welfare has clearly increased (at least in the advanced economies), but average welfare may be approaching an apogee, beyond which, absent collective action, decline will set in, perhaps irretrievably. Figure 7.4 depicts the situation as a function of what happens to renewable resources per capita (shown as a dashed line).

7.4 Conclusion

The call for a better understanding of stakeholders' responsibilities is ultimately: (1) a moral appeal for greater understanding of both *unintended* negative consequences (i.e. unpriced negative externalities occurring in ignorance) and *intended* negative consequences (i.e. morally indefensible losses imposed on others); and (2) either voluntary individual or collective action for redress. Stakeholder responsibilities must be disentangled from general moral responsibilities and citizenship responsibilities. It may be that stakeholder responsibilities, in effect, direct moral attention in specific ways, but direction of attention itself has repercussions or consequences that must be traced and considered. The essential issue is whether the moral appeal is for philanthropy—moral education concerning personal preferences, especially by the wealthy that can afford to reallocate resources from luxuries to benevolence—or for binding moral duties. Under certain circumstances, the moral appeal would be a duty amounting to an involuntary tax on consumption. Any tax may rapidly become extortion: the wealthier must reallocate resources or face higher costs from destructive action by the less advantaged. The latter posture can rapidly become an 'extraction' grounded in threat rather than a 'duty' grounded in conviction. The decision facing a stakeholder is initially one of greater information concerning that which the stakeholder would not otherwise do except for ignorance; but ultimately one of self-sacrifice for higher purpose.

Two general appeals are possible. Plato, in *The Republic*, dealing with the design of an ideal commonwealth, has Socrates produce arguments demonstrating that a just person has a better and happier life than does an unjust person. (The unjust person does self-harm as well as harm to others.) Adam Smith (1776) considered that rising wealth and moral education would enhance the natural sympathy of humans for the circumstances of others. These considerations still leave the matter of stakeholder responsibilities on a tightrope balancing between economic development (for the great and moral purpose of reducing poverty worldwide) and the negative consequences, for nature and people, generated by that economic development. That tightrope requires reflection and choice. The greater one's wealth, the greater one's freedom of choice and, hence, obligation of moral reflection.

The author suggests that the lessons for managers are perhaps more stringent than the lessons for other stakeholders. Other stakeholders' responsibilities arguably increase the responsibilities incumbent on managers themselves, rather than providing some degree of relief. The duties of other stakeholders to a focal firm are quite weak. Why should any employee, much less a consumer, exhibit loyalty or commitment to a firm in a rapidly changing marketplace? The conduct of the airline industry and the problems in software distribution do not indicate strong duties incumbent on other stakeholders. Managers must themselves define those duties, concretely, largely through moral conduct. And managers may find that they are increasingly leading the way—as in the Global Compact Network—towards collective action efforts, which by definition (Olson 1965) require that someone bears the initial burden of moral leadership (cf. Windsor and Getz 1999 on the economic costs of moral leadership for the global suppression of business corruption of public officials).

THE CARRIS COMPANIES: MAKING 100% EMPLOYEE GOVERNANCE THE PRACTICE
Shifting stakeholder and citizen rights and responsibilities to the employees[*]

Cecile G. Betit
Independent researcher, USA

In the *Long Term Plan* (LTP) (Carris 1994), the Carris Companies' owner and visionary CEO, William (Bill) H. Carris described a highly unusual and wide-ranging change process designed to integrate employees into corporate governance and transfer ownership rights to employees through an Employee Stock Ownership Plan (ESOP).[1] This form of worker ownership (30% minimum to qualify) and deferred benefit plan is recognised within the United States legal code. There are approximately 10,000 ESOPs within the United States.

> Technically, an ESOP is a deferred benefit plan in which a company purchases shares of its own stock and places them in trust for its employees who may claim their shares or sell them back to the company when they quit or retire (Lawrence 1997: 198).

[*] The assistance of the following is gratefully acknowledged: William H. Carris for providing full access to the Carris Companies; Mike Curran, Vice President, for sharing insights that are honed and generative; Karin McGrath, Human Resources Director, for providing ongoing status information (so essential for keeping the research current); and the employee-owners of the Carris Companies whose efforts in providing information and materials for this work are absolutely essential to its success. I appreciate the reviewers' suggestions for significant improvements. Thank you to Ownership Associates for the use of intellectual property.

[1] (a) Employee stock ownership plan (ESOP): Bill Carris in the LTP explained to employees that the 'first step in transferring ownership is to create a new organisation, . . . *The Carris Employee Stock Ownership Plan*. The Plan will have a trustee and an ESOP committee.' (b) Qualification to be an ESOP is 30% of employee ownership.

The Carris design for the transfer of ownership and citizen stakeholder rights and responsibilities had several unique features:

- The discounted sales price for the transfer of 100% ownership of the privately held family firm
- The one-person one-vote provision within the ESOP
- The commitment to teach employees the business
- 100% employee governance

The practice of governance, within the Carris Companies transfer of ownership, provided a model of extensive and intensive engagement of a particular stakeholder group—the employees—during a time of structural change. This direction, pursued boldly within the Carris Companies, with their human scale, multiple products and national reach, has implications for those interested in employee ownership, systemic change to increase employee participation and/or new forms of corporate governance encouraging full exercise of corporate citizenship rights.

Following a brief description of the methodology employed within this chapter, background information is provided on the Carris Companies. Changing stakeholder relationships highlighted in the segment on employee ownership provide a foundation for understanding the transitional process within the Carris Companies and, specifically, the practice of governance.

> Taking a practice-based stakeholder view of the corporation significantly alters the approach to the firm and its responsibilities, broadening the understanding of those to whom a firm is accountable. It moves the conversation directly toward the quality and nature of the relationships that companies develop with stakeholders and the assessment of the impacts of corporate activities on those stakeholders (Waddock 2002: 9).

The processes to increase participation and to prepare stakeholder citizens for changing roles and relationships are at the centre of the discussion of the Carris Companies' six-year effort to move governance deep into its infrastructure—as a practice that involves all of the sites and stakeholder citizens within the corporation. Examples of the practice (not as completed efforts) are provided through examples of the work of the Corporate Steering Committee and the North Carolina Governance Committee.

8.1 Methodology

The study of the transitions at the Carris Companies began in 1996. This chapter drew primarily from conversations, interviews and meeting notes over a five-year period. Conversations with Bill Carris about his goals and plans for the ESOP and corporate governance were routinely scheduled. The change co-ordinator provided information about training activities and other efforts to increase employee skills and participation in the ESOP. Conversations with managers provided background on Carris Companies' operations and suggested additional indicators for tracking corporate change. Regular attendance at employee-owners' training activities, corporate governance meetings, North Carolina governance meetings, state-of-the-company meetings (Vermont and Connecticut), strategic planning meetings, task force meetings, human resource presentations and information sessions, etc. provided a direct means of keeping abreast of changes. From its onset, Bill Carris provided an open environment for the research process. No restrictions were placed on access to information or personnel or to materials published.

The next section offers a brief description of the company, its structure, its products and locations.

8.2 The Carris Companies

8.2.1 Henry Carris: the company founder

In 1951, when Henry Miller Carris opened Carris Reels Inc., a manufacturer of plywood reels (for steel and wire cable), he had two employees. (This start-up was warmly celebrated with a large family-style 50th anniversary celebration on 9 June 2001 in Centre

Figure 8.1 *Some examples of Carris reels*

Photo credit: Marilyn Dalick

Rutland, Vermont.) By 1955, the company had added 20 employees and moved to larger quarters. In 1957, the company moved to Depot Lane, where the Centre Rutland Mill continues its manufacturing operations. Henry, who was born into a self-sufficient farm family in Iowa, had his first experience of Vermont as a summer camp counsellor. Later, managing a workshop for disabled veterans in Irvington, New York, he learned the rudiments of manufacturing. Following his marriage to Helen (Huntington), a native Vermonter, he sharpened his understanding during several experiences with wood manufacturing in Vermont prior to starting his own company in Rutland. The company made money. Its growth was steady.

8.2.2 Bill Carris: Carris Companies CEO

The Vermont way of life, during Bill Carris's 1950s childhood in Rutland, was rooted in the predominantly agricultural lifestyle and strong sense of stability, egalitarianism, independence, fiscal conservatism, fair play and social concern (Bryan and McLaughry 1989; Moats 2001). These were characteristics and values also of the Carris family. Bill Carris brought them forward when he took over from his father as CEO in 1980. A few years older than the company, he had grown up with it, learning reel manufacturing and its administration. In addition to this depth of experience, he had clearly defined strategies for growth through start-ups and acquisitions and professionalisation of management. With the exception of a few years away for education and military service, Bill Carris has always lived within the Rutland, Vermont, area. He and his wife, Barbara (Tracey), have four children.

Corporate sales were over US$120 million at the end of 2000, reflecting an increase of 570% from 1980. Assets increased 940% during this period, while the number of employees increased 551%. The company passed the milestone for 1,000 employees during 1998 and at the end of 2000 employed 1,106. Starting pay was US$7.00 per hour and the average hourly wage was US$9.05. The hourly benefit rate was US$3.44 (38.0%). In addition to the ESOP and profit-sharing, employee benefits included company-paid: insurance (health, short-term disability and life); 4% of wages contributed to the 401K retirement plan; and sick and vacation leave time. During its first five years, the Carris ESOP contribution averaged about 11% of pay with the national average as reported in the *Employee Ownership Report* at 8% (NCEO 1998: 3). Following the vote of employees on the recommendations of the Health Care Task Force (the origins of which are described below), in January 2001, employees started to pay US$5.00 each week for health insurance. During Bill's 21-year tenure, the Carris Financial Corporation[2] (CFC) was formed and in 2001 had several subsidiaries and product lines shown in Table 8.1.

The companies in the main avoided much of the status differentiation within the modern corporation. Workers, supervisors and managers, found at most sites, reflected the commitment to a flat organisational chart. Larger sites had production managers in place. Corporate management located in Rutland, Vermont, travelled as needed, to the sites. No one, including Bill Carris, had a personal secretary and everyone was on a first-name basis. Calls were not screened. Doors were open. There was no executive suite, no reserved parking places and no executive washrooms. Small offices held standard furniture, computer, filing cabinets and an extra chair. No visible symbols of power or rank

2   For additional information, see www.carris.com.

Subsidiary	Products/services
Carris Reels	Plywood, nailed-wood, plastic, hardboard, wood-metal and metal reels for wire and cable industry
Vermont Tubbs	High-quality home furnishings, beds and case goods
Killington Wood Products	Pallets
Carris Plastics and Groggins	Plastic, using custom moulding and extrusion processes
Carris Speciality Products	Product development: originally wood; since 2000, plastics
Carris Foundation	Corporate gifts processed for non-profit and other community organisations

Table 8.1 **Carris Financial Corporation (CFC) subsidiaries and products**

distinguished executives from other employee-owners. On the manufacturing floor, they were indistinguishable from other workers.

The 2001 economic downturn affected the Carris Companies. In an article for *The Real News* (formerly *The Reel News*), David Fitzgerald, CFO, explained to citizen stakeholders that the economy was a cause for concern rather than worry: downturns such as recessions occur as part of the regular economic cycle, most recently in 1981 and 1991. He noted that business could get much worse and the company would still be strong (Fitzgerald 2001: 2). Table 8.2 lists the location of the Carris Companies and the activities of the sites.

The rapid pace of technology and building development in Mexico created ideal market conditions for Carris Plastics to begin manufacturing reels and other plastics in Monterrey for sale in that country. Carris de México started operations in early 2000. A small assembly operation followed a customer to Brazil in 2001. Because of the complexities involved, the two international sites were not brought into the ESOP. Other forms of employee ownership recognised within the legal code of local governments may be utilised at some point in the future.

8.3 Changing stakeholder relationships: employee ownership

For this chapter, the following definition of stakeholder is used. 'A stakeholder in an organisation is any group or individual who can affect or is affected by the achievement of the organisation's objectives' (Freeman 1984: 46). Clearly, by definition, stakeholders

	Full manufacturing	Assembly only	Multi-handicapped	Corporate (C) International sales (X)
Brandon, Forestdale, Centre and West Rutland, VT	X			
Madera, CA; Enfield, CT; Brookville, OH (1997) Fincastle, VA (July 1999); Statesville, NC	X			
Kingman and Phoenix, AZ; Santa Maria, CA; New Carlisle, IN; Galien, MI		X		
Contract sites: Martin Luther Homes, Nebraska (with Lucent Technologies sheltered workshops); Alabama, 2 facilities		X	X	
Contract sites: Mantua, OH; Watsonville, PA		X		
Brazil (2001)		X		X
Rutland, VT, corporate offices				C
Monterrey, Mexico (2000)	X			X
Tacoma, WA				X

Note: purchase dates after the beginning of the ESOP

Table 8.2 *Carris Companies facilities*

have a relationship with a corporation. Clarkson moves this idea of relationship forward within the context of the fundamental purposes of the corporation.

> The economic and social purpose of the corporation is to create and distribute increased wealth and value to all its primary stakeholder groups, without favouring one group at the expense of others. Wealth and value are not defined only in terms of increased share price, dividends, or profits (Clarkson 1995: 92).

Employee ownership provides an example of boundary-spanning capacity for stakeholders within a corporation (Waddock 2002: 76) and brings the idea of changing stakeholder relationships to the forefront.

In *The Capitalist Manifesto*, Louis Kelso presented a vision of employee ownership and a compass for change of the 'partly capitalistic and partly labouristic economy to a well-balanced and completely capitalistic economy' within a democratic framework (Kelso and Adler 1958: 252). In this view, employee ownership not only changes stakeholder citizenship relationships, it provides an offset to the requirement of the mass-production economy for mass consumption to maintain a high standard of living. In 1973, inspired by Kelso's dogged efforts to promote populism, Senator Russell Long introduced ESOP legislation with tax incentives to further employee ownership. There was broad support for the idea that employees owning their companies would balance some of the deficiencies growing within the United States economic system (Rockefeller III 1973).

Three decades later, such thinking has contemporary advocates. Jeff Gates, for example, addresses the challenge of capitalism in the context of changing stakeholder citizenship relationship and stewardship. He sees the dilemma as 'fashioning a social contract that can channel financial capital's return-seeking properties in a way that balances financial with other goals—social, fiscal, political, cultural, environmental'. He offers *The Ownership Solution* as a means of meeting that challenge within a 'people-based, feedback-intensive, self-organised, self-designed system' (Gates 1998: 292-93), thus joining employee ownership with full participation of its stakeholder citizens. Participation has been found to be critically important. Early efforts to mount employee ownership had disappointing results in those areas involving productivity. For improvements in production, it appears that employee participation must accompany employee ownership. Multi-faceted approaches for increasing participation (Blasi 1990; Smith 1992) similar to those being implemented within the Carris Companies, seemed to be most effective. For example, Marens *et al.* found that ESOPs 'can be a useful mechanism for building a stakeholder relationship'. That usefulness might be in 'anchoring participation programs in a tangible and credible manner' (Marens *et al.* 1999: 73). Employing meta-analysis (a statistical technique for distilling a single estimate from a number of studies) of 43 studies, Doucouliagos estimated the 'average correlation between productivity and various forms of participation'. He found that:

> profit sharing, worker ownership and worker participation in decision making are all positively associated with productivity. All the observed correlations are stronger among labour-managed firms (firms owned and controlled by workers) than among participatory capitalist firms (firms adopting one or more participation schemes involving employees, such as ESOPs or quality circles) (Doucouliagos 1995: 58).

The distinction in the forms of participation is an important one. Discussed further in this chapter are the Carris Companies' efforts towards the practice of employee governance and shifting stakeholder and citizenship rights and responsibilities to employees. These reflect employee participation beyond that expected within the traditional ESOP.

8.4 Changing stakeholder relationships within the Carris Companies

8.4.1 The Long Term Plan

In *The Long Term Plan* (LTP), which he wrote in 1994 for his employees, Bill Carris described his vision for the transfer of ownership that would take place over an extended period of 10–15 years. With seasoned management and workers in place, good market conditions, and stable margins on product, he felt confident that the time was right to begin this company transformation through employee ownership and employee governance.

8.4.2 Influences on Bill Carris

Having the good fortune never to want for anything of consequence, Bill Carris came to believe that the all-American credo of the right to life, liberty and the pursuit of happiness also meant 'a right to share wealth, to manage our daily work and to ultimately be in control of our lives' (Carris 1994: 7). Well aware of the fact that many companies promoted emotional ownership, he decided to transfer actual ownership of his company to the employees.

In addition to those influences provided by his family and his life and work experience, Bill Carris prepared extensively to lead the corporate transition. Over a span of several years he examined other companies' best practices, attended Harvard Business School's Program for Executives and participated with other Carris corporate managers in workshops on employee ownership, corporate change and group process. He was moved by the long-term financial success of the Basque (Pyrenees) Mondragon Co-operatives, the broad stakeholder relationships formed and provisions for the common good. The co-operatives' emphasis on collaboration, friendship, principles, consensus and profit as means of serving the common good (Mollner 1991) tangibly demonstrated the positive dynamism that could be created simultaneously in business and people's lives when purpose and practice were joined.

Robert K. Greenleaf's (1977) writings provided a perspective from which to think through the role of personal leadership as service to facilitate the change from private ownership to employees' shared ownership. Bill Carris had personal experience working with those within Alcoholics Anonymous[3] and had the opportunity to learn Quaker

---

3 Bill Carris references Alcoholics Anonymous (AA) frequently in conversations regarding individual transformation, group process and organisational structure. He has attended 12-step meetings for over 20 years and notes, as do Fisher *et al.* (2000: 191), the fundamental equality within AA's membership. They point out the union of AA's foundational stability, transforma-

(Society of Friends) practices. These enhanced his skills and provided practical, experiential bases for working with change within groups. There were extended discussions with Carris management, consultants and others from whom Bill Carris requested feedback, all of which helped to frame the discussion and to develop implementation processes.

The LTP's (Carris 1994) publication and the subsequent movement towards its implementation followed a consensus[4] built within corporate management around its main principles: traditional corporate concerns for production, pragmatism and profitability within the context of stakeholder relationships, ethics and values. These emphases placed the Carris Companies in good company. In *Built to Last*, Collins and Porras noted that visionary companies 'pursue a cluster of objectives, of which making money is only one—and not necessarily the primary one' (Collins and Porras 1994: 8).

The first two paragraphs within the cover memorandum to the LTP established its context, invited participation as stakeholder citizens and made note of the unknowns ahead:

> This document is my idea for the future of Carris Reels, Inc. and its affiliates. In it I attempt to describe the model for an *employee-owned* and *governed* company. The corporate community I have described does not exist today nor has it ever existed. The change from a privately held company to an employee-owned and governed organisation is a break with tradition, but it is also a departure from a system, which rewards but a few, to one in which the rewards are enjoyed by many . . . I a msearching for the working mechanism to make an ideal concept such as this a reality here, at our company, and I need your help (Carris 1994: i [emphasis original]).

The ideas of changing stakeholder and corporate citizen relationships were expansive and inclusive within the LTP. The plan was replete with statements denoting the radical nature of the shift in scope and depth Bill Carris envisioned in stakeholder citizen relationships, responsibilities and rights. A primary goal within the governance effort was to shift stakeholder citizen responsibility; 'to give voice' to employee-owners in the 'distribution of wealth and the overall direction of the organisation' (Carris 1994: 3). The LTP outlined the rewards and risks of running the business.

8.4.3 *Strategic directions*

The strategic directions for the transition were interlaced with equality and fairness, values found throughout the LTP. Joined closely to these were transparency and understanding of how things work. 'Teaching employees the business' suggested how directly Bill Carris saw his role changing from simple authority to a multifaceted leader/mentor relationship, designed to ensure success of the transition to shift stakeholder citizenship rights and responsibilities to the employees. This willingness to pass on the know-how of the business implies both openness and 'ongoing regard' (Kegan and Lahey 2001: 185)

tional disequilibrium and the perception of its members that participation helps them to transform their lives. These three characteristics are those of a foundational community of inquiry.

4 Though well beyond the discussion within this chapter, one might make the point that decision-making by consensus reflects a shifting in stakeholder citizenship responsibilities from the owner to the larger group.

for the firm's employees as well as respect. Respect 'creates symmetry, empathy, and connections in all kinds of relationships . . . commonly seen as unequal' (Lawrence-Lightfoot 1999: 9).

In the LTP, Bill Carris joined employee ownership to the creation of 'a new style of corporate governance, one characterised by community, trust and inclusiveness'. Neal notes the role of respect and root of equality in such behaviour. 'The effort to develop an openness to the other . . . is one which we make toward those whose dignity as persons we respect but which we deny to those we treat as objects' (Neal 1997: 18). The Carris Companies' mission statement extends the discussion of the practice of governance and stakeholder citizenship rights and responsibilities into the idea of the corporate community.

8.4.4 Carris Companies' mission statement: bringing internal and external communities together

Bill Carris tells the story of how a crumpled sheet of paper was taped to his bookcase for a very long time as he worked on the ideas for the LTP. On it was written, 'to improve the quality of life for our growing corporate community'. This phrase, through the action of the Corporate Steering Committee, became the corporate mission, joining internal and external communities as stakeholders:

> As we, a community of companies, are united in our business and common interests toward the common good, so too should our dedication and concern encompass the outside community—those towns or districts where we live— (the general public) and thereby society as a whole (Carris 1994: 2).

Workplace community has been defined as 'a partnership of free people committed to the care and nurturing of each other's mind, body, heart and soul through participatory means' (Naylor et al. 1996: 42). These are also characteristics that come to mind in thinking through the qualities of corporate citizenship (Waddock 2002: 202). With stakeholder citizen partnership as a broad business strategy, there are certain requirements: namely, those at every level have a part in defining vision and values; can say no to a given course of action; share accountability and can be honest; thereby maintaining contact without abdication of responsibility (Block 1993: 29-30). Characteristics of workplace community include, among other things: shared vision, common values, empowerment, responsibility sharing, growth and development, and education (Naylor et al. 1996: 42-43). Community clearly involves processes of relationship and communication. 'Communities of practice are the shop floor of human capital, the place where the stuff gets made.' They are ubiquitous (though not always obvious), defined by the history they develop over time; their shared enterprise (rather than one specific agenda); shared learning and culture, developed and experienced through the long term with a product recognised as shared (Stewart 1997: 97). 'The common work is simply a way to define ourselves by asking the question . . . "What is the larger purpose we share with others?" ' (Olson and Harris 1997: 9).

The LTP encouraged increasing levels of participation throughout the Carris Companies for employee ownership and the practice of governance. Herman Miller Furniture Chairman, Max Depree, noted the inherently participative premise of leadership in his embrace of the concept of the leader as servant popularised by former AT&T executive Robert K. Greenleaf (1977). Peter Senge endorsed the concept of servant leadership as 'providing the enabling conditions for people to lead the most enriching lives they can' (Senge 1990: 140). Depree (1989) defines such leadership as liberating individuals to do what is expected of them in the most human way possible. In commenting on this, Senge states: 'One of the deepest desires underlying shared vision is the desire to be connected, to a larger purpose and to one another' (Senge 1990: 230). Providing opportunities for connection and giving voice were essential elements in the practice of governance and shifting stakeholder citizen responsibility within the Carris Companies.

Often Bill Carris used the metaphor of a pebble in a pool to denote the impact of actions and the interconnections of stakeholder relationships. At the Carris Companies' June 2001 50th anniversary celebration, Rutland's Mayor, John Cassarino, spoke about the many ways in which local Carris Companies exercised good citizenship, responding directly to individuals' and community needs. Mayor Cassarino remembered when, as Director of the Rutland House's homeless shelter, he witnessed the impact on individual and community life that such personal and corporate response can effect. This is reflective of the developing understanding of corporate citizenship: 'concerned with ideas of connectivity through understanding the way our local and global communities and environments interrelate' (McIntosh *et al.* 1998: 35).

Leipziger extends ideas of connectivity, relationship and interrelationship to her definition of an interested party: 'an individual or group concerned with or affected by the social performance of the company'. She is clear that interested parties are also ' "stakeholders", as they have a stake in the company'; her listing of possible stakeholders is broad and exhaustive moving across local and societal groups (Leipziger 2001: 94). Harman and Hormann (1990) also see companies becoming connective links as shared business principles become the language and know-how of the world. Whereas even a few years ago such a view may have been considered quite radical, there is a growing body of business and social science literature emphasising the common good in ways that heretofore may have been the arena of philosophy, political science or religion. Severyn Bruyn placed the Carris effort into this larger context—as a case to demonstrate the kind of entrepreneurial thinking in 'civil society' that 'could signal an advanced phase of freedom, democracy and justice' (Bruyn 2000: 104). His book also extended the role of a company, business and the market into service of the common good, noting that the market should begin to see its outcomes in terms of power as much as profit: a form of self-governance as applying to the market economy.

In the Carris Companies, the importance of the individual was not lost in the idea of shared ownership and the common good. It is one of the paradoxes of group life that:

> The only way for a group to become a group is for its members to express their individuality and to work on developing it as fully as possible and that the only way for individuals to become more fully individualised is for them to accept and develop more fully their connections to the group (Smith and Berg 1987: 99).

In the LTP, Bill Carris spoke similarly in terms of individual development and the common good. In terms of reward, he noted when 'workers and owners are the same people . . . the pie gets bigger' (Carris 1994: 6). For those trained in the typical analysis of the market economy with its ideas of scarcity and competitiveness, such paradoxical thinking may be offputting. Staying with the idea opens the possibility of the good of the whole—the common good. In a narrow sense, this returns us to the earlier discussion of employee ownership within the ideas presented above of Gates, Kelso and Rockefeller. In the broader sense, one may easily think of Senge's apt description of the hologram. 'Each shares responsibility for the whole, not just for his piece . . . Each represents the whole image from a different point of view' (Senge 1990: 212). This thought can be extended and linked directly to the ideas of participation and stakeholder citizenship within this chapter: 'We cannot truly participate in the whole of which we are a part, unless, we take responsibility for it' (Skolimowski 1994: 152).

Shifting perception slightly, one can also think of each individual as a whole who, in joining a group, becomes part of another whole. Ken Wilber defines these as holons: 'wholes that are parts of other wholes' (1995: 40).

Within the organisational context of this chapter, this brief exploration of holograms and holons is intended to broaden the discussion and move it to another level to incorporate interrelationship, interdependence and diffused responsibility as these relate to Carris Companies' efforts to practise their corporate governance.

8.4.5 Underpinnings of Carris corporate governance

Governance refers to the 'pervasive power, purpose and wealth of an organisation' in contrast to management, which is more 'defined, objective and neutral' (Block 1993: 6). The attempt to balance management and governance can be seen within the LTP:

> The company needs to be managed by professionally trained people . . . the key to effective management is a clear hierarchy . . . equality must be primary, and hierarchy secondary . . . if the goals and values are clear and fair, management style is given much more importance than it deserves . . . if everyone's interests are directed toward the same goal (profitability) and if we work at it, power and control will be diminishing issues as the organisation evolves (Carris 1994: 18-19).

In explaining the rationale for developing a corporate governance model, Bill Carris referred to current management practice with its large variety of corporate monarchies developing just too many ways to keep the 'profit pie . . . paid to workers as small as the market for jobs will allow' (Carris 1994: 4). Bill Carris redefined concepts of return on investment for the Carris Companies to include much more than financial capital. Essentially, within the movement towards employee ownership and governance, longevity became 'sweat equity'. This became a factor in accruing financial reward and having a say in the corporate future.

8.5 Corporate governance

8.5.1 Establishing corporate governance as the practice

Waddock distinguishes between various organisational stakeholders from the stance of relationship and responsibility, noting that in each instance the claim may be primary or secondary (Waddock 2002: 11). While Collins and Porras speak of the point of the role in corporate life of experimentation 'trial, error, opportunism, and quite literally—accident' for successful companies (1994: 9), Waddock, as noted above, suggested the advantages of taking a practice-based stakeholder view, in the sense of speaking directly in conversation—putting forward the questions rather than having formulae for all exigencies (2002: 12).

Though the basis of the structure of its governance is different, the *German Code of Corporate Governance* adds another dimension of practice—the need to live it—within daily and ordinary experience:

> Rules of governance must be actually lived. A culture of open discussion in the Management Board and Supervisory Board as well as between the organs is a decision success factor of corporate governance. Rules for corporate governance can then only develop positive effects if they are practised in earnest. Particular importance is thereby attached to active participation of all members of organs in the intended processes of information and decision. By establishing and supporting a culture of open discussion in and between the boards, it may be ensured that the tasks of management and supervision are fulfilled in a well-founded manner and after exploiting the expertise of all officers (Berlin Initiative Group 2000: 39).[5]

Waddock extends this idea into the infrastructure of the organisation in terms of its operations and 'lived set of principles':

> Companies . . . are responsible for monitoring the outcomes and impacts of their activities, and developing a 'lived' set of policies, procedures, and programs—practices—that help them achieve their vision and values as the following definition illustrates: Good corporate citizens articulate and live up to clear positive visions and core values, by treating well through operating policies and practices the entire range of stakeholders who have risked their capital in, have an interest in, or are linked to the firm through its primary and secondary impacts (Waddock 2001: 40).

This discussion extends the earlier one concerning holons and holograms. Together they show dimensions and patterns of change within stakeholder relationships at the core of the Carris Companies' six-year effort to move governance deep into the corporation's infrastructure. Bill Carris framed this aspect of stakeholder citizen rights and responsibilities in a very practical way:

> In a structure where all levels of employees have a voice in the distribution of wealth and the overall direction of the organisation and see it as a vehicle to help them personally develop, they should be very interested in keeping the organization healthy (Carris 1994: 3).

---

5 Employee representatives are members of the supervisory board. There is also the principle of codetermination within the *German Code*, which has a minimum of five workers on a worker's council at every plant.

8.5.2   *A first step in the practice of governance:*
The Long Term Plan *is shared with employees*

In December 1994 following the distribution of *The Long Term Plan* to the employees, there was a series of small group meetings to go over its content and to respond to questions. Following the vote of employees accepting the LTP, ideas on ownership culture (see Table 8.3) were presented to employees in the context of rights, benefits and responsibilities—stakeholder citizenship. In Table 8.3, showing stakeholder and citizenship relationships, personal rights and benefits are balanced by personal engagement in meeting responsibilities to the common good within the ownership culture.

Rights and benefits	*Responsibilities*
▪ Potential payback from stock ownership	▪ Work efficiently and up to full potential
▪ Board representation	▪ Actively pursue participation programmes
▪ Voting on key ownership decisions	
▪ Participatory decision-making	▪ Create company vision
▪ Relative job security: no sale of business	▪ Participate in company policy decisions
▪ Creates community: inclusion of all	▪ See the whole and act for the common good
▪ Open access to financial statements and other key information	
Ownership culture	

Table 8.3   *A Carris Companies transparency, Spring 1995*

Bill Carris and the change co-ordinator visited the sites to outline the work ahead: the creation of an ESOP advisory committee to design the ESOP and its allocation formula.

8.5.3   *The LTP steering committee*

In a memorandum on 28 April 1995 to the newly formed Carris ESOP Advisory Committee, in anticipation of that group's meeting on 11 and 12 May, Attorney Deborah Olson described the typical roles for the ESOP Advisory Committee, ESOP trustees, corporate board of directors, seller, Information Centrals/Participation Program (see Box 8.1) and, unique to the Carris Companies, the LTP Committee. For the purposes of this chapter, two roles at the first stage in the practice of corporate governance hold particular interest. Their descriptions were excerpted from the memorandum:

> The ESOP Advisory Committee reviews issues that arise in drafting an ESOP and potential changes in corporate governance and either approves, disapproves or proposes modifications to the corporate articles, bylaws, ESOP plan and trust; which it believes accommodate the needs of the employees, the Company and the IRS. They are advisors and do not have the final authority or the responsibility of trustees who serve as fiduciaries.

ATTORNEY DEBORAH GROBAN OLSON,* CAPITAL OWNERSHIP GROUP CHAIR, HAS specialised in employee ownership and equity compensation plans since 1981. The following extends the understanding of the ESOP structure and offers dimensions on shifting corporate stakeholder citizenship responsibility to employee-owners.

ESOP trustees

Small group of Carris employees who take on the chief responsibility of protecting the interests of the ESOP participants. They take on fiduciary responsibilities defined in ERISA . . . They will handle the voting on all pass-through issues, in a manner which protects the privacy of the participants. They will use their discretion to vote on those shareholder matters (if any) not passed through to the participants. They will hire the ESOP evaluation consultants. They will hire and supervise the ESOP record-keeper. They will deal with participant eligibility and distribution. They will interpret plan language when it is vague.

Corporate board of directors

These will be elected by all the shareholders . . . The composition of the board of directors [in the ESOP structure] . . . has not yet been decided . . . While the interests of the ESOP participants (represented by the ESOP trustees) and the shareholders (represented by the board of directors) may often be the same, they are not identical and may, at times, conflict.

Seller

In a company where a family is selling over a period of years to an ESOP that is intended ultimately to own 100% of the company, the seller has a complex role. He is leading a group that will ultimately replace him. He has to remove himself and his financial stake in the company in a manner which is fair to both his family and the ESOP.

He has to remove himself as leader in a time and manner that both he and the employees can accept. His job is to pass on leadership knowledge, skills and authority to others. His challenge is that in so doing, he loses the freedom of action he has exercised for many years, which has been successful for the company. No one wants the change in leadership to impede the company's flexibility or competitiveness. Yet group ownership by definition requires more group decision-making than individual ownership does, and is usually more cumbersome. Therefore serious thought must go into how decisions such as the purchase of companies will be handled as the company becomes majority employee-owned. These are the types of questions that the Long Term Planning Committee, . . . the ESOP Advisory Committee might tackle. The process of letting go is difficult for everyone. It can be made easier if: all the necessary parties are very conscious that it needs to be done; the mechanisms for shifting of control are discussed and clearly defined by everyone involved, so that important tasks do not fall through the cracks; the parties necessary for these discussions include, the seller, senior management and the board of directors. The Communication Centrals and Participation Program will be very important to this process as well. They will at least need to disseminate information that leadership tasks are changing hands. To the extent that these tasks go beyond senior management, they may also be involved in determining how these new tasks are handled.

Information Centrals/Participation Program

Currently, the Information Centrals provide a means for employees to ask and receive answers to questions about the ESOP process and the developments concerning implementation of the *Long Term Plan*. The company would like the Information Centrals to become a full employee participation program, created and organised by the employees. They were started as Information Centrals to allow each work group to create a participation system that is meaningful to its members. As participation bodies are formed in the workplace, representatives from those groups will meet periodically to determine ways in which participation concepts and methods may be shared at other locations or levels of the company. This may involve visiting or studying participation systems at other companies to get ideas.

* She can be reached at: Jackier, Gould, Bean, Upfal & Eizelman, PC1021 Nottingham Road, Grosse Pointe Park, MI 48230, USA; tel: (313) 331-7821; e-mail: dgo@esoplaw.com.

Box 8.1 *Committee roles, as described by Deborah Olson*

Source: Olson 1995: 2-5

> The *Long Term Plan* Committee is the keeper of the flame. It is the general oversight body for this whole process. Its job is to ensure that throughout the details of ESOP creation and of running the business we keep in mind the overall *Long Term Plan* goals. Its job is to consider the long-term implications of actions being proposed and/or taken by the Company or any of the above named bodies driving the process off course, its job is to steer it back on target. I know of no companies who have such a committee. So the Seller and the ESOP Advisory Committee must ask themselves: Who will serve as the *Long Term Plan* Committee? How will it be chosen? Who will have the power to change the *Long Term Plan*? (Olson 1995: 2, 5).

At the May meeting, the functions of the ESOP Advisory Committee were joined with those of the now renamed Long Term Plan Steering Committee (LTPSC). The LTPSC, comprising three senior managers and 13 employee representatives, was formed to design the ESOP. This action provided a dramatic shift in stakeholder citizen responsibility that was seen and experienced throughout the organisation. If this kind of enterprise level thinking-through had followed precedent, Bill Carris or Mike Curran (Carris Vice President) would have led the discussion with senior management. In the LTPSC, they were participants; the change co-ordinator chaired the meetings. Later, when Bill Carris and Mike Curran were asked their rationale for having the LTPSC design the ESOP, they each responded similarly. 'The employees needed to start somewhere and the design of the ESOP was as good a place as any.' The LTPSC provided a tangible way to prepare employees for the changing stakeholder relationships under way.

Of the 18 major decisions to be made, Bill Carris made two at the very outset:

- He continued the corporate tithe at 10% of profits (to which he tied the discounted sale price of the company).

- He chose a one-person one-vote structure[6] (rather than voting according to the percentage of stock owned) to foster equality and fairness throughout the corporation.

The other 16 decisions to structure the ESOP to meet legal and operational requirements were made by the LTPSC within the context of the overall ESOP design. The committee used consensus for its decision-making, reflecting the shifting stakeholder citizen relationship with the corporation and its emphasis on equality. Four ESOP allocation formulae, designed by the LTPSC to be non-hierarchical,[7] were later put to a vote of all employees. Employees, with one vote each—as shareholder citizens—chose a plan. In

6   One-person one-vote is also the structure within the Mondragon Co-operatives.
7   Full vesting takes seven years. The original formula called for 30% of the annual allocation to be evenly divided among all eligible employees; 20% was based on seniority; and 50% was based on salary up to a maximum of US$30,000 (adjusted annually for inflation). This was designed to reward those who had built the value of the company. During 1998, it became apparent that the formula was not supporting current company initiatives—it was not rewarding newer employees or contributing to retention efforts at a time when the companies were growing and hiring heavily. To resolve this dilemma, at its September 1998 meeting, the Corporate Steering Committee put forward revision plans for company vote. The voted allocation formula bases 90% on salary up to the US$30,000 maximum (in 2000: US$34,280 following the annual adjustments), and 10% on longevity. The change maintained the Carris ESOP's commitment to all employee-owners in an even-handed approach that contrasts sharply with compensation plans designed primarily to reward senior management.

May 1997, the ESOP Company of the Year announcement indicated that the Carris Companies' ESOP plan was the only one to be so designed (Horwedal 1997: 1).

Several elements are striking from an examination of meeting minutes. The first is the level of trust among those participating. When obstacles emerged and the consequences of certain problems could not be foreseen, such as when the discounted price might have been a tax issue, Bill Carris suggested the need to 'do the next right thing'.

Two elements were chosen as priorities from the very beginning of the process: trust and level of participation. Trust was emphasised in the LTP as an ethical and personal value. 'Trust is important enough to warrant working on it from both a formal, organisational level (i.e. classes, workshops, etc.) as well as on a personal basis' (Carris 1994: 11). 'Trust is the willingness to assume risk; behavioural trust is the assuming of risk' (Mayer *et al.* 1995: 724). Trust was seen as a key element for engaging participation to provide for shifting stakeholder citizen relationships. Bill Carris knew that employees trusted him. Many recognised that the design of the transfer reflected his real trust in them. Early in the process, seeing that a large number of future employee-owners were not as comfortable with risk as his experience allowed him to be, he knew it would be up to him to shape a way that would build trust and increase confidence. This is the kind of organisational 'commitment with integrity' that Waddock (2002: 172) used to exemplify 'inspiring people' in the clear contribution to something 'bigger than oneself' and to the employees' wellbeing over the long term.

The LTPSC consensually decided to have one elected representative for every 50 employees with a three-year term elected by local site. This was an important step for the success of the ESOP because of the relationship between increasing the level of participation of corporate citizens to the success of ESOPs (Marens *et al.* 1999). The decision also provided fair and predictable representation within the practice of governance and provided a tangible example of Bill Carris's intent to share stakeholder citizen responsibility with the employees. In *The Long Term Plan*, he wrote of the importance of employee participation to sound corporate functioning:

> Companies that take advantage of the intelligence and ideas of all their employees will be much more successful than those that rely on a few people to lead. In conventional companies, it is up to the leaders (managers) to both generate the information needed to make changes and then to come up with the ideas for making improvements. The process may involve moving information up and down several layers of the organization, slowing the process of decision-making considerably. Companies can no longer afford to be so limited. Employees are the best and most timely source of information, so this power should be utilized. The most effective organizations are those that strive to find ways to generate and process this knowledge in practical, efficient ways. This will happen when employees are owners and we move away from 'monarch-type' leadership to where everyone *participates* in decision-making. A structure for this to work still needs to be defined . . . The winners of the next decade will be those companies who have more people processing more information and making decisions faster. These will be the companies that stay ahead of the market (Carris 1994: 5, 7; emphasis original).

As a way of moving the cultural change forward as well as deeper into the organisation, it was decided to hold the September LTPSC meeting concurrent with the semi-annual managers' meeting at corporate headquarters in Rutland (11, 12, 13 September 1996).

Professor Emeritus Louis B. (By) Barnes (Harvard Business School) was invited to give a workshop on trust and to facilitate part of the meeting. A dramatic outcome of that meeting was arrived at consensually. The LTPSC joined with the management group (senior and site managers) to form the new Corporate Steering Committee (CSC). This was the second time in the Carris Companies' practice of governance that two stakeholder groups changed their relationship to each other (see the first above in the work of the LTPSC). This change increased not only the span of the work but the boundaries of relationships to do the work (for boundary-spanning functions, see Waddock 2002: 14).

8.5.4 Corporate Steering Committee

8.5.4.1 Second meeting: 23–24 January 1997

Corporate Steering Committee members, recognising the shifting stakeholder citizen relationships under way, took the following actions:

- Adopted the mission statement with community principles, corporate purpose and company goal for prominent posting at every location (see Box 8.2)

- Noted that the statements reflected the process of change to employee ownership and governance within a balanced perspective between stakeholder citizenship rights and responsibilities and the individual and group

8.5.4.2 Third meeting: 14–15 May 1997

Discussion involved several matters reflective of the shift in stakeholder citizenship responsibilities from Bill Carris and management to the Corporate Steering Committee:

- The CSC learned that the Carris Companies were the recipients of the ESOP Association's Annual Award and that involving the LTPSC in the ESOP design was one factor making it unique.

- The question was raised, 'What does it mean for employee-owners to own 20% of the company?'

- Several stakeholder questions were brought forward. These involved hiring practices, avoiding waste and what it meant to be an employee representative on the CSC. Employees wanted to know more about was happening at the corporate level.

- The CSC recognised that the stock transfer rate needed to be slowed. Per person limits within Section 415 of the federal income tax code were moving long-term employees' retirement and ESOP benefits into an excess benefits category with 401K contributions being returned.

- Grants and gifts distribution involved site employee committees.[8] Bill Carris noted that the idea of distribution of the wealth of the corporation was basic to

8 One of the few tenets within the LTP that did not receive universal acceptance was the goal for a tithe of 10% (currently at 7.5%) of profits to be given to non-profit organisations outside the

CARRIS COMMUNITY OF COMPANIES MISSION
to improve the quality of life for our growing corporate community

Community can be described as a group of people who are committed to a common purpose, depend on one another, make decisions together, and identify themselves as part of something larger than the sum of their individual relationships. They make a long-term commitment to their own wellbeing, the wellbeing of others in the community, and the health and vitality of the community itself.

Community principles

Trust. Trust is the foundation of positive human interaction. Without trust, we will be working at cross-purposes. Trust has two basic components: predictability (constancy) and caring. To earn and keep trust takes a great deal of hard work and courage, but the rewards will exceed this effort in the form of satisfaction and performance of the individual and corporate community.

Individuality. Respect for individuals is a cornerstone of our community. We can achieve the highest quality of life for our community members when we promote and encourage that individuals have freedom and take responsibility for their behaviour and results in the community.

Integrity. A respectful, trusting community requires that we be truthful and honest in our dealings with ourselves, each other and those outside our community.

Growth. We strive to use personal and corporate development as a way to improve the community for all of our members. Each of us has the responsibility to better our own lives and those within and outside our community. Growth is desirable in order to include more people in our corporate community.

Corporate purpose

Our corporate community has to be profitable and grow in order to achieve our mission. Profit is what sustains us and allows us to achieve our personal and our community's higher goals. This will be realised through providing quality products and services, which meet or exceed customer expectations.

Company goal

To change a job, a workplace, a company, to a vocation, an extended family, a community. We can work towards achieving these lofty goals by being honest, open-minded and willing. We will continuously strive for these elusive ideals. In the end, each of us is ultimately responsible for transforming these principles into workplace behaviour.

Box 8.2 *Statement adopted by the Corporate Steering Committee, January 1997*

the idea of ownership. It was important for employees to be a part of that process.

▪ Decision-making strategies. There was discussion regarding the decision-making strategies within the group and the time involved in deriving a consensus.

8.5.4.3 Fourth Meeting: 10–11 September 1997

Months later at their September 1997 meeting, Gregory Zlevor[9] worked with the CSC:

▪ To develop procedures for polling, voting or consensus for decision-making.

▪ A system was developed for flow of the agendas for CSC meetings. Each work group would be able to provide input as well feedback to an agenda being brought forward to the CSC. Criteria were established to review the agenda at the start of every CSC meeting to allow for items more appropriately addressed at a given site to be removed. This system, in conjunction with the CSC representation structure, provided every employee with a voice for input and for feedback within the practice of governance.

Bill Carris brought forward a discussion of a possible incentive compensation programme. There was extensive discussion of pros and cons. Consensus was reached that that the incentive programme should be tried on a small scale in locations where measures were in place (January 1998).

8.5.4.4 1998–99 meetings

With its process of agenda building and feedback to employees, the practice of governance within the Corporate Steering Committee had matured. Matters affecting stakeholder citizens within the company began to come forward within the agenda-building process; many of these at the outset related to human resources/personnel functions. Some were delegated to groups for additional research:

▪ Compensation: delegated to a committee for extended discussion

▪ Increasing participation

company. Some felt the percentage was too high while others felt such gifts should be tied to activities that benefited employees more directly. Requests for Carris Foundation donations and grants had traditionally been made directly to Bill Carris and some continue to go directly to him. In early 1996, reflecting the increasing portion of employee ownership and as a means of involving all levels of the Carris Companies, a formula was developed to allocate to each site a per capita ratio of 3.75% of annual profits. Each site formed a Charitable Giving Committee comprised of employee-owner representatives. Requests from non-profits are brought to the site Charitable Giving Committee, through site employee-owners, who in several instances also deliver the cheque. In developing the programme, it was recognised there might be some controversy about the causes supported. Local committees developed their own guidelines to meet Carris Foundation requirements, which are minimal: the request must be for more than US$100 from a recognised 501 charity. Corporate does not approve the requests—it takes care of the paperwork.

9   Greg Zlevor is founder of Westwood International, a consulting firm dedicated to process consulting and cultural change.

- Vermont Tubbs relocation to its new 1.2 hectare facility

- Closing on the purchase of a Brookfield, Ohio, reel company and Groggins Plastics

- Initiative into Mexico

- Healthcare costs (March 1998). A representative from the firm administering healthcare was present to go over the costs and options for the company. There was extended discussion about what the companies could do to reduce the costs of their self-insured healthcare insurance plan.

- At each meeting people remarked on the growing interest in the corporate and site reports. Participants saw these as directly related to the idea of 'teaching employees the business'. Many questions were raised about the strategic planning process and production.

- Information was made available regarding the change of company banks, international sales and a report of the compensation committee.

- Bill Carris put the question forward for discussion, 'At what point should the company have an employee on the board of directors?' That question led to an extended discussion on employees' roles in decision-making. A consensus evolved that the practice of governance should move forward more quickly to involve employees in decision-making.

- Health Care Insurance Task Force. Following up on the earlier discussion of dealing with healthcare insurance costs, it was decided to form a task force to research the matter and to develop recommendations for CSC deliberation

8.5.4.5 CSC 2000 meetings: defining ownership rights, responsibilities, risk and rewards

During the Health Care Insurance Task Force's work, it was frequently mentioned that the level of direct employee involvement was a real sign of how the firm was changing—practising governance. Up until the formation of the Task Force, Bill Carris, Mike Curran and Karin McGrath (Human Resources Director/Change Co-ordinator) would have worked on the changes. During 1999 and 2000, the human resources department had expanded its personnel at the corporate and site level partly because of company growth and partly to facilitate the change. The increased staff was seen as basic to increasing employee participation and direct involvement in the cultural and corporate changes under way in the process of becoming employee-owned and -governed. Human resources took on a leadership role in working with employees to frame the changes being undertaken by the firm and 'making meaning' for training and participative activities.

One of the ways that the firm brought the practice of governance into everyday life and a 'community of practice' was through the introduction of 'Lean Manufacturing'[10] to

---

10 Lean Manufacturing is the programme initiated by Toyota and developed at the University of Kentucky. An essential component is management's role in mobilising and pulling together the intellectual resources of all employees within the pull of serving the customer.

selected areas in the companies. This effort joined participation to manufacturing productivity, the 'common work'. The 'Lean' programme was one of the major ways that the Carris Companies implemented the strategic directive to 'teach employees the business'.

The CSC meetings in 2000 reflected dynamic change in stakeholder relationship. By year-end, a new compensation plan was rolled out, surveys concerning ownership culture were conducted and analysed and most of the employees in the Carris Companies had participated in a workshop presented by Ownership Associates (OA).[11] All of this had been done under the CSC's delegated authority.

In the following segment a few excerpts and comments are quoted from the Ownership Associates workshop at CSC meetings. It becomes quite clear that change in stakeholder citizen relationship was being undertaken in a very dynamic way and balance among components was key to success.

In 'Building an Ownership Culture' OA explained to the CSC that balance is key in implementing ownership values. For example, organisational life deals with rights and responsibilities (i.e. between the membership and people issues), while economic life deals with risks and rewards (business and money issues). This Powerpoint presentation used scales of justice to reflect the balance between rights and responsibilities, and risks and rewards:

Organisational (social)

Rights	Scale	Responsibilities
Voice	Social	Recognising expertise
Influence	Fairness	Commitment

Economic (business)

Risks	Scale	Rewards
Innovation	Economic	Fair bonus
Investment	Fairness	Economic

OA noted that, as rights areas increase, more responsibility needs to be expressed in the following areas: decision-making, information and learning, organisational fairness, accountability, work, pay, and entrepreneurship. Each employee-owner is responsible for learning and being accountable. 'You have the rights to have the rewards of ownership; there is some risk—your retirement is tied up in the company.'

---

11 Ownership Associates is an international consulting firm providing a range of services to corporations interested in broadening ownership and workplace participation opportunities for employees. It specialises in the design and implementation of education and training programmes concerned with ownership, participation and financial basics for employees, as well as in organisational development and corporate culture change initiatives. Chris Mackin, Loren Rodgers and Adria Scharf are working with Karin McGrath (Carris) on the decision-making governance model Frontiers and Boundaries. For additional information see www.ownershipassociates.com. Correspondence can be addressed to Ownership Associates, Inc., 6 University Road, Harvard Square, Cambridge, MA 02138, USA; tel: + 1617 868-4600; e-mail: oa@ownershipassociates.com.

Figure 8.2 graphically illustrates the need for balance in stakeholder relationships. Clarkson's observation about not favouring one group is apropos here (1995: 92). Note in the figure the management and employee-owners' attempts to 'have their cake and eat it, too' by excluding either rights (management excludes) or responsibilities (employee-owners exclude).

How do these ideas appear in the real world of companies trying to do this stuff?

	RIGHTS	RESPONSIBILITIES	RISKS	REWARDS
1. Management	−	+	+	−

Continental divide in the discussion of ownership

	RIGHTS	RESPONSIBILITIES	RISKS	REWARDS
2. Employee	+	−	−	+

1 = act like an owner—sit down and be quiet
2 = treat me like an owner and like an employee

Figure 8.2 **The continental divide: from notes and the OA Powerpoint slide**

OA recognised that, while there was a need to keep the scale balanced, some 'potholes' required continual attention. These four problem areas, if unavoidable, had to be counterbalanced to keep ownership culture balanced:

Heavy	Ownership type
Rights	Referendum
Rewards	Plundering
Risks	Scrooge
Responsibilities	Paternalistic

Chris Mackin said:

> Moving to employee ownership is an attempt to create a richer environment than that in which people are living. They need to have that taken seriously. The plant manager has more responsibility and training—he can't be successful unless he engages the mind and heart of shop floor people. The goal here: decision-making is to have a clear structure that is transparent to all involved.

Chris Mackin then presented a generic influence allocation chart (IAC; see Fig. 8.3 on page 180 for a Carris chart) noting the nature of roles with 22 generic organisational decisions presented. Bill Carris said:

> Over the next few years we have to do the constitutional stuff. This group will be the drafter for the constitution—this committee will make those decisions

just as the LTPSC made the decisions for the ESOP. Here is the template (the IAC) of the way to go about it. We would like to have people involved in it. It is important that we recognise this and ultimately how these decisions are made. The summation sometimes after the CSC meeting is blurt and duck. This template can change this. I think each individual site will have its way of doing this—coaching basketball vs. track team. Before this committee gets to 60 to 70 we need a constitution as to how it will run. I want to get people involved. We may need over the next few months to establish our own 22 items . . . This is a great learning process. We need to start learning our role.

This practice of governance seeks to make transparent how decisions are made within the company so that every individual knows the rights and responsibilities within the process at every step of the way.

8.5.5 Frontiers and boundaries by ownership associates at the CSC meetings: September 2000 and March 2001

Bill Carris pointed out:

This is the first real step toward codifying how decisions are brought to this group and from this group. This will ultimately say how we are going to do things. This is about governance. When we are satisfied with this then we can go to the sites with it. We are experimenting with all of this, developing a model. This is a different project than most businesses go through. The constitution metaphor is an important one. We want as much consensus as possible.

Chris Mackin began the next segment of the session framing the conversation:

Ownership implies power held by one person. How does a company owned by more than one person work? If Carris workers are like other workers and ownership means we have say, what is it that we have a say over?

He posted a standard list of 22 corporate decisions and the manner in which they are allocated in most companies. He added to the board of directors and management, employee participation and work teams and re-sorted the decisions (Fig. 8.3 is a Carris version with 38 decisions).

Groups like this as standing committees might make some decisions, and there may be some task forces for specific issues . . . The more general point is: how do you make ownership real? You need to get specific about what decisions are. The people you think might be most threatened by such are management. When they look at the whole picture, they say, 'Wouldn't that make life easier? I wouldn't have to do housekeeping or people management.' What this speaks to is one of the problems with speaking emotionally and rhetorically. Ownership is such an unspecific idea. Managers need a zone of safety. This model tries to make clear where the boundaries are; how ownership expectations can be managed. If I know that marketing is a green zone decision and my call, I am more comfortable in getting input. One of the challenges in creating an employee-owned company is making clear where the fences are . . . Setting and moving constitutional boundaries gets to this point. The constitutionality needs rules that are possible to change. It can't be easy but it has to be possible.

The decision at the end of the September meeting was made to go forward. At the beginning of the March 2001 CSC meeting, Karin McGrath provided a status report on the work done on governance in between CSC meetings:

> In preparation for this week's meeting, there was a meeting last week of the February Task Force with Ownership Associates. CSC representatives, Mike Curran, Bill Carris and I worked with OA to come up with a provisional influence allocation chart similar to the one that we looked at during the last CSC meeting. The Task Force took a look at OA's generic chart, and developed two charts: pre-ESOP and a present one for decision-making. The CSC will look at them in the next few days. We have a goal to set up a Corporate Governance Task Force and we have some suggestions as to how to do that. JF[12] will be staff to the Governance Task Force. Bill Carris, Mike Curran and I will also be part of it. The Governance Task Force will be responsible to work with the site that we have already picked as a pilot site to work through the influence allocation chart from a local point of view. North Carolina has a lot of history within the company. Dale Clary, the manager has been in place since the site's beginning. There are some obstacles for the site to work through in developing the chart. It is a bilingual site and it is among our larger sites. We felt it would be easier than OH, which had volunteered to be a pilot site. We thought Dwight Harder site manager in California might have volunteered. OA will work with North Carolina in the development of its site influence allocation chart. There will be charts to outline the day-to-day decisions to be made corporately and at the site. The (Corporate) Governance Task Force will work with the CSC to develop a constitution over the next few years.

Bill Carris added:

> This influence allocation chart will tell us who has the authority for most of the decisions. We've been asked about the hows of decision-making a great deal over the past few years. The chart will give us more structure than we have had. It should make life simpler and clearer for people.

Over the next few hours, issues were discussed as well as where decisions concerning them should be made. The context involved changing stakeholder citizenship rights and responsibilities in the Carris Companies. After one year, every employee becomes a shareholder (though unvested for seven years). Figure 8.3 was developed during the meeting to reflect the present decision-making structure within the Carris Companies. Each shade reflects a different group of decision-makers. The numbered items are issues to be addressed within most organisations and these were specifically addressed at the CSC meeting.

In addition to work on the present, Bill Carris looked at the near-term and future decision-making within the company. Please note that the charts are working items. (The numbers in Fig. 8.4 are in the opposite order from Fig. 8.3. In Fig. 8.3, 1, the Fate of the Company is 38 in Fig. 8.4) Of great interest to those present and the Governance Committee was the fact that Bill Carris's segment involving employees (the black segment) was larger than the whole CSC had foreseen. The shift in ownership responsibilities from Bill Carris to the employees became real in the conversation. At the Governance Com-

---

12 Carris employees named in the chapter are senior or site management or they have published a public article.

THE PRESENT AT CCC*

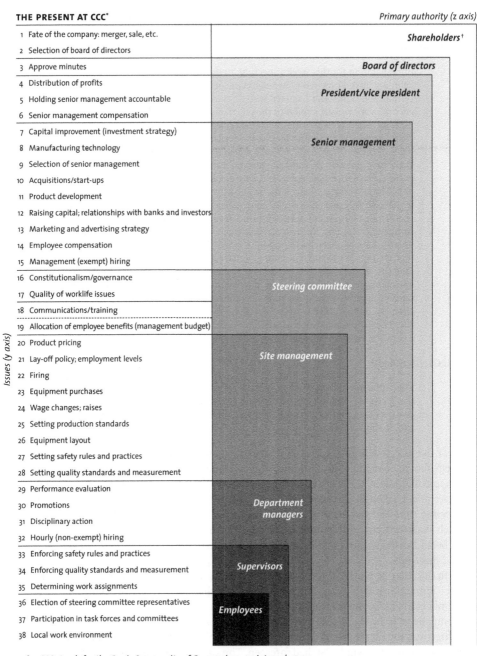

Primary authority (z axis)

1 Fate of the company: merger, sale, etc.
2 Selection of board of directors
Shareholders†

3 Approve minutes
Board of directors

4 Distribution of profits
5 Holding senior management accountable
6 Senior management compensation
President/vice president

7 Capital improvement (investment strategy)
8 Manufacturing technology
9 Selection of senior management
10 Acquisitions/start-ups
11 Product development
12 Raising capital; relationships with banks and investors
13 Marketing and advertising strategy
14 Employee compensation
15 Management (exempt) hiring
Senior management

16 Constitutionalism/governance
17 Quality of worklife issues
18 Communications/training
Steering committee

19 Allocation of employee benefits (management budget)
20 Product pricing
21 Lay-off policy; employment levels
22 Firing
23 Equipment purchases
24 Wage changes; raises
25 Setting production standards
26 Equipment layout
27 Setting safety rules and practices
28 Setting quality standards and measurement
Site management

29 Performance evaluation
30 Promotions
31 Disciplinary action
32 Hourly (non-exempt) hiring
Department managers

33 Enforcing safety rules and practices
34 Enforcing quality standards and measurement
35 Determining work assignments
Supervisors

36 Election of steering committee representatives
37 Participation in task forces and committees
38 Local work environment
Employees

Issues (y axis)

* CCC stands for the Carris Community of Companies—an internal name.
† Shareholders include the Carris family and the ESOP.

Figure 8.3 ***Carris Corporate Influence Allocation Chart developed at the March 2001 CSC meeting***

BILL CARRIS'S NEAR-TERM VISION FOR CCC*

38 Fate of the company: merger, sale, etc.	*Shareholders†*
37 Selection of board of directors	
36 Senior management compensation	*Board of directors*
35 Holding senior management accountable	
34 Approve minutes	
33 Distribution of profits	*Senior management*
32 Capital improvement (investment strategy)	
31 Manufacturing technology	
30 Selection of senior management	
29 Acquisitions/start-ups	
28 Product development	
27 Raising capital; relationships with banks and investors	
26 Employee compensation	
25 Marketing and advertising strategy	
24 Management (exempt) hiring	
23 Constitutionalism/governance	*Steering committee*
22 Quality of worklife issues	
21 Communications/training	
20 Allocation of employee benefits (management budget)	
19 Product pricing	*Site management*
18 Lay-off policy; employment levels	
17 Firing	*Department managers*
16 Equipment purchases	
15 Promotions	
14 Setting production standards	*Supervisors‡*
13 Equipment layout	
12 Setting safety rules and practices	
11 Setting quality standards and measurement	
10 Wage changes; raises	
9 Performance evaluation	
8 Disciplinary action	
7 Hourly (non-exempt) hiring	*Employees*
6 Enforcing safety rules and practices	
5 Enforcing quality standards and measurement	
4 Determining work assignments	
3 Election of steering committee representatives	
2 Participation in task forces and committees	
1 Local work environment	

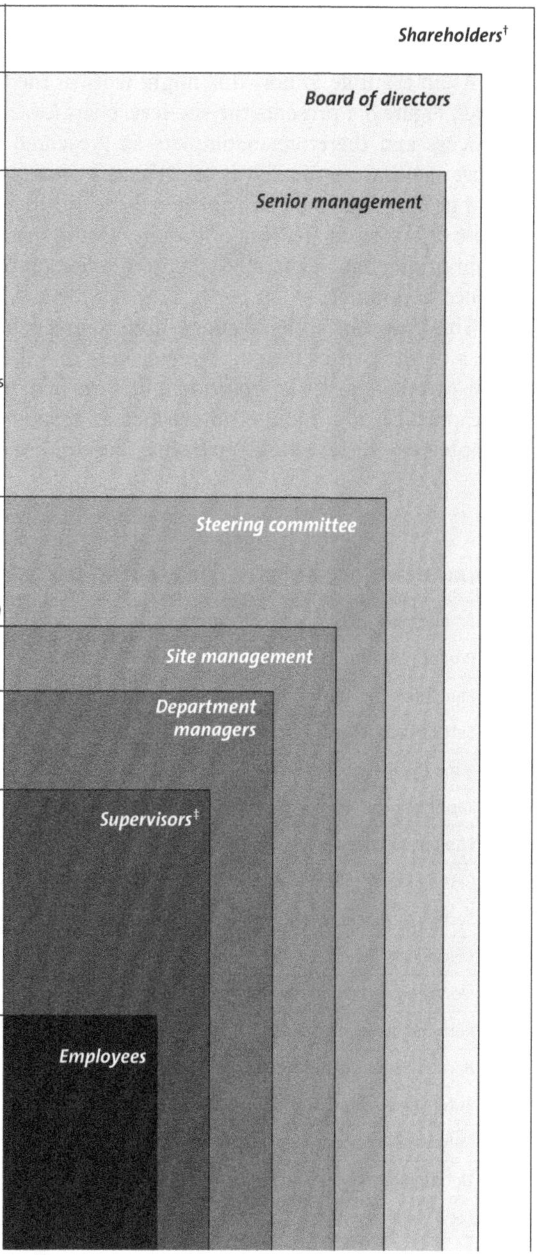

* CCC stands for the Carris Community of Companies—an internal name.
† Shareholders include the Carris family and the ESOP.   ‡ These can be combined where appropriate.

Figure 8.4 ***Bill Carris's Influence Allocation Chart developed at the March 2001 CSC meeting***

mittee Meeting in August 2001, Bill Carris noted that he would be very willing to survey the employees to see where they would like to see decisions made. He offered to work with OA to ensure that these 38 items are valid items for the Carris Companies.

As an example of how this might work at the local level in contrast to the corporate level, Figure 8.5 presents the site-level chart for Carris North Carolina. This work was in process and therefore incomplete as presented in this chapter. The North Carolina Governance Committee was selected as a prototype group to work through those items and groups that could be considered specific to a local site. Members of the committee were drawn from all areas of the site. Doing the IAC and the supporting discussion for each of the items generated intense interest on the part of the members of the Governance Committee.

This group also offered suggestions to make the process smoother. There was awareness on the part of the employee-owners that they were engaged in conversations that most workers never approach in a lifetime of work. This may be a significant aspect of the practice of corporate governance as responsibilities shift from Bill Carris to the employees—as stakeholder citizens. The employees were directly involved in the practice

PRIMARY RESPONSIBILITY FOR MAKING DECISIONS

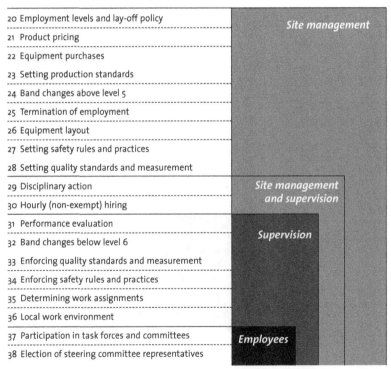

Figure 8.5 ***North Carolina Governance Committee Influence Allocation Chart, Spring 2001***

of governance. They were laying the groundwork for the system that will show everyone who makes a decision and responding to Bill Carris's invitation to be as involved as they want to be.

8.6 Conclusions

At the time of writing this chapter, William H. (Bill) Carris's vision of his company, as 100% employee-owned within an ESOP structure and 100% governed, was a work in process—a practice rather than a completed work. The Carris approach, with 100% employee governance, is unique. Deborah Olson and Ownership Associates, well-known consultants in the field of employee ownership, noted this fact to the Long-Term and Corporate Steering Committees.

Examples of the dimensions of the practice for changing stakeholder citizen relationships have been described. Among these were the Carris Companies' employee-owners' involvement in designing their own ESOP, distributing the wealth of their corporation, establishing the parameters for their healthcare insurance and—their current work—establishing the structure for their future governance and decision-making. The Carris Companies' six-year effort to move governance deep into the infrastructure as a practice reflects constancy and attention in involving their stakeholder citizens from throughout the corporation. Within the Corporate Steering Committee, management and elected representatives deliberate as colleagues for the common good. Equality and fairness, as essential values at the foundation of the corporate effort, are connected closely to the desire for transparency in decision-making. A goal is to have the stakeholder citizens understand their own rights and responsibilities and how decision-making works in the corporation. Profit-making as a goal within the firm has not been diminished by this effort. It has become another way to serve the common good.

The practice of governance led to increasing employee involvement. As employees were encouraged to be part of the building of a CSC agenda, the immediate results may have been a higher number of agenda items skewed in favour of those directly involving human resources and personnel related matters than might be expected later in the process. Until the parameters for the decision-making structure were fully in place, there were gaps and unknowns that needed to be resolved among management and employee-owners as to process and procedures. Distinctions between management and governance were not always clear. Implementing the practice of governance was a time-consuming, interactive activity. For managers accustomed to making decisions quickly, there were points in the process when the practice of governance was perceived as more of a hindrance than a help. As employees were involved in making decisions—for example, on healthcare insurance—it was recognised that more explanation and discussion were required beforehand but there was less justification and misunderstanding after the decision.

For CSC representatives, there was a real shift in stakeholder relationships with management. At CSC meetings, they were working together for the good of the whole. As comfort grew at meetings, there was more willingness to ask questions, confront and co-operate. Frequently the representatives and site managers travelled together to CSC meetings. They noted how many understandings were transferred and how trust and the relationship grew.

As shown throughout the chapter, taking a practice-based stakeholder view 'moves the conversation . . . toward the quality and nature of the relationships that companies develop with stakeholders and the assessment of the impacts of corporate activities on those stakeholders' (Waddock 2002: 9). This chapter examined the Carris Companies' practice of governance and the multifaceted process used to prepare the stakeholder citizens for their changing roles and relationships as shared owners. While it was too early in the process to assess impacts, the path of travel was clear.

THE DRIVERS OF STAKEHOLDER ENGAGEMENT

Reflections on the case of Royal Dutch/Shell*

Anne T. Lawrence

San Jose State University, USA

A small but significant number of corporations today are moving towards greater engagement with stakeholders. The term 'stakeholder' refers to persons and organisations that affect, or are affected by, a corporation's actions—that is, all those that have a stake in what a firm does. Stakeholders include such diverse groups as customers, employees, creditors, the media, governments, professional and trade associations, social and environmental activists, and non-governmental organisations (Freeman 1984; Post *et al.* 2002). In the stakeholder model of the firm, business organisations are seen as enmeshed in a network involving many participants, each of which shares to some degree in both the risks and rewards of the firm's activities (Donaldson and Preston 1995).

A venerable tradition in the study of business and society has sought to classify variations in the relationship between firms and their stakeholders. In an early and classic formulation, Preston and Post (1975) posited a progression of strategies of corporate response to public constituencies, ranging from reactive, to proactive, to interactive. Frederick (1978) described an evolution of firm behaviour from corporate social responsibility to corporate social responsiveness; he later (1986 and 1987) added corporate social rectitude—a stance in which corporate behaviour was deeply influenced by societal values. Logsdon and Yuthas (1997) classified companies according to their stage of moral development, with more ethically advanced firms actively promoting the welfare of stakeholders. More recently, theorists have proposed a stage model in which individual firms increase their level of engagement with stakeholders over time. In this view, in the

---

* I am grateful to Sandra Waddock, Ann Svendsen, Geoffrey Chandler, Gemma Crijns, Egbert Wesselink, and one anonymous reviewer for their comments on an earlier draft of this manuscript.

first stage, companies identify or map stakeholders and their interests; in the second stage, they attempt to manage stakeholders and the social issues of concern to them; and, in the third stage, they actively engage stakeholders for long-term value creation. Stakeholder engagement, in contrast to earlier stages, involves a stance of mutual responsibility, information-sharing, open and respectful dialogue, and an ongoing commitment to joint problem-solving (Svendsen 1998; Waddock 2002).

Although we now know a good deal about variations in the corporate–stakeholder relationship and the stages through which it may progress, we know less about the factors that drive firms forward through this process. Certainly, most firms are still in stages one or two; firms in stage three remain the exception. What external or internal factors increase the likelihood that corporations will embrace greater engagement with stakeholders? That is, what are the key drivers of stakeholder engagement? What are the necessary and sufficient conditions for companies and their stakeholders to attempt engagement? Once undertaken, what factors facilitate the success or failure of the process?

This chapter examines these questions in the context of a discussion of the experiences of a single firm: the multinational oil company Royal Dutch/Shell. Shell has been widely recognised by academics and practitioners alike as a leader in the process of stakeholder engagement. Since 1995, Shell has taken a series of interrelated initiatives to improve the company's social and environment performance, as well as to enhance the public's perception of its corporate citizenship. These initiatives have included a study of society's expectations; revision of the company's business principles; and adoption of a triple-bottom-line approach to auditing and verifying its social and environmental, as well as financial, performance. Shell has also entered into a series of interactive dialogues with a number of stakeholder organisations, including human rights groups, shareholder activists, community groups and environmentalists, on matters of mutual concern. Arguably, Shell is further along in the transition to full stakeholder engagement than any other major multinational corporation. The company is of theoretical interest not because it is typical but, on the contrary, precisely because it is not.

Over an 18-month period from 1999 to 2000, I was part of a team that conducted a study of the transformation of Shell, under the auspices of the Council on Ethics in Economics (CEE). Our immediate purpose was to produce a two-part multimedia case for use by business students and executives. As part of this process, we conducted videotaped interviews with around two dozen Shell executives, leaders of stakeholder organisations, consultants and academics in the United States, the United Kingdom, the Netherlands and Nigeria. These interviews ranged in duration from half an hour or so to several hours; they were professionally transcribed and reviewed for accuracy by the interviewees. We also reviewed a wide range of written and videotaped documentary evidence provided by Shell and its stakeholders. This effort produced two teaching cases, which were published online by the CEE under the titles 'Shell in Nigeria' and 'The Transformation of Shell'.[1]

1 Funding for the multimedia case project was provided by a grant from Shell to the Council on Ethics in Economics. Under the terms of agreement between the two organisations, Shell had the right to review for factual accuracy material provided by the company and its executives, but had no authority to edit the final cases. I am deeply grateful to my colleagues on this project, David C. Smith, Joel V. Copeland and John Drummond. However, the conclusions of this chapter, as well as any errors it contains, are solely my own. Quotations from the interviews are used here by permission of the Council on Ethics in Economics. The two multimedia

In this chapter, I draw on the interviews and documentary evidence collected during this project to reflect on Shell's experience and that of its stakeholders. My intention, in the tradition of inductive, grounded research, is to help build our theoretical understanding of the conditions that drive corporate–stakeholder engagement. My method, to the extent possible, is to allow the participants in the dialogue process to speak for themselves, to reveal the patterns of meaning by which they understood their own experiences. I focus, in particular, on the parties' **motivation** to seek engagement; their **goals** in the engagement process; the **organisational capacities** they employed; and the **dynamics** of effective dialogue. In constructing my argument, I draw mainly on one particular example of stakeholder engagement: Shell's productive ongoing dialogue with two human rights organisations, Amnesty International and Pax Christi International. I conclude with a discussion of the implications of the Shell case for stakeholder engagement theory.

9.1 Shell's crisis of reputation

In the mid-1990s, Shell faced a serious crisis of reputation. At the time, the Royal Dutch/Shell Group was the world's largest fully integrated petroleum company. 'Upstream', the conglomerate controlled oil and gas exploration and production; 'midstream', the pipelines and tankers that carried oil and gas; and 'downstream', the refining, marketing and distribution of the final product. The company also had interests in coal mining, forestry, chemicals and renewable energy. In all, the Anglo-Dutch conglomerate comprised over 2,000 separate entities, with exploration and production operations, refineries and marketing in scores of countries. Royal Dutch/Shell was, in both its ownership and scope, perhaps the world's most truly transnational corporation. In 1994, Royal Dutch/Shell made more money than any other company in the world, reporting annual profits of US$6.3 billion and, with 106,000 employees worldwide, had the largest workforce of any oil company.

The events that gave rise to the reputational crisis of this major global corporation have been extensively described elsewhere. Briefly, the key developments were these:

- **The Brent Spar incident.** The Brent Spar was an ageing oil storage buoy in the North Sea. In 1991, Shell took the Brent Spar out of service and began looking at options for disposal. In April 1995, after extensive study, Shell announced its intention to sink the Brent Spar in the Atlantic, and British authorities approved the plan. Some environmentalists expressed concern, however, that toxic residue in the Brent Spar's tanks could harm the marine environment. On 30 April activists from the environmental organisation Greenpeace boarded and occupied the abandoned buoy and remained there for three weeks. The Greenpeace occupation and resulting media coverage galvanised public opinion, especially in Europe. Government officials of Belgium, Denmark, Sweden, the Netherlands and Germany asked Shell to postpone sinking the Brent Spar, and a

cases produced by the project are available for classroom adoption and use, and may be previewed online at www.i-case.com.

consumer boycott gathered force, especially in Germany. On 20 June Shell abruptly changed course, announcing that it had decided to abandon its plan to sink the Brent Spar at sea and to look at various alternative methods of disposal.[2]

- **Human rights in Nigeria.** Just a few months later, the execution of Ken Saro-Wiwa and eight colleagues in Nigeria on 10 November 1995 led to further widespread public criticism of the beleaguered company. Saro-Wiwa was a leader of the Ogoni people of Nigeria and a charismatic environmental and human rights activist. In a series of campaigns, Saro-Wiwa had charged that that Shell's operations had despoiled the ecology of the Niger River delta, and that revenue-sharing practices that returned little to the people of the oil-producing regions were unjust. In 1995, the Nigerian military government had brought Saro-Wiwa and several colleagues to trial before a special tribunal on what many believed were trumped-up charges that he had ordered the murder of political opponents. In the wake of Saro-Wiwa's execution, environmentalists and human rights activists criticised Shell for failing to intervene with the authorities to stop the execution and called for an international boycott of Shell's gasoline and other products.[3]

In the wake of the Brent Spar incident and the Saro-Wiwa execution, Shell found itself the object of intense public scrutiny. Environmentalists, human rights activists and churches joined a chorus of criticism. Institutional shareholders in the UK, including public employee pension funds and religious organisations, called for reforms of the company's corporate governance. These campaigns against Shell interacted in a synergistic way to produce what many viewed as a profound challenge to the company's public image as a socially and environmentally responsible corporation. Shell was particularly vulnerable to attacks on its reputation because it marketed a well-known branded product—Shell gasoline sold under the familiar red and yellow seashell logo—in scores of countries. Consumers disappointed with Shell's environmental or human rights performance or responsiveness to its stakeholders could often easily switch allegiance to another brand of gasoline.

9.2 Changing course

Coincidentally, at the time that these campaigns against Shell erupted, a managed internal change process was already under way at the company. In 1994, the chairman of Shell's committee of managing directors (CMD), Cor Herkströter, had initiated a review

2   These events are further documented in 'The Transformation of Shell' (Lawrence 2000b). See also: 'The Brent Spar Incident: A Shell of a Mess', Harvard Business School Case 9-597-013 (1996), and 'Shell, Greenpeace, and Brent Spar', Stanford University Graduate School of Business Case P-19 (September 1995).

3   These incidents are further documented in 'Shell in Nigeria' (Lawrence 2000a). See also: 'Royal Dutch/Shell in Nigeria (A) and (B)', Harvard Business School Cases N9-399-126 and N9-399-127 (1999).

of the firm's organisational structure by management consultants McKinsey & Company, aimed at improving the company's financial performance relative to its competitors. Although Shell was highly profitable, other big oil companies—including rivals British Petroleum, Exxon and Mobil—enjoyed significantly higher returns on capital. In March 1995, Shell concluded the first phase of its internal review by announcing a plan to abandon its complex matrix structure and to reorganise into five worldwide business units. This restructuring was intended to enable the company to focus more efficiently on the needs of its business and retail customers.

Even as Shell announced its intended organisational redesign, however, external pressures on the company had the effect of shifting the focus of the change process to the 'softer' issues of the company's reputation and relations with stakeholders. In a series of executive retreats held in late 1995 and early 1996, consultants retained by Shell asked participants to develop a 'diagnosis of current reality' to serve as a starting point for further changes aimed at improving corporate profitability. To the apparent surprise of both the consultants and Shell's top leaders, discussion began to shift from strictly business matters to the company's social and environmental performance. Many participants at the retreats wanted to talk not about profitability but about the fact that Shell was being pilloried in the press for its failures of social and environmental responsibility.

Mark Moody-Stuart, then a managing director, framed Shell's problem as the need for a new mind-set that paid greater attention to societal expectations. One of the consultants present, Philip H. Mirvis, later observed:

> Mark Moody-Stuart should be credited with the intellectual framing of this. Shell was an engineering-type company . . . a very technical organisation and essentially a very bureaucratic organisation . . . What [Moody-Stuart] said was that the technical mind-set, our rational, logical approach, is blinding us to a world out there of human rights activists, of environmentalists, of governments with different wants and interests and changing customer tastes, expectations of the public, etc. We are so internally focused, so technical, that we are missing a whole set of opportunities and a whole new reality out there . . . We are not talking any more about a structural change in the organisation; we are not even talking about new leadership per se. We are talking about a new Shell.[4]

The crucial insight, for Shell's leaders, was that meeting the expectations of the 'world out there' was a *business* imperative. The company's reputation was a valuable asset that had to be managed, along with other commercial risks and opportunities. Moody-Stuart, who succeeded Herkströter as chairman of the CMD, described the company's motivation for moving towards greater interaction with civil society:

> [C]ommunication between ourselves and society [was] obviously not optimum, and in some areas it plainly wasn't working. Now, if that is the situation, it is a major situation that needs to be addressed, because, if an organisation is not in communication with society, it is not in communication with its customers. It is a commercial matter, because society is your customers. It is not

4   All quotations, unless otherwise noted, are taken from the interviews conducted for the multimedia cases. Full transcripts of all interviews are included with the cases and are available online.

> a soft and woolly thing, because society is what we depend on for our living. So we had better be in line with its wishes, its desires, its aspirations, its dreams and so on.

Later, contrasting the social and commercial obligations of the company, he underscored this point:

> You can't divorce the two. People sometimes try to do that. They say, all this societal stuff is woolly, we should stick to commerce. The two are absolutely linked . . . These soft issues are really business issues, because we are part of society, and members of society are our customers. So, our impact on society really matters commercially.

Once the CMD became convinced of this critical point—that meeting society's expectations was a *business* necessity—the directors undertook a series of interrelated initiatives to improve the public's perception of its corporate citizenship. Shell commissioned a major survey to provide its leaders with information about society's changing expectations in all regions of the world in which it did business. It established a board-level committee, allocated additional staff and resources to its external affairs department, and began exploring other ways to improve its social and environmental performance to meet its customers' expectations.

9.3 Seizing an opportunity

As Shell struggled to understand and respond to society's changing expectations, several non-governmental organisations (NGOs) recognised Shell's crisis as an opportunity to pursue their own objectives.

In December 1995, in the wake of Saro-Wiwa's execution, Pax Christi International (PCI)—a Catholic lay organisation devoted to promoting world peace, human rights and economic justice—wrote to Shell asking the company to speak out on human rights in Nigeria. Herkströter replied, responding to specific points and inviting the NGO to engage in further discussion. Independently, Amnesty International (AI) branches in both the United Kingdom and the Netherlands had also approached Shell to express concerns about Shell's actions in Nigeria. At the time, Amnesty International was probably the best-known human rights organisation in the world, with over a million members internationally. Herkströter met with AI representatives in January 1996 and indicated that the company was prepared to review its business principles. When the relevant leaders of the two NGOs discovered they were pursuing a similar agenda, they decided to draft a joint memorandum to Shell. Over the following three years, these two organisations engaged jointly in an ongoing discussion with Shell, involving face-to-face meetings, an exchange of position papers and debate in public forums.

Both Amnesty International and Pax Christi had recently developed an interest in working directly with the business community to promote human rights. Traditionally, these organisations had focused on pressuring governments—through grass-roots campaigns and other methods—to uphold their espoused commitments to the Universal Declaration of Human Rights and other international covenants. Many people in both organisations were fundamentally hostile to the business community. In the 1990s, however, some activists within both NGOs had increasingly sought to work directly with multinational corporations to promote their objectives. In 1991, a group of individual members of Amnesty International–UK, most of whom had industry experience, formed an internal Business Group with the objective of encouraging companies to adopt human rights policies and practices. Geoffrey Chandler, a former Shell executive who had been instrumental in drafting Shell's first Statement of General Business Principles, became chair of the group.[5] Pax Christi had also begun work in this arena, with a department of economic relations undertaking various corporate initiatives.[6]

A core group of activists in Amnesty International and Pax Christi recognised that both protest and persuasion were necessary components of a successful strategy to influence corporate behaviour. Unlike governments—which were constrained to some degree by international human rights agreements they had signed—most corporations could not be *legally* compelled to support human rights, beyond compliance with the laws of the nations in which they operated. As Gemma Crijns, a staff member of Amnesty International in the Netherlands who was active in the dialogue with Shell, put it to us plainly: 'There is no law that says that companies have to be concerned about human rights.' Crijns was convinced that the activist campaigns against Shell had been critical to bringing the company to the table. She put it this way: 'It is more efficient if you work with a company that is in trouble . . . A kind of urgency . . . is very important in this work.'

At the same time, she believed 'that just organising demonstrations or shouting before the door' was insufficient. Her British colleague, Geoffrey Chandler, similarly observed:

> I think very strongly that protest raises an issue, [but] . . . it cannot win the argument. You can only win the argument by engagement and discussion . . . Protest has a role. Protest and engagement are essentially complementary . . . In the end, there is gain from protest, [and] there is gain from argument, as long as it is honest.

Dialogue, unlike protest, offered the NGOs an opportunity to engage Shell, as well as other companies, in an extended discussion of specific actions they might take to improve their human rights records. Chandler commented:

> Companies are not stupid. They are pragmatic. Once they had accepted the problem, and recognised in themselves that they were at fault, they then sat down and said, what do we do? So, we then began to discuss with them how they might incorporate human rights into their own principles.

---

5 Private correspondence with Geoffrey Chandler. The website of AI–UK's Business Group may be found at www.amnesty.org.uk/business.
6 The growing interest of human rights organisations in engaging multinational corporations in a discussion of their ethical obligations to uphold human rights is explored by Garth Meintjes (2000).

9.4 Risks and rewards

Engaging in an open, interactive dialogue carried risks and rewards for both Shell and its NGO stakeholders. In order for the participants to enter and to continue a dialogue, all parties had to perceive the balance between risk and reward as favourable.

For the company, dialogue offered the potential benefits of learning about society's expectations, drawing on outside expertise, generating creative solutions and achieving stakeholder support for implementing them. It also could potentially disarm or neutralise dangerous critics and improve its reputation for taking constructive action. When asked to describe the benefits of stakeholder engagement, Robin Aram, Shell's vice president for external relations and policy development, commented:

> If you anticipate, and you get into dialogue, and you listen more carefully to those signals, and you become engaged with people, then you will . . . learn a lot of things which you can apply more generally, you'll get closer to your customers, and indeed your business will do better.

The risk of *not* engaging stakeholders, Aram noted, was the converse: the company would fail to meet society's expectations, thereby undermining its licence to operate. 'If the company operates in a way that is not acceptable in the communities and the society in which it operates,' he commented, 'over the long term it would not be allowed to operate.' Of course, dialogue also carried the risk of public failure, loss of control and of raising expectations beyond what the company could deliver. Egbert Wesselink, an officer of Pax Christi Netherlands, expressed his understanding of Shell's risk this way:

> The moment you make a promise you will be attacked ten times harder: that is their [the company's] fear. They fear they will be attacked ten times harder when they promise something and do not do it, than when they have the same behaviour but have never spoken out that they will not do it.

On this point, Geoffrey Chandler added: 'An additional risk in engagement to companies is the degree of disclosure that NGOs demand [when] there is real engagement and, even more, when there is partnership in looking at a problem.'[7]

For their part, the human rights organisations were also acutely aware of the potential risks of a dialogue strategy. Wesselink told us that he had been strenuously criticised for talking with Shell, an organisation that many of his colleagues viewed as 'a symbol of what a multinational enterprise should not do'. Chandler, who organised a series of meetings in the United Kingdom to facilitate dialogue between NGOs and multinational corporations on the topic of human rights, reported that he had been 'vilified' by other activists who thought he was, in effect, consorting with the enemy. In Chandler's view, this criticism was unwarranted:

> The criticism comes from a very narrow focus . . . [from] NGOs who are ideologically opposed to what they call the capitalist system. They would say, you are getting into bed with the transnationals; this is insufferable. My reply is, if we achieve what they are after, which is to get a commitment to the Universal Declaration of Human Rights, . . . [we] are helping them in what they are doing.

---

7   Private correspondence with Geoffrey Chandler.

The NGOs also expressed concern that their names might be misused to give a kind of seal of approval to company action.

Amnesty International and Pax Christi, like many NGOs, are voluntary organisations that depend to a great extent on the financial support of their members. A tension exists in the rank-and-file between those who support engagement with multinational corporations and those who oppose it. In order for those leaders who favour engagement to maintain membership support, they must achieve measurable results. Crijns, for example, told us that she would have to withdraw from the dialogue process if it showed no progress.

> If there was only the dialogue for the dialogue, if you couldn't show to a member—because Amnesty is a membership organisation—that it is worthwhile to talk to a company, and you talk for a year or two years, and you don't see any worthwhile concrete improvement, you have to stop a dialogue.

The supporters of dialogue on both sides had to be able to show results: for Shell, benefits to the company's reputation; for the NGOs, a change in the company's human rights performance.

9.5 The dynamics of successful dialogue

Despite the potential risks, the dialogue between Shell and the two human rights organisations proceeded. The discussion focused on several issues. The two NGOs criticised the vagueness of Shell's Statement of General Business Principles (SGBP) and urged the company to revise them to incorporate explicit support for the Universal Declaration of Human Rights. They recommended that Shell should appoint a director for human rights and undertake independent auditing of its human rights practices. Other portions of the discussion focused specifically on the situation in Nigeria, including Shell's security practices, its relationship to the military authorities, and its role during and after Saro-Wiwa's trial.[8]

As the dialogue continued, Shell took a number of actions that were responsive to the NGOs' recommendations. For example, the company undertook a revision of the SGBP. In the revised principles, published in 1997, the company declared its support for 'fundamental human rights in line with the legitimate role of business'. The principles also clarified the company's stand on political activity. The earlier formulation, which emphasised abstention from politics, was replaced with language stating the company's intention to abstain from party politics, while emphasising its right and responsibility to make its position known to governments on matters affecting the company or its stakeholders. Shell also reviewed its rules of engagement for security personnel and made specific changes to bring them into compliance with United Nations standards. It also initiated independent auditing of its social and environmental performance.

---

8   Pax Christi International later published a collection of letters, position papers and other documents exchanged by Shell and the two NGOs during their dialogue (Pax Christi International 1998).

In other respects, in contrast, Shell did not act on the NGOs' recommendations. For example, the company did not explicitly endorse the Universal Declaration of Human Rights in its revised principles (although it did endorse them elsewhere). It declined to appoint a director of human rights, saying that its current governance procedures were sufficient.

What characteristics of the **dynamics** of this dialogue kept the process moving forward? I believe that four elements of this particular dialogue were critical to its success; I will call these elements affinity, legitimacy, trust and incrementalism.

One important success factor, in this instance, was a basic cultural **affinity** between the parties. Royal Dutch/Shell was, of course, an Anglo-Dutch firm. This particular dialogue took place between company representatives and the British and Dutch offices of the two NGOs. Amnesty International's chief spokesperson in these talks was Geoffrey Chandler, who, prior to heading up AI's Business Group in the United Kingdom, had been a Shell executive for over two decades. With experience in both the business and human rights communities, he proved extremely effective in bridging the gap between them. Crijns made the point that she felt it had been easier for AI to initiate dialogue in the Netherlands, with its low-hierarchy culture, than it would have been in some other nations:

> It is cultural. I think that the way that I can get in touch with companies here is possible because in Holland our relations are not very hierarchical. It is easy for me to get in touch with the people [corporate executives]. It is much more difficult for my colleagues in the US or in France, for instance. These are really cultural differences.

In short, it helped that at least some individuals on both sides felt reasonably comfortable talking with one another, either because of shared experiences and assumptions, or because of a low-hierarchy setting that put them on a more level playing field. Although they differed on many points, the two parties had enough in common that they were able to work together productively.

Both sides acknowledged the **legitimacy** of the other party and the integrity of its people. Chandler made this point this way:

> We are dealing with human beings here. We don't uniquely have the moral high ground. Shell can only survive as a commercial entity if it can recruit the most intelligent [people] who also have ideals and principles . . . I think we are dealing with people who are increasing [their] belief in these principles in order to survive in the critical world.

Later, he added, 'If one is negotiating with someone, I think you have to assume their integrity is as good as yours, until they prove otherwise.' Similarly, Shell implicitly seemed to acknowledge the legitimacy of Amnesty International and Pax Christi as representatives of a broader community of concern about human rights. The tone of the dialogue, throughout, was respectful.

Both sides in this dialogue demonstrated a willingness to keep talking, even when progress was slow or obstacles emerged. **Trust** had to be earned, as the result of an ongoing process of making and keeping commitments. Relationship building took time. Aram, who participated in many dialogues on Shell's behalf, commented:

> Trust is something that is crucial and takes time to be learned. That's why dialogue needs to be a sustained process. It needs give and take on both sides.

> There are risks. There are risks, and people get surprises along the way. I think the key thing is to recognise, as you go in to these processes, that there will be surprises, there will be disappointments, and to keep your eye on the long-term ball, and to keep the process going trust is the key. But trust takes a long time to develop, so stick at it.

The human rights activists we spoke with indicated that, as the conversation proceeded, their trust in the company's motives had been enhanced. Crijns stated:

> I have been dealing with Shell . . . [for] four or five years now. I do have a feeling that they really are trying to do it in the right way. Human rights never can be a core issue of a company . . . But I have a feeling that really they are working very hard to do it in [the] right way.

Wesselink of Pax Christi Netherlands similarly described his growing confidence in the process as he participated over time: 'Many people [in the human rights community] . . . said it [stakeholder dialogue] was only window dressing . . . They are fooling you. Well, we did not really get the impression that we were being fooled.'

A final success factor was that both sides seemed willing to accept **incremental progress** towards their goals. Neither side got everything it wanted. Both sides clearly felt, however, that they had met at least some of their objectives and that they could continue to build on these partial successes. Crijns told us that she felt that Shell's commitment to human rights in the revised SGBP was an important 'first step':

> Talking with a company about a code of conduct was new. Quite a lot of [activist] organisations do have the feeling that a [corporate] code of conduct, a piece of paper, is worthless. If there are human rights in them, or not, does not matter. If does not change anything . . . In a sense, I agree with them. But, knowing that human rights are a very alien issue for Shell and other companies, I feel as though we need a piece of paper in which the company itself says, 'we are concerned with human rights'. That would be a first step. Later on, we could come back to them and say, 'you said that you are concerned about human rights . . . Look at what you are doing.'

Both sides saw this dialogue as a first step, with others to follow.

Shell's dialogue with AI and PCI, described here, was only one of a great many initiatives taken by the company after 1995, including several extended dialogues with other stakeholder organisations. Of these, the human rights dialogue was widely viewed as one of the most successful. It is beyond the scope of this chapter to discuss Shell's other stakeholder initiatives. But this model, I believe, may help to illuminate failures as well as successes. A number of commentators have observed, for example, that Shell's efforts at dialogue in Nigeria itself were generally unproductive.[9] In contrast to the instance discussed here, Shell Nigeria and its Ogoni critics were separated by vast cultural differences, failed to acknowledge each other's legitimacy, seemed unwilling to accept incremental gains and (in the case of Saro-Wiwa's trial) faced enormous time pressures that prevented the gradual emergence of trust. In short, none of the dynamics of successful dialogue present here was operative in the Nigerian situation. A painful paradox is that dialogue seems most productive where the parties have much in common and plenty of

---

9 See, for example, the thoughtful analysis of Shell's continuing difficulties in Nigeria by David Wheeler and colleagues (2000).

time to talk; yet it may be most needed where the parties have little in common and face a difficult and urgent problem.

9.6 Drivers of engagement

Drawing theoretical conclusions from the particulars of a single case is inherently risky. Nevertheless, I will offer some modest conclusions about what Shell's dialogue with its human rights stakeholders reveals about the factors that drive forward the process of stakeholder engagement.

Stakeholder engagement is, at its core, a **relationship**. Dialogue is a multi-party event: the participation of one focal business organisation and at least one stakeholder organisation is necessary, by definition, to constitute engagement. Thus, any analysis that seeks to explain what drives engagement forward that examines only one side of the relationship—whether the corporation or the stakeholder—is necessarily incomplete. As the common expression goes, 'It takes two to tango.' In this instance, I suggest, both Shell and its human rights stakeholders possessed the **motivation** to engage one another in a dialogue, a **goal** that could only be met with the participation of the other party, and the **organisational capacity** to engage with each other. Moreover, the **dynamics** of the dialogue process itself contributed to its success. Table 9.1 summarises the motivation, goals and organisational capacities of the two parties to this particular dialogue.

	Company (Shell)	*Stakeholders (AI/PCI)*
Motivation	Reputational crisis; Shell perceives it is not meeting society's expectations.	Governmental campaigns, protest perceived as inadequate to change corporate behaviour
Goals	To improve corporate reputation; to earn licence to operate; to win approval of society	To change corporate behaviour; to obtain corporate support for human rights principles and practices
Organisational capacity	Managed change process; leaders committed to dialogue; well-funded department of external affairs	Economic relations units in place; experienced staff; core group of activists committed to dialogue

Table 9.1 *Corporate and stakeholder perceptions of the engagement process: Shell and human rights organisations*

9.6.1 Motivation

Shell, for its part, was motivated largely by a serious crisis of reputation, caused by strenuous public criticism of its behaviour by environmentalists, human rights activists and institutional shareholders. These groups had had considerable success in focusing negative media attention on the company. In a process of internal discussion, Shell leaders concluded that its reputation was a core commercial asset and that it needed to act assertively to better meet society's expectations. Understanding society's expectations required dialogue with stakeholders. The two NGOs, for their part, were motivated by a growing realisation that meeting their objective of promoting human rights required the active involvement of corporations. A strategy focused exclusively on pressuring governments to uphold their commitments under international law had proved insufficient. Moreover, in the NGOs' view, while protest might motivate companies to act, it was ultimately inadequate because it did not help them to understand what specific actions to take.

9.6.2 Goals

Shell, for its part, sought to understand and meet society's expectations. As a commercial organisation, the firm needed its customers' trust and confidence in order to market its products successfully. In short, it needed a licence to operate. It felt that by winning the support of legitimate representatives of stakeholder interests it could further this objective. In contrast, Amnesty International and Pax Christi wanted Shell to change its behaviour to better support human rights. They wanted the company to endorse the Universal Declaration of Human Rights, to make specific changes in the way it provided security for its overseas operations, and to undertake changes in its corporate governance and reporting to its stakeholders.

9.6.3 Organisational capacity

Each side had the organisational capacity to engage the other in a productive dialogue. At the time of its crisis of reputation, Shell, quite coincidentally, was involved in a managed change process focused on improving its bottom-line results. As managers involved in this process struggled to make sense of growing public criticism of the company, the organisational change initiative was, in effect, deflected from its original course and redirected to a goal other than the one for which it was intended. Moreover, Shell moved quickly to augment its organisational capacity to respond to stakeholders by allocating resources to its department of external affairs, by assigning top executives to reputation management, and by undertaking intensive environmental scanning initiatives. For their parts, both Amnesty International and Pax Christi had organisational units dedicated to business initiatives, and both had a core group of individuals committed to a corporate dialogue strategy and willing to assume the internal political risks it posed.

As is evident from Table 9.1, the stakeholder engagement process here was fundamentally **asymmetrical**: that is, the motivation, goals and organisational capacities of the two parties were very different. Yet they complemented each other in a way that made interaction attractive to both.

This case offers an opportunity for commentary on earlier theoretical work on collaborative partnerships. In a review of this literature, Wood and Gray (1991) defined collaboration as occurring 'when a group of autonomous stakeholders of a problem domain engage in an interactive process, using shared rules, norms, and structures, to act or decide on issues related to that domain'. This instance of stakeholder engagement may be considered collaborative to the extent that it did indeed constitute an interactive process among autonomous actors, with the aim of producing tangible results. Yet it was unlike a conventional collaboration in that the parties arguably were able (at least partially) to accomplish their objectives without ever accepting a common definition of the problem domain. To Shell, the problem was a faltering reputation; to the NGOs, the problem was corporate disregard for human rights. Prompting this dialogue was not a common problem but rather an interdependent set of problems: each side needed the other to advance its own agenda. In this respect, this case appears to confirm Logsdon's (1991) finding that collaborations are most likely to emerge where the parties perceive that their problems are both salient and interdependent. It is also consistent with Gray's (1989) conclusion that parties are most likely to collaborate when they see no other way to solve an intractable problem.

9.6.4 Process dynamics

Finally, the process of dialogue itself, in this instance, favoured success in several respects. The parties to the dialogue shared certain common cultural values and assumptions. They were committed to taking the time necessary to build a relationship of trust. Both accepted incremental progress as positive and were able to make enough gains to satisfy the potential critics in their own camp that the process was worth pursuing. And both parties fundamentally respected the other side's legitimacy and integrity.

In short, Shell's dialogue with these human rights organisations suggests that engagement between a business firm and a stakeholder organisation or organisations will be most likely to emerge under the following conditions:

- The business firm faces a **crisis of reputation**. Significant public criticism highlights a gap between society's expectations and the firm's behaviour. Such crises are most likely in firms that sell or provide a branded product or service directly to the public.

- The company perceives that **it cannot improve its reputation unilaterally**. Rather, this requires winning the support of representatives of stakeholder interests. Moreover, these representatives are organised and are perceived by the firm as legitimate.

- The business firm possesses sufficient **organisational capacity** to engage with stakeholders. This may include support from top leadership and an adequately funded external affairs or similar department with a reporting relationship to top executives. It may also include a managed change process that provides an opportunity for leaders to identify and respond quickly to shifts in the external environment.

- The stakeholder organisation perceives that a core **goal** cannot be met without the active participation of the business firm. Unilateral action has not been effective in meeting its objectives.

- The stakeholder organisation possesses sufficient **organisational capacity** to engage with the business firm. This may include leadership or a significant faction that supports dialogue and an organisational unit with expertise in working with the business community.

- Both sides share a **cultural affinity**, recognise the other side's fundamental **legitimacy**, are able to dedicate considerable time to the process of building **trust**, and are willing to accept **incremental progress** towards their goals.

The stage model implicit in much recent work in stakeholder theory is correct in one sense: it accurately describes the sequence in which various types of stakeholder interaction occur. That is, stakeholder mapping generally precedes stakeholder management, and stakeholder management generally precedes stakeholder engagement. But using stage models to describe social phenomena is risky because the biological analogy can be taken too far. Stage models imply a developmental sequence: that is, one stage inexorably leads to another. A child, if properly nurtured, will pass through a series of physical and emotional stages as he or she becomes an adult. Unless illness, accident or some other catastrophe intervenes, these developmental stages are generally predicable—within limits—to paediatricians, child psychologists and experienced parents. Biology establishes a baseline.

In contrast, organisations are not biological entities, and there is nothing automatic about the process by which stakeholder mapping becomes stakeholder management, or by which stakeholder management becomes stakeholder engagement. On the contrary, the Shell case suggests that the transition from stakeholder management to stakeholder engagement is problematical and contingent. Full stakeholder engagement is likely, for now at least, to remain the exception, because it depends on a number of conditions that can be expected to occur simultaneously only infrequently. In this instance, a series of public relations debacles, a managed change process, the presence of NGOs prepared for dialogue, and some skilled and experienced participants all converged somewhat serendipitously to help drive forward engagement between Shell and its human rights stakeholders. In this sense, the experience of Shell, Amnesty International and Pax Christi must be considered a deviant case.

On the other hand, over time stakeholder engagement is likely to become more, rather than less, common. Companies that see others struggling with a crisis of reputation may elect to address stakeholder concerns proactively to avoid this eventuality. Or, they may do so simply because they become convinced that it is morally right or that it will confer a competitive advantage. NGOs and other stakeholders may see others like themselves succeed in influencing corporate behaviour and conclude that the political risks of engagement are worth taking. The globalisation of markets and the rapid dissemination of information technology will certainly accelerate the rate at which both business firms and stakeholder organisations are able to generalise from each other's best practices. Successful dialogues, such as the one described here, will encourage both companies and stakeholder organisations to engage more often in the difficult, but productive, task of listening to and learning from one another.

STAKEHOLDER AND CORPORATE RESPONSIBILITIES IN CROSS-SECTORAL ENVIRONMENTAL COLLABORATIONS

Building value, legitimacy and trust*

Dennis A. Rondinelli and Ted London

Kenan-Flagler Business School, University of North Carolina at Chapel Hill, USA

Corporations and external stakeholders are collaborating more intensively on social and environmental issues (Googins and Rochlin 2000). Until recently, companies mainly provided philanthropic support to environmental groups, assisting them with worldwide projects, and working with them on community activities aimed at protecting natural resources. Now, an increasing number of corporations are also exploring co-operative relationships with non-governmental organisations (NGOs) that address the management of companies' internal operations. McDonald's, United Parcel Service (UPS), Shell, DuPont, Starbucks, General Motors and the Ford Motor Company are only a few of the many corporations that collaborate with NGOs on a variety of internal environmental projects that provide tangible benefits to corporate operations. Yet relatively little is known about the factors that contribute to the success of these collaborations or how stakeholders and corporations perceive their responsibilities in cross-sectoral environmental relationships (Phillips and Reichart 2000; Harvey and Schaefer 2001).

Incorporating stakeholder perspectives in strategy design can help corporations to manage external change better (Freeman 1984) and has been shown to influence their financial performance positively (Preston and Sapienza 1990; Waddock and Graves 1997a; Hillman and Keim 2001). The increasing number of co-operative activities, in itself, indicates a growing belief among both stakeholder groups and corporations that there are mutual benefits from working together on environmental problems (Halal

* The research for this chapter was funded in part by the Nonprofit Sector Research Fund of the Aspen Institute, Washington, DC. The conclusions and interpretations, however, are those of the authors.

2001). Forming partnerships that effectively use the unique resources of corporations and NGOs also creates new demands and opportunities for both. By collaborating more effectively with corporations, NGOs can help to avert negative impacts on the environment before they occur. NGOs can promote practices that eliminate the causes of environmental degradation within manufacturing and distribution systems instead of simply reacting to the results.

The benefits from collaborating with stakeholders also accrue to corporations (Ullman 1985). Demands from powerful environmental stakeholders are becoming more salient (Pfeffer and Salancik 1978; Mitchell *et al.* 1997). Progressive companies now consider collaborating with stakeholders on environmental management as part of their corporate citizenship and social responsibility activities (Wood 1991a; Rondinelli and Berry 2000). Logan *et al.* (1997: 7) define corporate citizenship as the practices that reflect 'a corporation's direct responsibilities to employees, shareholders, or owners, customers, and suppliers and to the communities where it conducts business and serves markets'. Marsden and Andriof (1997) emphasise that corporate citizenship involves understanding an organisation's influences on the rest of society and managing relationships with external stakeholders in ways that minimise negative impacts and maximise positive ones. This includes obeying the law, engaging in ethical behaviour and giving back to the community through philanthropic activities (Carroll 1998).

In addition to fulfilling social responsibilities, companies are also recognising the possibility of accruing tangible internal benefits from cross-sectoral partnerships (Kanter 1999). While some companies focus on immediate returns in the form of cost savings and increased efficiency, others perceive longer-term returns—including stronger competitive advantage, preservation of crucial resources and raw materials, favourable corporate image, and opportunities for new product development—from working with external stakeholders. For example, more executives now understand that the benefits of a strong corporate reputation for environmental management can include greater access to capital, reduced operating costs, improved financial performance and enhanced brand image (Hansen and Gleckman 1994).

Although many companies and some NGOs see the advantages of collaborating on internal corporate environmental management problems, such partnerships add an additional layer of complexity (Kanter 1999). As a result, they do not always succeed. Long and Arnold (1995) note three psychological barriers that can undermine these collaborations: mistrust, fear of loss of control, and misunderstandings of the motivations and intent of each of the partners. Thus, in cross-sectoral environmental collaborations, as in corporate alliances, partners must find ways to create reciprocal value, learn from each other, establish legitimacy and overcome distrust (Cohen and Levinthal 1990; Rousseau *et al.* 1998).

In this chapter, we draw on archival data, a content analysis of corporate performance reports and in-depth interviews with 16 representatives of organisations that participated in corporate–stakeholder collaborations to identify the responsibilities that both partners must carry to ensure the effectiveness of cross-sectoral environmental relationships. Our surveys sought to answer the following questions: (1) In what ways are corporations and environmental NGOs collaborating? (2) What motivates corporations and external stakeholders to work together on internal environmental issues? and (3) What do participants in corporate–NGO environmental collaborations perceive to be the most important responsibilities of both parties in making the interactions effective?

10.1 Types of corporate–stakeholder collaboration

Our earlier research indicated that corporations and environmental stakeholders are collaborating in at least seven different ways (Rondinelli and Berry 2000; Rondinelli and London 2001a). They include:

1. Corporate contributions and gifts to NGO environmental programmes and activities

2. Corporate support for employee participation in environmental NGO activities

3. Corporate–NGO marketing affiliations

4. Corporate support for targeted NGO environmental projects

5. NGO certification of corporate business practices

6. Environmental awareness and education collaborations

7. NGO–corporate environmental management alliances

These different approaches to corporate–environmental NGO collaborations are summarised in Table 10.1.

The McDonald's and Environmental Defense Fund collaboration was among the first to demonstrate, in the early 1990s, that collaborative activities could successfully target internal company processes and practices. Using the capabilities of both partners, the project significantly reduced McDonald's packaging volume and wastes and involved suppliers, who began to use recycled materials in the paper and packaging products they sold to McDonald's (EDF–McDonald's 1991).

From the early 1990s, corporations and NGOs began working together more intensively. While most companies still work with stakeholders on joint activities in which tangible benefits primarily accrue to NGOs, as highlighted by the first four types of collaboration listed in Table 10.1, an increasing number are collaborating on activities that generate more tangible benefits for corporations, such as certification, information-sharing and education partnerships, and environmental management alliances (Rondinelli and London 2001a).

10.1.1 *Collaborations primarily benefiting NGOs*

In the first four types of relationship described in Table 10.1, tangible benefits flow mainly to the NGO partner, and the most prevalent type of interaction is philanthropic. Many corporate foundations or public affairs divisions make grants or gifts to environmental organisations. Hewlett-Packard's (1998) contribution to environmental and conservation groups of nearly US$4 million in cash, equipment and technology since 1991, and Motorola's (1999) gift of radio equipment worth more than US$1 million to the World Wide Fund for Nature to use in protecting wildlife in remote and environmentally endangered regions in the world, are examples of philanthropy that enhance corporate image, but primarily benefit NGOs. Such gifts give NGOs' programmes more visibility, allow them to tap new sources of funding and afford them the opportunity to give their activities more widespread publicity.

Types of corporate–NGO relationship	Examples of collaboration	Primary tangible benefit flow
1. Corporate contributions and gifts to NGOs	▪ Hewlett-Packard's donation of GIS and mapping equipment to 150 US conservation groups	NGO stakeholder
2. Corporate support for employee participation in NGO activities	▪ Ashland Inc.'s Chairman's Challenge Award ▪ AT&T's corporate programme to pay employees for a day dedicated to volunteering with NGO or community organisation	NGO stakeholder
3. Corporate–NGO marketing affiliations	▪ Milton Bradley licence for Sierra Club name on jigsaw puzzles ▪ Bushnell licence of National Audubon Society name on its binoculars	NGO stakeholder
4. Targeted project support	▪ Johnson & Johnson support for The Nature Conservancy project on biodiversity protection in Latin America ▪ Ford Motor Company support to Conservation International to establish Center for Environmental Leadership in Business	NGO stakeholder
5. NGO certification of corporate business practices	▪ Unilever and World Wide Fund for Nature establishment of the Marine Stewardship Council ▪ Forest Stewardship Council's certification of wood products corporations' timber purchasing practices	Corporate partner
6. Environmental awareness and education collaborations	▪ Business for Social Responsibility's 'Business and the Environment' programme	Corporate partner
7. Environmental management alliances	▪ Norm Thompson Outfitters project with the Alliance for Environmental Innovation to reduce energy and resource use ▪ SC Johnson and the Alliance for Environmental Innovation joint task force on assessing environmental impacts of new products	Corporate partner

Table 10.1 **Types of corporate–NGO environmental collaboration**

Source: adapted from Rondinelli and London 2001a

Some firms also offer incentives for their employees to work with external stakeholders and local communities to improve environmental conditions and prevent or clean up environmental degradation. Firms match their employees' contributions to, or encourage employees to volunteer for, NGO environmental programmes. Ashland Inc.'s Chairman's Challenge Award recognising its employee volunteers who participate in noteworthy environmental programmes in their communities; AT&T's programme to pay employees for a day of volunteering with environmental or community organisations; and Chevron's support for employees who volunteer each year to clean up beach areas during National Coastal Cleanup Day are examples of corporate support for NGO activities. NGOs benefit not only from the increased number of volunteers but also from the corporations' endorsement of employee participation in the environmental groups' activities.

When corporations license the name or logo of environmental organisations for their products, purchase the endorsements of environmental groups for their goods or services, or donate a portion of their sales to environmental NGOs, it is a way of affiliating with an environmental cause. Milton Bradley's licensing of the Sierra Club's name for its jigsaw puzzles and Bushnell's use of the National Audubon Society seal on its binoculars helped the NGOs to publicise environmental and social issues. These collaborations provide new sources of income and enhanced visibility for NGOs and help them to expand the market for 'green products'.

Finally, companies and NGOs also work together on specific stakeholder projects that focus on a particular region or a targeted activity. Johnson & Johnson (2001), for example, has worked with The Nature Conservancy on community health and resource conservation programmes in Latin America and the Ford Motor Company supported Conservation International's (CI) Center for Environmental Leadership in Business. CI's Center helps companies and environmental organisations to create solutions to crucial global environmental problems, promote business practices that contribute to conservation, and reduce industry's environmental impacts (Moyer 2001).

These traditional philanthropic relationships between corporations and NGOs offer something to both parties, although the primary tangible benefits—grants, employee volunteers, licensing fees and targeted donations—flow to the NGO. A newly emerging set of relationships provides greater flows of tangible benefits to the corporation.

10.1.2 *Collaborations primarily benefiting corporations*

Since the early 1990s corporations and stakeholder groups have been more aggressively exploring new forms of collaboration (relationships 5, 6 and 7 in Table 10.1) that focus on the internal management of corporations' environmental impacts and provide them with tangible benefits from working with NGOs. They include NGO certification of corporate business practices, environmental awareness and education partnerships, and NGO–corporate environmental management alliances.

Corporations in environmentally sensitive industries—such as natural resource exploitation or sales of natural resource products—are now developing more intensive relationships with environmental NGOs, often as the result of external pressures, to obtain third-party authentication of environmentally appropriate business practices. Examples include the joint effort by Unilever and the World Wide Fund for Nature (WWF) to establish the Marine Stewardship Council (MSC). The MSC became an independent certification programme that endorses environmentally responsible fishing practices and will help Unilever in purchasing all of its fish from certified fisheries by 2005. The Forest Stewardship Council certifies that timber wholesalers, retailers and users such as Home Depot, Wickes Inc., Lowes, 84 Lumber and the Andersen Corporation purchase their products from suppliers using environmentally and socially responsible harvesting processes and from forests in which environmental damage is minimised (Carleton 2000).

Some NGOs are also seeking to make stronger impacts on corporate practices by becoming a source of environmental information and a clearinghouse for effective practices for changing company products or processes to prevent pollution and environmental damage. The 'Business and the Environment' programme of Business for Social Responsibility (BSR), for example, helps companies to establish environmentally sustainable supply chain management, create value from sustainable development, design products to reduce negative environmental impacts, mitigate greenhouse gas emissions, and improve building design by providing information on environmental management best practices. BSR and other non-profit organisations not only disseminate environmental information but provide corporations with networking opportunities, carry out research on new environmental approaches, increase public awareness of environmental issues, and help companies to disseminate performance results.

Finally, as in the McDonald's–EDF partnership of the early 1990s, more stakeholder groups are now working with corporations to improve internal operations. The Alliance for Environmental Innovation (the Alliance) helped Norm Thompson Outfitters, a speciality retailer of apparel, gifts and home items, to revise its catalogue paper practices and to reduce energy, resource use and solid waste. The Alliance also collaborated with the international household products manufacturer SC Johnson to assess the environmental impacts of its new product development procedures and to reduce packaging.

These collaborations on internal management procedures help corporations to obtain access to environmental expertise, more diverse perspectives on environmental problems, and external endorsements for environmental solutions developed jointly by the corporation and stakeholder groups. When the improvements are successfully implemented, the collaborations provide corporations with favourable publicity for their partnering efforts.

In these newer types of collaboration, the tangible benefits flow primarily to the corporation, although both parties gain value from the partnership. Yet these relationships are also fraught with risks that did not characterise traditional philanthropic collaborations where the primary tangible benefits flowed to the NGO partner. In the more intensive collaborations, corporations must expose internal practices and processes to environmental advocacy groups and NGOs face the danger of having their credibility questioned by accusations of 'sleeping with the enemy'.

10.2 Motivations for corporate–stakeholder co-operation

Given these extraordinarily high stakes, why do corporations and NGOs engage in these relationships? Over the past decade, a complex set of factors and pressures has brought these seemingly dissimilar organisations together (Warhurst 2001). Many corporations have learned that customers often seek to align themselves with firms that have a reputation for social and environmental responsibility (Messelbeck and Whaley 1999). To stay competitive in global markets, multinational corporations have also found it important to develop strong supply chains through which they can influence their suppliers, vendors, distributors and contractors as well as their own divisions and subsidiaries to address environmental issues proactively. Other observers point out that public and shareholder expectations regarding corporate involvement in solving host-community problems have also risen dramatically as national and local government roles have been shrinking (Rondinelli and Berry 1997). For example, BSR (1998) notes that public demands for enforcement of regulations and for increased disclosure by investors, regulators and public-interest groups have played a strong role in increasing corporations' sensitivity to their environmental and social responsibilities.

NGOs are recognising the benefits of working proactively with corporations to address environmental issues before they occur rather than merely reacting to ecological damage. NGOs can build on the growing recognition in many corporations of the immediate and direct business benefits from proactive environmental management in the form of lower costs, fewer risks and liabilities, and more efficient operations. As corporations gave greater attention to and spent more money on their environmental management practices, environmental interest groups such as the Alliance for Environmental Innovation, the World Resources Institute, The Nature Conservancy, Conservation International and others began to forge active relationships with them to address these internal environmental issues (Hoffman 1997).

At the same time, more corporations are exploring the role that partnerships can play in addressing problematic operational practices, in supporting product development and marketing, and in dealing with suppliers and external stakeholders. NGOs offer corporations access to a different set of core competences than are typically available internally (Prahalad and Hamel 1990; Leonard 1998). Forming partnerships that effectively use the resources of both corporations and NGOs can create opportunities to promote strong environmental management practices while helping firms to earn profits. Properly structured, these collaborations allow both organisations to achieve their fundamental goals by creating value through mutual learning.

With increasing awareness of the potential benefits of working together, the number, scope and depth of corporate–NGO collaborations are likely to grow in the future. Yet, for these relationships to succeed, both organisations must focus not only on how their specific individual needs will be met, but also on the responsibilities they have to, and the demands they put on, their partner.

10.3 Stakeholder and corporate responsibilities in making environmental collaborations effective

In order to understand better the responsibilities of participants in corporate–NGO environmental collaborations, we analysed archival data and interviewed 16 participants from both corporations and NGOs that have been involved in the cross-sectoral environmental collaborations where the tangible benefits flow primarily to the corporate partner. Our examination of archival data, including a content analysis of the environmental performance reports of 50 multinational corporations, gave us insights into both the types and the goals of a large cross-section of corporation–environmental NGO collaborations (Rondinelli and London 2001b).

To gain greater understanding of the demands and responsibilities of both corporate and NGO stakeholders engaged in cross-sectoral environmental collaborations that mainly benefited the corporate partner, we interviewed 16 representatives from eight corporate–environmental NGO dyads. The dyads were selected based on secondary data and consultation with academic experts and knowledgeable practitioners. Corporate respondents included managers from DuPont, Starbucks, Bay Beyond, Norm Thompson, Westvaco, Collins Products and Shell. We also interviewed NGO representatives from the World Resources Institute, Conservation International, the Center for Compatible Economic Development, The Nature Conservancy, The Natural Step, the Alliance for Environmental Innovation, Business for Social Responsibility and SustainAbility (a hybrid organisation that operates as a think-tank, a campaigning organisation and a for-profit consultancy).

Through interviews with key managers from both corporations and NGO stakeholders, we were able to compare and contrast—in an exploratory fashion (Weick 1996)—the observations and perspectives from eight different corporate–environmental NGO dyads. The interviews ranged from 45 minutes to 90 minutes and consisted of a series of open-ended questions that probed the development and formation of a specific corporate–NGO partnership. Additionally, we asked our respondents to discuss their experiences with inter-sectoral alliances in general. Questions in this part of the interview included an analysis of mistakes made, an examination of past successes and an assessment of lessons learned.

Following from a systematic analysis of the archival data and the results of the interviews, we found that both corporate and NGO respondents consistently identified three crucial sets of mutual responsibilities: (1) creating value through learning; (2) establishing legitimacy; and (3) developing trust. Table 10.2 provides examples of the responses we received which are discussed more fully in the following sections.

10.3.1 Creating value through learning

In relationships where the benefits flow primarily to the NGO partner—such as grants, employee voluntarism, licensing fees and targeted donations—the transaction is more 'arm's-length'. In these collaborations, creating value through mutual learning typically is not of high importance. On the other hand, in collaborations in which the tangible benefits flow primarily to the corporate partners, participants point out that both corporations and NGOs have a responsibility to provide value in their joint activities. In the latter relationship neither type of organisation is likely to collaborate unless both perceive that the other will take seriously its responsibility for creating value.

Respondents noted, in particular, that each party has a responsibility to jointly develop new ideas through the sharing of different perspectives and complementary knowledge. Corporate respondents pointed out that the primary value that NGOs must bring to the collaboration is the generation of good ideas. Corporate participants also noted that it is difficult for firms to develop a broad perspective if they are isolated and that NGOs can bring a different perspective on issues. As pressures build on corporations to address

	Corporate respondents	*Non-profit respondents*
Joint responsibility #1: *Creating value through learning*		
The generation of new ideas	Prime benefit is the generation of good ideas and NGOs have good people with good ideas.	Each side has a unique perspective; working together, they can come up with better ideas than either alone.
Providing a different perspective and complementary expertise	Both sides can be teachers: ▪ Corporation can provide knowledge of the business process and commercial perspective. ▪ NGO partner can bring a sense of social trends as well as a conduit for getting ideas to external reviewers.	Corporations can get access to expertise; access to thought leaders who can help identify emerging issues.
Joint responsibility #2: *Establishing legitimacy*		
External legitimacy	NGO can proactively link relevant parties; facilitate meetings with diverse organisations.	NGOs offer risk management that can help avoid future potential advocacy issues. NGO can help in engaging stakeholders.
Internal cross-organisational legitimacy	NGO should be interested in making real changes, willing to be flexible, willing to move at a relatively slow pace, interested in 'proving the business case' over time.	NGO should look for corporation that is open, unprotected, and not defensive.
Internal intra-organisational legitimacy	Commitment by president; corporate culture; team approach; wide level of information dissemination all important.	Horizontal and vertical depth in the corporate participation; fully integrated into operations; organisation willing to conduct a broad internal investigation and understand global impacts of its activities.
Joint responsibility #3: *Developing trust*		
Initially developing trust	Good personal relationships between organisations that have continued to improve over time; partners have hung together in some relatively tough times.	Relationship started with a donation; needed time to develop a trusting relationship between organisations.
Maintaining trust during the collaboration	Transparency needed on both sides; risk losing credibility if not fully honest; also collaboration will not be able to survive the inevitable bumps.	Conservation organisation has to realise everything is not going to be perfect and corporation has to let its guard down.

Table 10.2 **Typical interview responses: corporate–NGO collaborations with benefits flowing primarily to corporate partner**

more numerous and complex environmental impacts of their operations, collaborations with NGOs can be a source of information and knowledge about creative ways of rethinking operational activities, identifying new products and marketing opportunities, and addressing stakeholder concerns (Leonard-Barton 1992; Kanter 1999). In addition to learning, working with NGOs may allow corporations to create value by both legitimising their internal environmental improvements and externally verifying their concern for environmental protection (Rogers 2000).

The project between Norm Thompson Outfitters and the Alliance for Environmental Innovation is an example of how a company seeks ideas from an external stakeholder group. The project was designed to identify, test and implement environmental improvements in the apparel manufacturer's catalogue paper practices. The partnership had three specific goals that required tapping into the expertise of both partners: first, to deliver significant reductions in energy and resource use, solid waste and pollution; second, to demonstrate that greener paper practices need not adversely affect cost or business performance; and, third, to drive positive change in the catalogue industry.

In successful collaborations, corporate participants identified the types of tangible benefit they expect to derive from collaborating with NGOs by developing specific objectives. Corporations especially value NGOs' expertise in areas where a company may not have much in-house capability. For example, Starbucks collaborated with an NGO on creating a line of biodiversity-friendly 'shade-grown' coffee, McDonald's on reducing its operational waste, UPS on using less environmentally harmful packaging materials, and Collins Products on improving the environmental performance of its timber manufacturing.

The NGO can be a critical reference point providing valuable information about stakeholders, expertise in specific aspects of environmental management and contacts with a wide range of other specialised organisations. A 'high level of public awareness motivating its stakeholders' and the partners' mutual recognition that pursuing common interests would help them to achieve similar goals led Unilever and the World Wide Fund for Nature to collaborate on certifying environmentally sustainable fisheries (Weir 2000). Westvaco used two primary criteria for selecting The Nature Conservancy (TNC) as a collaborator. First, TNC could bring technical competence through decision-making based on science and technical data to the partnership. Second, Westvaco was impressed with TNC's professionalism in operating on business and environmental criteria rather than emotional reaction.

NGO participants also emphasised the importance of both sides creating value, and pointed out that both parties must work to develop new ideas throughout a project. For TNC, for example, working with corporations provides access to large areas of private forests in which it can use its in-house capabilities to identify rare species and special natural habitats and then work with corporations to develop plans for efficiently protecting these resources. BSR sees partnerships as a way to achieve its objectives of providing training to companies and their key business partners on environmental issues, learning about emerging issues and gaining access to thought leaders in order to serve as an information clearinghouse.

The NGO respondents also noted that their organisations have expertise and a perspective that are different from those of companies and that collaborations may have the ability to facilitate organisational, and even industry-wide, change. NGOs can add value by helping corporations to test new ideas, developing and advancing new markets for products and services that are directly related to environmental issues (especially for natural resource-dependent companies), and assisting corporations to 'do the right thing' while advancing their own environmental objectives.

One stakeholder group, the Alliance for Environmental Innovation, for example, chooses companies and projects that can advance its core strategies. Those strategies focus on organisational and industry change and include defining new best practices in environmental management; greening the supply chain; demonstrating the business benefits of environmentalism; and environmentally improving product design. The Alliance develops partnerships with companies that have enough purchasing power to stimulate change in the supply chain and sufficient influence to establish new corporate environmental management best practices.

Similarly, the Conservation International–Starbucks partnership is an example of how joint learning-oriented activities can achieve tangible benefits for the corporation through the development of a new product line. In this case, Starbucks collaborated with Conservation International to develop and sell a new shade-grown coffee harvested from farms supported by the partnership. The coffee, 'Shade Grown Mexico', comes from farmers located in a buffer zone around Chiapas's El Triunfo Biosphere Reserve. Conservation International provides expertise on conservation-related issues, while Starbucks offers financial support to the project and technical advice to farmers to raise the quality of their coffee. The relationship between the two organisations is continuing to expand and develop.

10.3.2 Establishing legitimacy

A second essential set of responsibilities that both corporate and NGO participants in environmental collaborations identified was establishing legitimacy. Respondents emphasised the importance of two types of responsibility, one externally oriented and the other internally focused. Environmental NGOs provide public legitimacy to the actions of corporations that implement the recommendations or activities emerging from the collaboration. Internally, each party must establish both cross- and intra-organisational legitimacy. In other words, each organisation must demonstrate to its partner and its own members that it is seriously engaged in finding mutually beneficial solutions to environmental problems through co-operation.

Corporate respondents noted that, in addition to tangible value creation, corporations looked to collaborations with NGOs as a way to bring external legitimacy to the firm's internal efforts to solve or prevent environmental problems. They indicated that, while public relations-oriented projects alone typically do not result in strong relationships, an external stakeholder's help in legitimising a company's environmental management activities enhances the value of the tangible benefits. Corporate participants thought that NGOs have the capacity to establish legitimacy of the corporate–NGO activities by providing independent information on issues, proactively linking other relevant stakeholders, facilitating meetings with diverse organisations and creating goodwill for the corporation when it implements the recommendations coming out of a collaborative project.

The NGO respondents were clearly aware that in collaborating with corporations they were expected to confer public legitimacy on the outcome of the project. NGO participants did, however, worry that some companies—especially in businesses focused on natural resource exploitation or extractive activities—might be reacting to pressure from customers and were using external stakeholder collaborations only as a way to create good public relations or to avoid government intervention or more severe 'official' third-party certification processes. To avoid this type of partnership, many of the NGO respondents looked for specific actions on the part of companies as signs that they were legitimately interested in engaging in mutual problem-solving.

Both corporate and stakeholder respondents believed that, in order to create internal legitimacy across organisations, both parties—especially at initial meetings—should explore values and perspectives, determine common objectives and maintain flexibility when considering the nature, extent and importance of problems and potential solutions. For instance, rather than staking out positions prior to exchanging information, the UPS–Alliance team started with an open mind about the nature of the problems and the possible solutions. Corporate respondents also recognised that, to maintain NGO legitimacy, these external stakeholders would still have to be free to criticise, challenge and be objective in their collaboration with the company.

Selecting representatives from corporations and NGOs with qualifications to address core issues is considered another important responsibility in establishing cross-organisational legitimacy. For example, both corporate and NGO respondents noted that the NGO representatives must be able to understand business needs and constraints and to work co-operatively with business executives. The Alliance for Environmental Innovation–UPS (1998: 4) task force succeeded in part because NGO team members were knowledgeable about environmentally favourable materials and internal operating requirements. 'The project team was cross-functional both within and across the two organisations', the final report noted. The Alliance team had technical expertise in life-cycle analysis of paper and plastic materials and in waste reduction.

Both corporate and NGO respondents pointed out that in order to establish intra-organisational legitimacy the corporation must be able to put together a cross-functional team respected within the company to work with NGOs. UPS team members, for example, represented a variety of functional areas such as marketing, customer communications, package engineering, and materials management and purchasing, as well as environmental affairs, and they communicated critical decisions to corporate leaders. Prior to the president signing a memorandum of agreement with Conservation International, Starbucks aligned the company internally. The coffee department was given responsibility for dealing with product issues and the department of environment and community affairs was tasked with maintaining relationships with the NGO. Both partners indicated that the relationship prospered because specific responsibilities were properly aligned with Starbucks' business structure.

Similarly, strong commitment from high-level executives in the corporation is also crucial for intra-organisational legitimacy. Collaboration between the Alliance for Environmental Innovation and UPS (1998: 11), for example, succeeded in part because top corporate executives 'believed from the start that this environmental project could benefit its customers and its businesses in a tangible way. Because of that, there was high-level commitment to the goals of the project.'

In addition, both cross- and intra-organisational legitimacy arises out of the willingness of both parties in a collaborative arrangement to agree on a working process or procedure. The EDF–McDonald's partnership was effective because the joint task force was willing to develop a five-step procedure that included: (1) an inventory to measure and understand the materials that McDonald's used and discarded; (2) brainstorming to explore a wide range of potential solutions; (3) evaluation to develop priorities for action; (4) modification of existing management tools to bring environmental considerations into standard operating procedures and practices; and (5) accountability, to develop clear measurement systems and assignment of authority and responsibility (Prince and Denison 1994).

EDF further established legitimacy with McDonald's by learning about its business. The joint task force met with a cross-section of staff members, visited distribution centres, and talked with packaging and food suppliers.

10.3.3 Developing trust

The third set of responsibilities that respondents identified as crucial to the success of cross-sectoral environmental collaborations is the development of trust. Cross-sectoral collaborations often are not consummated, or fail in the early stages, because the participants cannot overcome ingrained feelings of mistrust. The long history of adversarial relationships between corporations and environmental interest groups makes trust creation and maintenance an especially demanding responsibility for both parties throughout the collaboration process.

In many of the cases we examined, participants initially created trust over an extended time through personal relationships. Several corporate respondents noted that the idea for collaboration emerged from personal relationships between the president or CEO of a company and the leaders of environmental NGOs who they met or worked with on public service committees. Other corporate respondents pointed out that they got to know the NGO community through internal awards programmes (some of the judges were from external organisations) and that interacting with those judges provided the opportunity to identify potential NGO partners.

Stakeholder participants also noted that, for them and their corporate counterparts, developing a trusting relationship often took time. One collaboration, for example, began with a specific individual from the NGO providing consulting to the corporation on how it could identify and cope with barriers to initiating internal sustainability and environmental changes. This study found that shareholders did not always see the value in environmental sustainability activities, that customers were not always willing to pay a premium for environmentally friendly products, that the corporation needed to develop a better framework for measuring and reporting on environmental impacts and activities, and that the company required more effective tools and training to manage change across the organisation. From this specific set of tasks, the NGO was able to develop activities to address important issues within the company and to expand its relationships with the corporation over time.

Similarly, Conservation International's partnership with Starbucks also expanded gradually from an initial contact in which CI sought (and received) a donation for its conservation site in Chiapas, Mexico. Starbucks became more interested in learning about the conservation site as a result of its donation and CI arranged visits for Starbucks executives to see the operations in Mexico. Over time, the interests of both sides grew to the point where Starbucks worked closely with CI on a coffee-purchasing agreement and marketing of the 'Shade Grown Mexico' coffee product. From its success, Starbucks began to talk with CI about expanding its purchasing of coffee from CI projects in Guatemala, Colombia and East Africa.

Moreover, both corporate and NGO respondents emphasised that trust is best maintained by open interaction and that transparency is required on both sides. Either party risks losing legitimacy and trust if its representatives are not open about problems and forthcoming with important relevant information. These collaborations, they argued, would not be able to survive the inevitable 'bumps' if one side believes that the other is withholding information.

To enhance information transfer, the NGO partner can often offer a 'safe space' in which corporate representatives can 'let their guard down', and discuss frankly the problems and issues of improving environmental performance. BSR, for example, allows companies to work comfortably with external groups on solving environmental problems, and provides benchmarking—through one-on-one consulting—of companies' innovative environmental practices.

As the relationship proceeds, developing mutually agreed protocols (including the negotiation of a clearly written memorandum of agreement on the purpose, scope, objectives, intended outcomes and duration of work) maintains and reinforces trust. The collaboration between the Alliance and Norm Thompson Outfitters, for example, included an agreement that clearly stated the scope of work, deliverables for each partner, confidentiality provisions, expected resource commitments and reporting conditions. By protecting the independence of the NGO and recognising the profit-making objectives of the corporation, a pre-existing agreement can help to prevent misunderstanding of responsibilities and avoid potentially detrimental disputes.

Respondents from both sectors also noted the importance of developing metrics for measuring environmental performance and assessing the problems under consideration. Trust is built when the collaborating team specifies rigorous outcomes and results that can be monitored and measured after solutions are applied. Using the principles of The Natural Step, Collins Products developed 'Journey Indicators', a tracking system that measured environmental performance improvements that led to better oversight and direction.

Similarly, the SC Johnson–Alliance task force, working on environmental design problems, developed new product concept screening strategies and design principles in areas of dematerialising products, conserving materials, reducing chemical intensity, reducing energy intensity, extending product life and enhancing functionality. The prospects for success of the collaboration were enhanced by initially establishing a 'scientifically sound conceptual framework for systematically driving value-added environmental improvement into the company's products' (Alston and Roberts 1999: 120).

Finally, assuring that the results of the collaborative activities are jointly announced also manifests trust. Both corporate and NGO respondents emphasised that in order to develop trust the team members from both organisations should maintain confidentiality throughout the collaboration processes and, once the project is completed and results are known, should issue public reports jointly and simultaneously.

10.4 Conclusions

Corporations and external stakeholders use a variety of relationships, which were summarised in Table 10.1 on page 204, to collaborate on addressing environmental problems.

These include both traditional arrangements such as supporting employee volunteerism, philanthropy and marketing affiliations, where tangible benefits flow to the NGO, and more direct and intensive collaborations such as certification programmes, education partnerships and environmental management alliances, where corporations are the primary recipient of tangible benefits.

The collaborative relationships with tangible benefits flowing to the corporation offer both greater risks and greater opportunities to both partners. These collaborations are relatively recent and not analysed extensively in the literature on cross-sectoral partnerships. We found that, while the risks associated with sharing internal practices and organisational reputations are greater, the benefits of sharing complementary knowledge across organisations are also more substantial. As such, these types of collaboration must be carefully planned and managed if they are to succeed.

Those whom we interviewed suggested that the effectiveness of these collaborations depends on the corporations' and the stakeholders' ability to create mutual value through learning, establish external and internal legitimacy, and develop trust. Mutual value through learning is primarily created by the joint generation of new ideas that capitalise on the different perspectives and complementary expertise that each partner brings to the collaboration. External legitimacy results mainly from the ability and willingness of the NGOs to create linkages with relevant stakeholders, facilitate relationships with diverse organisations, and help generate goodwill for the collaborative activities.

Our respondents indicated that internal legitimacy has both cross- and intra-organisational aspects. Cross-organisational legitimacy is developed by maintaining open minds, engaging in frank discussions, collaborating on defining problems, jointly exploring feasible solutions and ensuring that personnel with the appropriate experience are involved. Support from top management and strong, internally respected cross-functional teams are crucial for intra-organisational legitimacy. Trust is developed and sustained when partners have good personal relationships, view the collaboration as a long-term effort that will have inevitable bumps, and are able to preserve transparency in information-sharing and dialogue.

Although our research is exploratory, our findings provide insights into the responsibilities of corporations and external stakeholders that make cross-sectoral environmental collaborations with benefits flowing primarily to the corporate partner successful. Our findings offer a broad array of propositions about the need for both corporations and stakeholders to provide value through learning, legitimacy and trust that can be tested through more quantitative research methods as a larger sample of such relationships becomes available for analysis.

In sum, complex collaborations between corporations and external stakeholders are likely to increase in the future as the former face more intense pressures to pursue higher levels of social responsibility and corporate citizenship and the latter face greater pressures from supporters and the public to deliver on their goals of protecting the environment. The success of these collaborative efforts will depend on the ability of both corporations and external stakeholders to identify their respective responsibilities in cross-sectoral partnerships and to develop the capacity to manage complex inter-organisational relationships effectively.

TWO-WAY RESPONSIBILITY
The role of industry and its stakeholders in working towards sustainable development

Gretchen E. Hund and Jill A. Engel-Cox
Battelle Memorial Institute, USA

Kimberly M. Fowler
Pacific Northwest National
Laboratory, USA

Howard Klee
World Business Council for Sustainable
Development, Switzerland

In 2000, the World Business Council for Sustainable Development (WBCSD) awarded a contract to Battelle Memorial Institute as the lead research organisation on a project entitled 'Towards a Sustainable Cement Industry'. The project was sponsored by ten of the world's leading cement companies drawn together by the WBCSD for this project as the Working Group Cement (WGC). Battelle is a not-for-profit research institution with a long history of research in industrial sustainability, life-cycle analysis and stakeholder engagement. Their work has been with national and local government agencies and a wide variety of private industries, including chemical manufacturing, forestry, transportation and electronics. Battelle staff actively work with these industries not only on technical research related to sustainable development but also on the critical element of stakeholder communication and engagement.

WBCSD is a coalition of 150 international companies united by a shared commitment to sustainable development. Members are drawn from more than 30 countries and 20 industrial sectors. The Council's aim is to provide business leadership as a catalyst for change towards sustainable development, and to promote the role of eco-efficiency, innovation and corporate social responsibility towards sustainable development. The WBCSD co-ordinates a number of Council projects on topics relevant to the entire membership, such as Climate and Energy, and Sustainable Livelihoods, among others. The member-led sectoral projects research, analyse and recommend actions to promote sustainable development within an individual industry.

The purpose of the project was to provide a vision and roadmap for the cement industry to help it move towards long-term sustainability. By addressing the challenge of sustainable development, cement companies hope to better understand and meet stakeholder expectations, create a safe environment for their employees and surrounding communities, foster innovation in their products and services, and find new ways to create value for their shareholders. Figure 11.1 identifies the components of sustainable development: environmental stewardship, economic prosperity and social responsibility. Together, these three elements are frequently referred to as the 'triple bottom line' for corporate sustainability.

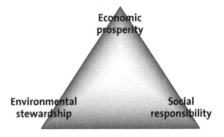

Figure 11.1 **The triple bottom line of sustainable development**
Source: Battelle 2002a

This project was built on the premise that engagement with a broad range of stakeholders is essential for successful business operations. Well-designed involvement leads to increased awareness and understanding by both the business community and their stakeholders. Some companies have always understood the value of engaging with the community; however, as communities grow, so does the circle of stakeholders with whom business needs to engage. Stakeholder input is playing an ever-growing role in helping to influence company decision-making. Figure 11.2 describes the types of stakeholder that are typically included in engagement activities.

The stakeholder engagement research from the Sustainable Cement project sought to provide a framework and tools for the industry to inform and engage external stakeholders across geographies, communities and interest groups. Research methods and results included:

- Benchmarks for 'best practices'

- Identifying critical stakeholder groups and their interests

- Determining priority issues and opportunities for the cement industry to advance its sustainable development goals

- Guiding companies in choosing appropriate communication and involvement methods to reach critical audiences and stimulate feedback

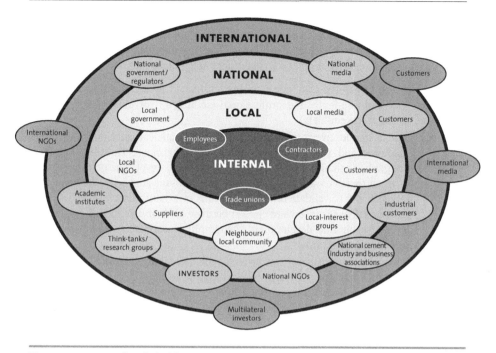

Figure 11.2 **Types of stakeholder**

Source: Hund *et al.* 2001

11.1 Methodology

Basic research consisted of gathering information from a variety of primary and secondary sources, including:

- **Cement staff interviews**. Conducted interviews with staff from a cement industry national group and a cement plant to prepare two case studies on communication approaches.

- **Questionnaires**. Provided a questionnaire to WGC members to determine current communication practices and future plans.

- **Literature and Internet searches**. Conducted a literature search followed by interviews to identify current best practices for communication and stakeholder engagement in cement and non-cement companies.

- **Research**. Conducted research on communication standards and guidelines currently used on environmental issues and sustainability, including environmental performance standards, sustainability performance programmes, sector-specific programmes and reporting initiatives.

- **Information requests.** Collected information from WGC members via written requests and numerous interviews with cement industry staff and their third-party stakeholder involvement experts in order to compile 17 short case studies on facility communication and stakeholder engagement programmes.

- **Dialogues.** Organised dialogue sessions, co-hosted by local cement companies[1] and independently and professional facilitated,[2] for local stakeholders and national stakeholders.

  - *Local stakeholders* from the business, non-governmental organisations (NGOs), academic and scientific communities in four cities: Curitiba, Brazil; Bangkok, Thailand; Lisbon, Portugal; and Cairo, Egypt. The objective was to learn their views on sustainability issues associated with the cement industry and to validate or refine previous efforts to identify stakeholder concerns. These cities were chosen because of their diversity in cultures, level of economic development, geographic location and high level of cement manufacturing.

  - *National and international stakeholders*, such as major NGOs and interested government agency officials, in Washington, DC, and Brussels, Belgium. These were aimed at gathering a broader geographic perspective and to include larger NGOs that had an interest in the more global issues confronting the cement industry.

- **External stakeholder interviews.** Conducted at dialogue locations.

Based on the information gathered, there was thorough analysis and the development of recommendations, presented in a detailed report to the WGC (Hund *et al.* 2002). Additionally, a stakeholder dialogue guidebook was prepared for use by individual cement facilities (Hund *et al.* 2001).

11.2 Significant cement industry findings

11.2.1 *Stakeholder perceptions*

Generalising about individual stakeholder perceptions is always difficult owing to several factors, including the stakeholder's relationship to the industry, the stakeholder's previous experience or exposure to the industry, location of the cement facility, and degree of economic development.

This section reports on feedback heard during the dialogue sessions, and the interviews and surveys conducted. This section first discusses perceptions that were consistently heard and then describes perceptions that varied greatly.

Consistent perceptions across the information gathering sessions were that:

---

1   The cement companies that co-hosted the local dialogues were Votorantim in Brazil, Siam Cement Industry in Thailand, CIMPOR in Portugal, and Holcim and CEMEX in Egypt.
2   John Ehrmann from Meridian Institute facilitated all four of the local dialogues.

1. The cement industry is important to the local economy.[3]

2. The industry has a dirty (polluting) image.[4]

3. Communication between the industry and its stakeholders is not adequate.

4. Employees want a more active role in representing their cement company in their community.[5]

5. The cement industry should do more to contribute to social development and citizens have a responsibility to define their priorities and communicate them to the industry.

Two of the above perceptions (3 and 5) require more explanation.

3. **Lack of industry transparency.** Stakeholders generally think that the cement industry is not transparent or open to its stakeholders and has been hesitant to initiate discussions with them on issues of concern. Communication typically occurs on an informal basis; opportunities for stakeholders to meet as a group and share their issues and concerns with industry occur but are not routine. Of course, some plants have better communication practices than others. Much of this is attributed to the individual efforts of the plant managers, though company policy does set the overall direction and tone for communications.

5. **Contributions to social development.** Stakeholders, on the whole, feel that industry could be more sensitive to society's needs. Community members are usually concerned about health, literacy, community infrastructure, worker safety and a clean environment. However, in some developing countries, the citizens may be most interested in job creation. Stakeholders feel that the industry needs to take responsibility for considering the surrounding community's rights, needs and interests, and for designing and operating its plants in a manner that protects public health and in some way helps the community. Some stakeholders also argue that citizens are responsible for defining their priorities and communicating them to the industry. They cannot assume that a company intuitively knows their concerns and they have a responsibility to communicate them to the company.

Critical areas of concern that were consistently raised by stakeholders in the dialogues and interviews and in the secondary sources reviewed include:

- Potential adverse health effects from facilities from dust inhalation and perceived toxic gases

- Environmental concerns such as CO_2, dust and gaseous pollutants

3 Some stakeholders from communities near cement plants expressed the view that concerns they had about environmental effects of the cement plant were tempered with positive feelings about the jobs and other economic impacts associated with the plant.

4 From dust around cement plants and from quarrying operations that can generate a great deal of noise and traffic.

5 This is particularly true if the company is one the staff respects and when staff feels the company has ethics and moral principles similar to their own. These staff members want to make a difference and be proud of working for a cement company.

■   Energy use and efficiency

■   Socioeconomic issues such as employment opportunities, traffic congestion, environmental justice issues, land use and visibility, and impacts on regional image and quality of life

Stakeholders also consistently made more complex suggestions of how the industry could improve. For example, they mentioned cement companies working with the community to create eco-industrial parks where other businesses would co-locate, sharing product and waste-streams efficiently, and creating jobs for the community. These areas of mutual responsibility are further explored in the 'Possible actions to enhance mutual responsibility' section.

There were also several **perceptions that varied among locations**. These included:

1. **Stakeholder knowledge of the industry**. In general, the industry has a low profile, but in some countries recent controversy has increased public awareness. For example, in Portugal, burning waste as a secondary fuel at cement plants has become highly politicised; as a result, citizens have heard a lot about cement industry operations. In contrast, Brazilian stakeholders have little awareness owing to little controversy. In Thailand, the public is familiar with the Siam Cement Industry, because the company helps surrounding communities (e.g. by providing water supplies and helping to build schools) and is partially owned by the royal family, but they are less familiar with other cement companies. In Egypt, stakeholders are familiar with the industry's operations, but have a negative impression since they feel the industry is responsible for environmental and social problems.[6] At the Washington, DC, dialogue, most stakeholders were unfamiliar with the industry except for those directly working with it. These stakeholders saw an opportunity for increasing stakeholder understanding through various forms of communication. However, one NGO group questioned whether the industry is ready for real community involvement or aware of the consequences of raising community expectations. The NGO group recommended that the industry make clear to communities how decisions are made and 'be a good listener'.

2. **Trust between the industry management and stakeholders**. Stakeholder perceptions ranged from considerable trust in Thailand (at least for Siam Cement Industry) to little trust in Egypt. Public trust was so poor in Egypt that some stakeholders argued for locating industries in remote regions far from current or future communities. Furthermore, the Egyptian stakeholders involved asked that a neutral, scientific institute, rather than the industry itself, provide information about technologies and environmental, safety and health issues to the public and the media. In both Egypt and Portugal, stakeholders believe that there is covert co-operation between business and government to maintain the status quo, particularly on such issues as burning waste as a secondary fuel in cement kilns. In contrast, in Thailand, the Siam Cement Industry is closely

---

6   In many areas of the world, cement facilities were owned and operated by the national government until quite recently, owing to a trend towards privatisation.

associated with the government, but stakeholders view this relationship positively.

3. **Stakeholder empowerment**. Stakeholder empowerment varied considerably. In Egypt, stakeholders feel they cannot raise issues since they fear retribution (e.g. job loss). In Brazil, stakeholders feel they could do more to influence the industry and be more proactive in raising issues, but they typically depend on academics for answers. In Thailand, local communities have recently been given more power and financial resources (in the form of tax allocations) as a result of a change in the Thai Constitution. They are therefore becoming more vocal on issues of concern, although local authorities frequently lack support from federal agencies to influence industry or to implement programmes. Over time, they are likely to gain knowledge of the system and have more influence. In Portugal, changes in governance have also left the public with a stronger voice than in the past, although industry representatives are not accustomed to interacting with NGOs and the public. As citizens are given more voice through political liberalisation, the public interest becomes vocalised and the powers to influence and even disrupt an industry's plans become possible.

4. **The use of alternative fuels and resources**. Opinion on the use of alternative fuels varied based on knowledge and past experiences. Brazilian stakeholders are intrigued by the idea of using wastes as fuels. They feel that primary fuels should be replaced to the degree possible with alternatives, but that potential environmental issues associated with heavy metals need to be addressed through third-party assessments of the environmental impacts. In Egypt some stakeholders feel that using alternative fuels is a good idea, but others feel that traditional fuel sources are so abundant that using alternatives is unnecessary. In Thailand, there is support for alternative fuels use, but issues have arisen about supply and collection (e.g. there is a 'black market' for used lubricating oil, making it difficult to secure for use as cement plant fuel). In Portugal, there is a controversy about burning waste as a secondary fuel. At the Washington, DC, dialogue, NGOs emphasised the need to conduct or support research to characterise and communicate the risks and benefits of alternative fuels and resources to workers and the community.

5. **Media's role in monitoring the industry**. Stakeholder views also varied on why the media is doing a poor job at monitoring the cement industry. The Brazilian press representatives interviewed were largely uninformed about cement industry operations. In Egypt, media representatives are familiar with the industry, but are often blamed by other stakeholders for not reporting more on problems caused by the industry. The media remain largely controlled by the government and members of the press are fearful of losing their jobs; they also feel it their duty not to cause the general public to panic. In contrast, stakeholders in Portugal and Thailand were sceptical about the objectivity of the media and complained that they focus on 'bad news' and create controversy.

11.2.2 *Case studies and discussion*

Overall, the information gathered emphasised the benefits of co-operation between the cement industry, the government and local stakeholders. One case study (Box 11.1) in Portugal illustrates how a company and government can work together to further sustainable development with the result being improved operating conditions, less environmental impact and social improvements.

IN 1999, CIMPOR, AS PART OF THE PORTUGUESE CEMENT SECTOR, ENTERED INTO AN agreement with the government of Portugal entitled 'Continuous Environmental Performance Improvement for the Cement Sector'. The goal of this agreement is to reduce dust emissions and improve other aspects of environmental performance.

CIMPOR agreed to take the following measures in its plants in Alhandra, Souselas and Loulé:

- Installing or retrofitting bag filters to control fixed particle emissions
- Controlling the sources of diffuse particle emissions, namely those related to conveying, and the handling and storing of raw materials and products
- Installing a network of instruments to monitor the quality of airborne emissions
- Abating the noise and vibration of equipment
- Restoring landscape altered by plant activities

The company is also analysing new technologies for quarrying, specifically alternatives to blasting.

In return, the Portuguese government (Ministry of the Environment and Ministry of the Economy) and local municipalities and councils have committed themselves to a three-year environmental and social rehabilitation programme for the same areas in which the plants operate.

Box 11.1 ***Case study of company/government co-operation for sustainable development: CIMPOR***

Source: Hund *et al.* 2001

Mutual responsibility by the cement industry and its stakeholders can be used to further sustainable development. Research shows that stakeholders feel that employment creation and 'keeping your job' are important. Yet these two issues can often be in direct conflict. A company can bring new jobs to a region by opening a new plant. However, residents can also perceive the proposed plant as damaging to current employment or way of life. For example, fishermen and others who use ocean resources vigorously protested against a proposed plant on the shores of Taiwan (to the point of sabotage and violence) because they felt that the cement plant would pollute the ocean and their fisheries (Fuertes 2000). Updating existing plants, bringing in new management and decommissioning are cases where a company can be mindful of its existing workforce and make decisions transparently with extensive communication. For example, positive company actions can show an interest in employees' concerns by minimising lay-offs, enabling employees to retire early or hiring local construction workers to make plant improvements. Box 11.2 shows an example of a company that has used a creative approach in decommissioning several plants and developing a new plant. The

IN THE UK, RMC SUBSIDIARY RUGBY CEMENT WAS OPERATING SEVEN OUT-OF-DATE kilns on four sites. The company decided to close all seven kilns and build a single new kiln on the site of an existing facility.

The company faced the challenge of announcing the plants' closures and responding to the reaction of employees and the public. The company realised the importance of giving employees time to make other plans. As soon as the company knew it was going to shut down a plant, it informed the staff. The feeling was that bad news was better than rumours. The company policy is to give a year's notice depending on the plant.

In addition, Rugby put announcements in local newspapers. Each of these plants employed 100–150 people, so the effect of the closures varied with the size of the community. Nonetheless, a total of 350 out of 1,000 jobs were lost. However, every person in the four closing sites had the option of applying for a job at the new plant. The company decided to completely change its culture in the new plant, moving to a team culture where everyone would be salaried and have input into operational decisions. Being chosen as one of the 130 to work at the new plant brought considerable status. The other options for employees were to retire early or to take a severance package and work elsewhere. Everyone was offered outplacement counselling and the company helped to place people. The transition occurred over a period of a year and a half.

Another major issue with decommissioning is planning what to do with obsolete facilities. Rugby owns a closed plant in the south-eastern part of the country (Kent). The company meets there with a community committee that cares very much about the future use of the site.

Another old, closed plant—Chinnor in Oxfordshire—was originally built away from a village but over time the village grew until it was directly next to the plant. In the past a relatively high proportion of residents worked at the plant, but now the village is in the London commuter belt. Here the company wants to develop its land for a multiplicity of uses including residential, small-scale industrial and public amenity. It is working with representatives of the village to draw up redevelopment proposals.

Debate about future site uses is commonly part of decommissioning a facility and active communications including stakeholder involvement can be critical in reaching a resolution.

Box 11.2 *Case study of decommissioning: RMC/Rugby Cement*

Source: Hund *et al.* 2001

company felt a responsibility to its workers and the communities. Likewise, the communities participated in the efforts to honestly identify workable solutions.

Land use and visibility are two further interrelated issues raised by stakeholders. At the Portugal dialogue, one stakeholder commented on an obsolete, tall stack left from a closed plant that she felt should have been removed long ago. Stakeholders are also concerned that quarries take up a large amount of land and often leave large holes or remove entire hills, significantly changing the landscape. In Java, the huge area of land used by cement plants and their associated quarries (minimum 1,000 hectares for lime and clay quarries) prompted the Ministry of Forestry in 1997 to ban the approval of any further plants in forested areas (*Jakarta Post* 1997). Overall, the extent to which people value the land they see around them cannot be underestimated. Box 11.3 gives an example of a company working with its government and local community to identify a mutually agreeable solution for obtaining the silica needed for making cement. This silica was

LAFARGE'S SANDSTONE QUARRY—ITS SOURCE OF SILICA FOR ITS EXSHAW PLANT near Banff, Alberta, Canada—is in the middle of an area that in the mid-1990s the provincial government designated as a Natural Area. The provincial government invited Lafarge to participate in the Yamnuska Natural Area Working Group to discuss the future of the quarry.

In responding to a suggestion by an environmental group representative during the ensuing negotiations, Lafarge agreed to take recycled glass containers from the surrounding region, including Banff National Park. The silica in the recycled glass supplements the silica that Lafarge mines from the quarry in the Natural Area. This arrangement gives the company the opportunity to display its logo on glass recycling containers throughout the region and to provide a public service. Lafarge agreed to reduce the 'footprint' of its operating area at the quarry and to progressively reclaim the quarry as mining progressed. It agreed to limit vehicle traffic around the quarry, and to confine its mining to the coldest months of the year when the fewest people are enjoying the Natural Area. The company helped to develop a management plan for the Natural Area. Lafarge has assumed more of an environmental stewardship role for the area by building trails, avoiding conflicting land uses and reducing the visibility of its fences.

An environmental group representative questioned whether Lafarge could obtain its sandstone from another source. Lafarge responded that the high-quality sandstone from the Mt Yamnuska quarry was necessary for the production of the high-quality cement the company manufactures for well casings for the oil and gas industry. To resolve this issue, the negotiating group brought in an expert from the Alberta Geological Society. The consulting geologist concluded that the Mt Yamnuska quarry was the only economically feasible supply of high-quality silica available to Lafarge's Exshaw plant. The environmental interests accepted this finding.

In 1997, the working group reached agreement that Lafarge could continue to operate its quarry in the Natural Area.

Box 11.3 *Case study on changing quarry operations: Lafarge*

Source: Hund et al. 2001

being mined in a quarry that had recently become part of a natural area designated by the government.

Impacts on regional image and quality of life are often of great public concern and are not immediately obvious to members of a potential incoming industry. The arrival of a new industry in a pristine area is often perceived as the beginning of a change from an agrarian rural way of life to an industrial urban culture. This can result in communities worrying that the change in character and presence of a cement plant will deter employers with less perceived environmental impact from locating in the region. Communities have also historically worried about the in-migration of non-local labour and subsequent impacts on the culture of their community (Cowell and Owens 1998). As with visual impact, qualitative issues can significantly influence siting and operations. While employment is important, it is not always the overriding interest; in many places, people take pride in their environment and traditional lifestyle (religious practices, farming, fishing) and want to see those respected.

11.3 Experience with other industries

The Sustainable Cement project offers a unique example of leading companies in one industry coming together to understand what actions are necessary to take positive steps towards a more sustainable future. There are many cases where individual companies have worked with stakeholders on specific projects and activities aimed at achieving a more sustainable society. For example, in the early 1990s Amoco Corporation formed a partnership with the United States Environmental Protection Agency to evaluate a wide variety of pollution control strategies and policies for a small refinery. Following a two-year study, the group found that substantially more pollution could be removed at lower cost than current environmental regulations demanded. Subsequent follow-up activities in both federal and state governments launched a number of pilot programmes aimed at testing new compliance approaches (Solomon 1993).

In the mid-1990s Dow Chemical joined forces with the Natural Resource Defense Council, Diane Hebert and Mary Sinclair (two Michigan residents), the Lone Tree Council, Citizens for Alternatives to Chemical Contamination, and the Ecology Center of Ann Arbor in Michigan under a project called the Michigan Source Reduction Initiative. Working together in a systematic way, they achieved dramatic pollution reductions over a two-year period at Dow's Midland Michigan manufacturing site, eliminating more than 4.8 million kg of waste and more than 0.6 million kg of releases: a 37% cut in pollution. The project also saved Dow more than US$5 million a year in operations and waste treatment costs for a US$3 million investment. This work was subsequently recognised with an award from the National Pollution Prevention Council (Meridian Institute 1999).

In the mid to late 1990s, the Chilean subsidiary of Henkel, a German Chemical company, identified a problem with a number of its adhesive products. At that time, toluene solvent in these products was attracting widespread illegal use by teenagers as an addictive inhalant. Used in this fashion, toluene was having serious and irreversible neurological effects on a significant fraction of Chile's youth. Henkel decided to reformulate a number of products to eliminate toluene. While the technical issues were solved relatively easily, Henkel built an effective coalition among the Universidad de Chile, the Centro de Información Toxicológica y de Medicamentos, the Chemical Industry Association of Chile and the Chilean Ministry of Health to promote the new product formulations, via a public education campaign. Henkel has institutionalised what it learned in Chile and now constantly seeks to eliminate solvents from its products where possible, reducing costs, environmental emissions and potentially dangerous exposures.

These examples illustrate companies that have taken responsibility for their actions and are working collaboratively with community groups and other stakeholders to achieve more sustainable development.

11.4 Possible actions to enhance mutual responsibility

Progress towards sustainable development requires thoughtful engagement and listening. Industry has the responsibility to involve and listen to its stakeholders and consider their feedback when making decisions. Management actions, strategic approaches and practical tools need to reflect that industry has considered stakeholder feedback in their design and implementation. Stakeholders have the responsibility of getting engaged in the challenges facing their community, identifying and communicating priorities, taking on assignments of their own, and developing partnerships with industry where appropriate.

11.4.1 Management actions

Sustainable development will only be successful if senior management is committed to it. Part of this commitment includes senior management actively communicating with stakeholders and articulating its specific commitments to sustainable development. Communication can take various different forms (see Fig. 11.3) that are appropriate for different types of situation.[7] In general, the more engaged stakeholders feel, when both the company and stakeholders are sharing knowledge and, ideally, stakeholders are involved in decision-making, the more company decisions will be viewed as acceptable to stakeholders and therefore implemented more easily.

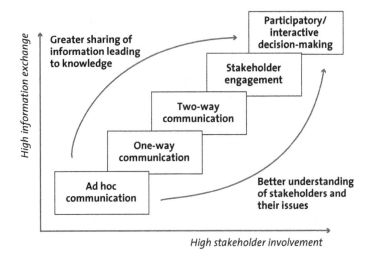

Figure 11.3 **Types of communication**

Source: Hund *et al.* 2001

Senior management need to participate in exchanges with stakeholders and provide feedback directly to them. The public often sees a plant manager as the face of a company. Therefore, it is ideal for these managers to have strong communication skills.

A communications strategy is needed with sufficient staff and financial resources to implement it. In situations where a communications team is available and actively working with stakeholders, senior management should involve them in internal decision-

---

7   See Hund *et al.* 2001 for a full discussion on types of communication.

making, particularly about major changes being considered, given the team's first-hand knowledge of stakeholder perceptions, concerns and expectations.

Staff of a company make excellent ambassadors in their community and can be an important part of a stakeholder engagement plan. Senior management is responsible for communicating its vision and involving staff in implementing sustainable development projects. Staff want to be proud of their company and feel that it reflects their values and morals. When such is the case, they can promote and implement sustainable actions in the plant and in their communities.

A continuous communications programme is critical to monitor changes and shifts in society and resulting stakeholder perceptions so that business priorities and strategies can be adjusted accordingly. One example mentioned in the cement dialogues was the recent shift in the political environment in some regions to encourage public participation in public policy development. In these regions, companies will need to consider how to engage a public that feels more empowered to take political action.

One specific management action that the WGC could take to further its message and plans for sustainable development would be to educate non-WGC companies about best practices. Small companies and quarry operators could be mentored to help them improve their operations.

11.4.2 *Strategic approaches*

Several strategic approaches could be used to further industry's responsibility in communicating with and engaging stakeholders such that sustainable development is encouraged. One approach for industry to consider is creating or enhancing its **sustainable development management and reporting mechanisms**. Stakeholders want more information about the industries that they perceive can affect them. Stakeholders are responsible for identifying the information they want and communicating it to industry. Likewise, industry is responsible for soliciting this information from global, regional and local stakeholders and considering it in designing their reporting approach. Stakeholders want information to be transparent and want a timeline of when particular performance goals will be met.

Industry wants a reporting approach that is manageable, and one that does not overburden the company with documentation requirements or release proprietary information. The development of performance measures needs to be done openly with stakeholders including the general public, regulators and shareholders. Items that may be of interest include air emissions, worker safety, contributions to community activities and financial performance. The performance measures and other relevant environmental, health and safety, social parameters and economic measures could be included in an annual Sustainable Development Report. This report can communicate the benefits of new technologies and processes being implemented. It can also discuss what the company needs from its stakeholders in order to be sustainable. A sustainable development report could be used as the reporting mechanism for a company's environmental management system, and health and safety management system and could become a key communication device aimed at keeping stakeholders informed and tracking progress towards sustainable development.[8]

---

8   All WBCSD members are required to produce such a report as a condition of membership.

There are many approaches that industry can consider, all centring on its commitment to **strategic engagement with communities** to determine their concerns and needs to build stronger communities (e.g. infrastructure support and education support), which leads to enhanced recruiting opportunities and overall stronger relations. Again, communities also have the responsibility to establish priorities and make them known to industry. Several collaborative approaches can be tailored to solicit stakeholder feedback:

- **Voluntary agreements** between a company and its surrounding community that establish sustainable development objectives and/or performance measures that would be tracked jointly by the company and the community.

- **Citizen advisory or community liaison groups** designed with a broad range of views that are seen as representative and credible to the community. These groups are helpful sounding boards for companies when considering major decisions.

- **Dialogues** where stakeholders are involved in decision-making (more than just public relations sessions). Dialogues are particularly critical for companies considering changes that will affect their communities.

- **Third parties** used to gather stakeholder feedback on how well the corporation is performing in a sustainable development manner. Interviews could be conducted as well as mail-in postcards. Such a solicitation could also be designed to determine how well the corporation is connecting to its various audiences. Results from these solicitations could be posted on the corporation's website to indicate its transparency and interest in continually improving.

- **Annual stewardship dinners** where stakeholders and the managing directors of critical business units are invited to meet and discuss sustainable development progress.

- **Sustainable business dinners** where the chief executive officer discusses sustainable development issues with a small number of policy-makers, NGOs and critical business leaders to receive feedback first-hand.

- **Community support projects** where a company and community work together to identify those projects most needing assistance that are supportive of sustainable development goals (e.g. technical assistance to a local waste-water treatment system, community health monitoring).

- **Partnerships with educational institutions** to provide training to broaden a community's skill base. Enhancing recruitment options would be a benefit to industry from such a partnership.

- **Partnerships between communities and industries to form industrial ecosystems** where the waste of one industry can be used as a feedstream for another industry. This partnership would enhance job creation and minimise pollution.

- **Partnerships between industry and appropriate stakeholders to influence policies that are supportive of sustainable development.** For example, a regulatory body interested in sustainable development could work with a national cement association to look for opportunities to modify policies and regulatory protocols to encourage sustainable development.

Finally, one approach the global cement industry could take to demonstrate its responsibility to stakeholders is to **establish a Sustainable Development Institute** that would be a voice for the cement and concrete industries to engage in all aspects concerning sustainable development.[9] If such an institute were to be created, it could identify areas for research and development where investments need to be made and co-ordinate the results of this research (including technical, economic and social topics). Communication approaches could be researched to determine those perceived as most appropriate and effective for different audiences. From a mission perspective, the institute could communicate information to and from stakeholders globally and serve as a resource for regional and local communications to all stakeholders. If the institute were formed, it would need an active communications division to gather stakeholder opinions, perceptions and reactions to influence research priorities and inform policies. In this role, the institute would need to co-ordinate information content and flow and to align industry messages at the various levels within industry.

Sustainable development can only occur if a company and its stakeholders are jointly committed. When a company is incorporating sustainability into its way of doing business, it needs its stakeholders to be engaged and involved in the transformation. Stakeholders need to become educated on the principles of sustainable development and prepared to communicate their ideas about how to achieve it. Where appropriate, partnerships need to be formed with roles and responsibilities outlined and supported by all parties. A joint commitment will help sustainable development succeed.

---

9 A thorough description of the vision and roles and responsibilities of this proposed institute is provided in Battelle *et al.* 2002b.

WHO CARES?

Community perceptions in the marketing of corporate citizenship[*]

Debra King and Alison Mackinnon
Hawke Institute of Social Research, University of South Australia

Corporations are increasingly coming under scrutiny as a well-educated community, informed by active media, becomes more aware of corporate misdemeanours in offshore settings, of high executive salaries and of an apparently never-ending litany of take-overs, downsizing and redundancies. However, at the same time, and sometimes in response to this scrutiny, corporations are becoming increasingly anxious to develop and showcase 'good' corporate citizenship practices. Community attitudes towards corporate behaviour and the relationship between business and society are widely regarded as influencing the development of responsible corporate citizenship practices (Nolan 1996; Marsden and Andriof 1998; Wartick and Wood 1998; Khoury *et al.* 1999; Peters 1999). Within specific corporations, community members have been asked for their opinions on corporate performance, and sometimes involved in identifying the ways in which a corporation can address its social responsibilities (for example, see the annual reports of corporations such as Shell [2000], WMC [1999] and The Body Shop [1998]). At a more general level, the community has been canvassed for its opinion on the generic performance of business and whether or not business as a whole should be more ethical, environmentally sustainable and socially responsible (Environics 1999). Research at both of these levels indicates that the community certainly does care about corporate behaviour. Indeed, with the community encapsulating a broad range of primary and secondary stakeholders in the corporate citizenship debates, when asking 'Who cares?' the relevance of community opinion cannot be overlooked.

[*] We would like to acknowledge the contribution of The National Heart Foundation of Australia for its its generosity in funding this research, and in particular of its former Marketing Director, Bill Hovey, for playing a key role in initiating and maintaining the research partnership; of David Curtis who provided essential statistical expertise and assistance; and of Caz Batson who is progressing the research project.

While both of these levels of analysis are important in understanding the relationship between community expectations and corporate citizenship practices, there is another level that offers new insights into this relationship. Between the macro level of the community's attitude to the general responsibilities of business and the micro level of stakeholders' attitudes towards a specific corporation's citizenship practices is a mesa level focusing on the community's attitude to particular corporate citizenship practices. It is this mesa level that we concentrate on in this chapter.

Mesa-level analysis interested us for two reasons. One reason was the gap in knowledge about corporate citizenship created by a focus on the micro and macro levels. What we sought to establish in this project was whether the general community valued some aspects of corporate citizenship over others and, if so, whether these differences were associated with particular demographic or stakeholder groups. The other reason was that the mesa level appeared to be more relevant for producing information required for increasing the take-up of responsible corporate citizenship practices among corporations. In effect, our project sought to find a way of effectively marketing corporate citizenship to corporations. This meant conceptualising the community as 'potential' stakeholders, who not only had an interest in corporate behaviour but could also influence a corporation's reputation and success. Once again our approach had a mesa-level focus. We have attempted to fill in some of the gaps between the macro level, which provides a generalised overview of the benefits of corporate citizenship, and the micro level, which provides information to corporations once they have already embarked on their corporate citizenship strategy. Our aim was to produce information that would be useful to corporations that had some knowledge about the benefits of corporate citizenship, but had not taken any steps to systematically incorporate corporate citizenship practices into the organisation.

This chapter provides an overview of the results of our research, which was conducted in Australia during the first half of 2000. Before discussing these results, however, a brief summary of the state of play of corporate citizenship in Australia is provided. We argue that one of the main drivers for increasing the take-up of corporate citizenship in Australia is likely to be reputation, and as such the research focuses on delineating the relationship between corporate citizenship practices, reputation and reputational value. In discussing the survey results, the value of this relationship as a tool for marketing corporate citizenship to corporations is highlighted. The chapter concludes with an appraisal of how these results might be used by corporations to develop and implement a corporate citizenship strategy.

12.1 Marketing corporate citizenship to Australian corporations

As a case study, Australia has its own particularities. Somewhat paradoxically from a marketing perspective, while Australians are among the most active in identifying and punishing irresponsible corporations (Hale 1999), the business sector has been comparatively reticent in adopting corporate citizenship practices. This is not to say that corporate citizenship is not being discussed. In 1998, the Prime Minister, John Howard, launched the Community–Business Partnership initiative aimed at encouraging greater corporate investment in Australia's social fabric (Howard 1998). In 1999, the first Australian Corporate Citizenship Conference was held, and at the same time the Business Council of Australia began to consider the issue in its Working Papers (BCA 1999: 47-64). To a large extent, however, corporations that have taken up corporate citizenship at an organisational level have tended to be those that are global/international, or those that have had their reputation damaged by previous irresponsible practices.

Part of this reticence to embrace corporate citizenship could be explained by the history of corporate–government–community relations in Australia. For example, Australia has had:

- Little history of widespread corporate philanthropy or social investment; instead the government has been a major player in delivering community and social welfare programmes

- Relatively strong unions in their advocacy of workers' rights

- A reasonably successful environmental movement in terms of mainstreaming many environmental issues

- A broad base of relatively acquiescent shareholders regarding issues of corporate governance

In this context, business has not had to take leadership in the areas encapsulated by corporate citizenship and the lack of clear leadership in this area has definitely been a problem for increasing the take-up of corporate citizenship (Cazalet 2000: 11-12). With this background, the project focused on developing a mesa-level analysis with a view to influencing the take-up of corporate citizenship activities by businesses.

One of the strategies used for increasing the take-up of corporate citizenship in the business community has been in relating the benefits of corporate citizenship to improved corporate reputation (Fombrun 1996; McIntosh *et al.* 1998; Peters 1999; PwC 1999a, 1999b; WalkerInformation 1999). A key argument for this strategy is that adopting 'good' corporate citizenship practices will not only increase corporate reputation but that this increased reputation will have a financial benefit as a result of improved competitive advantage (Fombrun 1996: 73; Burson-Marsteller 1998: 3). A difficulty with this argument is in defining what a 'good' corporate citizenship practice constitutes for particular corporations. Until corporations are prepared to go to the expense and trouble of conducting intensive research with their stakeholders to delineate the kinds of corporate behaviours that will improve their reputation, the notion of being a 'good' corporate citizen remains somewhat abstract. On the other hand, corporations are unlikely to conduct this kind of stakeholder research unless they can perceive some eventual benefit. Our research aimed to break this deadlock by providing corporations with generic information relating to the kinds of corporate citizenship activity that were likely to increase or decrease reputation and reputational value. Corporate citizenship advocates could then use this information to persuade corporations to develop and adopt an appropriate corporate citizenship strategy.

12.2 The research process

The research sought to determine the extent to which adopting corporate citizenship principles influenced reputation and the value of a corporation's reputation. As mentioned earlier, we took a mesa-level approach to the research in order to establish whether potential stakeholders, in this case members of the general community, differentiated between various corporate citizenship activities. With the view of using the results of the research to market responsible corporate citizenship to Australian corporations, we developed a questionnaire designed to examine the relationship between corporate citizenship, reputation and reputational value from the perspective of potential stakeholders. As each of these terms have been used in various ways, it is perhaps useful to delineate our definitions:

- **Corporate citizenship.** Following Maignan and Ferrell (1999: 456), corporate citizenship is taken to refer to the practices associated with a commitment to corporate social responsibility.

- **Reputation.** Drawing on Fombrun's (1996: 72) definition, reputation is the 'perceptual representation of a company's past actions and future prospects that describes the firm's overall appeal to all of its key constituents when compared with rivals'. Reputations are built from stakeholder perceptions of corporate behaviour and, because stakeholders are diverse (each group has particular interests and needs), they are often contested sites (King 2000), not only between corporations but also within each corporation. This contestation means that the ability to identify, respond to and mediate between the perspectives of different stakeholder groups is critical for corporations to gain, maintain and benefit from having a good reputation.

- **Reputational value.** As reputation is an intangible good, it is difficult to give it an objective value.[1] However, inasmuch as a reputation provides a corporation with a competitive advantage, one would expect financial benefits to follow. For this research the indicator of reputational value was the 'intentions to deal' of the potential stakeholders. That is, if a corporation engaged in a particular corporate citizenship practice, to what extent would this influence stakeholder behaviour? As consumers, investors, employees and community members, the behaviour of potential stakeholders is likely to have a real impact on corporate profitability through changes in consumption and investment patterns, employee satisfaction and productivity, and community acceptance.

- **Potential stakeholders.** This term was used to differentiate between the community as actual stakeholders of particular corporations, and the community as having the potential to be stakeholders based on their perception of a corporation's performance and activities. In this research, the corporation is hypothetical and the focus is on how the implementation of particular corporate citizenship practices will influence the potential stakeholders' perceptions of

1   Fombrun uses the notion of 'reputational capital' to refer to the 'the amount by which the company's market value exceeds the liquidation value of its assets' (1996: 92). However, this amount covers the value of all intangibles which may or may not relate to reputation.

that corporation and whether it will influence their intentions to deal with that corporation in the future.

Participants in the survey were asked their opinions about 40 corporate citizenship activities. These activities were grouped into four categories, some of which had sub-sets. The hierarchical relationships among the items are illustrated in Figure 12.1. In the survey, however, the order in which the corporate citizenship activities were listed was randomly selected. For each activity, participants were asked two questions about an unspecified corporation:

- To what extent would knowing about this aspect of corporate behaviour influence what you think about the corporation's reputation?

- To what extent would knowing about this aspect of corporate behaviour influence your decision to deal (use products/services, invest in, work for) with this business in the future?

A mail-out of 2,200 surveys was sent to randomly selected households throughout Australia. Of these, 213 were returned unopened or undelivered.[2] A phone follow-up was

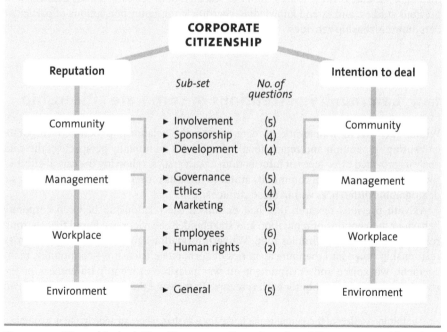

Figure 12.1 ***Hierarchical relationships among the sub-scales of the corporate citizenship inventory***

2   The random sample of residential addresses was drawn from the DeskTop Marketing Systems (DTMS) CD-ROM which lists all entries in the Australian *White Pages* telephone directory. An

conducted, giving an overall response from 279 participants, seven of which were incomplete and not used. The response rate of usable surveys was therefore 13.7% of those delivered, which was considered reasonable given the unsolicited and specific nature of the survey.[3]

In addition to the questions relating to corporate citizenship, reputation and reputational value, the survey also sought basic demographic details and information relating to the participants' identification with stakeholder groups. Although the survey was sent to a national random group, the respondents differed from the national average in significant ways. It is reasonable perhaps to infer from these differences that a certain group of Australians have an interest in corporate citizenship. Compared with national figures compiled by the Australian Bureau of Statistics (ABS 1999, 2000), the survey respondents were better educated, more likely to be between the ages of 35 and 54, slightly more likely to be female and have a slightly higher income (see Table 12.1).

Following the preliminary SPSS[4] analysis to establish data integrity, frequencies, scale reliability, basic multiple regressions and an exploratory factor analysis, the data was further subjected to two more levels of analysis. Quest was used to conduct a Rasch analysis (discussed below) of the validity of the scale that was used, while PLS Path was used to implement a partial least squares approach to determine the relationships between the major variables. The findings from our research both reinforce trends delineated in previous studies, and extend knowledge regarding community perceptions of particular corporate citizenship activities.

12.3 Community perceptions of corporate citizenship

Within the overall framework of determining the relationship between corporate citizenship, reputation and reputational value from a community perspective, the data analysis provided three types of information: a path analysis showing the causal effect of the relationship, a scale of community attitudes towards the relationship, and some basic demographic differences within these attitudes.

As with previous research that had examined the relationship between corporate behaviour, perceptions of reputation and stakeholder behaviour, we found that a strong relationship existed (Environics 1999; WalkerInformation 1999). In breaking this gross relationship down into the four categories of corporate citizenship—community, management, workplace and environment—it was possible to identify differences in the strength of the relationship for each category. To measure the relationship we used two

> unfortunate effect of the sampling methodology was that, where an address did not contain a specific unit or house number, the postal service returned the survey stamped 'insufficiently addressed'.

3 Nevertheless, this response rate is recognised as being low. Although piloted before distribution, it is possible that the complexity of the survey, as well as the fact that it was totally unsolicited, were the main reasons for this low rate. It is therefore likely that those responding to the survey had an interest either in the subject matter (as was indicated by the comments they made on the surveys) or in filling out surveys.

4 SPSS is a software package used to compute statistical analyses of data.

Demographic information	ABS national profile (%)	Survey respondents (%)
Gender		
▪ Male	49.4	44.9
▪ Female	50.6	55.1
	100.0	*100.0*
Age (years)		
▪ 15-34	37.5	20.8
▪ 35-54	36.2	52.6
▪ 55+	26.3	26.6
	100.0	*100.0*
Income ($)		
▪ Nil–19,999	41.4	34.0
▪ 20,000–39,000	30.1	28.8
▪ 40,000–59,000	14.9	18.6
▪ 60,000–79,000	6.2	6.6
▪ Over 80,000	7.7	8.0
▪ No answer		4.0
	100.0	*100.0*
Educational attainment		
▪ Secondary school (not completed)	46.6	17.9
▪ Secondary school (completed)	16.3	28.1
▪ TAFE or diploma	24.4	19.3
▪ Undergraduate degree	11.1	17.9
▪ Postgraduate degree	1.6	12.8
▪ No answer		4.0
	100.0	*100.0*

Table 12.1 ***Comparison of demographic profile of the Australian population and survey respondents***

methods of analysis. First, the correlation between reputation and intentions to deal was determined using the data from the Rasch-scaled scores. Compared with the standard SPSS raw scores, Rasch-scaled scores were considered to be the more reliable values as they are computed on the basis of the relative difficulties of the items that were completed and are not as affected by missed items. As shown in Figure 12.2, the correlations between reputation and intentions to deal for each of the sub-scales were all very high and extremely significant ($p < 0.000$), almost reflecting a ceiling effect (which would be reached at $r = 0.9$). By estimating the coefficient of determination (r^2) it was possible to begin to develop the grounds for arguing a causal relationship. From these figures, between 69% and 77% of the variation in future dealings can be explained by changes in perception of reputation.

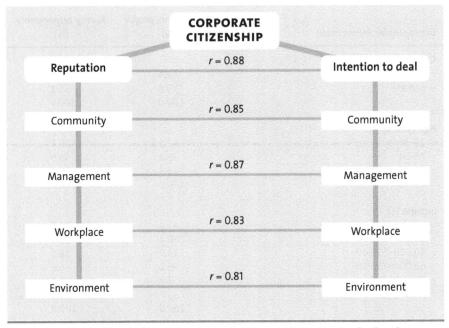

Figure 12.2 **Correlations between 'reputation' scales and 'intention to deal' scales (p <0.000)**

Second, a path analysis was conducted. Both reputation and intentions to deal are latent constructs that were measured in the survey through the manifest variables of the four sub-scales: community, management, workplace and environment. The relationships depicted in Figure 12.3 show that:

- Reputation is indicated by four 'observed' or manifest variables.

- Intentions to deal are reflected in four similar observed variables.

- There is a causal relationship between reputation and intentions to deal.

This is a path model and is based on both theory and observed data. Theory suggests the relationships and their direction of influence, and the data collected is used to indicate the validity of the model.

The model was tested using a partial least squares[5] approach to the estimation of model parameters. There are two components to the model: the relationship between the

---

5 Partial least squares path analysis (PLS) was preferred over structural equation modelling (SEM) due to concerns about both the complexity of the model, and the possibility that certain distributional assumptions associated with SEM might be violated due to the size of the sample. As PLS cannot estimate standard errors or confidence intervals for parameters, jack-knifing (the removal of individual cases and the re-estimation of parameters) was used to assess the stability of estimates. Low jack-knife standard errors indicated the estimates were stable.

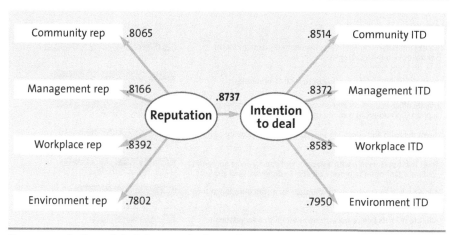

Figure 12.3 *Path model of the causal relationship between 'reputation' and 'intention to deal' and their manifest expressions in the sub-scales*

manifest variables to each latent construct is measured as a multiple regression relationship, while the inner path illustrates the causal relationship among the latent constructs. As expected from the preliminary analysis, the loadings of the outer model are all high; there is only slight differentiation between the community, management and workplace sub-scales. Although the environment is slightly lower than the others, it would be difficult on the basis of the data in the sample to say that one factor is definitively more influential than others in forming either reputation or intentions to deal.

The inner model path had a value of 0.8737 (standard error 0.025) which, considering the range is between –1.0 and +1.0, is very high. Its coefficient of determination at 0.763 indicates that 76% of the variation observed in intentions to deal can be explained by changes in perceptions of reputation. Overall, the model illustrates that the relationship between corporate citizenship, perceptions of reputation and intentions to deal is both highly coherent and causal.

The strength of the relationships between reputation and intentions to deal as indicated by the path analysis is further legitimated by the Rasch-scale analysis that was performed on the data. This analysis was conducted to determine whether the scale used in the questionnaire was a coherent measure of corporate citizenship. If it was, then the scale could be replicated and used either for specific corporations or on different sample groups (particularly stakeholder groups, for example). In effect, the Rasch method ensures that scales of attitude are 'sample-independent' inasmuch as it produces scale-free person measures and sample-free item difficulties (Hand and Trembath 1999: 64).

In developing a corporate citizenship scale, Rasch analyses were conducted to ascertain item fit. Infit mean square (IMS) statistics were generated and items were accepted as fitting if the IMS lay between 0.77 and 1.30. Of the 40 items tested, three did not fit the scale: that is, they were not a reliable measure of one variable, and were therefore eliminated. All further analyses of the data, including the path analysis discussed above, were therefore based on a 37-item scale of corporate citizenship. These items, grouped in their sub-scales, are listed in Figure 12.4. Opposite each item are two bar charts, one

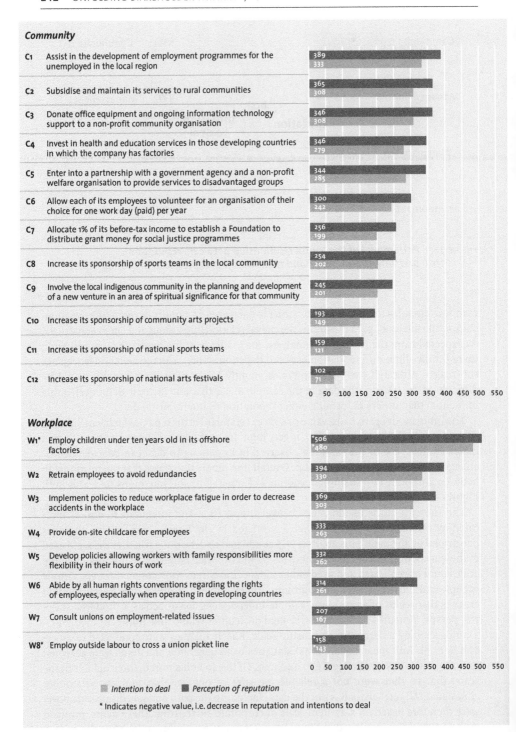

Community

C1 Assist in the development of employment programmes for the unemployed in the local region — 389 / 333

C2 Subsidise and maintain its services to rural communities — 365 / 308

C3 Donate office equipment and ongoing information technology support to a non-profit community organisation — 346 / 308

C4 Invest in health and education services in those developing countries in which the company has factories — 346 / 279

C5 Enter into a partnership with a government agency and a non-profit welfare organisation to provide services to disadvantaged groups — 344 / 285

C6 Allow each of its employees to volunteer for an organisation of their choice for one work day (paid) per year — 300 / 242

C7 Allocate 1% of its before-tax income to establish a Foundation to distribute grant money for social justice programmes — 256 / 199

C8 Increase its sponsorship of sports teams in the local community — 254 / 202

C9 Involve the local indigenous community in the planning and development of a new venture in an area of spiritual significance for that community — 245 / 201

C10 Increase its sponsorship of community arts projects — 193 / 149

C11 Increase its sponsorship of national sports teams — 159 / 121

C12 Increase its sponsorship of national arts festivals — 102 / 71

0 50 100 150 200 250 300 350 400 450 500 550

Workplace

W1* Employ children under ten years old in its offshore factories — *506 / *480

W2 Retrain employees to avoid redundancies — 394 / 330

W3 Implement policies to reduce workplace fatigue in order to decrease accidents in the workplace — 369 / 303

W4 Provide on-site childcare for employees — 333 / 263

W5 Develop policies allowing workers with family responsibilities more flexibility in their hours of work — 332 / 262

W6 Abide by all human rights conventions regarding the rights of employees, especially when operating in developing countries — 314 / 261

W7 Consult unions on employment-related issues — 207 / 167

W8* Employ outside labour to cross a union picket line — *158 / *143

0 50 100 150 200 250 300 350 400 450 500 550

□ Intention to deal   ■ Perception of reputation

* Indicates negative value, i.e. decrease in reputation and intentions to deal

Figure 12.4 **Corporate citizenship scale: changes in reputation and intention to deal**
(continued opposite)

Management

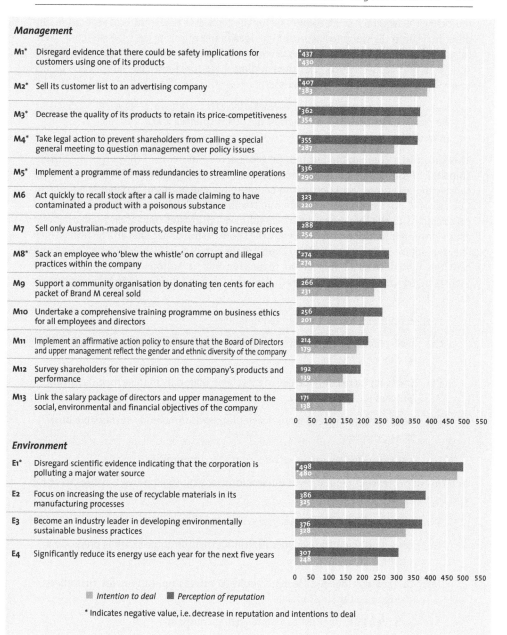

M1*   Disregard evidence that there could be safety implications for customers using one of its products — *437 / *430

M2*   Sell its customer list to an advertising company — *407 / *383

M3*   Decrease the quality of its products to retain its price-competitiveness — *362 / *354

M4*   Take legal action to prevent shareholders from calling a special general meeting to question management over policy issues — *355 / *287

M5*   Implement a programme of mass redundancies to streamline operations — *336 / *290

M6   Act quickly to recall stock after a call is made claiming to have contaminated a product with a poisonous substance — 323 / 220

M7   Sell only Australian-made products, despite having to increase prices — 288 / 254

M8*   Sack an employee who 'blew the whistle' on corrupt and illegal practices within the company — *274 / *274

M9   Support a community organisation by donating ten cents for each packet of Brand M cereal sold — 266 / 231

M10   Undertake a comprehensive training programme on business ethics for all employees and directors — 256 / 201

M11   Implement an affirmative action policy to ensure that the Board of Directors and upper management reflect the gender and ethnic diversity of the company — 214 / 179

M12   Survey shareholders for their opinion on the company's products and performance — 192 / 139

M13   Link the salary package of directors and upper management to the social, environmental and financial objectives of the company — 171 / 138

0   50   100   150   200   250   300   350   400   450   500   550

Environment

E1*   Disregard scientific evidence indicating that the corporation is polluting a major water source — *498 / *480

E2   Focus on increasing the use of recyclable materials in its manufacturing processes — 386 / 325

E3   Become an industry leader in developing environmentally sustainable business practices — 376 / 328

E4   Significantly reduce its energy use each year for the next five years — 307 / 248

0   50   100   150   200   250   300   350   400   450   500   550

▨ *Intention to deal*   ■ *Perception of reputation*

* Indicates negative value, i.e. decrease in reputation and intentions to deal

Figure 12.4   (continued)

indicating the weighted score for measuring the change in perceptions of reputation, the other indicating the weighted score for changes in intentions to deal. These scores were calculated by multiplying the number of responses for each of the five points on the Likert scale by a relevant weighting, and then adding these together. That is, for each item a score was generated using the formula:

Decrease a lot (N responses × −2) + *Decrease some* (N responses × −1) +
No change (N responses × 0) + *Increase some* (N responses × 1) +
Increase a lot (N responses × 2)

This provided a comparable meaningful score across all items of the corporate citizenship scale. From Figure 12.4, it is therefore possible to determine which items are likely to have the greatest effect in changing community perceptions of reputation and intentions to deal. For example, in the community sub-scale, the development of employment programmes in the local region (C1) would have far greater impact on reputation and future dealing intentions than increasing the sponsorship of national arts festivals (C12).

From Figure 12.4 it is possible to compare the extent to which corporate citizenship activities would have an impact on reputation and intentions to deal. In terms of increasing reputation and intentions to deal, the top five activities were for corporations to:

W2: retrain employees to avoid redundancies

C1: assist in the development of employment programmes for the unemployed in the local region

E2: focus on increasing the use of recyclable materials in their manufacturing processes

E3: become industry leaders in developing environmentally sustainable business practices

C2: subsidise and maintain services to rural communities

In terms of decreasing reputation and intentions to deal, the top five activities were for corporations to:

W1: employ children under ten years old in offshore factories

E1: disregard scientific evidence indicating that the corporation is polluting a major water source

M1: disregard evidence that there could be safety implications for customers using one of their products

M2: sell their customer list to an advertising company

M3: decrease the quality of their products to retain their price-competitiveness

In addition to enabling these comparisons, the above scale also illustrates the differences in the relationship between the change in reputation and the change in intentions to deal for each type of corporate citizenship activity. In the management sub-scale, for example, item M8, sacking a 'whistle-blower', generated equivalent scores in the change in perceptions of reputation and change in intentions to deal, while item M6, acting quickly to recall contaminated stock, generated a large change in perception of reputation, but a much smaller change in intentions to deal. Therefore, while the overall relationship between reputation and intentions to deal is very high, there is variation between items that needs to be considered if the aim is to change a corporation's reputational value, rather than simply its reputation.

Further delineation of differences in the data was achieved by examining the scale in terms of the following demographic and stakeholder variables:

- Demographic variables: gender, age, education, income

- Stakeholder variables:[6] employee, investor, union member, community volunteer, member of a professional association, a social movement organisation, a political party, an environmental organisation

Initial analysis compared the mean scores on each of the main corporate citizenship categories of community, management, workplace and environment for reputation and intentions to deal, as well as on the two major scales. In order to separate the influences of participants' demographic and stakeholder characteristics on the corporate citizenship scale, a series of multiple regression models were then run.

Table 12.2 summarises the results of the multiple regression analyses by allocating a numerical value from 1 to 10 relating to the statistical significance of the results. The strength of an influence is demonstrated by the size of the statistical significance (p value); where $p = 0.000$ the influence is extremely strong and has been allocated a '10', declining to the weakest influence of '1' when $p = 0.099$. With the exception of age (discussed below), all significant influences have been reported: that is, where $p < 0.1$.

Of the demographic and stakeholder variables tested, the most significant influence on changes in the combined sub-scales relating to reputation and to intentions to deal was membership of a social movement organisation, while being a woman or a union member also had a strong influence. In contrast, variables such as income level, educational attainment, being a member of a political party or a professional association exerted no influence on any of the indicators of corporate reputation or intentions to deal.

Within the four corporate citizenship sub-scales, however, there was greater differentiation. In these, being a woman exerted a strong influence on both reputation and intentions to deal in the community and workplace sub-scales, while being a member of a social movement organisation was a very strong influence in all sub-scales except for environment. In contrast, being a member of an environmental organisation influenced the intentions to deal, but not reputation, when environmental issues were at stake. In fact, being a volunteer was a stronger influence on changes in perceptions of reputation and intentions to deal within the environment sub-scale. Less surprising, perhaps, was the strong influence that union membership had on workplace reputation and intentions to deal. Union membership was also a significant influence in changes in perceptions of reputation in management corporate citizenship activities, as well as in the intentions to deal when environmental issues were at stake. While being in paid work had a strong influence on both reputation and intentions to deal within the environment category, being an investor had only a small influence on the reputation variable in environment.

---

6   It was assumed that all respondents would be consumers at some level, therefore this stakeholder group was not used as a variable in the research.

	Community reputation	Community intentions to deal	Management reputation	Management intentions to deal	Workplace reputation	Workplace intentions to deal	Environment reputation	Environment intentions to deal	All items reputation	All items intentions to deal
Woman	8	10			5	9		7	8	10
Investor						7	6			
Paid worker							10	8		
Volunteer worker							8	1		
Union member			6		10	10			5	6
Member of social organisation	10	10	10	10	10	10			10	10
Member of environmental organisation								7		

Note: Range goes from 10 = extremely high influence, to 1 = weak influence

Table 12.2 **Summary of analysis of the influence of demographic and stakeholder variables on corporate citizenship categories**

However, investors also had an influence on intentions to deal regarding workplace corporate citizenship activities.

Unlike the other variables reported in Table 12.2, age was not conducive to a multiple regression analysis. However, the comparison of mean scores relating to the three age categories indicated that respondents in the middle age group of 35–54 years were more concerned with reputation in the management category, and both reputation and intentions to deal with regard to environmental issues, than respondents in either of the other two age groups (15–34 or over 55 years).

In summarising this section, the data from the research provides a wealth of information for corporations to draw on in making decisions about whether corporate citizenship is worthwhile, and what kinds of corporate citizenship activity would be appropriate for them to adopt. In the following section, we discuss how these results might be used in the marketing of corporate citizenship.

12.4 Marketing corporate citizenship at the mesa level

This research reinforces claims made in previous research that being perceived as a 'good' or a 'bad' corporate citizen will have repercussions for corporations in terms of changes in stakeholder behaviour. Inasmuch as stakeholder behaviour influences a corporation's competitive advantage through purchasing and investing patterns and employee productivity, then changes in stakeholders' intentions to deal with a corporation could have very real bottom-line effects. Even when the aggregate category of corporate citizenship was broken down into the four sub-scales, it was found that there was only a slight variation in the relationship between reputation and intentions to deal for practices relating to the community, management, workplace and the environment. Therefore, while corporations could improve their reputation and reputational value by focusing on any one of the areas, unless they can sustain these in the remaining areas, they risk losing the benefits of any improvements. Indeed, given the strength of the relationship between reputation and intentions to deal, the most advantageous strategy would be to adopt 'good' corporate citizenship practices across all four areas. This means that, although corporate citizenship can have benefits when undertaken with a single focus, it is of greatest value when viewed in a more holistic way and integrated into corporate activities across all areas.

Undertaking wholesale corporate change is, however, a mammoth task requiring a high level of commitment from all sectors of a corporation. While obviously the best strategy in terms of maximising the benefits of being a good corporate citizen, the research also provided useful information for corporations wishing to stagger or target their corporate citizenship strategy. For corporations interested in staggering the implementation of a corporate citizenship strategy the path analysis indicated that, although all areas had a very high impact on reputation and intentions to deal, the workplace might be the best area in which to begin. While improvements in workplace practices were likely to have the greatest impact on both reputation and intentions to deal, corporations interested in undertaking a more community-oriented approach to their corporate citizenship strategy would still benefit significantly in terms of changes in stakeholder behaviour (and, therefore, their reputational value), even though the impact on their reputation may not be as high.

Although the environment sub-scale did not appear to have as great an impact on either reputation or intentions to deal as the other sub-scales, this should not be over-emphasised. It needs to be remembered that all of the correlations in the research were very highly significant, although there are two factors in particular that may have affected the slightly lower impact of the environment sub-scale. One factor is internal to the research and relates to the relatively small number of questions asked about environmental issues. As the research had a focus on the social rather than environmental responsibilities of business, it was this aspect that received the greatest attention. Nevertheless, of the environmental questions asked, three made it into the two 'top five' lists for activities that had the greatest impact on reputation and intentions to deal (refer to the discussion about Fig. 12.4), indicating that the environment has particular importance to the potential stakeholders surveyed.

The other factor relates to the nature of environmental issues. In Australia there is an extent to which the community expects corporations to be environmentally responsible.

For the past 15 years, Australia has had a very vocal and often very active environmental movement which has raised awareness not only of issues but also of the responsibilities of various groups in addressing these issues. Even though corporations are often found to be less than adequate in their environmental practices, the expectation that they should be responsible means that it may well be slightly more difficult for them to gain reputational benefits from implementing 'good' practice in this area.[7]

In addition to providing information to assist in staggering the implementation of a corporate citizenship strategy, the research also provides some preliminary data that allows corporations to target their strategy to particular stakeholders. Once again, in order to capitalise on the benefits of corporate citizenship, this targeting probably needs to be part of a more holistic strategy. However, it might help in providing a starting point for corporations considering implementing a corporate citizenship strategy. As a whole, the research suggests that ideas about corporate citizenship are of concern to a particular group of people: those aged between 35 and 54, comparatively well educated, and the larger proportion of whom are women. At a more specific level, differences were found in the impact of different demographic and stakeholder groups on the corporate citizenship sub-scales.[8] This has implications not only for whom a corporation wishes to target in adopting corporate citizenship practices, but also how they target the marketing of their corporate citizenship strategy to fully benefit from the changes in reputation and reputational value. Future research will be able to further delineate the groups to which particular corporate citizenship practices can be targeted.

It is also likely that future research will be able to build on the corporate citizenship scale that was developed in this project. As it is now, the scale can be used as a tool either for conducting further mesa-level research in producing data for use in advocating the take-up of 'good' corporate citizenship practices; or it can be easily adapted as a first stage for corporations considering a corporate citizenship strategy. For example, a particular corporation may want to conduct a quick survey on how it is currently perceived on each of the items, and the extent to which adopting any of the practices would benefit it in terms of improving its reputation or reputational value. The sample could comprise potential and/or actual stakeholders, and would provide a corporation with sufficient information to gauge the costs and benefits of implementing an appropriate corporate citizenship strategy as well as the extent to which such a strategy would involve widespread corporate change. In developing the survey further, however, it will be possible to create a comparative tool that will allow corporations to measure their performance relative to their competitors, or as a means of marketing themselves to potential stakeholders such as trade partners, investors and high-quality employees.

---

7   An indication that this may be the case came from the need to eliminate one of the environmental questions from the corporate citizenship scale. The question referred to corporations adhering to the 'minimum legal requirements' regarding environmental practices related to the business. Analysis of the question found that it was not a measure of a single variable and did not fit the scale. When the surveys were further examined, it was found that some of the respondents had underlined the word 'minimum' and written 'not enough' next to their answer. Other responses, however, had scored this highly, indicating that they thought that corporations deserved to be recognised for achieving this minimum.

8   While the sample was not large enough to break these groups down further for each item, there is certainly scope for this to be done in a larger project.

12.5 Conclusion

It is interesting to speculate that the demographic and stakeholder groups that stand out strongly in this research have some similarities with those willing to take their concerns to the streets, as we have seen in Seattle and Davos, in the belief that corporations are exceeding their legitimate boundaries and overlooking social issues. As with these more public protests, the research provides clear evidence that the community certainly does care about corporate behaviour and has shown that it is willing to punish and reward corporations on this basis. Indeed, the relationship between the community's perceptions of reputation and intentions to deal with a corporation was demonstrated to be very strong and highly significant. The mesa-level analysis of corporate citizenship described in this chapter provides a means of marketing corporate citizenship practices to corporations by using community perceptions of reputation as a lever. For corporations interested in best practice, stakeholder relations and maximising competitive advantage, the messages emanating from this research cannot be ignored.

However, the research is not simply about delivering this message, for in many ways it is not a new one for us to deliver. Instead, this research aimed to provide information to corporations that will facilitate the formulation of an appropriate corporate citizenship strategy. In making data available that enables corporations to stagger or target the implementation of a coherent set of corporate citizenship practices, this research acknowledges the practical difficulties of adopting such practices, while at the same time advocating their implementation as a strategy that will have reputational and financial benefits.

CITIZEN ADVOCACY GROUPS
Corporate friend or foe?

Tamara J. Bliss
Center for Corporate Citizenship at Boston College, USA

> Boycotts . . . letter-writing campaigns . . . take-over of corporate property . . . shareholder resolutions . . . picketing and demonstrations . . . lawsuits . . . websites devoted to criticising business practices.
>
> Joint task forces . . . technical assistance . . . policy dialogues . . . stakeholder engagement . . . collaborative strategic planning.

How can a corporate leader make sense out of the vast pot-pourri of strategies and tactics that citizen advocacy groups use to influence corporate behaviour? Should citizen activists be seen as annoying zealots and irresponsible critics or can they become valuable stakeholders that can engage in collaborative problem-solving with corporations?

Since the 1960s citizen advocacy groups have taken their demands directly to corporations. In a variety of ways, rational and radical, peaceful and violent, they have directly confronted the social, environmental and economic policies of private companies to make changes. Groups as diverse as Greenpeace, Amnesty International, Sweatshop Watch, Interfaith Center on Corporate Responsibility and The Moral Majority have developed strategies to pressure companies to be more responsive to the concerns of environmentalists, the Christian Right, college students and citizen organisations, concerned with issues that range from child labour to the packaging of hamburgers.

The advent of 24-hour news cycles and the Internet has increased the transparency of corporate behaviour. At the same time electronic communication has increased the visibility of citizen advocacy groups, their ability to organise worldwide campaigns and their power to destroy corporate reputations. Building on the success of prior generations of activists, today's advocacy groups regularly borrow the strategies and tactics of earlier issue campaigns. Analysing the advocacy group campaigns concerned about diverse issues over many decades can help to make sense of today's increasingly sophisticated activism by advocacy groups to influence corporate behaviour.

An in-depth analysis of over 100 issue campaigns waged over the past 40 years by advocacy groups to change corporate policies and practices reveals four distinct types of **pressure** campaign that advocacy groups use to influence corporate behaviour.[1] Beginning in the late 1980s a few pioneering advocacy groups and companies began to move beyond adversarial relationships to explore new **collaborative** ways of working together. Over time some of these collaborations moved from focusing on operational issues related to a specific business problem to a transformation of a company's values, strategy and approach to engaging with citizen advocacy groups. The rest of this chapter will give examples of how advocacy groups have used the four types of pressure campaign and the two types of collaborative relationship to change corporate policies and practices.[2] Table 13.1 summarises the characteristics of these six different types of relationship between advocacy groups and corporations.

13.1 Influencing corporate behaviour through pressure campaigns

13.1.1 'Enforce the rules' campaigns

When advocacy groups engage corporations in an issue campaign based on established rules, they use a legal strategy that relies on **analytical** tactics that emphasise facts, technical issues, laws and regulations. To change corporate behaviour by forcing companies to comply with existing laws and regulations, advocacy groups need highly skilled legal and technical expertise and sufficient funds to pay for the high cost of litigation.

In the 1970s and 1980s many environmental organisations employed an **enforce the rules** strategy when they sued companies for violating environmental regulations. When local neighbourhood organisations use existing zoning laws to stop a company from obtaining the necessary permits to build new facilities or expand existing ones, they are following an *enforce the rules* strategy.

An example of a successful *enforce the rules* campaign occurred in the late 1970s when the Environmental Defense Fund (EDF) waged a three-year legal battle to convince the California Public Utility Commission to require Pacific Gas & Electric Company (PG&E) to invest substantial resources in conservation and alternative energy rather than construction of new power plants. EDF focused on facts and rules to argue its case; it used a sophisticated computer simulation model that demonstrated that it would be more profitable for PG&E to invest in energy conservation than to construct costly new power plants. Even though the EDF spoke in the language of business and argued for a new approach to the utility business that would enable PG&E to make greater profits, the company's management was not receptive to taking advice from a group of environmen-

---

1 Most of the examples are described in greater detail in Bliss's (1996) study of how citizen advocacy groups influence corporate behaviour. Her data was drawn from academic studies, newspaper and magazine articles, business school cases and conversations concerning 100 issues campaigns targeted at major US corporations between 1990 and 1995.

2 The model of six types of issue campaign to influence corporate behaviour builds on Will McWhinney's identification of four distinct approaches to social change in McWhinney 1992.

Type of campaign	Key characteristics of campaigns	Advocacy group's goal
Adversarial campaigns		
Enforce the rules	▪ Legal strategy to enforce compliance with existing laws and regulations ▪ Emphasis on research and testimony based on data, facts and technical issues ▪ Economic analysis and computer modelling	▪ Use facts and existing rules to force company to change behaviour
Change the rules	▪ Political strategy ▪ Legal strategy that reinterprets the law ▪ Invention of new tactics	▪ Change the rules that affect corporate practices
Adopt my values	▪ Emphasis on ideological and ethical issues ▪ Confrontational and educational strategies that emphasise emotion	▪ Influence the values of the public and the target company
Change the economics	▪ Consumer boycotts combined with tactics that tarnish a company's image ▪ Shareholder resolutions ▪ Ethical investing	▪ Use economic pressure to change company practices
Collaborative campaigns		
New ways of working together	▪ Advocacy groups as technical consultants to companies ▪ Focus on inventing a win–win process to engage in creative problem-solving	▪ Use advocacy-group expertise to influence corporate behaviour
Stakeholder engagement	▪ Innovative approach to stakeholder engagement that may lead to a transformed vision for the company and a radical rethinking of the business in which the corporation is engaged	▪ Develop creative solutions that benefit the company and the common good

Table 13.1 **Characteristics of six types of issue campaign**

talists until they were pressured into changing their assumptions and practices (Roe 1984).[3]

EDF's campaign brought major changes in PG&E's approach to environmental issues. After years of trying to refute EDF's pro-conservation arguments, PG&E leaders stopped battling environmentalists and developed new ways of working with them. A cover story in *Fortune* in 1990 singled out PG&E as an example of a company that learned to change its approach to environmental issues as a result of the campaign waged by EDF. The company leased EDF's computer model to improve its ability to undertake conservation planning, appointed an environmentalist to serve on its board of directors and began to engage in regular discussions with environmental organisations (Kirkpatrick 1990).

3 The Environmental Defense Fund changed its name to Environmental Defense. Its tag line is 'Finding the ways that work'.

GOAL OF ADVOCACY GROUPS

- Use facts and existing rules to force a company to change its behaviour

CHARACTERISTICS OF *ENFORCE THE RULES* CAMPAIGNS

- Legal strategy, especially formal intervention in a regulatory hearing or suing a company to force compliance with existing laws or regulations
- Emphasis on research and testimony based on data, facts and technical issues
- Economic analysis and computer modelling

ARENAS OF ACTION

- Regulatory hearings
- Courts
- Media

Box 13.1 *'Enforce the rules' campaigns*

13.1.2 *'Change the rules' campaigns*

When advocacy groups believe that existing rules, even if enforced, do not require companies to adopt the types of policies and practices important to the groups, they may initiate a **change the rules** campaign to modify the rules that govern corporate behaviour. Advocacy groups waging this type of issue campaign can employ three very different strategies: political, legal and entrepreneurial.

Advocacy groups use a *change the rules* political strategy to change public policy and laws through legislation or ballot initiatives. These campaigns may change public policies that affect all companies, such as the Americans with the Disabilities Act, or policies that affect one industry, such as the Community Reinvestment Act that requires banks to invest in low-income communities. Once advocacy groups change public policy through the passage of legislation, they can shift to an *enforce the rules* campaign by monitoring corporate policies and practices to ensure that companies comply with the new laws.

A second type of *change the rules* campaign uses a legal strategy to obtain a judicial reinterpretation of existing laws. When an advocacy group uses a legal strategy to force corporate compliance with existing laws and regulations, they are waging an *enforce the rules* campaign. When they use a legal strategy to convince the courts to reinterpret the law, they are waging a *change the rules* campaign.

When social change occurs through reinterpretation of existing laws, the ensuing conflicts can be especially intractable. When one set of advocacy groups succeeds in changing the rules, other groups form to oppose the new interpretation of the law. Notable examples include the NAACP Legal Defense Fund's Change the Rules campaign that led to the landmark 1954 *Brown v. the Board of Education Supreme Court* decision. As a result of the NAACP's legal victory, new advocacy groups were organised to fight school desegregation. *Roe v. Wade* led to extreme polarisation between pro-life and pro-choice organisations. Companies such as AT&T have found themselves the target of pro-life groups because of their philanthropic gifts to Planned Parenthood.

Activists employ an entrepreneurial *change the rules* strategy when they invent a new tactic, such as shareholder resolutions, and then sue the government to win the right to use this strategy. When the Medical Committee for Human Rights used a shareholder's activism strategy in 1969 to pressure Dow Chemical into stopping the production of napalm, they first had to sue the Securities and Exchange Commission to change the rules regarding what information corporations must include on their proxy statements. When the US Court of Appeals of the District of Columbia ruled in 1970 that Dow must include the resolution in their proxy statement, the court opened the way for citizen organisations to use shareholder resolutions to require corporate management to include political and social issues in their proxy statements for shareholder consideration (Vogel 1978, 1983).

When Campaign GM used shareholder resolutions to address the issue of corporate accountability, they turned shareholder resolutions from a tactic to influence public policy to one that focuses on influencing corporate decision-making. Following these victories advocacy groups interested in a range of issues from animal rights to executive compensation began to systematically file shareholder resolutions to influence corporate behaviour. Thus a successful *change the rules* campaign can result in a permanent change in the rules that allow advocacy groups to wage successful *enforce the rules* campaigns. This enables advocacy groups to build on the success of activists concerned about entirely different issues.

GOAL OF ADVOCACY GROUPS

- Change the rules to force companies to change their behaviour

CHARACTERISTICS OF *CHANGE THE RULES* CAMPAIGNS

- Political strategy to change laws that regulate corporate behaviour by changing public policy through legislation or ballot initiatives and referenda
- Legal strategy that reinterprets the law
- Invention of new tactics

ARENAS OF ACTION

- National or regional legislative bodies
- Courts
- Elections

Box 13.2 *'Change the rules' campaigns*

13.1.3 *'Adopt my values' campaigns*

In sharp contrast to the behind-the-scenes facts and figures of an analytical *enforce the rules* campaign, activists waging **adopt my values** campaigns engage in highly emotional and symbolic tactics to attract media attention to their moral arguments, win the hearts of the public and attract new recruits to their cause. Focusing on ideological and ethical issues, *adopt my values* campaigns rely on confrontational, 'in your face' direct-action tactics, such as picketing, colourful demonstrations and civil disobedience. These campaigns are organised by advocacy groups composed of highly committed members who are willing to become involved personally in a direct-action campaign instead of just sending a cheque to their favourite cause.

Over the years activists have become very skilled in creating highly visual events that generate intense media coverage designed to embarrass the target company and to arouse public concern and sympathy with the activists' cause. Greenpeace's successful campaign that forced Royal Dutch/Shell Group to abandon its decision to sink its obsolete 40-storey-high Brent Spar oil platform into the North Atlantic was one of the most dramatic and highly publicised direct action campaigns in recent years.

Some of the most brilliant and flamboyant *adopt my values* campaigns were organised in the 1980s by AIDS activists to call attention to the plight of individuals dying from AIDS and the government's failure to actively address the AIDS crisis. When ACT UP (AIDS Coalition to Unleash Power) failed to convince Burroughs Wellcome to lower the price of AZT (the first drug available to fight AIDS), it staged a dramatic takeover of the New York Stock Exchange, displayed a huge banner that said 'Sell Wellcome' and forced the stock exchange to shut down for several hours. The next morning a banner headline on the front page of *The Wall Street Journal* read: 'Burroughs Wellcome reaps profits, outrage from its AIDS drug: Mounting protests over the cost of AZT tarnishing the firm and intensifying regulation'. Several days later Burroughs Wellcome significantly lowered the price of AZT (Nussbaum 1990; Emmons and Nimgade 1991).

But Greenpeace and ACT UP are far from the only advocacy groups that engage in emotionally charged tactics designed to develop public awareness of an issue and pressure companies into complying with activists' demands. Since the late 1970s animal rights activists have waged creative and highly emotional campaigns that package moral arguments into catchy one-line phrases. While the publication in 1964 of Rachel Carson's *Silent Spring* served as the catalyst for the environmental movement, the publication in 1975 of philosopher Peter Singer's clearly articulated set of values in his widely read philosophical treatise *Animal Liberation: A New Ethic for Our Treatment of Animals* galvanised thousands of animal lovers to launch the animal rights movement. Using costumes, props, slogans and Hollywood celebrities to attract attention, animal rights activists pioneered the use of melodramatic direct-action tactics to embarrass companies into compliance with their demands.

Henry Spira, the first leader in the emerging animal rights movement, rejected the conventional political and educational strategies popular with traditional animal welfare organisations. A former teacher, merchant seaman and veteran of both the labour and civil rights movements, Spira knew that 'power concedes nothing without a struggle'. He believed that the animal rights movement needed a specific target, a focused, achievable goal and a single, well-publicised victory (Jasper and Nelkin, 1992: 27).

Looking for a glaring abuse that would 'engage public sensibilities and attract media attention' (Jasper and Nelkin 1992: 103), Spira initiated a campaign against Revlon in 1979 to eliminate the Draize test that uses rabbits to test the toxicity of cosmetics. He deliberately chose this test because he believed rabbits would attract greater public sympathy than other test animals, such as rats or mice. From an ethical perspective Spira realised that cosmetic companies would have difficulty justifying hurting innocent rabbits for the sake of a new colour lipstick or mascara. Since cosmetic companies are selling beauty and image and their products are perceived as relatively frivolous, the industry is vulnerable to negative publicity that associates cosmetics with suffering, blinded rabbits.

Spira selected Revlon as the target company because it was the industry leader. When initial efforts to negotiate with Revlon management to make a substantial financial contribution to research alternatives to animal testing failed, he organised the Coalition to Stop the Draize Rabbit Blinding Test, composed of 400 traditional animal welfare groups and humane societies that operate animal shelters and spay clinics. He ran full-page advertisements in *The New York Times* with photographs of mutilated rabbits and a headline that asked: 'How Many Rabbits Does Revlon Blind for Beauty's Sake?' The advertisements alerted many consumers for the first time about the issue of animal testing and attracted individuals sympathetic to animal rights who were willing to join a protest. Adopting the direct-action tactics of the civil rights movement, he convinced 300 animal rights activists to dress up in bunny suits and demonstrate in front of Revlon's upmarket Fifth Avenue corporate headquarters in May 1980. Photographs of the demonstrators carrying signs accusing Revlon of blinding rabbits appeared in newspapers and on television. Thousands of supporters wrote letters to company executives.

Sensitive about its image and embarrassed by the negative publicity, Revlon capitulated to Spira's demands after six months of negotiations. Revlon fired the vice president who had refused to speak to Spira and agreed to donate US$750,000 over a three-year period to Rockefeller University to establish a research programme to identify alternatives to the Draize test (Finsen and Finsen 1994).

When advocacy groups engage in *adopt my values* campaigns, they are concerned with changing the values of the public and the companies they are criticising. These campaigns may appear to be religious crusades where there is little room for compromise. Because of their ideological nature, they can spawn very negative reactions and the formation of counter-groups organised by corporations and others who are opposed to the views of the campaign leaders.

GOAL OF ADVOCACY GROUPS

- Change corporate behaviour by embarrassing a company into adopting policies congruent with the values of the advocacy group

CHARACTERISTICS OF *ADOPT MY VALUES* CAMPAIGNS

- Emphasis on ideological and ethical issues
- Confrontational and educational strategies that emphasise expressive tactics and emotion
- Campaigns may spawn counter-groups that support corporate position

ARENAS OF ACTION

- Corporate facilities
- Media
- 'In the streets'

Box 13.3 *'Adopt my values' campaigns*

13.1.4 'Change the economics' campaigns

Change the economics campaigns focus on the marketplace where advocacy groups harness the economic power of consumers and investors to reward 'good' and punish 'bad' corporate behaviour. Ethical investing, consumer boycotts, selective buying and corporate recognition awards are *change the economics* tactics aimed at increasing the cost or the difficulty (and thus the price) of conducting business.

Companies fear boycotts and the negative publicity that accompanies them. According to a national survey of business leaders, boycotts are the most effective strategy that consumers can use to influence corporate behaviour (Friedman 1991; Putnam 1993). A company may be damaged by the threat of a boycott as well as by an actual boycott because of the negative impact on its image and reputation (Smith 1990). This is especially true for brand-conscious consumer product companies who spend millions of dollars on advertising. The very visible boycotts that began in the 1990s against Nike and other footwear and apparel companies to protest against sweatshop conditions and child labour among their Asian subcontractors are examples of *change the economics* campaigns.

Boycotts are most effective when they are aimed at consumer product companies that sell a non-essential or easily replaceable consumer product that is purchased frequently and is difficult to distinguish from competitors' products. If an advocacy group wants to organise a boycott against a company that does not sell consumer products, it must identify a suitable surrogate target. When Greenpeace and the Save the Earth Coalition wanted to protest DuPont's use of CFCs, they did not directly target DuPont, which sells only to other businesses. Instead they chose Seagrams, the liquor company that owns 25% of DuPont's stock, as a surrogate target.

The growth of transnational companies along with the increased transparency of electronic communication techniques has enabled advocacy groups to target companies along the entire supply chain. Advocacy groups can influence the practices of companies that sell to other businesses by targeting the retail stores at the end of the supply chain. To change the practices of timber companies that were cutting down trees in tropical rainforests, the Rainforest Action Network targeted Home Depot, the largest retailer of old-growth wood products in the world.

While consumer boycotts may lead to very visible *change the economics* campaigns, selective buying and ethical investing is mostly carried out by individuals who make purchasing and investing decisions based on specific performance criteria. To assist consumers and investors with their decisions, the Council for Economic Priorities conducts extensive research and rates the performance of companies on many different issues, including labour practices, advancement and treatment of women and minorities, charitable giving, animal testing and environmental practices. The Council publishes its findings in best-selling books such as *Shopping for a Better World* and *Better World Investment Guide*. Individual investors, financial advisers and institutional investor organisations (including major pension funds) use the Council's research to pressure companies to change their practices through the use of shareholder resolutions and ethical investing practices. The Council also recognises and publicises positive corporate policies and practices by presenting 'Corporate Conscience Awards' to companies they consider socially responsible.

Shareholder activism and ethical investing are other important *change the economics* tactics. The Interfaith Center on Corporate Responsibility, which represents 275 Protestant, Catholic and Jewish institutional investors, regularly introduces shareholder resolutions and has also been effective in encouraging investors to join the ethical investing movement. The percentage of investment dollars that are socially screened has risen dramatically in the past 20 years; as of 1999 over US$2,000 billion, accounting for one out of every eight professionally managed investment dollars, were invested in socially screened investments (Schueth *et al.* 1999).

GOAL OF ADVOCACY GROUPS

- Use economic pressure to make it too expensive in dollars or reputation for a targeted company to continue a policy or practice

CHARACTERISTICS OF CAMPAIGNS

- Consumer boycotts combined with tactics that damage a company's reputation
- Performance rating on social and economic criteria
- Socially screened investing
- Shareholder resolutions

ARENAS OF ACTION

- Corporate facilities
- Media
- 'In the streets'

Box 13.4 *'Change the economics' campaigns*

13.2 Influencing corporate behaviour through collaboration

13.2.1 New ways of working together

When advocacy groups and corporations break away from their traditional adversarial relationships and create opportunities for collaborative problem-solving, they are operating under totally new rules of engagement. In the late 1980s and early 1990s the leaders of the Environmental Defense Fund (EDF) and the Conservation Law Foundation (CLF) began to recognise the limits of improving the environment solely through *enforce the rules* and *change the rules* campaigns, which depended on the passage of new laws and tight government regulation of industry. They wanted to move beyond pressure tactics to create innovative and collaborative approaches to social change and corporate social responsibility by inventing new problem-solving processes, such as joint task forces, policy dialogues and cross-sector partnerships.

EDF's Executive Director Fred Krupp began to explore using market incentives to resolve environmental problems. Instead of hiring more lawyers, Krupp started hiring economists. Under Krupp's leadership EDF played a major role in the passage of the 1990 Amendments to the Clean Air Act, which created a trading system that allows utilities to use the free market to achieve reductions in pollution in the most cost-effective manner for each company. Krupp expressed his new philosophy of environmentalism in a speech before the Environmental Marketing Communications Forum:

> We cannot regulate our way out of every environmental problem—we have to innovate our way out—and that innovation has to come from the marketplace. To the environmental ethic we must add the entrepreneurial spirit. To harness that spirit will take finding and using the power of economic incentives (Krupp 1992: 658).

Fred Krupp's commitment to innovation led him to seek new ways to influence corporate behaviour. Realising that McDonald's had been widely criticised for the 'clamshells' it used for packaging its hamburgers, he saw an opportunity for his organisation to provide its expertise to help McDonald's solve its solid waste problem. When McDonald's accepted Fred Krupp's invitation to form a joint task force to develop new approaches to packaging and solid waste management, the company and the environmentalists were pioneering a new approach to environmental problem-solving.

According to Shelby Yastro, McDonald's Senior Vice President for Environmental Affairs, who was quoted in a McDonald's/EDF press release:

> EDF struck a responsive chord when they proposed to work with us . . . This is an entirely new process for us, and evidently for business in general. We're taking this leadership role hoping that we are going to find new ways to improve and to reduce solid wastes from our operations. This is going to be a difficult process but we want it to work (Livesey 1990: 15; emphasis added).

Why was McDonald's willing to form a partnership with an environmental advocacy group? To participate in the Waste Reduction Joint Task Force, McDonald's management had to give up its normal organisational autonomy and share proprietary operational processes and environmental data with an organisation well known for its hard-hitting *enforce the rules* campaigns. Sensitivity to maintaining its positive corporate image was a key element in McDonald's willingness to collaborate with EDF. McDonald's had been the target of the McToxic campaign, an aggressive *change the economics* campaign led by the Citizens Clearinghouse on Hazardous Waste (CCHW). CCHW urged their 7,000 affiliated grass-roots environmental groups to send dirty Styrofoam clamshells back to McDonald's headquarters to pressure them into reducing their production of solid waste. By agreeing to work collaboratively with a respected environmental group, McDonald's was creating a symbol of a company that wanted to be seen as environmentally responsible (Livesey 1990; Allen 1991; Hemphill 1994).[4]

At the end of the task force process, McDonald's committed US$100 million to source reduction and recycling. When McDonald's adopted the recommendations of the Joint Task Force, EDF Director Fred Krupp called the company's actions 'an environmental touchdown'. Both EDF and McDonald's received extensive favourable press for the work of the Joint Task Force.

---

4   For a detailed analysis of the different ways advocacy groups collaborate and compete in issue campaigns, see Bliss 1996: 281-94.

The collaborative problem-solving partnership between McDonald's and EDF marked a watershed in relationships between some types of advocacy groups and large corporations. The project's success and visibility increased EDF's credibility and clout as an effective environmental organisation that could build collaborative alliances with corporations. EDF organised a task force with six major companies to develop policies to promote the use of recycled paper. In co-operation with the Pew Charitable Foundation, EDF formed The Alliance for Innovation to provide technical assistance to leading consumer product companies, such as Starbucks and UPS, to reduce the negative impact of their business practices on the environment while helping them to reduce costs.

While some environmental groups remain fearful of being co-opted by 'the enemy', a growing number of environmental organisations have followed EDF's approach to forming partnerships with companies. Some collaborations involve a single advocacy group and one company, such as Conservation International's partnership with Starbucks to promote coffee cultivation practices that protect tropical rainforests while increasing profits for farmers (Waddock 2002). Others represent a collaboration between one or more advocacy groups and members of one industry, such as the Forest Stewardship Council, which the World Wide Fund for Nature and 120 companies established to develop a certification process for the timber industry (Marsden and Andriof 1998).

GOAL OF ADVOCACY GROUPS

- Use of advocacy group expertise to develop joint problem-solving approaches to changing specific policies and practices of one company or an entire industry

CHARACTERISTICS OF CAMPAIGNS

- Focus on inventing a win–win process to resolve problems, such as joint task forces and policy dialogues
- Emphasis on use of entrepreneurial skills to engage in creative problem-solving
- Advocacy groups may act as technical consultants to companies

ARENAS OF ACTION

- Corporate offices and boardrooms
- Neutral location or offices of advocacy groups

Box 13.5 *New ways of working together*

13.2.2 *Stakeholder engagement: a new way of doing business*

When advocacy groups engage with corporations to solve specific operational problems, they are using their entrepreneurial skills to create change. While the new processes can lead to major changes in corporate practices, the company's underlying values and strategy remain the same. This is in contrast to the rare company that makes a long-term commitment to active stakeholder engagement, dialogue and ongoing collaboration with advocacy groups. When a company moves beyond working with advocacy groups to change one or two specific practices and begins to redefine the nature of its business, its values and its relationships with advocacy groups, it has incorporated stakeholder engagement as a key part of its corporate strategy. When advocacy groups and corporations engage in long-term collaboration related to corporate values and strategy, they are involved in a radical change process that can create new meaning and vision for both organisations.

13.2.2.1 Energy conservation in the electric utility industry

An early example of long-term collaboration that led to a major change in one company's corporate strategy occurred in the electric utility industry in the late 1980s and early 1990s. Government regulators played a critical role in creating new processes to resolve the intense conflict between electric utilities and environmental groups over energy conservation and the construction of new power plants.

The Conservation Law Foundation (CLF), a New England-based scientifically and legally oriented environmental organisation, began an *enforce the rules* campaign to prevent the construction of additional power plants. CLF had conducted extensive research showing that the electric utilities needed to shift their focus from the supply side to the demand side of the business by investing in a massive conservation programme that would eliminate the need for new generating capacity, save money and reduce air pollution. CLF intervened in utility rate cases before the Public Utility Commissions in the six New England States to stop electric utility companies from building any new power-generating capacity in the region (Ellis 1989; Foster 1989; Cohen and Townsley 1990).

The Public Utility commissions of Connecticut and Massachusetts accepted CLF's argument and ordered the utilities to collaborate with CLF and other citizen organisations that had intervened in the regulatory process. Nine different New England utilities participated in formal demand-side management (DSM) collaborative planning with CLF between 1988 and 1990. Some of these collaborations involved other stakeholders, including the Massachusetts Public Interest Research Group and the Massachusetts Executive Office of Energy Resources.

To make DSM financially profitable to utilities, CLF shifted to a *change the rules* political strategy. However, this time it worked with electric utility companies to advocate significant changes in the regulations affecting rate setting and profitability. The new rules allowed electric utilities to invest directly in their customer facilities and promoted the building of long-term partnerships with their customers. With technical assistance and encouragement from CLF, the New England Electric Systems (NEES) began to work with customers to change their payback perspective from 10 to 30 years.

After the initial successful collaboration related to operational planning for energy conservation and DSM, the collaboration between CLF and the NEES moved far beyond the demands imposed by the regulators. NEES executives began to question their basic assumptions about the energy business by thinking of customer demand for power as a variable. They faced the challenge of developing a 20-year strategic plan that would enable the company to be competitive, meet customer demands for quality service at lower prices while at the same time meeting public policy goals for environmental sustainability. Appreciating the competitive advantage to be gained from forming an ongoing partnership with CLF, NEES's visionary CEO, John Rowe, expanded the relationship to encompass the company's strategic planning process.

Through active, ongoing dialogue with CLF, an organisation of highly educated scientists and economists with in-depth knowledge of environmental issues and a different perspective on the energy business, NEES executives were able to change their own vision of the electric business. In the process they transformed the company from an electrical supply company to an electrical services company that works collaboratively with customers to develop energy systems that minimise energy consumption, are cost-effective for the customer and profitable for the company. Instead of letting a citizen advocacy group continue to be an annoying and expensive thorn in its side, the company transformed a former foe into a sophisticated adviser and ally. Today under its new British owner, National Grid, the company continues to work in close partnership with CLF and continues to have a national reputation in the industry as a leader in DSM and energy conservation.

13.2.2.2 Royal Dutch/Shell Group and stakeholder engagement

In 1995 Royal Dutch/Shell's reputation was severely damaged by the disastrous publicity resulting from its highly visible conflicts with Greenpeace over the proposed sinking of the Brent Spar oil platform and with human rights and environmentalists over the execution of world-renowned author and environmental activist Ken Saro-Wiwa in Nigeria. These conflicts were major motivators for Shell to take a holistic approach to changing the way it conducts its business. The company organised a working group of executives to develop a better understanding of society's changing expectations of transnational companies and perceptions of Shell (Moldoveanu 1999; Paine 1999; Lawrence 2001).

Shell executives began to realise that the company was too internally focused and insensitive to its impact on the environment and society. They articulated a new set of business principles, developed a commitment to sustainable development and to greater transparency. Since 1998 Shell has published social and environmental annual reports. The company encourages feedback from the general public as well as activists through an interactive feature on its website and tear-off 'Tell Shell' cards in its corporate reports. Shell has also written and published on its website *Business and Child Labour: A Management Primer*.

Central to Shell's new strategy is a commitment to regularly engage in ongoing dialogue with a wide range of external stakeholders, including environmentalists and human rights advocacy groups who had been extremely critical of the company. Shell executives are learning that they can solve what appear to be intractable problems through active dialogue with stakeholders. To find a solution for the obsolete Brent Spar oil platform, the company launched an international competition; with assistance from the Environmental Council it conducted meetings in four European countries to discuss possible solutions. As a result of the contest and consultations, Shell identified a creative solution that recycles the notorious Brent Spar oil platform into a ferry quay in Norway (Lawrence 2001: 602).

Royal Dutch/Shell Group has undergone a profound transformation involving the re-examination of its corporate values, purpose and business practices and is actively engaged with a wide range of stakeholders. However, no major transnational corporation will ever satisfy all of its critics. As the world's largest energy supplier, Shell still finds itself the target of advocacy groups such as Corporate Watch, which accuses the company of greenwashing. However, Shell's commitment to ongoing stakeholder engagement makes it far less likely that it will be so completely blindsided by advocacy-group criticism as it was with Brent Spar and the execution of Ken Saro-Wiwa. Shell is leading the way in transforming the relationships between multinational companies and citizen advocacy groups through its ongoing commitment to stakeholder engagement.[5]

GOAL OF ADVOCACY GROUPS

- Finding creative transformation solutions through synergy between advocacy groups and corporations

CHARACTERISTICS OF CAMPAIGNS

- Collaborative strategic planning
- Joint ventures between corporations and advocacy groups
- Radical new approach to stakeholder engagement that may lead to a new vision for the company

ARENAS OF ACTION

- Corporate offices and boardrooms
- Offices of advocacy groups or neutral location

Box 13.6 **Stakeholder engagement**

13.2.3 Implications for corporate leaders

An analysis of the radically different approaches that advocacy groups use to influence corporate behaviour can help corporate leaders to distinguish between the different ways advocacy groups can affect their company's business practices, strategies and reputation. As executives become more aware of their vulnerability to advocacy group pressure and the potential damage to their reputation and 'licence to operate' in a networked global economy, they have an opportunity to move away from reactive and defensive behaviour to a new collaborative approach to engaging with advocacy groups and other external stakeholders.

Today more and more companies are actively pursuing strategies to engage in dialogue and form partnerships with a wide variety of advocacy groups, government agencies, universities and non-profit organisations. They are finding new allies for coalitions for legislative and regulatory changes as well as identifying ideas for new or enhanced products or services. They are gaining advice for solving difficult problems by working with customers and concerned citizens who bring a different perspective to the company.

By actively engaging in dialogue and problem-solving efforts with concerned citizens and former critics who bring a different perspective to the company, corporate leaders are finding creative and cost-effective solutions to what had appeared to be intractable problems.

---

5   For the story of the organisational transformation of Royal Dutch Shell, see Mirvis 2000.

It is critical to remember that, no matter how skilled corporate leaders become in engaging with their critics, they will never be able to meet the expectations of every stakeholder. They will sometimes find themselves the target of multiple groups making opposing demands on the company. However, by becoming more sophisticated about the strategies of advocacy groups and by engaging in dialogue with a wide range of stakeholders, they are less likely to be blindsided and are more sensitive to the needs and changing expectations of their customers, investors and the public at large.

PUBLIC-INTEREST GROUPS AS STAKEHOLDERS
A 'stakeholder salience' explanation of activism*

James E. Mattingly and Daniel W. Greening
University of Missouri, USA

A common joke among business executives involves recognising that it is going to be a bad day when the television crew for '60 Minutes' is at your doorstep when you get to work in the morning. It is ironic, however, that we joke about this because dealing with issues in the public domain is one of the aspects of managerial work in which managers are least confident. That this is the case should be hardly surprising. We generally do not teach courses to prospective managers preparing them to deal with social and political issues. We are much better at teaching them to deal with problems relating to the workplace and market competition. A sobering fact is that activism by sociopolitical actors has been on the rise since the 1960s (Vogel 1978; Heath and Nelson 1984; Greening 1992; Shepard 1997). These groups have used a number of assertive tactics, such as boycotts, strikes, embargoes, lobbying, media coverage and terrorism (Greening and Gray 1994), to ensure that their interests become plainly within the organisation's awareness. In light of these trends, it is a non-trivial problem that practising managers often do not know where to turn to begin to make sense of their interactions with actors of the sociopolitical environment.

Our objective in exploring this topic is to begin to provide practising managers with the scholarly tools that are currently available in order to allow them to begin to make sense of the interactions they witness and experience with sociopolitical actors—such as governmental and public-interest groups. Our secondary purpose is to provide an integration and extension of the little literature that exists to inform those who wish to study interactions between firms and sociopolitical actors. Along the way, we argue that prior models of stakeholder action (Frooman 1999) could be improved by recognising the

* We gratefully acknowledge helpful input on earlier drafts of this chapter from Felissa Lee, Rick Johnson, Pursey Heugens and anonymous reviewers.

potential for a stronger form of collaborative response. Also, we suggest that prior theo-rising has ignored the strength of the reciprocity norm (Gouldner 1960) in predicting and explaining interactions between firms and activist stakeholders. We believe that both of these concepts are key for scholarly understanding of these types of interaction and for practising managers to take into account when planning and navigating exchanges with sociopolitical actors.

To accomplish the above objectives, we first assess the current state of scholarly contri-bution to our understanding of when and how these sociopolitical actors interact with the firm. Correspondingly, we propose a model of the specific behaviour in which these actors might engage and the factors that explain such action. Then we explore various conditions, informed by the study of both organisational stakeholders and social move-ments, which might alter the model's predictions. Finally, we assess the implications of our work for both the practice of management and the extension of scholarship.

14.1 Stakeholder action

A stakeholder is an individual or group having a legitimate claim on the firm—someone who can affect or is affected by the firm's activities (Freeman 1984). The stakeholder approach rejects the primacy of the shareholder, instead recognising the intrinsic value of all stakeholders' claims (Donaldson and Preston 1995). This is a controversial norma-tive position, however, among management scholars. It is clear that CEOs hold no such notion of the intrinsic value of stakeholders. A study of CEOs reveals that they prioritise stakeholders by their relative importance (Posner and Schmidt 1984; see Table 14.1). As illustrated in the table, customers are most important, followed by employees, owners, the general public, stockholders, elected public officials and administrative bureaucrats. Some typical stakeholders discussed in management literature but absent from this list are suppliers, labour unions, the local community and the natural environment.

There are numerous types of stakeholder, with non-trivial implications for the expla-nation of stakeholder action. For the purpose of this analysis, we focus solely on the public-interest group stakeholder segment. We expect there to be substantial variation in firm–stakeholder interactions involving various types of stakeholder. Therefore, by hold-ing constant the type of stakeholder under consideration we simplify our model in order to gain a clearer understanding of interactions between a firm and stakeholders of this important segment. One cannot assume that the same conditions and motivations would similarly impact interactions between a firm and stakeholders of a different type—such as customers, employees or stockholders.

14.1.2 When stakeholders act

The study of interactions between firms and public-interest groups first began to emerge when Vogel (1978) noted the rise of 'corporate accountability' movements, whereby public-interest groups began to directly 'lobby' firms for redress of social issues.[1] Jones

---

1   An example is the protest by many groups over firms' business activities in South Africa during

Stakeholder	Ranking
Customers	6.4
Employees	6.0
Owners	5.3
General public	4.5
Stockholders	4.5
Elected public officials	3.8
Government regulators	2.9

Note: Rankings were calculated on a 7-point scale, where 7 = most important and 1 = least important

Table 14.1 ***Importance to executives of various stakeholders***

Source: Adapted from Posner and Schmidt 1984

(1983) provided a classificatory scheme of governance mechanisms that citizen groups use with firms in their efforts to create social change. More recent treatments have suggested that a public-interest stakeholder group is more likely to mobilise when it has some past experience with collective action, is embedded in a relatively dense web of inter-organisational relations and when members share a common identity (Rowley and Moldoveanu 2000). Past mobilisation experience makes it easier for a stakeholder group to act because it removes some of the uncertainty regarding how to go about mobilising and the outcomes that members might expect from participation. A dense network provides a pool of potential allies on which a stakeholder group might rely in its mobilisation effort. When participants share a common identity, stakeholder groups may just as readily form and mobilise in order to express or reinforce belonging to a group as to protect the group's interests. It is not the question of when stakeholders act that we attempt to explain but how stakeholders act and the forces that explain their actions. For this analysis, we assume that the public-interest stakeholder group is motivated to act, indicating that a conflictual social issue exists between a focal firm and a public-interest stakeholder group.[2]

the reign of apartheid. Groups not only led boycotts of firms' products, but also attempted several more direct-governance mechanisms, such as public-interest shareholder resolutions and securing participation in annual shareholder meetings as well as the support of institutional investors for policy proposals (Vogel 1978).

2 It is commonly recognised that firm–stakeholder interactions arise as a result of emerging social issues. Especially for public-interest stakeholder groups, this may be the result of a perceived legitimacy gap (Sethi 1979). A legitimacy gap is described as the difference between the behaviour a social actor expects of a firm and the behaviour that the social actor observes of the firm. These expectations of, or preferences for, a firm's behaviour need not be narrowly defined as an objective conception of stakeholders' interests. For example, what interests do 'pro-life' activists have in defending the rights of unborn children?

14.1.3 *How stakeholders act*

To understand the specific collective behaviour in which stakeholders engage, we must first understand the factors that explain such behaviour. Stakeholders' 'influence strategies' have previously been theorised as a function of the power-dependence relationship between the firm and stakeholder group (Frooman 1999). Citing resource-dependence theory (Pfeffer and Salancik 1978), the level of the firm's dependence on the stakeholder's resources is proposed to determine the path of the stakeholder's influence effort—whether directly with the firm or indirectly through a third party. Conversely, the level of the stakeholder's dependence on the firm's resources determines the stakeholder's resource-control strategy—whether usage or withholding. Withholding strategies terminate resource flows to the firm whereas usage strategies restrict the conditions under which the firm will maintain access to resources. Relatively dependent stakeholders are proposed to adopt usage strategies whereas those less dependent are expected to withhold resources altogether. Although this lone formulation provides a valuable contribution to the stakeholder literature, it fails to recognise the potential for a stronger form of collaboration between firm and stakeholder. Rather than withhold or restrict the use of resources, a stakeholder may choose to maintain a resource flow to the firm while simultaneously seeking a jointly optimal solution to a social issue, thereby exercising active participation in the firm's activities. We propose a model of stakeholder action that provides for this potentiality.

14.1.4 *A revisited model of stakeholder action*

A resource-dependence model of stakeholder action has room also for a stronger form of firm–stakeholder collaboration than the earlier model provided. The model's two dimensions are pathway of influence, whether direct or indirect, and outcome orientation, whether integrative or distributive (see Fig. 14.1). Direct paths of influence involve a stakeholder group interacting directly with a firm in order to redress its claim, whereas indirect action refers to the stakeholder group's mediation of the claim through a third party or parties. Integrative orientations seek to maximise joint outcomes,

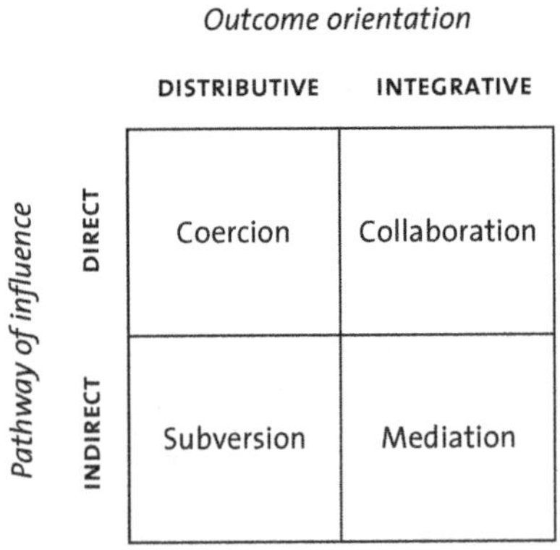

Outcome orientation

		DISTRIBUTIVE	INTEGRATIVE
Pathway of influence	DIRECT	Coercion	Collaboration
	INDIRECT	Subversion	Mediation

Figure 14.1 *Styles of stakeholder action*

perceiving possible simultaneous gains for both parties, whereas distributive orientations imply a zero-sum game whereby one party's gain necessarily is at the other's expense (Walton and McKersie 1965). The two dimensions are depicted in Figure 14.1 as comprising an explanatory model of four styles of stakeholder response. We label the four styles collaboration, mediation, coercion and subversion.

- **Collaboration**. High stakeholder salience and high firm salience encourages a direct, integrative response that we label 'collaborative'. A collaborative stakeholder intends to maximise outcomes relating to interests common to both it and the firm, instead of maximising only its own interests. The firm and stakeholder negotiate to find a solution to the issue that maximises the parties' common interests. Adoption of a superordinate goal is key to successful collaboration (Sherif 1958). A superordinate goal is one that is shared by the parties and subordinates all other goals and agendas—both shared and unilateral.

- **Mediation**. High firm salience and low stakeholder salience encourages a stakeholder to seek mediation. A non-salient stakeholder lacks the perceived power, legitimacy and urgency on the part of the firm to elicit its co-operation in addressing the stakeholder's issue. Therefore, the stakeholder will seek an alliance with a third party or parties that may be able to get the firm's attention. This may involve filing suit against the firm to gain the state's position of salience or coalescing with a better organised or resource-endowed organisation that may be sympathetic to the stakeholder's claim with the firm.

- **Coercion**. Low firm salience and high stakeholder salience encourages a coercive approach of the stakeholder with the firm. In this case, the stakeholder perceives that it can defeat the firm through direct action—given the firm's reliance on resources in the stakeholder's possession. This is illustrated by Firestone's recent multi-million-dollar settlement with a family whose Ford Explorer rolled over when a tyre exploded, resulting in the mother's permanent paralysis. In this case the family possessed resources of legitimacy and potential allied jurors that the firm apparently perceived to be overwhelming.

- **Subversion**. Low firm salience and low stakeholder salience produces subversive stakeholder action. Neither firm nor stakeholder holds resources substantial enough to create dependence on the part of the other, yet the stakeholder takes issue with the firm's actions. Assuming that the issue is important enough to the stakeholder to continue to pursue its resolution, the stakeholder will do so through indirect channels—perceiving that it warrants little priority in the eyes of the firm's managers. Public protest, sabotage and terrorism are examples of specific behaviour in which the subversive stakeholder might engage. This indirect action is subversive because the stakeholder, lacking dependence on the firm's outcomes, will seek to advance its own interests without consideration of the consequences to the firm.

Stakeholders' actions in resolving a conflictual social issue with a firm can be explained by the extent of the stakeholder's salience to a firm (Fig. 14.2). The salience to a firm of a stakeholder and its claims (and vice versa) are thought to vary with the extent of power, legitimacy and urgency the managers of each party assign to the other's claims (Mitchell

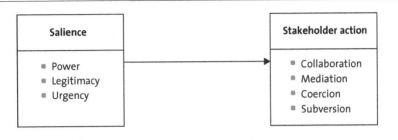

Figure 14.2 *Factors explaining stakeholder action*

et al. 1997). Power is explained, from the resource-dependence perspective, as the opposite of dependence (Pfeffer and Salancik 1978). It can be inferred from this theory that a stakeholder on whose resources a firm relies heavily will have power in its relationship with the firm. Similar to Emerson's (1962) and Blau's (1964) formulations of social exchange, power from this perspective is attributed to the nature of the relationship instead of the actor. Legitimacy indicates that the firm acknowledges the authenticity of the stakeholder's claim to interest in the firm's activities. Urgency refers to the time-sensitive nature of the stakeholder's claim and places additional pressure on the firm to act in a timely manner. According to Mitchell *et al.* (1997), public-interest groups having at least two of these would have a good chance of obtaining the firm's acknowledgement as a stakeholder.[3]

A stakeholder group pursues a path of influence—either direct or indirect—as a result of the stakeholder's perceptions regarding its salience to the firm. A salient stakeholder, especially one enjoying a position of relative power in its relationship with the firm, will pursue direct action with the firm; otherwise it will pursue indirect action through alliance with others that have the necessary resources to gain the firm's serious consideration. We also expect the stakeholder's outcome orientation along the integrative-distributive dimension to be, *ceteris paribus*, a function of salience and resource dependence, but this time of the firm relative to the stakeholder. Absent a prior or expected future relationship with the firm (which we later revisit), a stakeholder group adopts a distributive orientation unless it is forced to adopt an integrative response due to the firm's position of relative power resulting from the stakeholder's dependence on the firm's resources. If the firm and its interests are salient to the stakeholder, it pursues jointly beneficial outcomes with the firm: an integrative approach. On the other hand, the stakeholder adopts a distributive approach—ignoring the firm and its interests—if conditions of salience are unmet, including resource dependence. It is important to note here that these calculations of salience are subjective assessments by the stakeholder group, based on its situational perceptions, which explain the stakeholder's interactions with the firm. They are not objective 'facts' that can be verified independently of the stakeholder group's subjective evaluations.

---

3   We suggest, however, that power is a key determinant of firms' responsiveness to stakeholders and that the other two dimensions are distant cousins.

Proposition 1: Stakeholder action is observable as four distinctive styles of collective behaviour—including collaboration, mediation, coercion and subversion—and explainable as a function of the joint consideration of the salience—involving power, legitimacy and urgency—of the firm and stakeholder each to the other.

14.2 Conditions of stakeholder action

The consideration of determinants of stakeholder action, thus far, has been based on a narrowly rational and temporally naïve conception of interaction between stakeholder and firm. We now expand the scope of the model to account for those factors that help to explain the conditions that influence the extent to which the relative salience of firm and stakeholder explains observed stakeholder action. Some factors that add explanatory power to the model are the stakeholder group's culture, the nature of the firm's interactive response to stakeholder action, and the nature of the stakeholder's relationships with both the firm and third parties (Fig. 14.3).

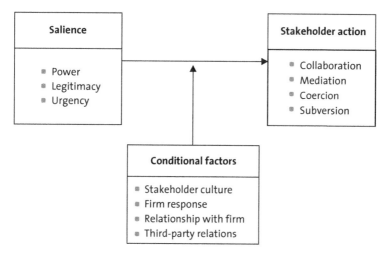

Figure 14.3 **Conditions of stakeholder action**

14.2.1 *Stakeholder culture*

The degree to which stakeholder action can be explained by mutual firm–stakeholder salience is partially conditional on the stakeholder group's culture. As previously discussed, a stakeholder group's motivation to act may be more a function of participants' penchant for expression of their collective identity than an indication of a perceived legitimacy gap or conflict of interest (Rowley and Moldoveanu 2000). Jasper (1997) explains that protest groups tend to adopt strategic 'tastes' around the kinds of tactics they employ and objectives they pursue. This is generally a function of the culture that emerges in the group. Especially when this is the case, one might expect to find this collective identity expressed through rituals having symbolic meaning that continually reproduce the group's culture through its routine use of certain styles of action. In lay terms, this means that a public-interest stakeholder group's participants may get intrinsic rewards merely from the act of protesting. Through years of the practice of protest, they may have come to identify themselves as a 'protest' group. Protesting may be a socialising activity for them, conjuring memories of past events and relationships and offering them a sense of security and belonging. Under these circumstances, an observer would be frustrated in trying to explain the group's actions as a function of relative salience. The rational explanation of stakeholder action ceases to be of much assistance in this case and the group's culture takes centre stage in terms of its power to explain the group's actions.

> Proposition 2: The presence of a strong group culture, especially one that provides participants with a sense of collective identity, provides a more powerful explanation than mutual salience of the nature of stakeholder action.

14.2.2 The firm's response to stakeholder action

Until now, we have discussed the stakeholder's salience to the firm only in terms of the stakeholder group's assessment of how the firm might perceive it and respond to action it might take in redressing the group's social issue with the firm. We will now consider the effects of the firm's response to stakeholder action, recognising that firm–stakeholder actions and responses are interwoven in a web of interaction that influences the course of events.

Debate rages among management scholars regarding the extent to which managers have discretion to respond to pressures in the firm's external environment, including stakeholders' needs. While some perceive inertia as a factor limiting managerial alternatives (Staw et al. 1981; Hannan and Freeman 1984), others suggest that managers can and do exercise considerable discretion in choosing courses of action, despite environmental constraints, that may or may not bode well for long-term firm outcomes (Child 1972; Fama and Jensen 1983; Hrebeniak and Joyce 1985; Perrow 1986). The point of divergence between these alternative viewpoints seems, primarily, to involve the degree to which managers are believed to control the consequences of their actions through control of the firm's environment. We suggest that managers do choose from among various alternative courses of action and that their choices have consequences for the firm in terms of stakeholder actions. In fact, we believe that one of the key contributions of this chapter is in recognising the substantial effect that the firm's response has on subsequent stakeholder action.

The firm's response, similar to the stakeholder group's initial reaction, can be described using the same typology used to describe stakeholder action. Particularly important is the dimension of outcome orientation, whether integrative or distributive. The reciprocity principle in social exchange theory (Gouldner 1960; Emerson 1962; Blau 1964) provides the explanatory mechanism that predicts strong effects of the firm's response on subsequent stakeholder action. The reciprocity principle suggests that the stakeholder group will tend to respond to the firm in the same way that the firm responded to the stakeholder's initial action. For instance, if the stakeholder group initially protests but the firm counters with an integrative response, the stakeholder will be more likely to respond integratively—despite the stakeholder's initial calculations of relative salience. On the other hand, the stakeholder will be more likely to choose a distributive response if the firm's response to initial stakeholder action is distributive. Research in conflict management has found the norm of reciprocity to have strong explanatory effects for conflict behaviour (Thomas 1992). The key point to glean from this discussion is that the norm of reciprocity creates strong social pressures such that a firm can often motivate and should expect a stakeholder group to reciprocate the firm's action.

> *Proposition 3:* Firms' responses to stakeholders' initial action create strong social pressures for the stakeholder to reciprocate the response in subsequent interactions with the firm.

14.2.3 The firm–stakeholder relationship

The analysis of stakeholder action to this point has revolved around a cross-sectional or episodic consideration of the factors explaining a stakeholder group's observed behaviour. Firm–stakeholder interactions, however, are not always limited to a single transaction. Multiple interactions between a firm and stakeholder may produce relational familiarity that alters our expectations for encounters between the parties (Schuppisser 1998; Greening *et al.* 2001). For our purposes, these encounters may be situated in an historical or future expected relationship that alters the stakeholder group's behaviour from that predicted by our original relative salience model. Past relationships and future expectations have divergent effects on a stakeholder group's action, but both hold important consequences for explaining the stakeholder group's collective behaviour.

14.2.3.1 Past relationship

Past interactions between a firm and stakeholder provide an occasion for balance or imbalance in the rewards or detriment provided to one party by the other. Again, the reciprocity norm provides a strong explanation for stakeholder action depending on the obligation the stakeholder assumes in a current interaction. For instance, if past interactions have left the stakeholder group with the perception that it has received excess rewards from the firm in the past, the stakeholder group will assume the obligation of returning those rewards to the firm in the current interaction. Therefore, the mutual salience model might predict that a distributive response would be expected but the investigator would observe an integrative action on the part of the stakeholder. Conversely, past interactions may leave the stakeholder group with the perception that the firm can be expected to behave opportunistically—seeking distributive outcomes. This shapes the stakeholder group's expectations regarding the behaviour it can expect of the firm in the current interaction and, again, the strong effect of the reciprocity norm prompts the stakeholder group to pursue a distributive outcome—behaving either coercively or subversively, depending on whether a direct or indirect approach is adopted.

Another source of complexity in the explanation of stakeholder action stems from the potential for personal relationships developing between boundary spanners in each organisation (Seabright et al. 1993). Both personal and structural attachments develop between organisations that have constraining effects on rational choices regarding concern for the other's outcomes. Structural attachments are agreements and covenants made between two actors that specify conditions of interaction between the two. These may have some explanatory power for stakeholder action, but the personal attachments are the phenomenon of interest here. If public relations managers from a firm and stakeholder group were, for instance, domestic partners one could imagine drastic departures from a rational calculation of firm–stakeholder interactions. Certainly, one would expect a more thorough exchange of information and a deeper sense of shared fate. It would be difficult to imagine, under such circumstances, that the two actors would accept distributive outcomes as plausible.

> Proposition 4(a): Past firm–stakeholder interactions sometimes produce asymmetries of obligations or personal relationships between boundary spanners that better explain stakeholder actions than our original salience model.

14.2.3.2 Future expectations

Expectations about the future may also serve to either strengthen or nullify the rational calculation for predicting stakeholder action provided in our original mutual salience model. The study of conflict management suggests that the 'length of the shadow of the future' is a strong predictor of integrative bargaining (Pruitt 1981). If the stakeholder group expects its relationship with the firm to last for the foreseeable future, it might reconsider adopting a distributive response. In particular, if a stakeholder expects its position of resource dependence relative to the firm to continue into the future, the salience explanation of stakeholder action is strengthened. Alternatively, if the stakeholder group perceives an impending decrease in its dependence on the firm's resources, the stakeholder would be somewhat more likely to adopt a distributive response with the firm. For example, this might be brought about by the potential for obtaining needed resources from a third party, which we discuss next.

> Proposition 4(b): Future expectations for the maintenance of a relationship with the firm strengthens the explanatory power of the salience model, whereas expectations for a decline in the importance of the relationship weakens the model's explanatory power.

14.2.4 Third-party relationships

The argument advanced in the previous section assumed an isolated dyadic relationship between the firm and the stakeholder in explaining the effects of the relationship on the stakeholder group's actions. This is a limiting assumption, however, in that the dyadic relationship is embedded in a larger web of relationships that provides both constraints and opportunities for both parties, and has substantial consequences for the stakeholder's behaviour. Rowley (1997) proposes that network density (the number of existing relationships between collective actors in an inter-organisational network) and actor centrality (the actor's prominence relative to other actors in the network), which is usually interpreted as indicative of the actor's influence relative to other network actors, affect the extent to which a firm can resist a stakeholder's demands.

From the stakeholder's perspective, then, network density offers opportunities for stakeholders to find alternative resource providers and potential alliance partners when seeking, in its conflict with the firm, support from a salient stakeholder in achieving its own salience with the firm. Additionally, whether the firm or stakeholder group is more central to the network is a function of resource dependence—previously described as the opposite of relational power. In the network setting, however, centrality is not merely a function of resource dependence of one party on another but of the entire network of actors on each of the parties. When considering the entire network, for example, the calculation of resource dependence between the firm and stakeholder may favour the firm while the centrality calculation favours the stakeholder. This is possible because, while the stakeholder may be relatively more dependent on the firm's resources than is the firm on the stakeholder's resources, there may be many other actors in the network that are more dependent on the stakeholder's than the firm's resources. For instance, in the 1960s and '70s, public-interest groups forged alliances with pension funds to gain support for public-interest resolutions in their conflicts with managers regarding public issues such as the firm's business involvement in South Africa (Vogel 1978). Of course, just as third-party relationships can work to the stakeholder group's advantage they can similarly work to the firm's advantage. This could dramatically alter the calculation of power when compared with the dyadic calculation and may present a completely different explanation of stakeholder action from that of the salience model.

> *Proposition 5:* Relationships between stakeholders and third parties may alter the resource-dependence calculation between the firm and stakeholder, changing power and, therefore, salience dynamics—thereby altering predictions of stakeholder action.

14.3 Conclusions

In our quest to review and extend the study of interactions between firms and public-interest group stakeholders, we have suggested that initial formulations of these interactions overlooked the potential for a strong form of collaboration. We have stretched original formulations to account for this possibility and explore the conditions that might explain its occurrence. We have applied the model of stakeholder salience to include a more thorough accounting of when and how public-interest stakeholders will interact with a firm. We have suggested that the firm's response to the stakeholder's actions may have a strong effect on subsequent interactions between the parties. Finally, we have integrated the scholarly literature addressing relations between firms and public-interest stakeholders—including recent contributions in the study of social movements—to provide a practical model to explain these complex interactions.

14.3.1 *Implications for discovery*

Our theorising in this chapter has focused on the relationship and response between a focal stakeholder—a public-interest group—and a particular firm, most commonly thought of as a large, publicly held organisation. We suggest that future research investigates not only the relationships proposed here but how these relationships might generalise to those between different kinds of stakeholder with larger, complex firms and also in relationships with smaller to medium-sized firms. We suggest that a finer-grained analysis that breaks stakeholders into meaningful categories might yield insight into why certain stakeholders take integrative or distributive, direct or indirect responses in their relationships with specific firms. Even the variance within the particular stakeholder categories might be more easily examined within the context of a certain stakeholder group. For example, would labour unions tend to take a particular strategic response towards their focal firms, or, if they would take different strategic responses, what factors and what contingencies would account for the variation in their predominant response? Understanding these factors would allow scholars to determine across which firm–stakeholder relationships and in what contexts we could generalise certain research findings.

14.3.2 *Implications for application*

Initially, managers may wish to consider the model of relative salience (Fig. 14.1, page 270) to understand a sociopolitical actor's fundamental motives for collective action. Locating the stakeholder's actions within the framework can begin to provide clues about its evaluation of the public issue context—especially regarding the relative power, legitimacy and urgency of each of the parties to the conflict. On grasping this initial understanding, the manager may wish to consider each of the conditions that are proposed to alter the stakeholder's contextual motives, thereby providing a better explanation of its actions. In particular, when the manager cannot seem to make sense of the stakeholder's behaviour he or she might turn to those conditions to provide some insight into the nature of the particular stakeholder under consideration.

We suggested earlier in the chapter that one of our key contributions would be to extend a prior model of stakeholder action by considering the potentiality for, and consequences of, a strong form of collaboration between a firm and a stakeholder group. Monsanto's contrasting fortunes from the 1980s to the 1990s clearly illustrates our thesis. In the early 1980s, under CEO Louis Fernandez, Monsanto enjoyed substantial benefits from 'creative co-operation' with public interests, especially environmental groups (Littlejohn 1987). Fernandez participated in the National Wildlife Federation's Corporate Conservation Council, lobbied for increased funding for EPA (Environmental Protection Agency) research, and helped establish Clean Sites, Inc.—a co-operative partnership between industry and environmental groups to promote effective clean-up of hazardous waste. Also during this time-period, the company established the Dialogue Project, a Washington-based group designed to facilitate discussion between industry groups, think-tanks, public-interest groups and scholars, regarding various policy areas—including among them biotechnology regulation. After completing a successful campaign in co-operation with the Sierra Club to tighten environmental regulation in Ohio, one Monsanto employee concluded, 'At the beginning, it was a challenge to work with people who see things differently, but after a few meetings we found that we agreed on a surprising number of issues' (Monsanto 1984).

Later, however, Monsanto abandoned its inclusive strategy of co-operation with public interests and began to lobby executive and administrative agencies directly for policies favourable to adoption of agricultural biotechnology (Eichenwald 2001). Company executives predicted that their efforts in producing biotech food would be met with much less public approval than its related expansion into biotech pharmaceutical products. Monsanto was successful in persuading the US Food and Drug Administration (FDA) to allow only voluntary testing of the safety of new biotech food products before releasing them into the market. Also, they successfully defended against a campaign by consumer groups to require mandatory labelling of genetically modified foods. Winning these battles for Monsanto proved, however, detrimental to the company's survival. These events launched a groundswell of public-interest group protest. The number of these groups lobbying for stronger regulation has grown from just a few in 1992 to 54 more recently (Eichenwald 2001). As a result, agricultural biotechnology has begun to lose its lustre. US farmers have slowed biotech food production (Barboza 2000). The European Union has virtually halted production and distribution of genetically modified food products, as producers, distributors and consumers have rejected them (McNeil 2000). For example, Novartis, a major European food distributor, has ceased marketing genetically modified food products (Pollack 2000).

In a written report, Robert Shapiro, then chairman of the Pharmacia Corporation—which had recently acquired Monsanto's food and pharmaceutical divisions—offered an explanation for the dramatic turn of events:

> We've learned that there is often a very fine line between scientific confidence on the one hand and corporate arrogance on the other . . . It was natural for us to see this as a scientific issue. We didn't listen very well to people who insisted that there were relevant ethical, religious, cultural, social and economic issues as well (Eichenwald 2001).

Monsanto's earlier strong form of collaboration, best exemplified in the Clean Sites, Inc. project in which Louis Fernandez participated, opened the possibility for a superordinate structure that allowed economic, governmental and public interests a forum for inclusion and negotiation. This direct form of mutual involvement assisted Monsanto, we argue, in eliciting a co-operative response from public-interest groups. The company's more recent clashes with public-interest groups regarding agricultural biotechnology is predictable, we suggest, using our model. The reciprocity principle indicates a strong effect of competitive behaviour on the part of public-interest groups when faced with Monsanto's attempts to gain unilaterally favourable public policies. The company recognised and acknowledged its error. Recently, Shapiro attended a conference sponsored by Greenpeace—one of the environmental groups that opposed the adoption of agricultural biotechnology (Eichenwald 2001)—in an apparent attempt to rekindle the relatively co-operative environment the company once enjoyed.

Undoubtedly, this formulation has been incomplete in its coverage of both the initial motives that explain stakeholder actions and the conditions that can cause departures from those explanations. It is our hope, however, that these ideas will provide a complete enough understanding of the nature of interactions between a firm and its sociopolitical stakeholders in order to be able to forgo introductions to the '60 Minutes' camera crew.

BIBLIOGRAPHY

ABS (Australian Bureau of Statistics) (1999) *Income Distribution, Australia* (Catalogue 6523.0; Canberra: ABS).

—— (2000) *ABS 2000 Year Book, Australia* (Catalogue 1301.0; Canberra: ABS).

Ackerman, R.W., and R.A. Bauer (1976) *Corporate Social Responsiveness: The Modern Dilemma* (Cambridge, MA: Harvard University Press).

Ackoff, R.L. (1975) *Redesigning the Future* (New York: John Wiley).

—— (1999) *Re-creating the Corporation: A Design of Organizations for the 21st Century* (New York: Oxford University Press).

Adams, E.S. (1969) 'Public Role of Private Enterprise', *Michigan Business Review*, May 1969: 12-17.

Agle, B.R., R.K. Mitchell and J.A. Sonnenfeld (1999) 'Who Matters to CEOs? An Investigation of Stakeholder Attributes and Salience, Corporate Performance, and CEO Values', *Academy of Management Journal* 42.5 (October 1999): 507-25.

AIDEnvironment (2001) *Multiple Stakeholder Dialogues and Thinktanks on Complex Environmental Issues* (www.aidenvironment.org/online/stakeholder.php, accessed 5 June 2001).

Alford, H.J., and M.J. Naughton (2001) *Managing as if Faith Mattered* (Notre Dame, IN: University of Notre Dame).

ALI (American Law Institute) (1994) *Principles of Corporate Governance: Analysis and Recommendations* (Vol. 1 of 2, Pt II; St Paul, MN: ALI Publishers).

Alkhafaji, A.R. (1989) *A Stakeholder Approach to Corporate Governance: Managing in a Dynamic Environment* (New York: Quorum Books).

Allen, F. (1991) 'McDonald's to reduce waste in plan developed with environmental group', *Wall Street Journal*, 17 April 1991: B1, B6.

Allen, G.B., and J.S. Hammond (1975) *A Note on the Boston Consulting Group Concept of Competitive Analysis and Corporate Strategy* (Vol. 9; Boston, MA: Intercollegiate Case Clearing House): 197-201.

Alliance for Environmental Innovation–UPS (1998) *Achieving Preferred Packaging: Report of the Express Packaging Project* (Boston, MA: Alliance for Environmental Innovation).

Alston, K., and J.P. Roberts (1999) 'Partners in New Product Development: SC Johnson and the Alliance for Environmental Innovation', *Corporate Environmental Strategy* 9: 110-28.

Ambler, T., and A. Wilson (1995) 'Problems of Stakeholder Theory', *Business Ethics: A European Review* 4.1: 30-35.

Amnesty International and Pax Christi International (Dutch branches) (1998) *Multinational Enterprises and Human Rights* (www.paxchristi.nl/mne).

Anderson, J.W., Jr (1989) *Corporate Social Responsibility* (New York: Quorum Books).

Anderson, R., K.N. Cissna and R.C. Arnette (1994) *The Reach of Dialogue: Confirmation, Voice and Community* (Cresskill, NJ: Hampton Press).

Andrews, K.R. (1971) *The Concept of Corporate Strategy* (Homewood, IL: Dow Jones–Irwin).

Andriof, J. (1998) 'Corporate Citizenship: Stakeholder Strategies for Responsible Companies', in VDI (ed.), *Werte erfolgreich managen* (Munich: VDI): 211-30.

—— (2001) 'Patterns of Stakeholder Partnership Building', in J. Andriof and M. McIntosh (eds.), *Perspectives on Corporate Citizenship* (Sheffield, UK: Greenleaf Publishing): 215-38.

Andriof, J., and C. Marsden (1999) 'Corporate Citizenship: What Is It and How to Assess It?', *Personalführung* 8: 34-41.

Ansoff, H.I. (1965) *Corporate Strategy: An Analytic Approach to Business Policy for Growth and Expansion* (New York: McGraw–Hill).

—— (1984) *Implanting Strategic Management* (Englewood Cliffs, NJ: Prentice Hall).

Aram, J. (1989) 'The Paradox of Interdependent Relations in the Field of Social Issues in Management', *Academy of Management Review* 14.2: 266-83.

Argenti, J. (1997) 'Stakeholders: The Case Against', *Long Range Planning* 30.3 (June 1997): 442-45.

Argenti, J., and A. Campbell (1997) 'Stakeholders: The Case Against/the Case in Favour', *Long Range Planning* 30.3: 442-50.

Arrow, K.J. (1964) 'The Role of Securities in the Optimal Allocation of Risk Bearing', *Review of Economic Studies* 31.86: 91-96.

Ashforth Blake, E., and B.W. Gibbs (1990) 'The Double-Edge of Organisational Legitimation', *Organisation Science* 1.2: 177-94.

Astley, W.G. (1984) 'Toward an Appreciation of Collective Strategy', *Academy of Management Review* 9.3: 526-35.

Astley, W.G., and C.J. Fombrun (1983) 'Collective Strategy: Social Ecology of Organisational Environments', *Academy of Management Review* 8.4: 576-87.

Atkinson, A.A., J.H. Waterhouse and R.B. Wells (1997) 'A Stakeholder Approach to Strategic Performance Measurement', *Sloan Management Review*, Spring 1997: 25-37.

Aupperle, K.E., A.B. Carroll and J.D. Hartfield (1985) 'An Empirical Examination of the Relationship between Corporate Social Responsibility and Profitability', *Academy of Management Journal* 28.2: 446-63.

Austin, R.W. (1965) 'Responsibility for Social Change', *Harvard Business Review*, July/August 1965: 45-52.

Baker, W.E. (1990) 'Market Networks and Corporate Behaviour', *American Journal of Sociology* 96: 589-625.

Bakhtin, M.M. (1981) *The Dialogic Imagination: Four Essays* (ed. M. Holquist; trans. C. Emerson and M. Holquist; Austin, TX: University of Texas Press).

Banfield, E.C. (1985) *Here the People Rule: Selected Essays* (New York: Plenum Press).

Barboza, D. (2000) 'Farmers are scaling back genetically altered crops', *New York Times*, 1 April 2000: A6.

Barker, E. (1960) *Social Contract: Essays by Locke, Hume, and Rousseau* (Oxford, UK: Oxford University Press [1947]).

Barlow, J. (2001) 'Putting the Hurt on Greedy Pirates', *Houston Chronicle* 100.317 (26 August 2001): 1D.

Barnard, C.I. (1938) *The Functions of the Executive* (Cambridge, MA: Harvard Business School Press).

Barney, J.B. (1986) 'Strategic Factor Markets: Expectations, Luck, and Business Strategy', *Management Science* 32.10: 1231-41.

—— (1991) 'Firms Resources and Sustained Competitive Advantage', *Journal of Management* 17.1: 99-120.

Barton, S.L., N.C. Hill and J.D. Sundaram (1989) 'An Empirical Test of Stakeholder Theory Predictions of Capital Structure', *Financial Management* 18.1: 36-44.

Battelle (2002a) *World Business Council for Sustainable Development toward a Sustainable Cement Industry: Summary Report* (Battelle, March 2002).

—— (2002b) *World Business Council for Sustainable Development toward a Sustainable Cement Industry: Integration Report* (Battelle, March 2002).

BCA (Business Council of Australia) (1999) BCA *Papers* 1.2 (Melbourne: BCA).

Beaulieu, S. (2001) 'La légitimité professionnelle: Une ressource qui se gère. Une application en contexte professionnel' (unpublished doctoral dissertation; Université du Québec à Montréal).

Beaver, W. (1999) 'Is the Stakeholder Model Dead?', *Business Horizons* 42.2: 8-13.

Becker, L.C., and C.B. Becker (eds.) (2001) *The Encyclopedia of Ethics* (New York: Garland Publishing, rev. edn).

Belliveau, M.A., C.A. O'Reilly III and J.B. Wade (1996) 'Social Capital at the Top: Effects of Social Similarity and Status on CEO Compensation', *Academy of Management Journal* 39.6: 1568-93.

Berle, A.A., Jr, and G.C. Means (1932) *The Modern Corporation and Private Property* (New York: Commerce Clearing House).

Berlin Initiative Group (2000) *German Code of Corporate Governance* (www.gccg.de).

Berman, S.L., A.C. Wicks, S. Kotha and T.M. Jones (1999) 'Does Stakeholder Orientation Matter? The Relationship between Stakeholder Management Models and Firm Financial Performance', *Academy of Management Journal* 42.5 (October 1999): 488-506.

Blair, M.M. (1995) *Ownership and Control: Rethinking Corporate Governance for the Twenty-first Century* (Washington, DC: Brookings Institution).

—— (1998) 'For whom should Corporations be Run? An Economic Rational for Stakeholder Management', *Long Range Planning* 32.2: 195-200.

Blasi, J.R. (1990) *Employee Ownership: Revolution or Ripoff?* (New York: HarperCollins/Harper Business).

Blau, P.M. (1964) *Exchange and Power in Social Life* (New York: John Wiley).

Bliss, T. (1996) *Leveling the Playing Field: How Citizen Advocacy Group Influence Corporate Behavior* (unpublished doctoral dissertation; Santa Barbara, CA: Fielding Graduate Institute).

Block, P. (1993) *Stewardship: Choosing Service over Self Interest* (San Francisco: Berrett-Koehler).

Body Shop (1998) *The New Bottom Line* (Australia and New Zealand: The Body Shop).

Bohm, D. (1996) *On Dialogue* (ed. L. Nichol; New York: Routledge).

Boissevain, J. (1974) *Friends of Friends* (Oxford, UK: Basil Blackwell).

Borch, O.J., and M.B. Arthur (1995) 'Strategic Networks among Small Firms: Implications for Strategy Research Methodology', *Journal of Management Studies* 32.4: 419-41.

Boulding, K.E. (1953) *The Organizational Revolution: A Study in the Ethics of Economic Organization* (with a commentary by Reinhold Niebuhr; New York: Harper).

—— (1968) *Beyond Economics: Essays on Society, Religion, and Ethics* (Ann Arbor, MI: University of Michigan Press).

Bourdieu, P. (1986) 'The Forms of Capital', in J.G. Richardson (ed.), *Handbook of Theory and Research for the Sociology of Education* (New York: Greenwood): 241-58.

Boutilier, R., and A. Svendsen (2001) *Stakeholder Bridging and Bonding in Clayoquot Sound* (unpublished manuscript, Centre for Innovation in Management, Simon Fraser University, Vancouver, BC).

Bowden, A.R., M.R. Lane and J.H. Martin (2001) *Triple Bottom Line Risk Management: Enhancing Profit, Environmental Performance, and Community Benefits* (New York: John Wiley).

Bowen, H.R. (1953) *The Social Responsibilities of the Businessman* (New York: Harper & Row).

Bowie, N. (1988) 'The Moral Obligations of Multinational Corporations', in S. Luper-Foy (ed.), *Problems of International Justice* (Boulder, CO: Westview Press): 97-113.

Brandenburger, A.M., and B.J. Nalebuff (1996) *Co-opetition* (New York: Doubleday).

Braybrooke, D., and A. Monahan (1992) 'Common Good', in L.C. Becker and C.B. Becker (eds.), *Encyclopedia of Ethics* (New York: Garland Publishing): 175.

Brenner, S.N. (1993) 'The Stakeholder Theory of the Firm and Organizational Decision Making: Some Propositions and a Model', in J. Pasquero and D. Collins (eds.), *Proceedings of the Fourth Annual Meeting of the International Association for Business and Society, San Diego* (San Diego, CA: International Association for Business and Society [IABS]): 205-10.

—— (1995) 'Stakeholder Theory of the Firm: Its Consistency with Current Management Techniques', in J. Näsi (ed.), *Understanding Stakeholder Thinking* (Helsinki: LSR Publications): 75-95.

Brenner, S.N., and P.L. Cochran (1991) 'The Stakeholder Theory of the Firm: Implications for Business and Society Theory and Research', *International Association for Business and Society* (Sundance, UT: International Association for Business and Society [IABS]): 43-61.

Bresser, R.K.F. (1988) 'Thatching Collective and Competitive Strategies', *Strategic Management Journal* 9: 375-85.

Brummer, J.J. (1991) *Corporate Responsibility and Legitimacy: An Interdisciplinary Analysis* (New York: Greenwood Press).

Bruyn, S. (2000) *A Civil Economy: Transforming the Market in the Twenty-first Century* (Ann Arbor, MI: University of Michigan Press).

Bryan, F., and J. McLaughry (1989) *The Vermont Papers: Recreating Democracy on a Human Scale* (Chelsea, VT: Chelsea Publishing).

Bryson, J.M., and S.R. Anderson (2000) 'Applying Large-Group Interaction Methods in the Planning and Implementation of Major Change Efforts', *Public Administration Review* 60.2: 143-62.

BSR (Business for Social Responsibility) (1998) *Introduction to Corporate Social Responsibility* (San Francisco: BSR).

Buber, M. (1970) *I and Thou* (New York: Scribner).

Buchholz, R.A. (1977) 'An Alternative to Social Responsibility', *MSU Business Topics* 25.3: 12-16.

Buchholz, R.A., W.M. Evan and R. Wagley (1994) *Management Responses to Public Issues: Concepts and Cases in Strategy Formulation* (Englewood Cliffs, NJ: Prentice Hall).

Burgers, W.P., C.W.L. Hill and W.C. Kim (1993) 'A Theory of Global Strategic Alliances: The Case of the Global Auto Industry', *Strategic Management Journal* 14: 419-32.

Burke, E.M. (1999) *Corporate Community Relations: The Principle of the Neighbor of Choice* (Westwood, CT: Praeger).

Burson-Marsteller (1998) *Maximizing Corporate Reputation* (report with Wirthlin Worldwide; www.bm.com/expertise/rep_mgmt2.html).

Burt, R.S. (1992a) *Structural Holes* (Cambridge, MA: Harvard University Press).

—— (1992b) 'The Social Structure of Competition', in N. Nohria and R. Eccles (eds.), *Networks and Organizations: Structure, Form, and Action* (Boston, MA: Harvard Business School Press): 57-91.

—— (1997) 'The Contingent Value of Social Capital', *Administrative Science Quarterly* 42: 339-65.

Business Roundtable (1990) *Corporate Governance and American Competitiveness* (Washington, DC: Business Roundtable).

Calhoun, J.C. (1853) *A Disquisition on Government and Selections from the Discourse* (Indianapolis, IN: Bobbs-Merrill).

California Global Accountability Project (1999) *Hard Issues, Innovative Approaches: Improving NGO–Industry Dialogue on Corporate Responsibility and Accountability: Report of a Roundtable* (Berkeley, CA: The Nautilus Institute, www.nautilus.org, 9 November 1999).

Calton, J.M. (1997) 'On the Positive Duty of Managers: Moral Agency in Community Conversations', in J. Weber and K. Rehbein (eds.), *Proceedings of the Eighth Annual Meeting of the International Association of Business and Society (IABS)* (Destin, FL: IABS): 279-84.

Campbell, A. (1997) 'Stakeholders: The Case in Favour', *Long Range Planning* 30.3 (June 1997): 446-49.

Campbell, A., and M. Alexander (1997) 'What's Wrong with Strategy?', *Harvard Business Review* 75.6 (November/December 1997): 42-44, 46, 48-51.

Capra, F. (1995) *The Web of Life* (New York: Anchor Doubleday).

Carleton, J. (2000) 'Against the Grain: How Home Depot and Activists Joined to Cut Logging Abuse', *Wall Street Journal*, 26 September: A1, A12.

Carris, W.H. (1994) *The Long Term Plan* (Rutland, VT: Carris Financial Corporation).

Carroll, A.B. (1979) 'A Three-dimensional Conceptual Model of Corporate Social Performance', *Academy of Management Review* 4: 497-505.

—— (1989) *Business and Society: Ethics and Stakeholder Management* (Cincinnati, OH: South-Western).

—— (1991) 'The Pyramid of Corporate Social Responsibility: Toward the Moral Management of Organizational Stakeholders', *Business Horizons* 34.4 (July/August 1991): 39-48.

—— (1993) *Business and Society: Ethics and Stakeholder Management* (Cincinnati, OH: South-Western, 2nd edn).

—— (1995) 'Stakeholder Thinking in Three Models of Management Morality: A Perspective with Strategic Implications', in J. Näsi (ed.), *Understanding Stakeholder Thinking* (Helsinki: LSR Publications): 47-74.

—— (1998) 'The Four Faces of Corporate Citizenship', *Business and Society Review* 100–101: 1-7.

Carroll, G.R., and M.T. Hannan (1989) 'Density Delay in the Evolution of Organizational Populations: A Model and Five Empirical Tests', *Administrative Science Quarterly* 34: 411-30.

Cazalet, G. (2000) *Generating Social Responsibility* (report prepared for the Myer Foundation; Sydney: St James Ethics Centre).

Chandler, G. (1998) 'Oil Companies and Human Rights', *Business Ethics: A European Review* 7.2 (April 1998): 69-72.

Child, J. (1972) 'Organizational Structure, Environment and Performance: The Role of Strategic Choice', *Sociology* 6: 1-22.

Child, J.W., and A.M. Marcoux (1999) 'Stakeholder Theory in the Origional Position', *Business Ethics Quarterly* 9.2: 207-23.

Clark, J.M. (1916) 'The Changing Basis of Economic Responsibility', *Journal of Political Economy* 24.3: 209-29.

Clarkson Centre for Business Ethics (1999) *Principles of Stakeholder Management: The Clarkson Principles* (Toronto: The Clarkson Centre for Business Ethics, Joseph L. Rotman School of Management, University of Toronto).

—— (2000) *Research in Stakeholder Theory, 1997–1998* (Toronto: Joseph L. Rotman School of Management, University of Toronto).

Clarkson, M.B.E. (1991) 'Defining, Evaluating, and Managing Corporate Social Performance: A Stakeholder Management Model', in J. Post (ed.), *Research in Corporate Social Performance and Policy* (Greenwich, CT: JAI Press): 331-58.

—— (1994) 'A Risk Based Model of Stakeholder Theory', in *Proceedings of the Second Toronto Conference on Stakeholder Theory* (Toronto: Centre for Corporate Social Performance and Ethics, University of Toronto).

—— (1995) 'A Stakeholder Framework for Analysing and Evaluating Corporate Social Performance', *Academy of Management Review* 20.1 (January 1995): 92-117.

—— (ed.) (1998) *The Corporation and its Stakeholders: Classic and Contemporary Readings* (Toronto: University of Toronto Press).

Clarkson, M.B.E., *et al.* (1994) 'The Toronto Conference: Reflections on Stakeholder Theory', *Business and Society* 33.1 (April 1994): 82-131.

Clarkson, M.B.E., M.C. Deck and N. Shiner (1992) 'The Stakeholder Management Model in Practice', paper presented at the *Annual Meeting of the Academy of Management, Las Vegas, NV* (Washington, DC: Academy of Management).

Climate Friendly Technology (2001) *2000 Forum on Climate Change* (www.oecd.org/env/docs/cc/comenvepocieaslt(2000)1.pdf, accessed 6 June 2001).

Coase, R.H. (1960) 'The Problem of Social Cost', *Journal of Law and Economics* 3 (October 1960): 1-44.

Cochran, P.L., and R.A. Wood (1984) 'Corporate Social Responsibility and Financial Performance', *Academy of Management Journal* 27.1: 42-56.

Cohen, A., and M. Townsley (1990) 'Perspectives on Collaboration as Replacement for Confrontation', *Public Utilities Fortnightly*, 1 March 1990: 9-13.

Cohen, W.M., and D.A. Levinthal (1990) 'Absorptive Capacity: A New Perspective on Learning and Innovation', *Administrative Science Quarterly* 35: 128-52.

Coleman, J.S. (1990) *Foundations of Social Theory* (Cambridge, MA: Belknap Press of Harvard University Press).

Collins, J.C., and J.I. Porras (1994) *Built to Last: Successful Habits of Visionary Companies* (New York: Harper Business).

Compaq Computer Company (2001) *Environment, Health and Safety 1999–2000 Leadership Report* (Houston, TX: Compaq).

Cools, K., and M. van Praag (2000) *The Value Relevance of a Single-Valued Corporate Target: An Empirical Analysis* (Social Science Research Network eLibrary at: http://papers.ssrn.com/paper=244788).

Corlett, J.A. (1989) 'The "Modified Vendetta Sanction" as a Method of Corporate Collective Punishment', *Journal of Business Ethics* 8: 937-42.

Cornell, B., and A.C. Shapiro (1987) 'Corporate Stakeholders and Corporate Finance', *Financial Management* 16: 5-14.

Cowell, R., and S. Owens (1998) 'Suitable Locations: Equity and Sustainability in the Minerals Planning Process', *Regional Studies* 32.9 (December 1998): 797-811.

Cyert, R.M., and J.G. March (1963) *A Behavioral Theory of the Firm* (Englewood Cliffs, NJ: Prentice Hall).

D'Aveni, R.A., and I. Kesner (1993) 'Top Managerial Prestige, Power and Tender Offer Response: A Study of Elite Social Networks and Target Firm Cooperation during Takeovers', *Organization Science* 4: 123-51.

Danielsson, C. (1979) 'Business and Politics: Toward a Theory beyond Capitalism, Plato, and Marx', *California Management Review* 21.3 (Spring 1979): 17-25.

Darwin, C. (1859) *On the Origin of Species and the Descent of Man* (New York: Random House [1995 edn]).

Davidson, W.N., D.L. Worrell and A. El-Jelly (1995) 'Influencing Managers to Change Unpopular Corporate Behavior through Boycotts and Divestitures: A Stock Market Test', *Business and Society* 34: 171-96.

Davis, G.F., and T.A. Thompson (1994) 'A Social Movement Perspective on Corporate Control', *Administrative Science Quarterly* 39: 141-73.

Davis, K. (1973) 'The Case for and against Business Assumption of Social Responsibilities', *Academy of Management Journal* 16: 312-22.

Davis, K., and R.L. Blomstrom (1975) *Business and Society: Environment and Responsibility* (New York: McGraw-Hill).

Day, R., and J.V. Day (1977) 'A Review of the Current State of Negotiated Order Theory: An Appreciation and A Critique', *Sociological Quarterly* 18: 126-42.

Dean, K.L. (1998) 'The Chicken and the Egg Revisited: Ties between Corporate Social Performance and the Financial Bottom Line', *Academy of Management Executive* 12.2: 99-100.

Debreu, G. (1959) *Theory of Value* (New York: John Wiley).

Denzin, N.K., and Y.S. Lincoln (1997) *Handbook of Qualitative Research* (London: Sage).

Depree, M. (1989) *Leadership is an Art* (New York: Doubleday).

Derber, C. (1998) *Corporation Nation: How Corporations are Taking Over our Lives and What we can Do about it* (New York: St Martin's Press).

Dey Report (1994) *Where are the Directors? Guidelines for Improved Corporate Governance in Canada* (Toronto Stock Exchange Committee on Corporate Governance in Canada).

Dierickx, I., and K. Cool (1989) 'Asset Stock Accumulation and Sustainability of Competitive Advantage', *Management Science* 35.12: 1504-11.

DiMaggio, P.J. (1988) 'Interest and Agency in Institutional Theory', in L.G. Zucker (ed.), *Institutional Patterns and Organizations: Culture and Environment* (Cambridge, MA: Ballinger): 3-21.

DiMaggio, P.J., and W.W. Powell (1983) 'The Iron Cage Revisited: Institutional Isomorphism and Collective Rationally in Organization Fields', *American Sociological Review* 46: 147-60.

Dodd, E.M., Jr (1932) 'For whom are Corporate Managers Trustees?', *Harvard Law Review* 45: 1145-63.

Donaldson, T. (1989) *The Ethics of International Business* (New York: Oxford University Press).

—— (1995) *American Anti-management Theories of Organizations: A Critique of Paradigm Proliferation* (Cambridge, UK: Cambridge University Press).

—— (1999) 'Making Stakeholder Theory Whole', *Academy of Management Review* 24.2 (April 1999): 237-41.

Donaldson, T., and T.W. Dunfee (1994) 'Towards a Unified Conception of Business Ethics: Integrative Social Contracts Theory', *Academy of Management Review* 19.2: 252-84.

—— (1999) *Ties that Bind: A Social Contracts Approach to Business Ethics* (Boston, MA: Harvard Business School Press).

Donaldson, T., and L.E. Preston (1995) 'The Stakeholder Theory of the Corporation: Concepts, Evidence, and Implications', *Academy of Management Review* 20.1 (January 1995): 65-91.

Doucouliagos, C. (1995) 'Worker Participation and Productivity in Labor-Managed and Participatory Capitalist Firms: A Meta-analysis', *Industrial and Labor Relations Review* 49.1: 59-77.

Drucker, P.F. (1980) *Management in Turbulent Times* (London: Heinemann).

—— (1993) *Post-capitalist Society* (Oxford, UK: Butterworth).

—— (1999) *Management Challenges for the 21st Century* (New York: HarperBusiness).

Dubar, C., and P. Tripier (1998) *Sociologie des professions* (Paris: Armand Colin).

Dussauge, P., and B. Garrette (1999) *Cooperative Strategy: Competing Successfully through Strategic Alliances* (New York: John Wiley).

Dworkin, R. (1978) *Taking Rights Seriously* (Cambridge, MA: Harvard).

Dyer, J.H. (1996) 'Specialized Supplier Networks as a Source of Competitive Advantage: Evidence from the Auto Industry', *Strategic Management Journal* 17.3: 271-92.

Dyer, J.H., and H. Singh (1998) 'The Relational View: Cooperative Strategy and Sources of Inter-organizational Competitive Advantage', *Strategic Management Journal* 23.4: 660-79.

Economist (1996) 'Blair Raises the Stakes', *The Economist*, 13 January 1996: 57.

EDF (Environmental Defense Fund)–McDonald's (1991) *Waste Reduction Task Force Final Report* (New York: Environmental Defense Fund).

Eichenwald, K. (2001) 'Biotechnology Food: From the Lab to a Debacle', *New York Times*, 25 January 2001: A1.

Eide, A., H.O. Bergesen and P. Rudolfson Goyer (2000) *Human Rights and the Oil Industry* (Antwerp: Intersentia).

Elbing, A.O., Jr (1970) 'Value Issue of Business: The Responsibility of the Businessman', *Academy of Management Journal* 16 (March 1970): 79-89.

Elkington, J. (1997) *Cannibals with Forks: The Triple Bottom Line of the 21st Century Business* (Oxford, UK: Capstone Publishing).

Elliott, C. (2001) 'Saturday Night's All Right: Airlines Ease Ticket Restrictions that Irked Travelers', *US News and World Report* 131.8 (3 September 2001): 34.

Ellis, W.B. (1989) 'The Collaborative Process in Utility Resource Planning', *Public Utilities Fortnightly*, June 1989: 9-12

Emerson, R.M. (1962) 'Power-Dependence Relations', *American Sociological Review* 27: 31-41.

Emmons, W., and A. Nimgade (1991) *Burroughs Wellcome and AZT (A) (B) (C) Cases and Teaching Note* (Boston, MA: Harvard Business School).

Emshoff, J., and R.E. Freeman (1981) 'Stakeholder Management: A Case Study of the US Brewers and the Container Issue', *Applications of Management Science* 1: 57-90.

Enterprise Development Group (2001) *Enterprise Development Workshops for Large Group Stakeholder Enrollment* (www.enterprisedevelop.com/w_stakeholder.htm, accessed 6 June 2001).

Environics (1999) *The Millennium Poll on Corporate Social Responsibility: Executive Briefing* (www.environicsinternational.com/news_archives/mpexecbrief.pdf).

EPE (European Partners for the Environment) (2001) *Leadership and Strategy in the Age of the Knowledge Economy* (www.epe.be, accessed 7 June 2001).

Epstein, E.M. (1987) 'The Corporate Social Policy Process: Beyond Business Ethics, Corporate Social Responsibility, and Corporate Social Responsiveness', *California Management Review* 29.3: 99-114.

—— (1998) 'Business Ethics and Corporate Social Policy: Reflections on an Intellectual Journey, 1964–1996, and Beyond', *Business and Society* 37.1 (March 1998): 7-39.

Etzioni, A. (1988) *The Moral Dimension* (New York: Basic Books).

Evan, W.M., and R.E. Freeman (1993) 'A Stakeholder Theory of the Modern Corporation: Kantian Capitalism', in T.L. Beauchamp and N.E. Bowie (eds.), *Ethical Theory and Business* (Englewood Cliffs, NJ: Prentice Hall, 4th edn): 75-84.

Evered, R. (1983) 'Contrasting Conceptions of Strategy', in R.B. Lamb (ed.), *Advances in Strategic Management* (Greenwich, CT: JAI Press): 24-32.

Fama, E.F., and M.C. Jensen (1983) 'Agency Problems and Residual Claims', *Journal of Law and Economics* 26: 327-49.

Finsen, L., and S. Finsen (1994) *The Animal Rights Movement in America: From Compassion to Respect* (New York: Twayne Publishers).

Fisher, D., D. Rooke and B. Torbert (2000) *Personal and Organisational Transformations through Action Inquiry* (Boston, MA: Edge/Work Press).

Fitzgerald, D. (2001) 'The CCC and the Economy', *The Real News*, Spring 2001: 2.

Fombrun, C.J. (1996) *Reputation: Realizing Value from the Corporate Image* (Boston, MA: Harvard Business School Press).

—— (1997) 'Three Pillars of Corporate Citizenship: Ethics, Social Benefit, Profitability', in N.M. Tichy, A.R. McGillis and L. St Clair (eds.), *Corporate Global Citizenship: Doing Business in the Public Eye* (San Francisco: New Lexington Press): 27-42.

Ford, J.D. (1999) 'Conversations and the Epidemiology of Change', in W.A. Pasmore and R.W. Woodman (eds.), *Research in Organizational Change and Development*. Vol. XXII (Stamford, CT: JAI Press): 1-39.

Foster, C. (1989) 'Making Conservation Profitable', *The Christian Science Monitor*, 28 November 1989: 3.

Frank, R.H. (1988) *Passions within Reason: The Strategic Role of Emotions* (New York: Norton).

Frederick, W.C. (1978) *From CSR1 to CSR2: The Maturing of Business-and-Society Thought* (Working Paper 279; Pittsburgh, PA: Graduate School of Business, University of Pittsburgh).

—— (1986) *Toward CSR3: Why Ethical Analysis is Indispensable and Unavoidable in Corporate Affairs*', *California Management Review* 28.2 (Winter 1986): 126-41.

—— (1987) 'Theories of Corporate Social Performance', in S.P. Sethi and C.M. Falbe (eds.), *Business and Society: Dimensions of Conflict and Co-operation* (Lexington, MA: Lexington Books): 142-61.

—— (1994a) 'From CSR1 to CSR2', *Business and Society* 33.2 (August 1994): 150-64.

—— (1994b) 'The Virtual Reality of Facts vs. Values: A Symposium Commentary', *Business Ethics Quarterly* 4: 171-73.

—— (1995) *Values, Nature, and Culture in the American Corporation* (New York: Oxford University Press).

—— (1998a) 'Moving to CSR4: What to Pack for the Trip', *Business and Society* 37.1: 40-59.

—— (1998b) 'Creatures, Corporations, Communities, Chaos, Complexity', *Business and Society* 37.4: 358-89.

—— (1999) 'An Appalachian Coda: The Core Values of Business', *Business and Society* 38.2 (June 1999): 206-11.

Freeman, R.E. (1984) *Strategic Management: A Stakeholder Approach* (Boston, MA: Pitman)..

—— (1994) 'The Politics of Stakeholder Theory: Some Future Directions', *Business Ethics Quarterly* 4: 409-21.

—— (1995) 'Stakeholder Thinking: The State of the Art', in J. Näsi (ed.), *Understanding Stakeholder Thinking* (Helsinki: LSR Publications): 35-46.

—— (1999) 'Divergent Stakeholder Theory', *Academy of Management Review* 24.2 (April 1999): 233-37.

Freeman, R.E., and R.G. Daniel, Jr (1988) *Corporate Strategy and the Search for Ethics* (Englewood Cliffs, NJ: Prentice Hall).

Freeman, R.E., and W.M. Evan (1990) 'Corporate Governance: A Stakeholder Interpretation', *Journal of Behavioral Economics* 19.4: 337-59.

Freeman, R.E., and J. Liedtka (1997) 'Stakeholder Capitalism and the Value Chain', *European Management Journal* 15.3: 286-97.

Freeman, R.E., and D.L. Reed (1983) 'Stockholders and Stakeholders: A New Perspective on Corporate Governance', *California Management Review* 25.3: 88-106.

Friedman, D. (2001) 'Gone From the USA: Not a Superpower without a Strong Manufacturing Base', *Houston Chronicle* 100.310 (19 August 2001): 1C, 5C.

Friedman, M. (1970) 'The Social Responsibility of Business is to Increase its Profits', *New York Times Magazine*, 13 September 1970: 32-33, 122, 124, 126.

—— (1991) 'Consumer Boycotts: A Conceptual Framework and Research agenda', *Journal of Social Issues* 1: 149-68.

Friedrich, C.J. (1963) 'Influence and the Rule of Anticipated Reactions', in C.J. Friedrich (ed.), *Man and his Government: An Empirical Theory of Politics* (New York: McGraw–Hill): 199-215.

Frooman, J. (1999) 'Stakeholder Influence Strategies', *Academy of Management Review* 24.2: 191-205.

Fuertes, Y. (2000) 'Giant clams 1st casualties of cement plant wars', *Philippine Daily Inquirer*, 3 June 2000: 15.

Fukuyama, F. (1995) *Trust: The Social Virtues and the Creation of Prosperity* (London: Hamish Hamilton).

Furlong, V. (2001) 'Researchers say, with government help, wind power could blow away coal', *Houston Chronicle* 100.317 (26 August 2001): 9D.

Galbraith, J.K. (1958) *The Affluent Society* (Boston, MA: Mentor Books).

—— (1967) *The New Industrial State* (Boston, MA: Houghton Mifflin).

Garrett, D.E. (1987) 'The Effectiveness of Marketing Policy Boycotts', *Journal of Marketing* 51: 46-57.

Gates, J. (1998) *The Ownership Solution: Toward a Shared Capitalism for the 21st Century* (Reading, MA: Addison-Wesley).

Gerde, V.W., and R.E. Wokutch (1998) '25 Years and Going Strong: A Content Analysis of the First 25 Years of the Social Issues in Management Division Proceedings', *Business and Society* 37.4: 414-17.

Gioia, D.A. (1999) 'Practicability, Paradigms, and Problems in Stakeholder Theorizing', *Academy of Management Review* 24.2 (April 1999): 228-32.

Gnyawali, D.R. (1996) 'Corporate Social Performance: An International Perspective', *Advances in International Comparative Management* 11: 251-73.

Goodpaster, K.E. (1991) 'Business Ethics and Stakeholder Analysis', *Business Ethics Quarterly* 1.1: 53-72.

—— (1998) 'Bridging East and West in Management Ethics: Kyosei and the Moral Point of View', in K.E. Goodpaster, L.L. Nash and J.B. Matthews (eds.), *Policies and Persons: A Casebook in Business Ethics* (New York: McGraw–Hill, 3rd edn): 529-39.

Googins, B.K., and S.A. Rochlin (2000) 'Creating the Partnership Society: Understanding the Rhetoric and Reality of Cross-Sectoral Partnerships', *Business and Society Review* 105: 127-44.

Gordon, R.A., and J.E. Howell (1959) *Higher Education for Business* (New York: Columbia University Press).

Gouldner, A.W. (1960) 'The Norm of Reciprocity', *American Sociological Review* 25: 161-78.

Goyder, M. (1998) *Living Tomorrow's Company* (Aldershot, UK: Gower).

Granovetter, M.S. (1973) 'The Strength of Weak Ties', *American Journal of Sociology* 78: 1360-80.

—— (1985) 'Economic Action and Social Structure: The Problem of Embeddedness', *American Journal of Sociology* 91: 481-510.

Gray, B. (1989) *Collaborating: Finding Common Ground for Multiparty Problems* (San Francisco: Jossey-Bass).

Greening, D.W. (1992) 'Organizing for Public Issues: Environmental and Organizational Predictors of Structure and Process', *Research in Corporate Social Performance and Policy* 13: 83-117.

Greening, D.W., and B. Gray (1994) 'Testing a Model of Organizational Response to Social and Political Issues', *Academy of Management Journal* 37: 467-98.

Greening, D.W., J.E. Mattingly and K.R. Evans (2001) 'Factors Affecting the Rational Evolution of Firm–Stakeholder Relationships', in C. Dunn and D. Windsor (eds.), *Proceedings of the 12th Annual Meeting of the International Association for Business and Society*: 228-33.

Greenleaf, R.K. (1977) *Servant Leadership: A Journey into the Nature of Legitimate Power and Greatness* (Mahwah, NJ: Paulist Press).

Griffin, J.J., and J.F. Mahon (1997) 'The Corporate Social Performance and Corporate Financial Performance Debate: Twenty-five Years of Incomparable Research', *Business and Society* 36.1 (March 1997): 5-31.

Halal, W.E. (2001) 'The Collaborative Enterprise: A Stakeholder Model Uniting Profitability and Responsibility', *Journal of Corporate Citizenship* 2 (Summer 2001): 27-42.

Hale, B. (1999) 'Ethics: Do Good, or Else, the Public Warns', *Business Review Weekly* 21.43 (5 November 1999): 94-95.

Hampel Report (1998) *Committee on Corporate Governance: Final Report* (London: European Corporate Governance Institute).

Hand, T., and K. Trembath (1999) *The Course Experience Questionnaire Symposium* (Canberra: Department of Education, Training and Youth Affairs).

Hanks, J.L. (1994) 'From the Hustings: The Role of States with Takeover Control Laws', *Mergers and Acquisitions* 29.2 (September/October 1994).

Hannan, M.T., and J. Freeman (1984) 'Structural Inertia and Organizational Change', *American Sociological Review* 49: 149-64.

Hansen, M., and H.R. Gleckman (1994) 'Environmental Management of Multinational and Transnational Corporations: Policies, Practices and Recommendations', in R.V. Kolluru (ed.), *Environmental Strategies Handbook* (New York: McGraw–Hill): 749-95.

Hardin, G. (1968) 'The Tragedy of the Commons', *Science* 162.3859 (13 December 1968): 1243-48.

Hardin, G., and J. Baden (eds.) (1977) *Managing the Commons* (San Francisco: W.H. Freeman).

Harman, W., and J. Hormann (1990) *Creative Work: The Constructive Role of Business in a Transforming Society* (Munich: Schweisfurth Foundation).

Harrison, J.S., and R.E. Freeman (1999) 'Stakeholders, Social Responsibility, and Performance: Empirical Evidence and Theoretical Perspectives', *Academy of Management Journal* 42.5 (October 1999, special issue): 479-85.

Harrison, J.S., and C.H. St John (1996) 'Managing and Partnering with External Stakeholders', *Academy of Management Executive* 10.2: 46-60.

Harvey, B., and A. Schaefer (2001) 'Managing Relationships with Environmental Stakeholders: A Study of UK Water and Electricity Utilities', *Journal of Business Ethics* 30: 243-60.

Hay, R.D., E.R. Gray and J.E. Gates (1976) *Business and Society* (Cincinnati, OH: South-Western Publishing).

Hayek, F.A. (1960) 'The Corporation in a Democratic Society: In whose Interest ought it and will it be Run?' in M. Anshen and G.L. Bach (eds.), *Management and Corporation 1985* (New York: McGraw–Hill): 99-117.

—— (1988) 'The Fatal Conceit', in W.W. Bartley (ed.), *The Collected Works of F.A. Hayek* (Chicago: University of Chicago Press): 14.

Heath, R.L., and R.A. Nelson (1986) *Issues Management: Corporate Public Policymaking in an Information Society* (Beverly Hills, CA: Sage).

Heilbroner, R.L. (1953) *The Worldly Philosophers: The Lives, Times, and Ideas of the Great Economic Thinkers* (New York: Simon & Schuster).

Hemphill, T. (1994) 'Strange Bedfellows Cozy up for a Clean Environment', *Business and Society* 90 (Summer 1994): 38-44.

Hewlett-Packard (1998) *Hewlett-Packard's Commitment to the Environment* (Palo Alto, CA: Hewlett-Packard).

Hill, C.W.L., and T.M. Jones (1992) 'Stakeholder-Agency Theory', *Journal of Management Studies* 29.2: 131-54.

Hillman, A.J., and G.D. Keim (2001) 'Shareholder Value, Stakeholder Management, and Social Issues: What's the Bottom Line?', *Strategic Management Journal* 22: 125-39.

Hirschman, A.O. (1982) 'Rival Interpretations of Market Society: Civilizing, Destructive, or Feeble?', *Journal of Economic Literature* 20.4 (December 1982): 1463-84.

Hofer, C.W., and D. Schendel (1978) *Strategy Formulation: Analytical Concepts* (New York: West Publishing).

Hoffman, A.J. (1997) *From Heresy to Dogma: An Institutional History of Corporate Environmentalism* (San Francisco: New Lexington Press).

Holman, P., and T. Devane (1999) *The Change Handbook: Group Methods for Shaping the Future* (San Francisco: Berrett-Koehler).

Hood, J.N., J.M. Logsdon and J.K. Thompson (1993) 'Collaboration for Social Problem Solving: A Process Model', *Business and Society* 32.1: 1-17.

Horwedal, M. (1997) 'Our Trip to DC', *The Reel News*, June 1997: 1.

Howard, J. (1998) 'Opening Comments by the Prime Minister, the Hon. John Howard MP', unpublished paper delivered at the *Business and Community Partnerships Round Table*, 25 March 1998, Canberra, Australia.

Hrebeniak, L.G., and W.F. Joyce (1985) 'Organizational Adaptation: Strategic Choice and Environmental Determinism', *Administrative Science Quarterly* 30: 336-49.

Hund, G., J. Engel-Cox, K. Fowler, T. Peterson, S. Selby and M. Haddon (2001) *Communication and Stakeholder Involvement Guidebook for Cement Facilities* (Battelle and ERM).

Hund, G., J. Engel-Cox, K. Fowler, S. Selby and M. Haddon (2002) *World Business Council for Sustainable Development toward a Sustainable Cement Industry. Sustainable Cement Substudies 1 and 2: Communications and Stakeholder Involvement in the Cement Industry* (Battelle and ERM, March 2002).

Huselid, M. (1995) 'The Impact of Human Resource Management Practices on Turnover, Productivity, and Corporate Financial Performance', *Academy of Management Journal* 38: 635-72.

Husted, B. (2001) 'Taking Friedman Seriously: Maximizing Profits and Social Performance', *Proceedings of the International Association for Business and Society*, forthcoming.

Husted, B., and D.B. Allen (2001) 'Toward a Model of Corporate Social Strategy Formulation', paper presented at The Academy of Management Annual Meeting, Washington, DC, August 2001 (Washington, DC: Academy of Management).

Hutton, W. (1997) 'Six Stakeholder Propositions', *Business Strategy Review* 2: 7-10.

Hybels, R.C. (1995) 'On Legitimacy, Legitimation, and Organisations: A Critical Review and Integrative Theoretical Model', *Academy of Management Best Papers Proceedings 1995*, Briarcliff Manor, NY: 241-50.

Isaacs, W. (1999) *Dialogue and the Art of Thinking Together* (New York: Currency Doubleday).

Ittner, C., D.F. Larcker and M.W. Meyer (1997) *Performance, Compensation, and the Balanced Scorecard* (unpublished, Philadelphia, PA: Wharton School, University of Pennsylvania).

Jacobson, M.Z., and G.M. Masters (2001) 'Energy: Exploiting Wind versus Coal', *Science* 293.5534 (24 August 2001): 1438

Jacobs, J. (1965) *The Death and Life of Great American Cities* (London: Penguin Books).

Jakarta Post (1997) 'No New Cement Plants', *Jakarta Post*, 14 August 1997.

Jasper, J.M. (1997) *The Art of Moral Protest: Culture, Biography, and Creativity in Social Movements* (Chicago: University of Chicago Press).

Jasper, J.M., and D. Nelkin (1992) *The Animal Rights Crusade: The Growth of a Moral Protest* (New York: The Free Press).

Jensen, M.C. (2000) 'Value Maximization and the Corporate Objective Function', in M. Beer and N. Nohria (eds.), *Breaking the Code of Change* (Boston, MA: Harvard Business School Press): 37-57.

Jensen, M.C., and W.H. Meckling (1976) 'Theory of the Firm: Managerial Behavior, Agency Costs, and Ownership Structure', *Journal of Financial Economics* 3: 305-60.

—— (1992) 'Specific and General Knowledge, and Organization Structure', in L. Werin and H. Wijkander (eds.), *Contract Economics* (Oxford, UK: Basil Blackwell, available from the Social Science Research Network eLibrary at: http://papers.ssrn.com/paper= 6658): 251-74 (repr. in M.C. Jensen, *Foundations of Organizational Strategy* [Cambridge, MA: Harvard University Press, 1998], and *Journal of Applied Corporate Finance*, Fall 1995: 4-18).

Johanson, J., and L.G. Mattsson (1987) 'Interorganizational Relations in Industrial Systems: A Network Approach Compared with the Transaction-Cost Approach', *International Studies of Management and Organization* 17: 34-48.

Johnson & Johnson (2001) *Healthy People, Healthy Planet: Environmental, Health and Safety 2001 Sustainability Report* (New Brunswick, NJ: Johnson & Johnson).

Johnson, R.A., and D.W. Greening (1999) 'The Effects of Corporate Governance and Institutional Ownership Types on Corporate Social Performance', *Academy of Management Journal* 42.5: 564-76.

Jones, T.M. (1980) 'Corporate Social Responsibility Revisited, Redefined', *California Management Review* 22.3: 59-67.

—— (1983) 'An Integrating Framework for Research in Business and Society: A Step toward the Elusive Paradigm?', *Academy of Management Review* 8: 559-64.

—— (1994) 'The Toronto Conference: Reflections on Stakeholder Theory', *Business and Society* 33.1: 50-82.

—— (1995) 'Instrumental Stakeholder Theory: A Synthesis of Ethics and Economics', *Academy of Management Review* 20 (April 1995): 404-37.

—— (1996) 'Missing the Forest for the Trees: A Critique of the Social Responsibility Concept and Discourse', *Business and Society* 35.1: 7-41.

Jones, T.M., and A.C. Wicks (1999a) 'Convergent Stakeholder Theory', *Academy of Management Review* 24.2 (April 1999): 206-21.

—— (1999b) 'Letter to AMR Regarding Convergent Stakeholder Theory', *Academy of Management Review* 24.4 (October 1999): 621.

Jones, T.M., C.W.L. Hill and P.C. Kelly (1989) 'A Generalized Theory of Agency: A Paradigm for Business and Society', paper presented at the Annual Meeting of the Academy of Management, Washington, DC (Washington, DC: Academy of Management).

Jowett, B. (1920) *The Republic, The Dialogues of Plato* (Book VII; New York: Random House): 773-800.

Jussawalla, M. (1992) *The Economics of Intellectual Property in a World without Frontiers: A Study of Computer Software* (Westport, CT: Greenwood Press).

Kaku, R. (1997) 'The Path of Kyosei', *Harvard Business Review* 75.4 (July/August 1997): 55-63.

Kanter, R.M. (1999) 'From Spare Change to Real Change', *Harvard Business Review* 77: 122-32.

Kaplan, R.S., and D.P. Norton (1992) 'The Balanced Scorecard: Measures that Drive Performance', *Harvard Business Review*, January/February 1992: 71-79.

—— (1996) *The Balanced Scorecard* (Boston, MA: Harvard Business School Press).

Kapp, K.W. (1950) *The Social Costs of Private Enterprise* (Cambridge, MA: Harvard University).

Kay, J. (1996) *Foundations of Corporate Success: How Business Strategies Add Value* (Oxford, UK: Oxford University Press).

Kegan, R., and L.L. Lahey (2001) *Seven Languages for Transformation: How the Way we Talk can Change the Way we Work* (San Francisco: Jossey-Bass).

Kelso, L.O., and M. Adler (1958) *The Capitalist Manifesto* (New York: Random House).

Keynes, J.M. (1936) *The General Theory of Employment, Interest and Money* (New York: Harcourt Brace).

Khoury, G., J. Rostami and P.L. Turnbull (1999) *Corporate Social Responsibility: Turning Words into Action* (Canada: Conference Board of Canada).

King, D. (2000) *Stakeholders and Spin Doctors: The Politicisation of Corporate Reputations* (Hawke Institute Working Paper No. 5; Magill, Australia: Hawke Institute, University of South Australia).

Kirkpatrick, D. (1990) 'Environmentalism in the 1990s', *Fortune*, 12 February 1990: 45-48.

Kohlberg, L. (1969) 'Stages and Sequences: The Cognitive-Development Approach to Socialisation', in D.A. Goslin (ed.), *Handbook of Socialization Theory and Research* (Chicago: Rand McNally): 347-480.

Kreps, T.J. (1940) 'Measurement of the Social Performance of Business', in *An Investigation of Concentration of Economic Power for the Temporary National Economic Committee* (Monograph No. 7; Washington, DC: US Government Printing Office).

Krupp, F. (1992) 'Business and the Third Wave: Saving the Environment', delivered at a meeting of the 1992 Environmental Marketing Communications Forum, New York, 15 August 1992, *Vital Speeches of the Day* 58.1: 656-59.

Lampe, M. (2001) 'Mediation as an Ethical Adjunct of Stakeholder Theory', *Journal of Business Ethics* 31.2: 165-73.

Langtry, B. (1994) 'Stakeholders and the Moral Responsibilities of Business', *Business Ethics Quarterly* 4: 431-43.

Lash, J. (1998) 'A Shrewd Business Strategy: Opportunities to Create Sustainable Earning', *Future. The Hoechst Magazine* 2: 54-55.

Laulan, Y. (1981) *The General Theory of Employment, Interest, and Cheating* (trans. J. Weeks; New York: Richardson & Snyder).

Lawrence, A.T. (1997) 'Employee Stock Ownership Plans', in P.H. Werhane and R.E. Freeman (eds.), *The Blackwell Encyclopedic Dictionary of Business Ethics* (Malden, MA: Blackwell Business): 198-99.

—— (2000a) 'Shell and its Stakeholders: Shell in Nigeria' (multimedia case; Columbus, OH: Council on Ethics in Economics, www.i-case.com).

—— (2000b) 'Shell and its Stakeholders: The Transformation of Shell' (multimedia case; Columbus, OH: Council on Ethics in Economics, www.i-case.com).

—— (2001) 'Case Study: The Transformation of Shell', in J. Post, A. Lawrence and J. Weber (eds.), *Business and Society: Corporate Strategy, Public Policy, Ethics* (New York: McGraw–Hill, 10th edn): 593-603.

Lawrence-Lightfoot, S. (1999) *Respect: An Exploration* (Reading, MA: Perseus Books).

Leigh, J.S.A. (2001) 'Developing Corporate Citizens: Linking Organizational Development Theory and Corporate Responsibility' (unpublished paper; Boston, MA: Carroll School of Management, Boston College).

Leipziger, D. (2001) *SA 8000: The Definitive Guide to the New Social Standard* (London: Financial Times).

Leonard, D. (1998) *Wellsprings of Knowledge: Building and Sustaining The Sources of Innovation* (Boston, MA: Harvard Business School Press).

Leonard-Barton, D. (1992) 'Core Capabilities and Core Rigidities: A Paradox in Managing New Product Development', *Strategic Management Journal* 13 (special issue): 111-25.

Levinas, E. (1989) *The Levinas Reader* (Oxford, UK: Blackwell).

Levitt, E. (1983) 'The Globalization of Markets', *Harvard Business Review*, May/June 1983: 92-102.

Levitt, T. (1958) 'The Danger of Social Responsibility', *Harvard Business Review* 36.5: 41-50.

Lewis, M. (2000) 'Exploring Paradox: Toward a More Comprehensive Guide', *Academy of Management Review* 25.4: 760-76.

Littlejohn, S.E. (1987) 'Competition and Cooperation: New Trends in Issue Identification and Management at Monsanto and Gulf', in A.A. Marcus, A.M. Kaufman and D.R. Beam (eds.), *Business Strategy and Public Policy* (New York: Quorum): 43-60.

Litz, R.A. (1996) 'A Resource-Based View of the Socially Responsible Firm: Stakeholder Interdependence, Ethical Awareness, and Issue Responsiveness As Strategic Assets', *Journal of Business Ethics* 15: 1355-1663.

Livesey, S. (1990) McDonald's and the Environment: Case and Teaching Note (Boston, MA: Harvard Business School).

LLRC (Low-Level Radiation Coalition) (2001) Stakeholder Dialogues: Is it Worth Getting Involved? (www.llrc.org, accessed 7 June 2001).

Locke, E.A. (1999) 'Some Reservations about Social Capital', Academy of Management Review 24.1: 8-9.

Lodge, G.C. (1970a) 'Top Priority: Renovating Our Ideology', Harvard Business Review, September/October: 43-55.

—— (1970b) 'Why an Outmoded Ideology Thwarts the New Business Conscience', Fortune, October 1970: 106, 107, 148, 150-52.

Logan, D., D. Roy and L. Regelbrugge (1997) Global Corporate Citizenship: Rationale and Strategies (Washington, DC: The Hitachi Foundation).

Logsdon, J.M. (1991) 'Interests and Interdependence in the Formation of Social Problem-Solving Collaborations', Journal of Applied Behavioral Science 27.1: 23-37.

Logsdon, J.M., and K. Yuthas (1997) 'Corporate Social Performance, Stakeholder Orientation, and Organizational Moral Development', Journal of Business Ethics 16.12–13: 1213-26.

Long, F., and M.B. Arnold (1995) The Power of Environmental Partnerships (Orlando, FL: Harcourt Brace).

Loury, G.C. (1977) 'A Dynamic Theory of Racial Income Differences', in P.A. Wallace and A.M. La Monde (eds.), Women, Minorities and Employment Discrimination (Lexington, MA: Lexington Books): 153-86.

Lukowski, J. (1991) Liberty's Folly: The Polish-Lithuanian Commonwealth of the Eighteenth Century, 1697–1785 (London: Routledge).

MacMillan, I.C. (1982) Strategic Initiative in Competitive Dynamics (working paper; New York: Strategy Research Center, Graduate School of Business, Colombia University).

Maignan, I., and O.C. Ferrell (1999) 'Corporate Citizenship: Cultural Antecedents and Business Benefits', Journal of the Academy of Marketing Science 27.4: 455-69.

Maines, D.R. (ed.) (1991) Social Organization and Social Process: Essays in Honor of Anselm Strauss (New York: Aldine de Gruyter).

Manne, H., and H.C. Wallich (1972) The Modern Corporation and Social Responsibility (Washington, DC: American Enterprise Institute for Public Policy Research).

Manning, M.R., and G.F. Binzagr (1996) 'Methods, Values, and Assumptions Underlying Large Group Interventions Intended to Change Whole Systems', International Journal of Organizational Analysis 4.3: 268-84.

March, J.G., and H.A. Simon (1958) Organizations (New York: John Wiley).

Marens, R.S., and A.C. Wicks (1999) 'Getting Real: Stakeholder Theory, Managerial Practice and the General Irrelevance of Fiduciary Duties Owed to Shareholders', Business Ethics Quarterly 9.2: 273-93.

Marens, R.S., A.C. Wicks and V.L. Huber (1999) 'Cooperating with the Disempowered: Using ESOPs to Forge a Stakeholder Relationship by Anchoring Trust in Workplace Participation Programs', Business and Society 38.1: 51-82.

Margolis, J.D., and J.P. Walsh (2001a) People and Profits? The Search for a Link between a Company's Social and Financial Performance (Mahwah, NJ: Lawrence Erlbaum Associates).

—— (2001b) 'Misery Loves Companies: Shareholders, Scholarship, and Society', University of Michigan Business School Working Paper, presented at the Academy of Management Annual Meeting, Washington, DC (Washington, DC: Academy of Management).

Markandya, A. (1999) Analysis of the Distribution of Rents from Mining Operations (Mining and Energy Research Network Working Paper, No. 167; Warwick, UK: University of Warwick).

Marsden, C., and J. Andriof (1997) Understanding Corporate Citizenship and How to Influence It (working paper; Coventry, UK: BP Corporate Citizenship Unit, Warwick Business School).

—— (1998) 'Towards an Understanding of Corporate Citizenship and How to Influence It', *Citizenship Studies* 2.2: 329-52.

Maslow, A.H. (1954) *Motivation and Personality* (New York: Columbia University Press).

Maturana, H.R., and F.J. Varela (1998) *The Tree of Knowledge: The Biological Roots of Human Understanding* (Boston, MA: Shambala Press, rev. edn).

Mayer, C. (1996) *Corporate Governance, Competition and Performance* (WP-164; Paris: OECD Economics Department).

Mayer, R.C., J.H. Davis and F.D. Schoorman (1995) 'An Integrative Model of Organisational Trust', *Academy of Management Review* 20: 709-34.

Mazlish, B., and R. Buultjers (1993) *An Introduction to Global History* (Boulder, CO: Westview Press).

McCoy, T.R. (1992) 'The Whys and Ways of Mediation', *Business Law Today* 2: 22-26.

McGee, J. (1998) 'Commentary on "Corporate Strategies and Environmental Regulations: An Organizing Framework" by A.M. Rugman and A. Verbeke', *Strategic Management Journal* 19: 377-87.

McGee, J., and H. Thomas (1985) *Strategic Management Research: A European Perspective* (New York: John Wiley).

McGowan, R.A., and J.F. Mahon (1995) 'The Ends Justify the Means: The Ethical Reasoning of Environmental Public Interest Groups and their Actions', *International Journal of Value-Based Management* 4: 135-47.

McGuire, J.B. (1963) *Business and Society* (New York: McGraw–Hill).

McGuire, J.B., A. Sundgren and T. Schneeweis (1988) 'Corporate Social Responsibility and Firm Financial Performance', *Academy of Management Journal* 31.3: 354-72.

McIntosh, M., D. Leipziger, K. Jones and G. Coleman (1998) *Corporate Citizenship: Successful Strategies for Responsible Companies* (London: Financial Times/Pitman).

McLaughlin, C., and G. Davidson (1994) *Spiritual Politics: Changing the World From the Inside Out* (New York: Ballantine Books).

McNamee, S., and K.J. Gergen (1999) *Relational Responsibilities: Resources for Sustainable Dialogue* (Thousand Oaks, CA: Sage).

McNeil, D.G. (2000) 'Protests on New Genes and Seeds Grow More Passionate in Europe', *New York Times*, 14 March 2000: AI.

McTaggart, J.M., P.W. Kontes and M.C. Mankins (1994) *The Value Imperative: Managing for Superior Shareholder Returns* (New York: The Free Press).

McWhinney, W. (1992) *Paths of Change* (Newbury Park, CA: Sage).

Meintjes, G. (2000) 'An International Human Rights Perspective on Corporate Codes', in O.G. Williams (ed.), *Global Codes of Conduct: An Idea whose Time has Come* (Notre Dame, IN: University of Notre Dame Press): 83-99.

Meridian Institute (1999) *Preventing Industrial Pollution at its Source* (final report; Denver, CO: Michigan Source Reduction Initiative).

Messelbeck, J., and M. Whaley (1999) 'Greening the Health Care Supply Chain: Triggers for Change, Models for Success', *Corporate Environmental Strategy* 6: 38-47.

Meyers, J.W., and B. Rowan (1977) 'Institutional Organizations: Formal Structures as Myth and Ceremony', *American Journal of Sociology* 80: 340-63.

Mill, J.S. (1859) *On Liberty* (ed. E. Rapaport; Indianapolis, IN: Hackett Publishing, 1978 edn).

—— (1861) *Considerations on Representative Government* (rendered into HTML on 12 April 1998 by Steve Thomas for The University of Adelaide Library Electronic Texts Collection, www.library.adelaide.edu.au/etext/m/m645r/).

Miller, W.H. (1998) 'Citizenship: A Competitive Asset', *Industry Week* 247.15: 104-108.

Mintzberg, H., and J. Lampel (1999) 'Reflecting on the Strategy Process', *Sloan Management Review*, Spring 1999: 21-30.

Mintzberg, H., B. Ahlstrand and J. Lampel (1998) *Strategy Safari: A Guided Tour through the Wilds of Strategic Management* (London: Prentice Hall).

Mirvis, P.H. (2000) 'Transformation at Shell: Commerce and Citizenship', *Business and Society Review* 105.1 (January 2000): 63-84.

Mitchell, R.K., B.R. Agle and D.J. Wood (1997) 'Toward a Theory of Stakeholder Identification and Salience: Defining the Principle of Who and What Really Counts', *Academy of Management Review* 22.4 (October 1997): 853-86.

Mitroff, I.I. (1983) *Stakeholders of the Organizational Mind: Toward a New View of Organizational Policy Making* (San Francisco: Jossey-Bass).

Moats, D. (2001) 'Backing Jeffords', *Rutland Daily Herald*, 27 April 2001 (http://rutlandherald.nybor.com/Archive/Articles/Article/25156).

Moldoveanu, M. (1999) *Royal Dutch/Shell in Nigeria (A) and (B) Cases* (Boston, MA: Harvard Business School).

Mollner, T. (1991) *The Prophets of the Pyrenees: The Search for the Relationship Age* (Northampton, MA: Trustee Institute).

Monsanto (1984) 'Industry–Environmental Cooperation can Get Results', *Monsanto World News*, August 1984.

Moran, P., and S. Ghoshal (1996) 'Value Creation by Firms', in J.B. Keys and L.N. Dosier (eds.), *Academy of Management Best Paper Proceedings* (Washington, DC: Academy of Management): 41-45.

Moss Kanter, R. (1994) 'Collaborative Advantage: Successful Partnerships Manage the Relationship, not Just the Deal', *Harvard Business Review* 31 (July/August 1994): 96-108.

—— (1999) 'From Spare Change to Real Change: The Social Sector as Beta Site for Business Innovation', *Harvard Business Review* 3: 122-32.

Motorola, Inc. (1999) *The Journey to a Sustainable World: Progress for 1999* (Schaumburg, IL: Motorola).

Moyer, P. (2001) 'Conservation International and Ford Motor Company Join Forces to Create the Center for Environmental Leadership in Business' (press release; Washington, DC: Conservation International, 11 June 2001).

Nahapiet, J., and S. Ghoshal (1998) 'Social Capital, Intellectual Capital, and the Organisational Advantage', *Academy of Management Review* 23.2: 242-66.

Näsi, J. (1995a) 'What is Stakeholder Thinking? A Snapshot of A Social Theory of the Firm', in J. Näsi (ed.), *Understanding Stakeholder Thinking* (Helsinki: LSR Publications): 19-32.

—— (ed.) (1995b) *Understanding Stakeholder Thinking* (Helsinki: LSR Publications).

Nathan, M.L., and I.I. Mitroff (1991) 'The Use of Negotiated Order Theory as a Tool for the Analysis and Development of an Interorganisational Field', *Journal of Applied Behavioral Science* 27.2: 163-80.

National Center for Employee Ownership (1998) *Employee Ownership Report* 18.2: 1-3.

Naughton, M., H. Alford and B. Brady (1996) 'The Common Good and the Purpose of the Firm: A Critique of the Shareholder and Stakeholder Models from the Catholic Social Tradition', in J. Donahue and M.T. Moser (eds.), *Religion, Ethics and the Common Good* (Mystic, CT: Twenty-Third Publications): 206-35.

Naylor, T.H., W.H. Willimon and M.R. Naylor (1994) *The Search for Meaning* (Nashville, TN: Abingdon Press).

Naylor, T.H., W.H. Willimon and R. Osterberg (1996) 'The Search for Community in the Workplace', *Business and Society Review* 97: 42-47.

NCEO (National Center for Employee Ownership) (1998) *Employee Ownership Report* (www.nceo.org).

Neal, S.M.A. (1997) 'Sociology and Community Change', in *Themes of a Lifetime* (Boston, MA: Emmanuel College).

Nolan, P. (1996) 'Angels in the Boardroom', *Potentials in Marketing*, June 1996: 10-18.

Nunan, R. (1988) 'The Libertarian Conception of Corporate Property: A Critique of Milton Friedman's Views on the Social Responsibility of Business', *Journal of Business Ethics* 7.12 (December 1988): 891-906.

Nussbaum, B. (1990) *Good Intentions: How Big Business and the Medical Establishment are Corrupting the Fight against AIDS* (New York: Atlantic Monthly Press).

O'Faircheallaigh, C. (1998) 'Indigenous People and Taxation Regime', *Resources Policy* 24.4: 187-98.

Ocasio, W. (1997) 'Towards an Attention-Based View of the Firm', *Strategic Management Journal* 18: 187-206.

Ogden, S., and R. Watson (1999) 'Corporate Performance and Stakeholder Management: Balancing Shareholder and Customer Interests in the UK Privatized Water Industry', *Academy of Management Journal* 42.5 (October 1999): 526-38.

Oliver, C. (1991) 'Strategic Responses to Institutional Processes', *Academy of Management Review* 16.1: 145-79.

Olson, D.G. (1995) 'Employee Participation in Carris Reels Restructuring as an ESOP Company', memorandum to Carris Reels ESOP Advisory Committee from Deborah Groban Olson, 28 April 1995.

Olson, K., and T.G. Harris (1997) 'Defining Common Work: A Conversation with Rob Lehman', *Institute of Noetic Sciences: Connections* 2: 8-10.

Olson, M. (1965) *The Logic of Collective Action: Public Goods and the Theory of Groups* (Cambridge, MA: Harvard).

—— (2000) *Power and Prosperity: Outgrowing Communist and Capitalist Dictatorships* (New York: Basic Books).

Orts, E.C. (1992) 'Beyond Shareholders: Interpreting Corporate Constituency Statutes', *George Washington Law Review* 61: 14-135.

Owen, B. (2001) *Resource Tools for Open Space* (www.albany.edu/cpr/gf/resources/OpenSpaceTechnology.html, accessed 10 June 2001).

Owen, H. (1991) *Riding the Tiger: Doing Business in a Transforming World* (Potomac, MD: Abbott).

—— (1997a) *Open Space Technology: User's Guide* (San Francisco: Berrett-Koehler).

—— (1997b) *Expanding Our Now: The Story of Open Space Technology* (San Francisco: Berrett-Koehler).

Paine, L. (1999) *Royal Dutch/Shell in Transition (A) and (B) Cases* (Boston, MA: Harvard Business School).

Papandreou, A.G. (1952) 'Some Basic Problems in the Theory of the Firm', in B.F. Haley (ed.), *A Survey of Contemporary Economics* (Homewood, IL: Irwin): 183-219.

Pasquero, J. (1996) 'Stakeholder Theory as a Constructivist Paradigm', in J. Logsdon and K. Rehbein (eds.), *Proceedings of the International Association for Business and Society Conference* (7th Annual Conference, Santa Fe, AZ; www.iabs.net): 584-89.

Paul, K., and S.D. Lydenberg (1992) 'Applications of Corporate Social Monitoring Systems', *Journal of Business Ethics* 11: 1-10.

Pava, M.L., and J. Krausz (1995) *Corporate Responsibility and Financial Performance: The Paradox of Social Cost* (London: Quorum Books).

—— (1996) 'The Association between Corporate Social-Responsibility and Financial Performance: The Paradox of Social Cost', *Journal of Business Ethics* 15: 321-57.

Pax Christi International (1998) *Multinational Enterprises and Human Rights: A Documentation of the Dialogue between Amnesty International/Pax Christi and Shell* (Utrecht: Pax Christi Netherlands).

Perrin, T. (1996) 'Inside "The Balanced Scorecard"', *Compuscan Report*, January 1996: 1-5.

Perrow, C. (1986) *Complex Organizations: A Critical Essay* (New York: Random House, 3rd edn).

Peters Report (1997) *Corporate Governance in the Netherlands: Forty Recommendations* (Amsterdam: Committee on Corporate Governance).

Peters, G. (1999) *Waltzing with the Raptors: A Practical Roadmap to Protecting your Company's Reputation* (New York: John Wiley).

Peters, T. (1987) *Thriving on Chaos: Handbook for a Management Revolution* (New York: Excel, a California Limited Partnership).

Pettigrew, A.M. (1985) 'Contextualist Research: A Natural Way to Link Theory and Practice', in E.E. Lawler III, Jr, A.M. Mohrman, S.A. Mohrman, Jr, G.E. Ledford and T.G. Cummings (eds.), *Doing Research that is Useful for Theory and Practice* (San Francisco: Jossey-Bass): 222-73.

Pfeffer, J. (1981) *Power in Organizations* (Boston, MA: Pitman).

—— (1997a) *Competitive Advantage through People: Unleashing the Power of the Work Force* (Boston, MA: Harvard Business School Press).

—— (1997b) *New Directions for Organization Theory* (Oxford, UK: Oxford University Press).

Pfeffer, J., and G.R. Salancik (1978) *The Eternal Control of Organizations: A Resource Dependence Perspective* (New York: Harper & Row).

Phillips, R.A., and J. Reichart (2000) 'The Environment as a Stakeholder: A Fairness-Based Approach', *Journal of Business Ethics* 23: 185-97.

Pierson, F.C. (1959) *The Education of the American Businessman: A Study of University College Programs in Business Administration* (New York: McGraw–Hill).

Pollack, A. (2000) 'Novartis Ended use of Gene-Altered Foods', *New York Times*, 4 August 2000: C4.

Porter, M.E. (1980) *Competitive Strategy: Techniques for Analyzing Industries and Competitors* (New York: The Free Press).

—— (1990) 'The Competitive Advantage of Nations', *Harvard Business Review*, March/April 1990: 73-93.

—— (1998) 'The Microeconomic Foundations of Economic Development', in *Reprint Series, Division of Research* (Boston, MA: Harvard Business School Press).

Portes, A., and J. Sensenbrenner (1993) 'Embeddedness and Immigration: Notes on the Social Determinants of Economic Action', *American Journal of Sociology* 98: 1320-50.

Posner, B.A., and W.H. Schmidt (1984) 'Values and the American Manager: An Update', *California Management Review* 26.3: 206.

Post, C.G. (ed.) (1953) 'Introduction', in J.C. Calhoun, *A Disquisition on Government and Selections from the Discourse* (Indianapolis, IN: Bobbs-Merrill).

Post, J.E. (1999) 'Meeting the Challenge of Global Corporate Citizenship', unpublished paper.

Post, J.E., and B.W. Altman (1992) 'Models of Corporate Greening: How Corporate Social Policy and Organizational Learning Inform Leading-Edge Environmental Management', *Research in Corporate Social Performance and Policy* 3: 3-29.

Post, J.E., A.T. Lawrence and J. Weber (2002) *Business and Society: Corporate Strategy, Public Policy, Ethics* (New York: McGraw–Hill, 10th edn).

Post, J.E., E.A. Murray, Jr, R.B. Dickie and J.F. Mahon (1982) 'The Public Affairs Function in American Corporations: Development and Relations with Corporate Planning', *Long Range Planning* 15.2 (April 1982): 12-21.

Post, J.E., L.E. Preston and S. Sachs (2002) *Redefining the Corporation* (New York: Oxford University Press).

Powell, W.W. (1990) 'Neither Market nor Hierarchy: Network Forms of Organization', in B. Staw (ed.), *Research in Organizational Behavior* (Vol. 23; Greenwich, CT: JAI Press).

Powell, W.W., and P.J. DiMaggio (1991) *The New Institutionalism of Organizational Analysis* (Chicago: University of Chicago Press).

Prahalad, C.K., and G. Hamel (1990) 'The Core Competence of the Corporation', *Harvard Business Review* 68 (May/June 1990), 79-91.

Preston, L.E. (1986) *Social Issues and Public Policy in Business and Management: Retrospect and Prospect* (College Park, MD: University of Maryland, Center for Business and Public Policy, College of Business and Management).

—— (1998) 'Agents, Stewards, and Stakeholders', *Academy of Management Review* 23.1 (January 1999): 9.

Preston, L.E., and J.E. Post (1975) *Private Management and Public Policy: The Principle of Public Responsibility* (Englewood Cliffs, NJ: Prentice Hall).

Preston, L.E., and H.J. Sapienza (1990) 'Stakeholder Management and Corporate Performance', *Journal of Behavioral Economics* 19.4: 361-75.

Preston, L.E., and D. Windsor (1997) *The Rules of the Game in the Global Economy: Policy Regimes for International Business* (Dordrecht, Netherlands: Kluwer Academic Publishers, 2nd edn).

Preston, L.E., H.J. Sapienza, and R. Miller (1991) Stakeholders, Shareholders, Managers: Who Gains what from Corporate Performance?', in A. Etzioni and P.R. Lawrence (eds.), *Socio-economics: Toward a New Synthesis* (Armonk, NY: M.E. Sharpe): 149-65.

Preston, L.E., T. Donaldson and L.J. Brooks (1999) *Principles of Stakeholder Management* (Toronto: Clarkson Centre for Business Ethics, Joseph L. Rotman School of Management, University of Toronto).

Prince, J., and R. Denison (1994) 'Developing an Environmental Action Plan for Business', in R.V. Kolluru (ed.), *Environmental Strategies Handbook* (New York: McGraw–Hill): 239-58.

Pruitt, D.G. (1981) *Negotiation Behavior* (New York: Academic Press).

Pruitt, S.W., K.C. Wei and R.E. White (1988) 'The Impact of Union-Sponsored Boycotts on the Stock Prices of Target Firms', *Journal of Labor Research* 9: 285-89.

Pruzan, P. (1998) 'From Control to Value-Based Management and Accountability', *Journal of Business Ethics* 17.13: 1379-94.

Putnam, R. (1993) 'The Prosperous Community: Social Capital and Public Life', *The American Prospect* 13: 35-42.

—— (1995) 'Bowling Alone: America's Declining Social Capital', *Journal of Democracy* 6: 65-78.

Putnam, T. (1993) 'Boycotts are busting out all over', *Business and Society Review* 85 (Spring 1993): 47-51.

PwC (PricewaterhouseCoopers) (1999a) *Earning Your Reputation: What Makes Others Respect your Company* (London: PwC).

—— (1999b) *Reputation Assurance: Safeguarding a Valuable Asset* (London: PwC).

Quinn, D.P., and T.M. Jones (1995) 'An Agent Morality View of Business Policy', *Academy of Management Review* 20.2: 1053-89.

Quinn, J.J. (1996) 'The Role of "Good Conversation" in Strategic Control', *Journal of Management Studies* 33.3: 381-94.

Rachels, J. (1999) *The Elements of Moral Philosophy* (New York: McGraw–Hill, 3rd edn).

Rahman, S. (2000) *The Global Stakeholder's Message, the Firm's Response, and an Interpretation of the Ensuing International Dilemma: Moving Children from Tin Sheds to Brick Houses* (PhD dissertation; Fort Lauderdale, FL: Nova Southeastern University).

RAND Environment (2001) *Stakeholder Dialogues and Consensus Building* (www.rand.org/scitech/environment/services/stakeholder.html, accessed 5 June 2001).

Rapaport, E. (1978) 'Editor's Introduction', in J.S. Mill, *On Liberty* (Indianapolis, IN: Hackett Publishing): vii-xxi.

Rawls, J. (1971) *A Theory of Justice* (Cambridge, MA: Belknap Press of Harvard).

Reeler, D. (2001) *Open Space Technology* (www.albany.edu/cpr/gf/resources/OpenSpaceTechnology.html, accessed 10 June 2001).

Rhenman, E. (1968) *Industrial Democracy and Industrial Management* (London: Tavistock [1964, in Swedish]).

Rhenman, R., and B. Stymne (1965) *Corporate Management in a Changing World* (Swedish language; Stockholm: Aldus/Bonniers).

Richardson, V. (1999) 'Stakeholders: What do "they" Know? Opening a Dialogue', *Public Manager* 28.2: 31-33.

Ring, P.S. (1994) 'Fragile and Resilient Trust and their Roles in Cooperative Interorganizational Relationships', in J. Pasquero and D. Collins (eds.), *Proceedings of the Fourth Annual Meeting of the International Association for Business and Society, San Diego* (San Diego, CA: International Association for Business and Society [IABS]): 107-13.

Robertson, J. (1999) *The New Economics of Sustainable Development: A Briefing for Policy Makers* (Luxembourg: Kogan Page).

Robin, D.P., and R.E. Reidenbach (1988) 'Integrating Social Responsibility and Ethics into the Strategic Planning Process', *Business and Professional Ethics Journal* 7.3–4: 29-46.

Rockefeller III, J.D. (1973) *The Second American Revolution: Some Personal Observations* (New York: Harper & Row).

Roe, D. (1984) *Dynamos and Virgins* (New York: Random House).

Rogers, C. (2000) 'Making it Legit: New Ways of Generating Legitimacy in a Globalizing World', in J. Bendell (ed.), *Terms for Endearment: Business, NGOs and Sustainable Development* (Sheffield, UK: Greenleaf Publishing): 40-48.

Roman, R.M., S. Hayibor and B.R. Agle (1999) 'The Relationship between Social and Financial Performance', *Business and Society* 38.1 (March 1999): 109-25.

Rondinelli, D.A., and M.A. Berry (1997) 'Industry's Role in Air Quality Improvement: Environmental Management Opportunities for the 21st Century', *Environmental Quality Management* 7: 31-44.

—— (2000) 'Environmental Citizenship in Multinational Corporations: Social Responsibility and Sustainable Development', *European Management Journal* 18: 70-84.

Rondinelli, D.A., and T. London (2001a) *Partnering For Sustainability: Managing Nonprofit Organization-Corporate Environmental Alliances* (Washington, DC: Aspen Institute).

—— (2001b) 'Making Corporate and Stakeholder Environmental Partnerships Work', EM: *Environmental Manager*, November 2001: 16-22.

Rose, D.C. (1999) *Teams, Firms, and the Evolution of Profit Seeking Behavior* (unpublished manuscript; St Louis, MO: Dept of Economics, University of Missouri–St Louis, available from the Social Science Research Network eLibrary at: http://papers.ssrn.com/paper=224438).

Rouda, R.H. (1995) *Background and Theory for Large Scale Organizational Change Methods* (http://alumni.caltech.edu/~rouda/background.html, accessed 2 June 2001).

Rousseau, D.M., S.B. Sitkin, R.S. Burt and C. Camerer (1998) 'Not So Different After All: A Cross-Discipline View of Trust', *Academy of Management Review* 23: 393-404.

Rousseau, J.-J. (1762) 'The Social Contract', in E. Barker (ed.), *Social Contract: Essays by Locke, Hume, and Rousseau* (Oxford, UK: Oxford University Press, 1960 edn): 167-307.

Rowley, T.J. (1997) 'Moving beyond Dyadic Ties: A Network Theory of Stakeholder Influences', *Academy of Management Review* 22: 887-910.

Rowley, T.J., and M. Moldoveanu (2000) 'When Will Stakeholders Act? An Interest—and Identity—Based Model of Stakeholder Mobilization', paper presented at the Annual Meeting of the Academy of Management, Toronto.

Royal Dutch/Shell (1998) *Profits and Principles: Does there have to be a choice?* (London: Royal Dutch/Shell).

Royce, J. (1885) *The Religious Aspects of Philosophy: A Critique of the Bases of Conduct and of Faith* (Gloucester, MA: Peter Smith): 131-70.

Rudolph, R., and S. Ridley (1986) *Power Struggle: The Hundred-Year War Over Electricity* (New York: Harper & Row).

Rugman, A.M., D.J. Lecrew and L.D. Booth (1985) *International Business, Firm and Environment* (New York: McGraw–Hill).

Rumelt, R.P. (1984) 'Towards a Strategic Theory of the Firm', in R.B. Lamb (ed.), *Competitive Strategic Management* (New York: Prentice Hall): 556-70.

—— (1991) 'How much does industry matter?', *Strategic Management Journal* 12.2: 167-85.

Rumelt, R.P., D. Schendel and D.J. Teece (1991) 'Strategic Management and Economics', *Strategic Management Journal* 13: 5-29.

Sachs, S., E. Rühli, R. Schmitt and D. Peter (1999) 'Redefining the Corporation: A Case Study of Shell, a Multinational Corporation', in D.J. Wood and D. Windsor (eds.), *Proceeding of the 10th Annual Conference of the International Association of Business and Society* (Paris: International Association for Business and Society [IABS]): 149-54.

Salomon, J., F.R. Sagasti and C. Sachs-Jeantet (1994) *The Uncertain Quest: Science, Technology, and Development* (New York: United Nations University Press).

Savage, G.T., T.H. Nix, C.J. Whitehead and J.D. Blair (1991) 'Strategies for Assessing and Managing Organizational Stakeholders', *Academy of Management Executive* 5: 61-75.

Scholes, E., and D. Clutterbuck (1998) 'Communication with Stakeholders: An Integrated Approach', *Long Range Planning* 31.2: 227-38.

Schueth, S., A. Gravitz and T. Larsen (1999) *1999 Report on Social Responsible Investing Trends in the United States* (www.socialinvest.org/areas/research/trends/1999-Trends.htm; Social Investment Forum Industry Research Program).

Schumpeter, J.A. (1934) *The Theory of Economic Development: An Inquiry into Profits, Capital, Credit, Interest, and the Business Cycle* (trans. R. Opie; Cambridge, MA: Harvard University Press).

Schuppisser, S.W. (1998) 'A Framework to Analyze the Evolution of Relationships between Firms and Non-market Stakeholder Organizations (NMSOs)', in J. Calton and K. Rehbein (eds.), *Proceedings of the 9th Annual Meeting of the International Association for Business and Society*: 531-36.

Schwartz, P., and B. Gibb (1999) *When Good Companies Do Bad Things: Responsibility and Risk in an Age of Globalization* (New York: John Wiley).

Scott, R.W. (1987) 'The Adolescence of Institutional Theory', *Administrative Science Quarterly* 32: 493-511.

Scott, R.W., and J.W. Meyer (1994) *Institutional Environments and Organisations: Structural Complexity and Individualism* (Thousand Oaks, CA: Sage).

Scott, W.R. (1987) *Organizations: Rational, Natural, and Open Systems* (Englewood Cliffs, NJ: Prentice Hall).

Seabright, M.A., D.A. Levinthal and M. Fichman (1993) 'Role of Individual Attachments in the Dissolution of Interorganizational Relationships', *Academy of Management Journal* 35: 122-60.

Selekman, B.M. (1958) 'Is Management Creating a Class Society?', *Harvard Business Review* 36.1 (January/February 1958): 37-46.

Selekman, B.M., and S. Selekman (1956) *Power and Morality in a Business Society* (New York: McGraw–Hill).

Selznick, P. (1957) *Leadership in Administration: A Sociological Interpretation* (New York: Harper & Row): 21-22.

Senge, P.M. (1990) *The Fifth Discipline: The Art and Practice of the Learning Organization* (New York: Currency Doubleday).

Sethi, S.P. (1970) *Business Corporations and the Black Man* (Scranton, PA: Chandler).

—— (1977) *Up Against the Corporate Wall: Modern Corporations and Social Issues of the Seventies* (New York: Prentice Hall).

—— (1979) 'A Conceptual Framework for Environmental Analysis of Social Issues and Evaluation of Business Response Patterns', *Academy of Management Review* 4: 63-74.

Shell (Royal Dutch Petroleum) (2000) *How Do We Stand? The Shell Report 2000* (www.shell.com).

Shepard, J.M. (1997) 'The Proactive Corporation: Its Nature and Causes', *Journal of Business Ethics* 16: 1001-10.

Sherif, M. (1958) 'Superordinate Goals in the Reduction of Intergroup Conflict', *American Journal of Sociology* 63: 349-56.

Shipp, S. (1987) 'Modified Vendettas as a Method of Punishing Corporations', *Journal of Business Ethics* 6: 603-12.

Skolimowski, H. (1994) *The Participatory Mind: A New Theory of Knowledge and of the Universe* (New York: Penguin Books).

Smith, A. (1759) *The Theory of Moral Sentiments* (ed. K. Haakonssen; New York: Cambridge University Press, 2002 edn).

—— (1776) *An Inquiry into the Nature and Causes of the Wealth of Nations* (ed. E. Cannan; Chicago: University of Chicago Press, 1977 edn).

Smith, K.K., and D.N. Berg (1987) *Paradoxes of Group Life: Understanding Conflict, Paralysis and Movement in Group Dynamics* (San Francisco: Jossey-Bass).

Smith, N.C. (1990) *Morality and the Market: Consumer Research for Corporate Accountability* (London: Routledge).

Smith, N.C., and E. Cooper-Martin (1997) 'Ethics and Target Marketing: The Role of Product Harm and Consumer Vulnerability', *Journal of Marketing* 61: 1-20.

Smith, W. (1992) 'The ESOP Revolution: Will it Increase Employee Involvement?', *SAM Advanced Management Journal* 57.3: 14-19.

Solomon, C. (1993) 'What Really Pollutes?', *Wall Street Journal*, 29 March 1993.

Starik, M. (1994) 'Reflections on Stakeholder Theory', *Business and Society* 33: 82-141.

—— (1995) 'Should Trees have Managerial Standing? Toward Stakeholder Status for Non-human Nature', *Journal of Business Ethics* 14.3 (March 1995): 204-17.

State of the World Forum (2001) *Multi-Stakeholder Dialogues* (www.worldforum.org/commission/dialogues.html, accessed 6 June 2001).

Staw, G.M., L.E. Sandelands and J.E. Dutton (1981) 'Threat-Rigidity Effects in Organizational Behavior: A Multilevel Analysis', *Administrative Science Quarterly* 26: 501-25.

Steiner, A.G. (1975) *Business and Society* (New York: Random House).

Sternberg, E. (1994) *Just Business: Business Ethics in Action* (Boston, MA: Little, Brown).

—— (1996) Stakeholder Theory Exposed', *Corporate Governance Quarterly* (Hong Kong) 2.1: 4-18.

—— (1999) *The Stakeholder Concept: A Mistaken Doctrine* (Issue Paper No. 4; London: Foundation for Business Responsibilities; also available from the Social Science Research Network at: http://papers.ssrn.com/paper=263144; Foundation for Business Responsibilities, UK).

—— (2000) *Just Business: Business Ethics in Action* (New York: Oxford University Press).

Stewart, T.A. (1997) *Intellectual Capital: The New Wealth of Organizations* (New York: Doubleday).

Stigson, B. (2000) 'Sustainable Development and Business: Organisation for Economic Cooperation and Development', *The OECD Observer* 221–222: 36-37.

Stone, C.D. (1975) *Where the Law Ends: The Social Control of Corporate Behaviour* (New York: Harper Colophon Books).

Strand, R. (1983) 'A Systems Paradigm of Organisational Adjustment to the Social Environment', *Academy of Management Review* 8: 90-96.

Strauss, A.L. (1978) *Negotiations: Varieties, Contexts, Processes and Social Order* (San Francisco: Jossey-Bass).

Struvidant, F.D., and H. Vernon-Wortzel (1990) *Business and Society: A Managerial Approach* (Homewood, IL: Irwin).

Suchman, M.C. (1995) 'Managing Legitimacy: Strategic and Institutional Approaches', *Academy of Management Review* 20.3: 571-610.

Svendsen, A. (1998) *The Stakeholder Strategy: Profiting from Collaborative Business Relationships* (San Francisco: Berrett-Koehler).

Swanson, D.L. (1995) 'Addressing a Theoretical Problem by Reorienting the Corporate Social Performance Model', *Academy of Management Review* 20.1: 43-64.

—— (1999) 'Toward an Integrative Theory of Business and Society: A Research Strategy for Corporate Social Performance', *Academy of Management Review* 24.3: 506-21.

Tawney, R.H. (1948) *The Acquisitive Society* (New York: Harvest Books, 2nd edn 1950).

Teece, D.J., G. Pisano and A. Shuen (1997) 'Dynamic Capabilities and Strategic Management', *Strategic Management Journal* 18.7: 509-33.

Thomas, K.W. (1992) 'Conflict and Negotiation Processes in Organizations', in M.D. Dunnette (ed.), *Handbook of Industrial and Organizational Psychology* (Chicago: Rand McNally): 651-717.

Thompson, J.D. (1967) *Organizations in Action* (New York: The Free Press).

Thompson, J.K., S.L. Wartick and H.L. Smith (1991) 'Integrating Corporate Social Performance and Stakeholder Management: Implications for a Research Agenda in Small Business', *Research in Corporate Social Performance and Policy* 12: 207-30.

Thorelli, H.B. (1965) 'The Political Economy of the Firm: Basis for a New Theory of Competition?', *Schweizerische Zeitschrift für Volkswirtschaft und der Statistik* 101: 248-62.

Tobias, A. (2001) 'What The Economy Means to You', *Houston Chronicle Parade Magazine* 100. 303 (12 August 2001): 4-5.

Trevino, L.K., and G.R. Weaver (1999) 'The Stakeholder Research Tradition: Converging Theorists—Not Convergent Theory', *Academy of Management Review* 24.2 (April 1999): 222-28.

Tuzzolino, F., and B.R. Armandi (1981) 'A Need-Hierarchy Framework for Assessing Corporate Social Responsibility', *Academy of Management Review* 6: 21-28.

Ullman, A.A. (1985) 'Data in Search of a Theory: A Critical Examination of the Relationships among Social Performance, Social Disclosure, and Economic Performance of US Firms', *Academy of Management Review* 10.3: 540-57.

Uyterhoeven, H.R., R.W. Ackerman and J.W. Rosenblum (1973) *Strategy and Organization: Text and Cases in General Management* (Homewood, IL: Irwin).

Vaara, E. (1995) 'Linking Social Construction of Success and Stakeholder Thinking', in J. Näsi (ed.), *Understanding Stakeholder Thinking* (Helsinki: LSR Publications): 215-35.

Vogel, D. (1978) *Lobbying the Corporation: Citizen Challenges to Business Authority* (New York: Basic Books).

—— (1983) 'Trends in Shareholder Activism: 1970–1982', *California Management Review* 3: 68-87.

Waddell, S. (1998) 'Market–Civil Society Partnership Formation: A Status Report on Activity, Strategies and Tools', *IDR Reports* 13.5.

—— (2000) *Business–Government–Civil Society Collaborations: A Brief Review of Key Conceptual Foundations* (working paper; Cambridge, MA: Interaction Institute for Social Change).

Waddock, S.A. (1989) 'Understanding Social Partnerships: An Evolutionary Model of Partnership Organizations', *Administration and Society* 12.1 (May 1989): 78-100.

—— (2001) 'Corporate Citizenship Enacted as Operating Practice', *International Journal of Value-Based Management* 14.3: 237-46.

—— (2002) *Leading Corporate Citizens: Vision, Values, Value Added* (Boston, MA: McGraw–Hill).

Waddock, S.A., and M.-E. Boyle (1995) 'Dynamics of Change in Corporate Community Relations', *California Management Review* 37.4 (Summer 1995): 125-40.

Waddock, S.A., and S.B. Graves (1997a) 'The Corporate Social Performance–Financial Performance Link', *Strategic Management Journal* 18.4: 303-19.

—— (1997b) 'Quality of Management and Quality of Stakeholder Relations: Are they Synonymous?', *Business and Society* 36.3 (September 1997): 250-79.

Waddock, S.A., and N. Smith (2000) 'Relationships: The Real Challenge of Global Corporate Citizenship', *Business and Society Review* 105.1: 47-62.

Waddock, S.A., C. Bodwell and S.B. Graves (2001) 'Responsibility: The New Business Imperative' (working paper).

WalkerInformation (1999) 'Your Reputation: Asset or Liability?', in *WalkerInformation Corporate Reputation Report* (WalkerInformation Global Network, May 2000; www.walkerinfo.com).

Walton, R.E., and R.B. McKersie (1965) *A Behavioral Theory of Labor Negotiations: An Analysis of a Social Interaction System* (New York: McGraw–Hill).

Warhurst, A. (1998a) *Corporate Social Responsibility and Human Rights: A Pro-active Approach* (report for Royal Institute of International Affairs, Chatham House, London).

—— (1998b) 'Evaluating and Reporting Corporate Social Responsibility', paper presented at World Business Council for Sustainable Development Conference, Geneva (Geneva: World Business Council for Sustainable Development).

—— (2001) 'Corporate Citizenship and Corporate Social Investment: Drivers of Tri-Sector Partnerships', *Journal of Corporate Citizenship* 1 (Spring 2001): 57-73.

Wartick, S.L. (1988) 'How Issues Management Contributes to Corporate Performance', *Business Forum* 13.2: 16-22.

Wartick, S.L., and P.L. Cochran (1985) 'The Evolution of the Corporate Social Performance Model', *Academy of Management Review* 10.4: 765-66.

Wartick, S.L., and J.F. Mahon (1994) 'Toward a Substantive Definition of the Corporate Issue Construct: A Review and Synthesis of the Literature', *Business and Society* 33.3 (December 1994): 293-311.

Wartick, S.L., and D.J. Wood (1998) *International Business and Society* (Malden, MA: Blackwell Publishers).

WBCSD (World Business Council for Sustainable Development) (2001) *An Overview of Our Work* (www.wbcsd.ch/aboutus/index.htm, accessed 5 June 2001).

Weaver, G.R., L.K. Trevino and P.L. Cochran (1999) 'Integrated and Decoupled Corporate Social Performance: Management Commitments, External Pressures, and Corporate Ethics Practice', *Academy of Management Journal* 42.5: 539-52.

Weick, K.E. (1996) 'Drop your Tools: Allegory for Organizational Studies', *Administrative Science Quarterly* 41: 301-13.

Weiner, J.L. (1964) 'The Berle–Dodd Dialogue on the Concept of the Corporation', *Columbia Law Review* 64: 1458-67.

Weir, A. (2000) 'Meeting Social and Environmental Objectives through Partnerships: The Experience of Unilever', in J. Bendell (ed.), *Terms for Endearment: Business, NGOs and Sustainable Development* (Sheffield, UK: Greenleaf Publishing): 118-24.

Werhane, P.H. (1999) *Moral Imagination and Management Decision Making* (New York: Oxford University Press).

—— (2000) 'Exporting Mental Models: Global Capitalism in the 21st Century', *Business Ethics Quarterly* 10.1 (January 2000): 353-62.

Wernerfelt, B. (1984) 'A Resource-Based View of the Firm', *Strategic Management Journal* 5: 171-80.

Wheeler, D., H. Fabig and R. Boele (2000) 'Paradoxes and Dilemmas for Aspiring Stakeholder Responsive Firms in the Extractive Sector: Lessons from the Case of Shell and Ogoni', paper presented to the *Conference on Corporate Governance and Corporate Responsibilities in Developing Economies*, York University, Toronto, April 2000; also accepted for publication in *Journal of Business Ethics*.

Wicks, A.C., and R.E. Freeman (1998) 'Organization Studies and the New Pragmatism: Positivism, Anti-positivism, and the Search for Ethics', *Organization Science* 9.2 (March/April 1998): 123-40.

Wicks, A.C., D.R. Gilbert, Jr, and R.E. Freeman (1994) 'A Feminist Reinterpretation of the Stakeholder Concept', *Business Ethics Quarterly* 4.4: 475-97.

Wilber, K. (1995) *Sex, Ecology, Spirituality: The Spirit of Evolution* (Boston, MA: Shambala Publications).

Williamson, O.E. (1975) *Markets and Hierarchies* (New York: The Free Press).

—— (1985) *The Economic Institutions of Capitalism* (New York: The Free Press).

—— (1991) 'Strategizing, Economizing, and Economic Organization', *Strategic Management Journal* 12: 75-94.

Wilson, J.Q. (1989) 'Adam Smith on Business Ethics', *California Management Review* 32.1 (Fall 1989): 59-72.

Windsor, D. (1992) 'Stakeholder Management in Multinational Enterprises', in S.N. Brenner and S.A. Waddock (eds.), *Proceedings of the Third Annual Meeting of the International Association for Business and Society, Leuven, Belgium* (IABS): 121-28.

—— (2002) 'Practising Corporate Citizenship in a Global Information Economy', in J. Park and N. Roome (eds.), *The Ecology of the New Economy: Sustainable Transformation of Global Information, Communications and Electronics Industries* (Sheffield, UK: Greenleaf Publishing): 72-84.

Windsor, D., and K.A. Getz (1999) 'Regional Market Integration and the Development of Global Norms for Enterprise Conduct: The Case of International Bribery', *Business and Society* 38.4 (December 1999): 415-49.

WMC (Western Mining Corporation) (1999) *WMC Limited Community Report 1999* (Melbourne: WMC).

Wood, D.J. (1991a) 'Corporate Social Performance Revisited', *Academy of Management Review* 16.4 (October 1991): 691-718.

—— (1991b) 'Social Issues in Management: Theory and Research in Corporate Social Performance', *Journal of Management* 17.2: 383-404.

—— (1991c) 'Toward Improving Corporate Social Performance', *Business Horizons* 34.4 (July/August 1991): 66-73.

Wood, D.J., and B. Gray (1991) 'Toward a Comprehensive Theory of Collaboration', *Journal of Applied Behavioral Science* 27.2: 139-62.

Wood, D.J., and R.E. Jones (1995) 'Stakeholder Mismatching: A Theoretical Problem in Empirical Research on Corporate Social Performance', *International Journal of Organizational Analysis* 3.3 (July 1995): 229-67.

Wood, D.J., and J.M. Logsdon (forthcoming) 'Business Citizenship: From Individuals to Organizations', *Business Ethics Quarterly*.

Wright, P., and S.P. Ferris (1997) 'Agency Conflict and Corporate Strategy: The Effect of Divestment on Corporate Value', *Strategic Management Journal* 18: 77-83.

Yosie, T.F., and T.D. Herbst (1998) *Using Stakeholder Processes in Environmental Decision Making: An Evaluation of Lessons Learned, Key Issues, and Future Challenges* (www.riskworld.com/Nreports/1998/ STAKEHOLD/HTML/nrg8aao1.htm, accessed 20 June 2001).

Yuthas, K., and J.F. Dillard (1999) 'Ethical Development of Advanced Technology: A Postmodern Stakeholder Perspective', *Journal of Business Ethics* 19: 35-49.

Zadek, S., P. Pruzan and E. Richard (1997) *Building Corporate Accountability: Emerging Practices in Social and Ethical Accounting, Auditing and Reporting* (London: Earthscan Publications).

Zan, L. (1990) 'Looking for Theories in Strategy Studies', *Scandinavian Journal of Management* 6: 89-108.

Zenisek, T.J. (1979) 'Corporate Social Responsibility: A Conceptualization Based on Organizational Literature', *Academy of Management Review* 4: 359-68.

ABBREVIATIONS

AA	Alcoholics Anonymous
ABS	Australian Bureau of Statistics
ACT UP	AIDS Coalition to Unleash Power
AI	Amnesty International
AIDS	acquired immuno-deficiency syndrome
ALI	American Law Institute
AZT	azidothymidine
BCA	Business Council of Australia
BCSD	Business Council for Sustainable Development
BSR	Business for Social Responsibility
CA	chartered accountant
CC	corporate citizenship
CCHW	Citizens Clearinghouse on Hazardous Waste
CD-ROM	compact disc read-only memory
CEBC	Center for Ethical Business Cultures (USA)
CEE	Council on Ethics in Economics
CEO	chief executive officer
CFC	chlorofluorocarbon
CFC	Carris Financial Corporation
CFO	chief financial officer
CI	Conservation International
CICA	Canadian Institute of Chartered Accountants
CIRIA	Construction Industry Research and Information Association (UK)
CLF	Conservation Law Foundation
CMA	certified management accountant
CMD	committee of managing directors
CO_2	carbon dioxide
CR	corporate responsibility
CSC	Corporate Steering Committee (Carris Companies)
CSP	corporate social performance
CSR (CSR1)	corporate social responsibility
CSR2	corporate social responsiveness

CSTD	Centre for Science and Technology for Development (UN)
DSM	demand-side management
DTMS	DeskTop Marketing Systems
EDF	Environmental Defense Fund (USA)
EPA	Environmental Protection Agency
EPE	European Partners for the Environment
ESOP	Employee Stock Ownership Plan
EVA	economic value added
FDA	Food and Drug Administration (USA)
GNP	gross national product
GRI	Global Reporting Initiative
IABS	International Association for Business and Society
IAC	influence allocation chart
ICC	International Chamber of Commerce
IFCB	International Forum on Capacity Building
IMS	infit mean square
IRS	Internal Revenue Service (USA)
ISEA	Institute for Social and Ethical Accountability
ISO	International Organisation for Standardisation
KLD	Kinder, Lydenberg and Domini
LGIM	large-group interaction methods
LLRC	Low-Level Radiation Coalition
LTP	Long Term Plan (Carris Companies)
LTPSC	Long Term Plan Steering Committee (Carris Companies)
MBV	market-based view
MNC	multinational corporations
MSC	Marine Stewardship Council
MSLD	multi-stakeholder learning dialogue
NAACP	National Association for the Advancement of Colored People (USA)
NCEO	National Center for Employee Ownership (USA)
NEES	New England Electric Systems
NGO	non-governmental organisation
OA	Ownership Associates
OD/C	organisational development/change
OECD	Organisation for Economic Co-operation and Development
PC	personal computer
PCI	Pax Christi International
PG&E	Pacific Gas & Electric Company
PLS	partial least squares
PTO	Patent and Trademark Office (USA)
PwC	PricewaterhouseCoopers
R&D	research and development
RBV	resource-based view
SAIP	Self-Assessment and Improvement Process
SEM	structural equation modelling
SGBP	Statement of General Business Principles (Shell)
SRI	Stanford Research Institute
TNC	The Nature Conservancy

TNC	transnational corporation
UN	United Nations
WBCSD	World Business Council for Sustainable Development
WGC	Working Group Cement
WICE	World Industry Council for the Environment
WMC	Western Mining Corporation
WWF	World Wide Fund for Nature

BIOGRAPHIES

Jörg Andriof joined KPMG Corporate Finance Frankfurt in April 2000. During and after studying business and engineering in Berlin and Leicester, UK, he worked with Daimler-Benz, BMW Rolls-Royce, KPMG Corporate Finance and Corporate Recovery. Jörg received his PhD in industrial and business studies from Warwick Business School, UK, his thesis focusing on the development of a concept for strategic partnering. As a Research Fellow of the Centre for Creativity, Strategy and Change at Warwick Business School, he was one of the founding members of the Corporate Citizenship Unit. At KPMG Corporate Finance in Frankfurt, Jörg works as an advisor for Mergers and Acquisitions. In addition, he is Associated Fellow of Warwick Business School. Jörg's areas of expertise are corporate citizenship, stakeholder management, corporate development and value-based management. He is a member of the editorial board of The Journal of Corporate Citizenship.
joerg@andriof.de

Suzanne Beaulieu is professor in accounting at the University of Sherbrooke (Québec). She is a member of two professional accounting corporations: CA and CMA. Her PhD in organisational theory is from the University of Québec at Montréal. Her research interests include organisational legitimacy, corporate social responsibility, corporate reputation and related topics.
sbeaulieu@adm.usherb.ca

As an independent researcher, **Cecile G. Betit**, PhD, East Wallingford, Vermont (A.B. Emmanuel College; PhD Temple University), has been studying the transformative change within the Carris Companies toward employee ownership and employee governance since 1996. This study of the whole-system transformative change has involved individuals (surveys of all employees and interviews), groups (meetings of work teams, ad hoc task groups, and ongoing) within the organisational context and Bill Carris's Long Term Plan. Her research is currently focusing on corporate citizenship, corporate governance and organisational developmental stages.
cgbetit@sover.net

Tamara J. Bliss, PhD is the major curriculum designer for The Center for Corporate Citizenship at Boston College. She has conducted extensive research on how citizen advocacy groups influence corporate behaviour. She designs workshops and consults with corporations on building strategic alliances with citizen advocacy and other stakeholder groups.
tjbliss@verizon.net

Jerry Calton's research interests focus on ethical governance processes for building and sustaining trust in stakeholder networks. His recent publications have appeared in *Business Ethics Quarterly*, *Business and Society* and *Human Systems Management*. He is a past president of the International Association for Business and Society.
calton@hawaii.edu

Jill Engel-Cox is a principal research engineer for Battelle Memorial Institute's Environmental Policy and Management group. Her research focuses on sustainable development, environmental monitoring, cleaner production and public communication. She holds a master's in mechanical/ environmental engineering and bachelors' degrees in mechanical engineering and liberal arts.
engelcoxj@battelle.org

Kimberly Fowler is a senior research engineer for Battelle's Environmental Technology Division. Her research has focused on sustainable design, pollution prevention, life-cycle analysis and environmental planning. She is adjunct faculty at Washington State University and holds a master's in civil/environmental engineering and bachelor's degree in political science.
kim.fowler@pnl.gov

Kenneth Goodpaster earned his AB in mathematics from the University of Notre Dame and his AM and PhD in philosophy at the University of Michigan. He taught graduate and undergraduate philosophy at the University of Notre Dame throughout the 1970s before joining the Harvard Business School faculty in 1980, where he developed the ethics curriculum. In 1990, Goodpaster left Harvard to accept the David and Barbara Koch Endowed Chair in Business Ethics at the University of St Thomas, St Paul, Minnesota. His publications include numerous articles in a variety of professional journals and (with Laura Nash) *Policies and Persons: A Casebook in Business Ethics* (1st edn 1985, 2nd edn 1991, 3rd edn 1998). His research has spanned a wide range of topics, from conceptual studies of ethical reasoning to empirical studies of the social implications of management decision-making.
kegoodpaster@stthomas.edu

Daniel W. Greening received his PhD degree in business administration from the Pennsylvania State University, USA. He is an associate professor of management at the University of Missouri–Columbia, College of Business. His research interests concern issues management, crisis management, firm governance, organisation design and measuring corporate social performance.
GreeningD@missouri.edu

Gretchen Hund is a Research Leader for Battelle, specialising in evaluating technology acceptance through innovative public involvement approaches. She is also a lecturer at the University of Washington's School of Business on international technology commercialisation. She holds a BA in Geology and MS in Political Science.
hund@battelle.org

Bryan W. Husted is a Professor of Management at the Instituto Tecnológico y de Estudios Superiores de Monterrey (Mexico) and Alumni Association Chair of Business Ethics at the Instituto de Empresa (Spain). His research focuses on cross-cultural business ethics and corporate social and environmental performance. His work has appeared in such publications as *The Journal of International Business Studies*, *Business Ethics Quarterly*, *The Journal of Environment and Development*, *Business and Society* and *The Journal of Business Ethics*. He is currently a member of the editorial board of *The Journal of International Management*.
bhusted@egade.sistema.itesm.mx

Michael Jensen is Managing Director of The Monitor Group's Organizational Strategy Practice, as well as Chairman of Social Science Electronic Publishing. He is also Jesse Isidor Straus Professor of Business Administration Emeritus of the Harvard Business School and Visiting Scholar at the Amos Tuck School of Business at Dartmouth College.
MJensen@hbs.edu

Debra King is a lecturer in The Flexible Learning Centre, University of South Australia. She was previously a Research Associate at the Hawke Institute of Social Research, and has a work portfolio covering areas such as volunteer work; work and identity; the relationship between passion, creativity and knowledge work; and activist (social change) work.
debra.king@unisa.edu.au

Howard Klee works with the World Business Council for Sustainable Development and is Program Manager for the Sustainable Cement project. Previously, Howard worked in the private sector in numerous executive and business functions, including strategic planning, business development, environmental affairs and manufacturing. He received his bachelor's degree in chemistry and doctorate in chemical engineering.
klee@wbcsd.org

Anne T. Lawrence is Professor of Organisation and Management at San Jose State University, USA. She is co-author of *Business and Society: Corporate Strategy, Public Policy, Ethics*, 10th edition (Irwin/ McGraw–Hill, 2002).
atlawrence@aol.com

Ted London is pursuing a PhD degree in strategic management at the Kenan-Flagler Business School, University of North Carolina at Chapel Hill, USA. Prior to entering the PhD programme, he worked in both the corporate and non-profit sectors in Asia, Africa and the US. Ted has an MBA (Peter F. Drucker Management Center, Claremont University) and a BS in Mechanical Engineering (Lehigh University).
londont@bschool.unc.edu

Alison Mackinnon is the Director of the Hawke Institute of Social Research, University of South Australia, which conducts research and promotes debate in the areas of globalisation and sustainability, participation, equity and citizenship in the workplace, cultural identity and Australia's position in international and regional contexts. Her personal research portfolio covers areas such as higher education and its impact on personal life, demographic change, changing relations between men and women and the impact of information technology.
alison.mackinnon@unisa.edu.au

Dean Maines is project director for the Caux Round Table Self-Assessment and Improvement Process and a research associate in business ethics at the University of St Thomas, USA. Prior to assuming these roles, he spent 16 years in various capacities for Cummins Engine Company. He was also a Sloan Fellow at Stanford University's Graduate School of Business, earning a Master of Science in Management. He holds undergraduate degrees in philosophy and mechanical engineering from Cornell University.
tdmaines@stthomas.edu

James E. Mattingly is a doctoral student in organisation science at the University of Missouri, USA, where he studies strategic management, organisation theory and political sociology. He is concerned with socially sustainable business practices and the role of business in social organisation. His current research interests are in the areas of firm–stakeholder interactions, corporate political activities and corporate governance.
Jim.Mattingly@missouri.edu

Jean Pasquero is full professor in strategic management at the University of Québec at Montréal. He is a past president of IABS (International Association for Business and Society) and of ASAC (Administrative Sciences Association of Canada). He holds a doctorate from the University of Grenoble (France). His research interests include social constructionist approaches to stakeholder theory.
pasquero.jean@uqam.ca

Steve Payne has been actively pursuing issues related to management and ethics education since the mid-1970s and has published 50 or more articles in journals ranging from the *Academy of Management Review* to *Human Relations*.
spayne@mail.gcsu.edu

Sandra Sutherland Rahman earned her BSBA and MBA from Suffolk University and her DBA from Nova Southeastern University, USA. She has taught international business courses at Bentley College, Suffolk University, Regis College and Newbury College before joining the faculty at Framingham State College. She has presented her work at conferences in Turkey, Singapore, Hong Kong, Belgium, Canada and Hawaii, as well as other venues in the USA. Rahman has spent many years studying labour issues in manufacturing facilities in Bangladesh. Her dissertation is entitled 'The Global Stakeholder's Message, The Firm's Response, and an Interpretation of the Ensuing Dilemma: From Tin Sheds to Brick Houses'.
hrahman@attbi.com

Dennis A. Rondinelli is the Glaxo Distinguished International Professor of Management at the Kenan-Flagler Business School, University of North Carolina at Chapel Hill, USA. Rondinelli has done research on corporate environmental management, international competitiveness issues, economic reform and market transition policies, and private enterprise development in emerging market economies. He has carried out research in Asia, Central Europe, Latin America and Africa. He has authored or edited 16 books and published more than 200 book chapters and articles in scholarly and professional journals.
dennis_rondinelli@unc.edu

Michelle Rovang is programme co-ordinator for business ethics at the University of St Thomas, USA. She also has ten years' experience in corporate positioning, corporate culture and communication management. Rovang earned her BA in communications from the University of Notre Dame and is completing her Master of Business Communications at the University of St Thomas.
mdrovang@yahoo.com

Sandra Waddock is Professor of Management at Boston College's Carroll School of Management, USA, and Senior Research Fellow at Boston College's Center for Corporate Citizenship. She received her MBA (1979) and DBA from Boston University (1985) and has published extensively on corporate responsibility, corporate citizenship and inter-sector collaboration in journals such as *The Academy of Management Journal*, *Strategic Management Journal*, *The Journal of Corporate Citizenship*, *Human Relations* and *Business and Society*, among many others. Her book, *Not by Schools Alone*, was published by Praeger in 1995. Her 1997 paper with Sam Graves, entitled 'Quality of Management and Quality of Stakeholder Relations: Are They Synonymous?', in *Business and Society*, won the 1997 Moskowitz Prize. Her latest book is *Leading Corporate Citizens: Vision, Values, Value Added* (McGraw–Hill, 2002). She was Senior Fellow at the Ethics Resource Center in Washington, DC, from 2000–2002 and a founding faculty member of the Leadership for Change Program at Boston College.
waddock@bc.edu

Duane Windsor (BA, Rice; PhD, Harvard) is Lynette S. Autrey Professor of Management at Rice University's Jesse H. Jones Graduate School of Management, where he has been on the faculty since 1977. He has published in the areas of corporate social responsibility and citizenship, international regime theory and stakeholder theory.
odw@rice.edu

INDEX

For Product Safety Concerns and Information please contact our EU representative GPSR@taylorandfrancis.com Taylor & Francis Verlag GmbH, Kaufingerstraße 24, 80331 München, Germany

Printed and bound by CPI Group (UK) Ltd, Croydon, CR0 4YY
08/05/2025
01864424-0001